MARKETING

AJAY K. SIRSI
Schulich School of Business
York University

a roadmap to SUCCESS

Pearson Canada
Toronto

To Tammara, Belvedere, and BC—F.E.L.T.

—AKS

Library and Archives Canada Cataloguing in Publication

Sirsi, Ajay K., 1960–
    Marketing : a roadmap to success / Ajay K. Sirsi.

Includes bibliographical references and index.
ISBN 978-0-13-713812-8

    1. Marketing—Textbooks. I. Title.
HF5415.S55 2009   658.8   C2009-900694-4

ISBN-13: 978-0-13-713812-8
ISBN-10: 0-13-713812-1

Vice-President, Editorial Director: Gary Bennett
Acquisitions Editor: Don Thompson
Marketing Manager: Leigh-Ann Graham
Developmental Editors: Pamela Voves, Victoria Naik
Production Editor: Avivah Wargon
Copy Editor: Kelly Coleman
Proofreader: Caroline Kaiser
Production Coordinator: Sarah Lukaweski
Composition: Macmillan Publishing Solutions
Photo and Permissions Research: Glen Herbert, Heather L. Jackson
Art Director: Julia Hall
Cover Designer: Anthony Leung
Interior Designer: Anthony Leung
Cover Image: Veer Inc.; Drive Carefully Sign: Jupiterimages

For permission to reproduce copyrighted material, the publisher gratefully acknowledges the copyright holders listed on page 299, which is considered an extension of this copyright page.

8   16

Printed and bound in the United States of America.

Contents

Part 1 Understanding Customers 1

Chapter 1
What Do Winning Organizations Do Well? 2

Chapter 2
Understanding Customer Needs 24

Chapter 3
Choosing Which Customers to Serve 46

Part 2
Creating Customer Value

Chapter 4
Developing a Strong Marketing Plan

Chapter 5
Product and Brand Strategies

Chapter 6
Pricing Strategies

Chapter 7
Channel Strategies

Chapter 8
Marketing Communications
Strategies   170

Part 3
Delivering
Customer
Value   195

Chapter 9
Marketing Planning to Sales
Execution   196

Part 4
Managing
Customer Value   231

Preface

As a business school professor, I spend my days pursuing two activities—creating knowledge and then applying it. Accordingly, I spend a lot of time reading, thinking, and writing. But the knowledge has to stand the test of application. That is why I enjoy interacting with students in the classroom. I teach at three different levels: executive (for business practitioners who are taking a course to further themselves), graduate (MBA), and undergraduate (BBA).

I also apply my knowledge in corporations, helping them in either an educational or a consulting capacity. There is nothing quite as sobering as testing your ideas with a group of practitioners. This is where I have my successes and make my mistakes, but above all, this is where I learn. And that knowledge goes back into the classroom. The process then starts all over again.

I love having one foot in the conceptual paradigm and one in the application paradigm. I have always wanted to write a book that imparts my love for the field of marketing.

Currently, there are two problems with the discipline of marketing: the way it is taught and the way it is practised. I suspect there is a correlation between the two—pedagogy impacts practice. First, let us look at practice.

I am currently advising two students who are taking part in a competition sponsored by a major professional marketing organization. Participants are required to develop a marketing plan for a fictitious organization. The problem is, even though the organization is calling it a "marketing plan," it is really a marketing *communications* plan. So students are asked to design marketing communications strategies (advertising, direct marketing, online efforts, etc.).

As marketing professionals, we should all be very concerned about this example because we see it every day in business practice. When someone asks: "What is your marketing budget?" they are really asking, "What is your marketing communications budget?" This kind of practice perpetuates the thinking that marketing is all about marketing communications (i.e., such things as advertising and marketing collateral). What gets missed is the fact that, first and foremost, marketing is a *strategic* activity, one that ideally should be the engine of corporate competitive acuity and corporate transformation (the focus of Chapter 12 in this book).

It took a while for the problems facing this discipline to surface, but they have been well documented in the recent literature.[1] Across industries, marketing is being asked to prove what value it brings to the corporation. And I am not just talking about demonstrating the return on investment (ROI) on marketing expenditures. My colleagues and I are arguing that marketing has failed to capture its seat at the executive table. But there are examples of corporations where marketing has demonstrated that it can be the engine of corporate transformation (at American Express, Procter & Gamble, Mercedes-Benz, Diageo, and Google, to name a few).

As I argued earlier, practice is related to the way marketing is taught. Pick up most marketing texts and you see that they are crammed full of terms and definitions. Seriously, how many instructors reading this have actually taught students what a "rack jobber" is? The focus on many books is on teaching students theory. The application of the theory is not given as much prominence; the books do not tell a story.

I wanted to write a book that would do the following:

- Instill in the student a love for the discipline of marketing.
- Instill in the student a love for business and an appreciation that, in spite of all the nasty things corporations do, they can do a lot of good through practising corporate sustainability.
- Help the student understand that they will have to think about marketing issues (customers, competitors, brands, etc.) *regardless* of whether they work in marketing, sales, finance, human resources, or the supply chain. For example, the role of the Chief Financial Officer (CFO) has dramatically changed from one of a singular focus on financial matters to one of strategic thinking and acting. Recently, some of my consulting engagements have involved helping CFOs realize their potential for driving change within the organization—a role that traditionally would have fallen into the laps of the marketing function.
- Provide the student with a holistic view of marketing— that first and foremost, it is a disciplined process used by an organization to solve business problems. Gone are the days when a graduate could aspire to toil away in the accounting department, safe from the vicissitudes of the marketplace. Businesses expect employees to be part of cross-functional teams solving a given problem. And students today aspire to become serial entrepreneurs. This new generation of students wants to know how to apply theoretical concepts in the workplace.
- Train the student for a job beyond the consumer packaged-goods industry (a bias I see in many texts). The fact is, most students will work in a business-to-business environment.

- Highlight the interrelationship between marketing and sales, two functions that need to work very closely together to enable the organization to win in the marketplace.

So this book is aimed at the following readers:

- The reader who wants to develop and implement winning strategies.
- The instructor who is fed up with the status quo.
- The reader who wants to know what marketing is and how it can help solve business problems.

In order to achieve this goal, I have developed a virtual "roadmap" for business students that guides them throughout the curriculum and points out the routes that will empower them to drive the engine of business success—marketing.

I have successfully taught in this fashion for over 20 years. When I get together with ex-students, they can recite material from my lectures years ago. They often comment on how my teaching approach focuses on how to apply the material, rather than on memorizing the theory. This helps them be successful in their careers. Therefore, I have applied the same approach in writing this text. Examples of marketing at work in the business world are presented first and then connected to theoretical concepts. Because I teach using examples, the student attains an immediate grasp of the theory that the example illustrates. Thus, theory and practice are more firmly linked.

How This Book Is Organized

The book is organized into four sections: Understand customers, create customer value, deliver the value, and manage value-creation efforts. I have taken this approach because this is how successful organizations run their businesses.[2]

- The first section on **understanding customers** has three chapters: what winning businesses do, understanding customers, and selecting which customers to serve (market segmentation and targeting).
- The second section on **creating customer value** has five chapters and starts with a chapter on developing marketing plans. The other chapters in this section focus on developing marketing strategies using the marketing mix (product, price, channel, and marketing communications strategies).
- The third section on **delivering customer value** has two chapters and acknowledges that many marketing strategies are actually implemented by other functions such as sales and customer service. In many organizations the sales and marketing functions do not work well together, with disastrous consequences for the customer. And when all functions are not focused on the customer, the

organization is not as successful. The first chapter in this section is on how to translate marketing strategy into sales execution, while the second chapter describes how to develop a customer-focused business.

- The final section on **managing customer value** has two chapters: the first covers customer attraction, satisfaction, and retention strategies, and the second, building the marketing organization of the future.

I chose to write about building a marketing organization because in organizations where marketing has a seat at the executive table, the marketing function has been successful in demonstrating what value it creates for the enterprise—contextualizing the market for other functions as well as spearheading corporate sustainability efforts (what one reviewer of this book referred to as "reduce, recycle, reuse" efforts).

Key Features of the Book

- I have written this book in a style I have successfully used in class—I conduct **a conversation with the reader**, inviting him or her to appreciate the material and learn how to use it.
- I have tried not to bombard the reader with terms, definitions, or excessive theorizing. Rather, the focus is on providing the reader with enough rigour (theory) to provide a holistic view of marketing and apply the material in a practical setting—how to craft and implement superior marketing strategies.
- To help the student understand how the material in each chapter is applied in the real world, I have included a **running case** at the end of each chapter. This case is based on a five-year consulting engagement with an organization that went from an internal, cost-focused business to a customer-focused, market leader.
- All instructors will appreciate one fact: given that the marketplace is a dynamic entity, content in a book often needs updating. For example, there is the case about Dell and channel strategy in Chapter 7. Since I wrote this chapter, Dell has made changes to its channel strategy (making more of a push into the retail sector to attract the consumer market and compete more effectively with HP).

So how can I help instructors keep up to date? To solve this problem, I will maintain a **blog**, which will be updated almost weekly. In it, I will post content updates and interesting articles. Also, I will send instructors separate communiqués informing them of the implications of a blog post (for example, what the Dell situation means and how to communicate the implications to students).

- Opening a channel for dialogue through the blog also means that I can **customize the book** for each instructor.

An instructor can send me a request to provide material on a topic not discussed in detail in the book, and I will respond quickly (with written content, resources, etc.), enabling the instructor to use the material in class.

- For each chapter, the reader will find **audio interviews** by content experts to help explain the material or provide examples.

- Each semester I invite **guest speakers** to my class to speak on a range of topics—from marketing-specific topics to general ones such as career advice for students. These speakers will be videotaped, and the **videos** will be available online for instructors and students to view.

- Terms and definitions appearing in the **Glossary** are bolded in the text for easy reference.

- This book contains **new material** that will set it apart from other texts:
  - Marketing–sales alignment
  - Cross-functional alignment to focus on the customer
  - Marketing metrics and return on investment (ROI) of marketing expenditures
  - Demonstration of marketing's productivity
  - Social media (blogs, Facebook, MySpace, Twitter, YouTube, etc.) and how to take advantage of them
  - Beyond the sale: building customer loyalty and retention

Pedagogy

Each chapter contains several features designed to increase student interest in, and understanding of, the material being presented. These features are as follows:

Chapter Learning Objectives

A list of numbered learning objectives is presented at the beginning of each chapter. These objectives, which guide students in determining what is important, are also referred to in the margins opposite the relevant content in the chapter.

In this chapter you will

1. Understand the *strategic* definition of product and why you need to know this to successfully build brands.

2. Learn strategies and tactics that will help you build a strong brand and differentiate yourself from your competitors.

Checkpoint: Where We've Been/Where We're Going

This feature appears at the beginning of each chapter and at appropriate intervals in the text. It acts as a guidepost for the student's journey, recapping what has been discussed in previous sections and indicating what to expect on the road ahead.

CHECKPOINT

Where We've Been
- We have learned that a crucial marketing task is to determine which customers to serve and to assess their needs.
- Successful businesses serve customers by utilizing all elements of the marketing mix—product, price, channel, and marketing communications strategies.
- Marketing strategies are "packaged" in the form of a marketing plan.

Where We're Going
- We will start by examining the first marketing mix element in this chapter—product.
- Other chapters in this part of the book will discuss price, channel, and marketing communications strategies.

Key Points

These points highlight important concepts discussed in the chapter.

KEYPOINT

A brand is a differentiated offering in the marketplace.

Quotations

Interspersed throughout each chapter are quotations that succinctly capture the essence of the discussion. For example, Theodore Levitt's words "People buy expectations, not things," in the chapter on product strategies reminds us not to focus narrowly on product features but on the total benefits the customer gets from the offering.

People buy expectations, not things.

THEODORE LEVITT

Marketing Drives Success

Each chapter contains at least four **Marketing Drives Success** vignettes that show a practical application of the material being discussed. These cases appear where the student needs them most to place the content in a practical context, rather than at the end of the chapter.

Tammy and Belle enjoying a latte at Starbucks

Are You on the Right Track?—Chapter Challenge

Also provided in each chapter are exercises that challenge students to check whether they are on the right track in terms of their comprehension of the material. **Are You on the Right Track?—Chapter Challenge** questions pretest students' knowledge of marketing or elicit critical thinking about topics discussed earlier in the text.

Visuals

Marketing is a visual subject, so throughout each chapter we feature a variety of colourful figures, photographs, and advertisements to help reinforce key concepts and applications.

MyMarketingLab Support

Each chapter contains an audio component. Marginal references direct students to the text's MyMarketingLab, where they can access the author's introduction to each chapter and marketing advice from industry experts (**audio interviews**), as well as the **author's blog**.

End-of-Chapter Materials

Several important pedagogical features are found at the end of each chapter. These are designed to help students better understand the contents of the chapter.

Summary of Learning Objectives

The material in each chapter is concisely summarized using the learning objectives as the organizing scheme. This helps students understand the main points that were presented in the chapter.

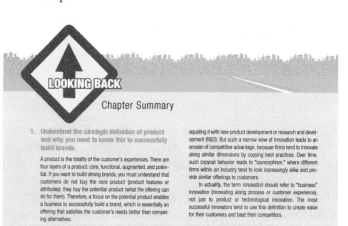

Critical Thinking Questions

After reading the chapter, a student is ready to apply the material. These end-of-chapter questions challenge students to find additional examples to support chapter content or conduct additional research to enhance their learning. They can also put students in a decision maker's shoes and ask them what action they would choose and why.

Running Case with Case Assignment

A running case based on a five-year consulting assignment, appears at the end of each chapter. Using the material presented in the chapter, each case highlights how the company advanced toward its goal of moving from an internal, product-focused organization to a market-oriented one.

Suggested Readings

At the end of each chapter, a set of readings is suggested for students interested in learning more about the topic. These readings have been very carefully selected to represent classic or essential thinking about a topic by experts in the field.

Notes

A comprehensive list of references provides sources for the information and examples discussed in each chapter.

End-of-Text Materials

Appendix I: Marketing Plan

Chapter 4 teaches students how to develop a winning marketing plan. Appendix I presents an example of a winning marketing plan for the business featured in the running case. In combination, the two sections should give students the confidence to develop strong marketing plans on their own, a critical skill for any business student to acquire.

Appendix II: Were You on the Right Track?
Answers to Chapter Challenges

Students are provided with answers to these in-chapter exercises so that they can check their progress.

Glossary

Key terms are bolded when first discussed in the text, and definitions are provided in the glossary.

Key Takeaways

Printed on perforated paper, the takeaways can be removed from the text and included in class notes. Written in a "top-10" format, they outline the core information covered and indicate exactly what students should be "taking away" from any chapter.

Supplementary Materials

A comprehensive supplements package accompanies the text.

MyMarketingLab

MyMarketingLab is a powerful web-based resource designed to save time and improve student results. Access to MyMarketingLab accompanies every new copy of this textbook.

MyMarketingLab Features and Benefits

Self-Assessment. MyMarketingLab offers robust self-assessment tests to determine individual mastery of key content areas. Organized by major section or chapter, these diagnostic tests contain questions that are mapped to the Learning Objectives within the text. Quizzes are randomized so students have numerous opportunities to retest areas they do not understand. This varied assessment program enables instructors and students alike to accurately measure student progress.

Customized Study Plan. Generated from chapter pre-tests and post-tests, the study plan identifies strengths and weaknesses to help students focus their attention and efforts where they're needed the most.

Multimedia Resources. MyMarketingLab also houses the array of digital media assets that accompany this text. Videos, weblinks, audio interviews, and links to the author's blog can all be found in MyMarketingLab.

Instructor's Resource Centre Instructor resources are password protected and available for download via www.pearsoned.ca. For your convenience, these resources are also available on the Instructor's Resource CD-ROM (ISBN-13: 978-0-13-815782-1).

MyTest from Pearson Canada is a powerful assessment generation program that helps instructors easily create and print quizzes, tests, and exams, as well as homework or practice handouts. Questions and tests can all be authored online, allowing instructors maximum flexibility and the ability to efficiently manage assessments at any time and from anywhere.

Instructor's Resource Manual This manual contains chapter outlines, teaching tips, and suggestions on how to use the text effectively. The manual also provides answers to the end-of-chapter questions and case assignments.

PowerPoint® Presentations outlining the key points in the text are available for each chapter.

Image Library This supplement provides selected full-colour ads from the text.

Technology Specialists Pearson's Technology Specialists work with faculty and campus course designers to ensure that Pearson technology products, assessment tools, and online course materials are tailored to meet your specific needs. This highly qualified team is dedicated to helping schools take full advantage of a wide range of educational resources by assisting in the integration of a variety of instructional materials and media formats. Your local Pearson Education sales representative can provide you with more details about this service program.

CourseSmart

CourseSmart is a new way for instructors and students to access textbooks online anytime from anywhere. With thousands of titles across hundreds of courses, CourseSmart helps instructors choose the best textbook for their class and gives their students a new option of buying the assigned textbook as a lower-cost eTextbook. For more information, visit www. coursesmart.com.

Author Blog

The author will maintain a blog that will be updated almost weekly. The blog will contain updates to chapter material (the latest theory and examples). In this way the book will bring to fruition the concept of "marketing in real time." The blog will also enable readers to form an online community and ask questions of the author.

Separate instructor sites on the blog will provide instructors with the opportunity to learn how to incorporate the blog material into their classes. They can also communicate with the author and request material customized to their needs (added details on a particular topic, material on a topic not explicitly covered in the book, etc.).

Acknowledgments

I would like to thank the reviewers for their thoughtful comments and suggestions, many of which have been incorporated into the book (I may have used some suggestions in a different part of the book than expected). My thanks to the following:

Marina Jaffey, Camosun College

Geoffery Malleck, University of Waterloo

Robert J. Palmer, Bishop's University

Robert Soroka, Dawson College

Marla Spergel, Carleton University

My sincere thanks go to the audio interviewees as well. By giving generously of their time and expertise, they have enhanced this book:

Susan Abbott, Abbott Research & Consulting

Joseph Amati, Loblaw Companies

Shakeel Bharmal

William Bruce

Paul Coleman, Logic Communications

Florence Furlong, Solo Cup

Livia Grujich, On Q Communications

Mike Jurincic, Bayer

Victoria Jurincic, Amgen

Mandy Kan, Dessert Lady

Keshia Khan, G&K Services

Klara Kolcze

Ennio Longo

Gloria Mogavero

Jacqueline Sava, Soak

Rob Schmeichel, Farm Credit Canada

Lisa Shepherd and Leah Andrew, Mezzanine Consulting

Craig Wilson, Travelers

Chen Yongjian, Hillsdale Investments

Pamela Voves, Senior Developmental Editor at Pearson, told me that the preface should be "inspirational." I hope it is. She was fantastic in making sure I was on track with the manuscript, gently guiding my efforts. Acquisitions Editor Don Thompson, Editorial Director Gary Bennett, and I had a meeting to discuss my vision for the book, and they were on board right away. Their commitment has never wavered. I thank them for the support.

The entire production team at Pearson was wonderful to work with. I thank everyone there for their dedication in making sure this book was produced on time, including those I did not get to meet. My special thanks to Avivah Wargon and to researchers Heather Jackson and Glen Herbert for their tireless efforts to make sure we had the right visuals for chapter content. I enjoyed our conversations, Avivah! As well, many thanks to editor Kelly Coleman and proofreader Caroline Kaiser. Both of you made the content more user-friendly and clean. And thanks also to Jennifer Parks, Media Content Developer, for her diligent work on the audio interviews, on setting up my blog, and on the rest of the MyMarketingLab, and to the New Media team alongside her.

Finally, my thanks go out to my wife, Tammara. For the year or so I was working on this book she was a "book widow." I could not spend time with her, even on weekends. She would patiently wait for me to finish. Her part in this book goes beyond mere support. When I started writing the book, I shared with her the chapters I was going to write. She then spent countless hours securing relevant advertisements and articles for me. She has always been my inspiration with her wisdom and strong work ethic.

Notes

1. Many articles have been written about this topic and its resolution recently. I am highlighting only a few. David C. Court, "A New Model For Marketing," *The McKinsey Quarterly*, 2004, No. 4, pp. 4–5; George Harter, Edward Landry, and Andrew Tipping, "The New Complete Marketer," *Strategy + Business*, Issue 48, Autumn 2007, pp. 78–87; Frederick Webster Jr., Alan J. Malter, and Shankar Ganesan, "The Decline and Dispersion of Marketing Competence," *MIT Sloan Management Review*, Summer 2005, pp. 35–43.

2. See, for example, Nitin Nohria, William Joyce, and Bruce Roberson, "What Really Works?" *Harvard Business Review* 81(7), July 2003, pp. 42–52. Successful businesses are good at creating and implementing superior strategies.

PART 1

Understanding Customers

describes the transformative power of marketing strategy.

CHAPTER 1   Provides marketing frameworks, tools, and techniques to succeed in business.

CHAPTER 2   Provides tools and techniques to develop a superior understanding of customer needs.

CHAPTER 3   Discusses market segmentation and target marketing strategies, the pillars of business success.

Understanding Customers
PART 1, P. 1

Creating Customer Value
PART 2, P. 67

Delivering Customer Value
PART 3, P. 195

Managing Customer Value
PART 4, P. 231

What Do Winning Organizations Do Well?

Before you begin, visit your MyMarketingLab to hear the author's **Audio Chapter Intro.**

CHAPTER INTRODUCTION

Each time I teach an introductory course in marketing, I ask students a question in the first class: "What is marketing?" And, in over 20 years of teaching this material, the answers always remain the same. "Marketing is advertising." "Marketing—is selling." "Marketing is trying to get me to buy something I don't want!"

Each of these answers is understandable, but wrong. Understandable, because there are many organizations that indeed take such an approach to marketing—they use high-pressure sales tactics to get the customer to buy, or they try to woo the customer by means of glitzy advertising. Wrong, because it is the *application* that is faulty, not the discipline of marketing itself.

Marketing is not advertising, nor is it selling. As we will see much later in this book (Chapters 7, 8, and 9), both advertising and selling are tools used by a marketing strategist to accomplish certain goals. Also, no one can make you buy something you don't want, unless they do so by coercion. Successful businesses know that the best they can hope for is to understand the needs of their customers and develop an offering that resonates more than what their competitors are offering in the marketplace.

In this chapter you will

1. Be primed for success by understanding what winning organizations do well.

2. Learn the discipline of marketing that will lead you to success over your competitors.

3. Get on the roadmap to success by learning how to use this book.

4. Master the 10 secrets of successful marketing organizations.

5. Learn to avoid mistakes made by organizations that are not marketing led.

OBJECTIVE 1

What Sets Winning Organizations Apart From Their Competitors?

Since the beginning of time (just joking—since the beginning of systematic business research), observers have asked one basic question: "What separates winning companies from their counterparts?" In other words, researchers have studied what companies that outperform their industry peers excel at. This question is important because less than 5% of all publicly traded companies maintain a total return to shareholders greater than their industry peers for more than 10 years.[1] One such research study is worth noting.

Researchers Nohria, Joyce, and Roberson followed 160 companies over a 10-year period. They divided these companies into 40 industry groups of 4 each. At the start of the study, they ensured that all 4 companies in a group were reasonably equivalent—similar to one another in terms of financial numbers and apparent future prospects. At the end of the study period, they noticed that some companies in a group were winners (as measured by **total shareholder return**), while others were losers. They asked the question: "What separates winning companies from losing companies?"

The researchers found that the top two factors that account for a company's success over its competitors are *strategy* and *execution*. Let us examine these two factors in detail.

> *The key to achieving excellence in strategy . . . is to be clear about what your strategy is and consistently communicate it to customers, employees, and shareholders.*
>
> NOHRIA, JOYCE, AND ROBERSON

MARKETING DRIVES SUCCESS

1.1 THE HOME DEPOT

Objective: Strategy and Its Execution Are Key to an Organization's Success

Arthur Blank and Bernie Marcus had a simple idea when they started The Home Depot[2]: unlike other hardware stores that simply sold a customer a can of paint and a brush, they would guide customers through the entire process, giving them the confidence to do the job without the help of a contractor. (You will find more about this strategy in Chapter 5.) In this way, the founders revolutionized an entire industry by creating a whole new way of serving the customer. To execute their strategy, Blank and Marcus hired professionals (such as painters and carpenters) to sell goods and offer advice in their stores. Their approach was a phenomenal success, leading to Home Depot's sales of nearly $90 billion (2006 figures).

A new chief executive officer (CEO), Bob Nardelli, was hired in 2000. Nardelli had no previous experience running a retail operation. His strategy was different from the founders': he pushed the contractor business, cut costs, streamlined operations, and pushed the vaunted customer service strategy down the company's priority list.[3] Many full-time workers were replaced with part-time employees, and workers' incentives (a profit-sharing plan) for good customer service fell from $90 million to $44 million.

This about-turn in strategy and execution did not go unnoticed by customers, who were getting grumpy (hear the audio interview in Chapter 10 as Lynn and Bill, two customers, discuss their vastly different customer service experiences at a Home Depot and at a Lowe's). Customers began defecting to the competition in droves. Home Depot's share price dropped 24% during one of the biggest home improvement booms in history. And its customer satisfaction scores went down. Lowe's, a major competitor, was the main beneficiary.

In a sudden move, Bob Nardelli announced he was leaving Home Depot in January 2007. Frank Blake, the new CEO, has vowed to return the retailer to its former strategy and execution. He has started consulting with Blake and Marcus, the founders. Only time will tell whether Home Depot can return to its roots.

continue

Home Depot is trying to get its marketing strategy on track.

Winning Organizations Devise and Maintain a Clearly Stated, Focused Marketing Strategy

Companies that succeed over their competitors begin with a simple value proposition that is based on a deep understanding of their customers. This is known as their **marketing strategy** and, as shown by the researchers, is the number one factor that accounts for an organization's success. Two contrasting examples from the research will illustrate this point.

Dollar General is a U.S. retailer that sells quality products at a low price to low- and fixed-income customers. It locates its stores in small towns and low-income urban areas, stocks merchandise that will appeal to its target customers, and prices its items at rock bottom. In the 10-year time period, Dollar General was clearly a winner, based on its laser-like focus on its marketing strategy.

In contrast, another retailer, Kmart, struggled throughout the 10-year time period because it could never get its marketing strategy straight. It couldn't seem to decide what type of customer it was trying to attract. To avoid direct competition with Wal-Mart, it decided to go upscale by making deals with Martha Stewart (before she went to jail!). This diluted its marketing strategy and confused customers because it had always focused on low- and middle-income customers. Realizing its mistake, Kmart retreated from the upscale strategy and went head-to-head with Wal-Mart, trying to compete on low prices. This, of course, confused customers even more, and they stopped going to Kmart, leading to Kmart's eventual filing for bankruptcy.

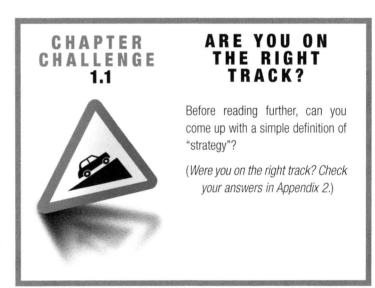

CHAPTER CHALLENGE 1.1

ARE YOU ON THE RIGHT TRACK?

Before reading further, can you come up with a simple definition of "strategy"?

(*Were you on the right track? Check your answers in Appendix 2.*)

Dollar General succeeds because its marketing strategy is focused.

Kmart failed because its marketing strategy was unclear.

Chapters 9 and 10 in this book focus on the all-important topic of executing marketing strategy.

Other than the actual decision to start the business, the sales and marketing aspects are the most important function of your business. If there is no sales and marketing, there are no clients to service. If there are no clients, there is no revenue. If there is no revenue, there is no business.

STEPHEN FAIRLEY

Winning Organizations Execute Their Marketing Strategy Flawlessly

The research shows that the second factor that separates winners from losers is their ability to execute their marketing strategy. Let us take an example.

I was at a grocery store in the checkout line. The person ahead of me was leaving with her bags when the checkout clerk called to her in a loud voice, "Hey! Come back!" The startled customer approached the clerk, wondering what she had done wrong. The clerk said to her, "Have a nice day." Seeing the equally startled looks on the other customers' faces, the clerk explained, "Management has told us that we should wish all customers a good day."

This example clearly illustrates the gap between *devising* and *implementing* a good strategy. Obviously, someone in top management had a bright idea that customer service was a strategic priority for this business. Accordingly, front-line employees were given instructions on what to tell customers. But while the *strategy* of customer service was noble, its *execution* was poor, perhaps because employees were not properly trained. The lesson we learn is that unless the organization wins the hearts of employees, the execution of the strategy is likely to be weak. As a result, the strategy will fail.

Where We've Been

■ We have seen that winning organizations earn their success by developing and implementing superior marketing strategies.

Where We're Going

■ We will learn what marketing is and how it can help a business succeed over its competitors.

CHECKPOINT

OBJECTIVE 2

What Is Marketing?

CHAPTER CHALLENGE 1.2

ARE YOU ON THE RIGHT TRACK?

Before reading further, can you come up with a one-line definition of "marketing"?
(*Were you on the right track? Check your answers in Appendix 2.*)

Before reading further, respond to Chapter Challenge 1.2.

We now know what the research shows—winning organizations design and implement superior marketing strategies. But what is marketing?

For the moment, let us just say that *marketing is a disciplined process used by organizations to solve business problems.* A list of typical business problems faced by an organization, and tackled by marketing, is shown in Table 1.1.

Of course, saying that marketing is a disciplined process used by organizations to solve business problems is not enough. We need to elaborate on this point.

TABLE 1.1   Problems Solved by Marketing

Type of organization	Typical problems faced by the organization
For-profit organization	■ Low-priced competitors are flooding the marketplace with cheap goods. ■ It is becoming more and more difficult to differentiate our goods and services from our competitors' goods and services. ■ How can we generate more revenue? ■ How do we manage the explosion in media and channels? ■ Our customers are becoming more sophisticated and more price-sensitive. ■ How do we build an organization where everyone is focused on the customer?
Non-profit organization	■ How can we differentiate ourselves from other non-profit organizations? ■ How can we increase the awareness of our brand? ■ How can we increase funding from donors? ■ How can we build partnerships with for-profit organizations? ■ How do we motivate our volunteers?

MARKETING DRIVES SUCCESS

1.2 SNAP-ON TOOLS

Objective: What Is Marketing?

Snap-on Tools is one of the best examples of a *marketing* organization.[4] It sells tools to primarily one target customer—the auto mechanic. Although it continues to sell traditional products such as wrenches and tool cabinets, it has kept pace with cars, becoming more sophisticated over time. As a result, Snap-on's product line includes computerized diagnostic equipment as well.

What kind of tools does Snap-on make? It puts superior steel in its products, guaranteeing them never to break. As a result, the warranty on the tool is just an afterthought for the customer. As Snap-on says, "If a mechanic is fixing a car that is due by 4:00 p.m. and the tool breaks at 3:00 p.m., what use is the warranty to the mechanic?"

Keeping in line with a superior product, Snap-on charges price premiums—from 10% over rival brands such as Mac to twice the amount charged for tools made by Sears. The crucial point is that their customers never complain about the price; they willingly pay.

How does Snap-on sell its tools? Does it have retail stores? The answer is no. Retail stores would not make sense, as the mechanic does not have time to go to the store. Therefore, the store comes to the mechanic. Snap-on has dealers who drive the familiar white Snap-on van and visit auto mechanics. Each dealer has tens of thousands of dollars of inventory in that van.

When a dealer visits a customer, he watches the mechanic at work without disturbing him. He might casually say something like, "I have a tool that will make that job a lot easier." The dealer's visit is always a welcome break from gruelling work, a chance for the customer to chat and learn what latest tools Snap-on has to offer. Here is an example of an interaction that might take place between the Snap-on dealer and the auto mechanic.

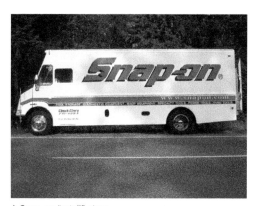

A Snap-on "retail" store

DEALER: "I want to show you a new tool that will make diagnosing the health of engines a lot easier."

CUSTOMER: "I am interested because that way I can repair many more engines in one day. How much does the tool cost?"

DEALER: "$1000."

CUSTOMER: "Where am I going to get $1000 to pay for the tool? I don't have that kind of money sitting in one spot!"

DEALER: "Look, I will give you the tool and finance it without interest. On a weekly basis you pay me what you can afford. Take your time to pay off the loan on the machine. I will give you the interest-free loan simply based on our relationship."

It is this one-on-one relationship building that makes the difference between the Snap-on brand and its competitors. As a result, Snap-on does not spend any money on traditional advertising to build its brand.

Marketing Is a Disciplined Process to Solve Business Problems

Before reading further, respond to Chapter Challenge 1.3.

Businesses like Snap-on succeed because, year after year, they follow a disciplined marketing process. It is rather like going to the gym for a workout—people who want healthy, strong bodies have to work at it. The disciplined marketing process is shown in Figure 1.1.

Marketing Process Step #1: Understand Customers   The very first step is to understand customer needs. Snap-on understands the needs of its customers very well: (1) auto mechanics are often maligned in society and are not regarded as "professionals"; (2) a mechanic's time is money—if a tool breaks, he cannot

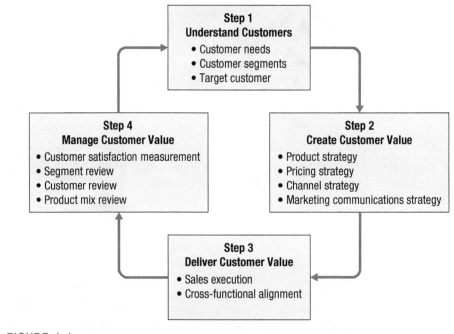

FIGURE 1.1

Marketing is a disciplined process used to solve business problems.

fulfill his promise of on-time car delivery to *his* customer, the car owner; (3) if a mechanic is more productive, he can work on more cars; (4) the mechanic does not have the cash flow to pay for a tool that costs thousands of dollars; and (5) the mechanic does not have time to go to a retail store to buy parts. Respond to Chapter Challenge 1.4 before reading further.

In Chapter Challenge 1.4, if you answered, "Different customers have different needs," you would be absolutely correct. This might sound rather obvious, but in marketing this statement takes on profound significance and is fundamental to any organization's success.

The fact that different customers have different needs means that a business must ask itself one crucial strategic question: "Which customers do we want to serve?" This marketing task is called **market segmentation** and **targeting (target marketing)**. It involves recognizing different sets or groups of customers based on their needs (and other criteria). Chapter 3 deals exclusively with this topic. Snap-on demonstrates tremendous discipline in this regard—it has made a commitment to serve the needs of the auto mechanic, foregoing other needs (segments) such as home building, construction, and non-professional consumers. Such focus earns it significant loyalty from its target segment—the auto mechanic.

At the end of Marketing Process Step #1, you should have segmented your customers and chosen a target customer or a set of target customers to serve. Do not be greedy; you cannot serve everyone.

KEYPOINT

Winning organizations know that they cannot serve all needs; they need to choose which customer needs they want to serve.

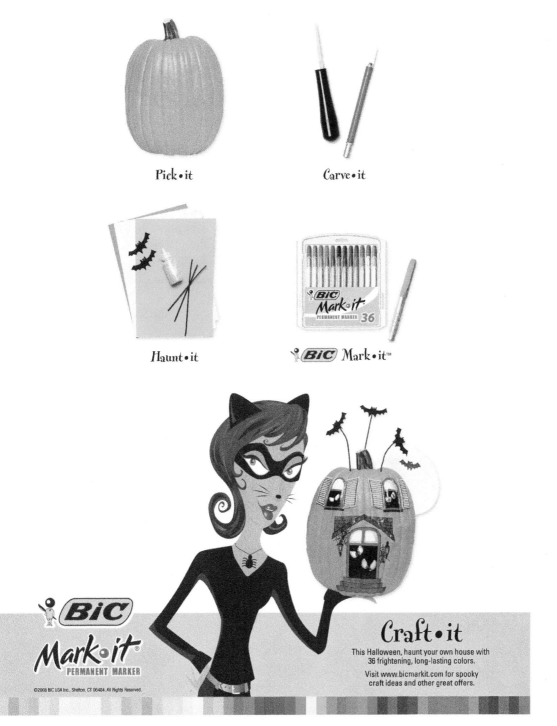

Bic is focused on serving one target segment: the customer who wants writing materials.

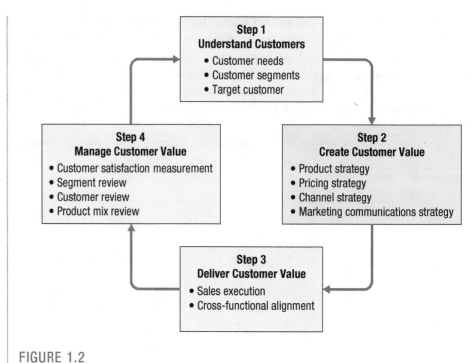

A business that tries to be all things to all people ends up being nothing to no one.

FIGURE 1.2

Customer value is created using the marketing mix.

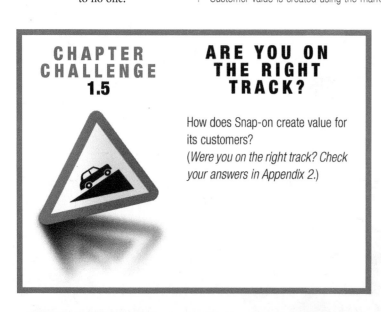

CHAPTER CHALLENGE 1.5

ARE YOU ON THE RIGHT TRACK?

How does Snap-on create value for its customers?

(*Were you on the right track? Check your answers in Appendix 2.*)

Marketing Process Step #2: Create Customer Value   Once a business understands customer needs and segments the market, the next marketing step is to create value for the chosen target segment, as shown in Figure 1.2. Respond to Chapter Challenge 1.5 before reading further.

Table 1.2 shows how Snap-on creates value for its customers.

Taken together, product, price, channel, and marketing communications strategies are called the **marketing mix**. Table 1.3 lists some cautions regarding this topic.

Marketing Process Step #3: Deliver Customer Value   As we will see in Chapter 4, the understand-create-deliver-manage customer value marketing

TABLE 1.2 Marketing Process Step #2: Create Customer Value		
Snap-on understands that	**It creates customer value by**	**This is called**
If a tool breaks, the mechanic cannot fulfill a promise made to his customer.	Putting superior steel in its products so they do not break. Essentially, Snap-on makes warranties inconsequential. As cars have become more sophisticated, Snap-on has developed diagnostic tools to make the mechanic more productive.	Product strategy
The mechanic cannot pay for an expensive tool.	Providing the customer with flexible financing mechanisms.	Pricing strategy
The mechanic does not have time to go to a retail store.	Having the store go to the mechanic.	Channel strategy
The mechanic will not be impressed by TV advertising.	Communicating with the customer by developing one-on-one relationships.	Marketing communications strategy

TABLE 1.3 Cautions Regarding Marketing Mix Elements

Caution #	Caution	Rationale
1.	Do not use the term "place" to denote channel strategies. Also, the preferred term is channel strategies, not channel of distribution strategies.	"Place" refers to a place of conducting a business. As we will see in Chapter 7, channels can be virtual, and they go way beyond merely performing distribution of goods or services.
2.	Do not use the term "promotion" to denote marketing communications strategies.	"Promotion" can also refer to short-term tactics used by a business to attract customers (such as coupons or giveaways). As we will see in Chapter 8, marketing communications play a very strategic role in any business.
3.	Never equate "marketing" with "marketing communications."	Using the two terms synonymously undermines the strategic and analytical nature of marketing. It perpetuates the misconception that marketing is all about advertising and other tools such as marketing collateral material (e.g., brochures).

process is captured in a strategic document called the **marketing plan**. Think of a marketing plan as an organization's "go-to-market" strategy, which specifies what target segments it will serve, how it will serve them, and how it will win by differentiating itself from its competitors.

Although many strategies in the marketing plan are implemented by the marketing function (building strong brands, for example), many marketing strategies are implemented by other functions such as sales, customer service, and shipping (see Figure 1.3). Let us take an example.

Travelers is an insurance company that serves residential and corporate customers. A visit to www.travelers.com reveals that the marketing function clearly wants to project the image of a "customer-focused" company (advertisements for Travelers also reinforce this point). It caters to Spanish-speaking customers by having a separate section on the website. To project an image of prestige, it sponsors a golf tournament. It makes it easy to do business with the company: the website offers insurance tips and makes it easy to find an agent or file a claim.

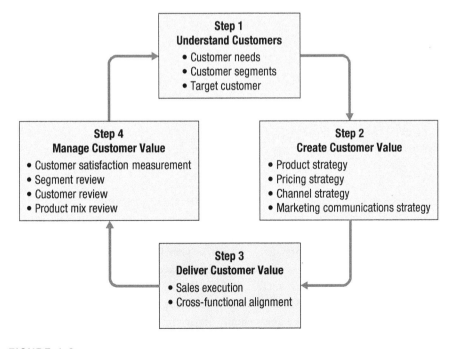

FIGURE 1.3

Many marketing strategies are implemented by other functions.

FIGURE 1.4

To achieve customer focus, the marketing plan has to be translated into functional plans.

Now, picture the following: What would happen if a Travelers salesperson visiting a business customer lacked product knowledge on a new insurance product? Or, what if the customer service representative serving a customer on the phone was not friendly? All of us can relate to such experiences with different suppliers. In these cases, the marketing strategy of customer focus is not being implemented because another function is responsible for implementing it.

It is for this reason that the third step in the marketing process is to deliver the value created for the customer. To accomplish this step properly, two things have to happen: (1) marketing strategies have to be translated into sales strategies and other functional strategies (Chapters 4 and 9 are devoted to this topic) and (2) the organization has to align all its functions to focus on the customer (this cross-functional alignment is called **customer focus** and Chapter 10 is entirely devoted to this topic).[5]

> *When an entire organization is focused on marketing, the need for a separate [marketing] department often disappears.*
>
> GEORGE, FREELING, AND COURT

This message is captured in Figure 1.4, where we see that the marketing plan is translated into functional plans. As we will see in Chapter 4, the marketing plan plays a very important role—it contextualizes the market for the other functions by outlining market conditions, customer segments being targeted, how the organization is going to create value for customers, and how the business is going to differentiate itself from its competitors. Such a context helps other functions to develop their functional plans. Without this crucial alignment, the organization cannot hope to be customer focused.

Craig Wilson, VP Marketing Strategy and Communications at Travelers, discusses the importance of marketing to business success.

Marketing Process Step #4: Manage Customer Value   The final marketing step is a feedback loop to review marketing strategies and make changes to ensure the business is keeping pace with changing market conditions (or, ideally, staying ahead of changing market conditions). This final step is shown in Figure 1.5.

To explain this last marketing step, I would like to tell you a story about my brother-in-law, Tim. Right after high school, he started a business selling pressure washers (a machine that cleans dirt and oil residue by injecting water at a high pressure). He works very hard and is a very successful business person. One day, I asked him to reveal his secrets for business success. This is what he told me.

> *Some customers are needy but greedy. . . . I "fire" them and hope they go to my competitors.*
>
> TIM

"My secrets are no secrets at all; they are just *four* practices every business should engage in *every* year. Whenever I visit a customer, I always ask how I can serve them better and what areas need improving. When I first got into this business, I only

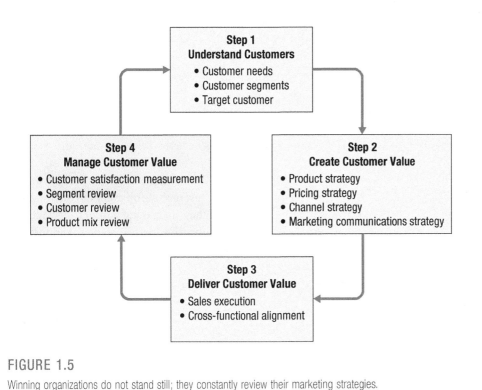

FIGURE 1.5

Winning organizations do not stand still; they constantly review their marketing strategies.

MARKETING DRIVES SUCCESS

1.3 SIEMENS MEDICAL SOLUTIONS

Objective: Delivering Customer Value Requires a Focus on the Customer

Companies that serve the needs of medical professionals are usually organized around functions that, in many cases, do not communicate well with each other.[6] So, for example, a sales professional may call on a hospital to sell an ultrasound machine. But the same sales professional may lack the technical knowledge to really serve the needs of the customer. The end result is that the customer does not get served in the best possible fashion.

Siemens Medical Solutions recognized that there was an opportunity to focus on the customer's total needs—from early diagnostic and detection technology to patient care. So, it set out to create the world's first fully integrated diagnostics company. This meant creating a company where all employees, regardless of functional affiliation, are focused on the customer. Today, Siemens has brought together imaging and lab diagnostics, therapy and healthcare information technology solutions, and consulting and support services for the customer. This means that the entire organization is totally focused on serving the customer's needs, regardless of what they may be.

Siemens Medical Solutions is a customer-focused business.

KEYPOINT

At the end of every year, a business must conduct a review of four items: customer satisfaction, segments, customers, and product mix.

The business enterprise has two and only two basic functions: marketing and innovation. Marketing and innovation produce results; all the rest are costs.

PETER DRUCKER

sold pressure washers to automobile garages. Over time, I realized that gas stations were a very lucrative segment to serve. Initially, I used to sell only the hardware, that is, the pressure washer. Over time, I realized that there was more money to be made in detergents, so I added them to my mix. Finally, at the end of each fiscal year, I review my customer list. You know, some customers are needy but greedy. They want a lot from me, but they do not want to pay me anything. So I 'fire' them and hope they go to my competitors!"

"I'm always thinking about what is next and where my business is headed. For example, the next frontier in cleaning dirt and grease is bacteria. Scientists have discovered a species of bacteria that loves to eat dirt, oil, and grease (they are completely harmless to humans). My competitors, on the other hand, are content just to show up every day and do business. They are happy if they are making money today; they do not think about where their business is headed. And they are surprised when the market changes and they are caught unawares. Many of them go out of business."[7]

I have captured what Tim told me in Table 1.4.

TABLE 1.4	**Tim's Secrets to Business Success**
What Tim does	**What we call it**
At each customer visit he asks customers how he can serve them better.	**Customer satisfaction measurement.** We will discuss this in Chapters 11 and 12.
He is always looking for new types of market segments to serve.	**Segment review.** We will discuss this in Chapters 3, 4, and 12.
He always ensures that the goods and services he sells are in line with customers' changing needs and technological advances.	**Product mix review.** We will discuss this in Chapters 4, 5, and 12.
He regularly "fires" his worst customers—the ones who want a lot from him, but do not want to pay for the value they are receiving.	**Customer review.** We will discuss this in Chapters 3, 4, 6, and 12.

Where We've Been

- We have seen that successful businesses win because they develop and implement superior marketing strategies.
- Marketing is a disciplined process used by an organization to solve business problems.
- The marketing process is to understand-create-deliver-manage customer value.

CHECKPOINT

Where We're Going

- This book is your roadmap to success; you will learn how to navigate this roadmap.

This Book: Your Roadmap to Success

Your roadmap to success begins with this book. As the research demonstrates, if you follow the disciplined process of understand-create-deliver-manage customer value, you will have accounted for 90% of the factors that are key to your business success. In other words, the research shows that although some factors are beyond your control (for example, the price of raw materials or governmental regulations), business success depends on how well you handle the factors you *can* control—strategy and implementation. Figure 1.6 shows you the key marketing steps and the chapters in this book that are associated with them.

OBJECTIVE 3

KEYPOINT

If you follow the marketing discipline recommended in this book, you will account for 90% of your success in business.

The author discusses how you can use this book as your roadmap to success.

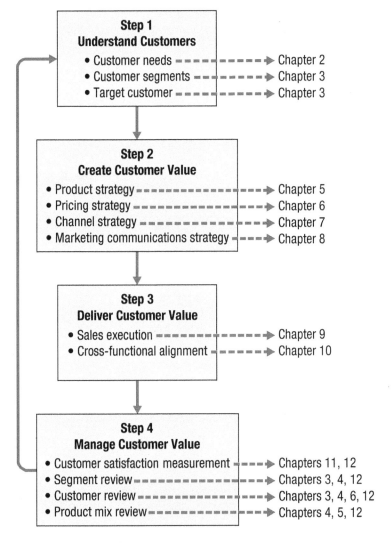

FIGURE 1.6

Your roadmap to success

Where We've Been

■ We have learned that if you use this book correctly, you will have accounted for 90% of the factors that determine business success.

Where We're Going

■ We will learn the 10 tasks every world-class marketing organization performs.

■ The final section of the chapter examines what organizations that are not marketing led look like.

CHECKPOINT

OBJECTIVE 4

KEYPOINT

Successful chief marketing officers (CMOs) live the 10 tasks of marketing every day.

What Do World-Class Marketing Organizations Do?

Whether marketing is a function within a larger organization or a set of tasks performed by an entrepreneur running a small business, all world-class marketing functions perform a set of common tasks.[8]

The 10 Tasks of Marketing

Table 1.5 captures the major tasks of marketing. The examples that follow illustrate these tasks.

TABLE 1.5   The 10 Tasks of Marketing

Task	Description
(1) Identify opportunities	Many organizations have a formal strategic planning department that is responsible for identifying which businesses to enter and which ones to exit. But if these departments are not being advised by marketing, their efforts are often not successful.[9]
(2) Segment and target markets	Within the chosen markets, a crucial marketing task is to segment customers and make recommendations on which customer segments to serve.
(3) Develop a marketing strategy	Using the marketing mix elements of product, price, channel, and marketing communications, marketing must design the marketing offer in such a way that the offer resonates with the customer and provides the company a differentiated positioning in the marketplace. The marketing plan encapsulates the firm's marketing strategy.
(4) Implement the marketing strategy	While marketing implements many aspects of the marketing plan, the rest of the organization ultimately has to implement the organization's marketing strategy. For this reason, marketing has to engage other functions by helping them develop functional plans.
(5) Assess and innovate	The world's best marketing organizations do not sit still; they assess their marketing strategies, make changes, and innovate by focusing on new product development.
(6) Provide a competitive advantage to the sales force	If marketing is not providing a competitive advantage to the sales force, it has failed. It does so by market segmentation efforts, target marketing, and brand building. More details are found in Chapter 9.
(7) Be the customer's champion within the organization	Marketing is the only function within an organization whose prime focus is on the customer. Therefore, it is the task of marketing to be the "voice of the customer" within the organization.
(8) Build a customer-focused business	Every function and every employee in a business has to be focused on the customer. Without this focus, the business will fail.
(9) Make marketing accountable	Weak marketing organizations believe that the way to build strong brands is to throw money at the problem. Such marketing functions are exposed in the end for what they are—charlatans posing as marketing strategists.
(10) Be a change agent within the organization	The motto of the world's best marketing organizations is "If it is not broken, fix it." In this way, they become transformation agents within their organizations. The worst marketing organizations' motto is "Leave well enough alone."

Example 1 Smucker's has identified an opportunity to expand its food portfolio. Hence, it purchased Folgers coffee, Jif peanut butter, and Crisco shortening from Procter & Gamble (P&G). P&G, on the other hand, wants to focus more on its health and beauty business. Marketing's role in this context is to provide advice on which businesses (markets) to enter and which ones to exit.

Example 2 Paul, a manager in the supply chain department of a major brewery, knows his firm's marketing function is weak.[10] "They think the way to build a strong beer brand is to do a lot of advertising. But, after spending heavily for years on this brand, it still continues to perform poorly. You know what, though? They do not want to change because this situation suits them just fine. They go with the advertising agency to exotic locations like Brazil and Australia to shoot commercials. Why would they want to change? And our advertising agency, whom we pay $1.5 million a year, is not going to tell them any different. In the end, our company is going to get into a lot of trouble."

In this company, the role of marketing is not clearly defined, perhaps because the strategic nature of marketing is not clearly understood by senior management. So marketing tries to build strong brands by spending heavily on advertising—a total contrast to the strategic nature of marketing we have discussed in this chapter.

Example 3 Procter & Gamble is keeping marketers and researchers in their positions longer to enable them to develop a deeper understanding of their business and their customers. Traditionally, this has not been the case at P&G. A focus on developing deep customer insights also means going to laundromats and homes to observe customers doing laundry and gathering data from such websites as www.tide.com. These consumer observations do not get filed away in a drawer, never to be used. Rather, they are disseminated throughout the organization, so everyone is focused on the customer.

Example 4 Beth Comstock, president of NBC Universal Integrated Media, works closely with the chief financial officer (CFO) to develop metrics to measure the return on marketing investment. Sometimes, though, there is no clear-cut way to measure the return on the marketing investment. In that case, she advocates starting a dialogue with the CFO, offering alternative measurement methods that might satisfy the CFO that she is undertaking the right move that will generate growth.

Example 5 Procter & Gamble's disposable diaper division learned a valuable lesson from its chief marketing officer (CMO). Previously, it had focused on the technological aspects of diapers—how they fit, stay on, and keep the baby dry. But the CMO focused them more on parents, who were more concerned about how P&G could help them with the baby's overall development and health. This enabled greater coordination between the diaper marketing team and the research and development (R&D) team, leading to greater brand growth, new market opportunities, and change within the organization.

In this example, marketing shows how it can be a powerful agent of organizational transformation.

> *[Ongoing research shows that] growth in revenue and profitability is strongest among those companies that elevate marketing's role to the strategic level.*
>
> HARTER, LANDRY, AND TIPPING

> *I can't imagine doing a marketing job without connecting with the CFO. Marketing must be a finance team partner. In fact, the worst thing a marketer, or for that matter, a business leader, can do is say, 'Just trust me; I'll show you when I make my numbers.'*
>
> BETH COMSTOCK[11]

KEYPOINT

World-class marketing organizations do not view marketing as a function, but as a force that transforms the entire organization.

1.4 OPERATION EYESIGHT

Objective: Marketing Is Important for Non-profit Organizations as Well

Operation Eyesight is a Canadian organization that has been working since 1963 to prevent and eliminate avoidable blindness in developing countries in Africa and South Asia. To achieve this goal, the organization has to use marketing principles to create value for its main stakeholders—donors (individuals and corporations) and eye care partners (hospitals and doctors). How does it do this? First, it carefully uses research to understand the unique needs of each segment: donors have different needs from eye care partners. For example, an eye care clinic needs equipment and infrastructure (bricks and mortar), while a donor wants to contribute to greater social good (vision and values).

Operation Eyesight ensures not only that it builds awareness for its brand, but also that the message communicated by the brand appeals to various stakeholders. To accomplish its objectives, Operation Eyesight partners with eye clinics, hospitals, and ophthalmologists to help patients in need. In essence, this becomes its channel strategy. Finally, it uses such marketing communications means as advertising and speaking engagements to inform various stakeholder segments (the public, potential partners, government, and so forth) about its mission to help eliminate avoidable blindness.

A world of unavoidable beauty, lost to avoidable blindness.

Millions of people in developing countries are needlessly losing their sight to treatable, and often preventable, eye disease. That's why Operation Eyesight, a Canadian non-profit organization, supports the efforts of eye doctors, educators and others in South Asia and Africa. Together, through surgeries, outreach clinics, treatment programs and more, we're curbing the spread of eye disease and blindness. But more people are waiting every day and we need your support. Your donation will help someone keep a world of beauty in sight. Find out how by visiting operationeyesight.ca.

1-800-585-8265 | www.operationeyesight.ca

OPERATION EYESIGHT™
For All The World To See

Operation Eyesight uses the principles of marketing to achieve its goals.

Where We've Been

- We have seen how successful businesses develop and implement superior marketing strategies.
- World-class marketing organizations perform 10 essential tasks, from identifying opportunities to transforming the organization.

Where We're Going

- In the final section of this chapter, we will see the mistakes made by businesses that are not marketing led.

CHECKPOINT

Characteristics of Organizations That Are Not Marketing Led

OBJECTIVE 5

In Figure 1.7, we see what happens when an organization is not marketing led. To begin with, these organizations do not have a clear agreement on what marketing is and what its role should be in the firm. Typically, such organizations are led by CEOs who are solely focused on the financial community. Lacking a customer focus, the business is focused on cost reduction and market share, not on long-term revenue growth and profitability driven by the development of a stable of strong brands.

We will have more to say about this in the next chapter.

KEYPOINT

Success in business is not accidental. Winning organizations earn their success.

Key Dimensions	When Marketing Is *Not* Influential in Corporate Decisions	When Marketing Is Influential in Corporate Decisions
Definition of marketing	Wide disagreement and ambiguity about the role and importance of marketing and customer orientation	Clear and shared understanding of the role of marketing: strong customer orientation in the corporate culture
Top-management objectives	Focused on current stock price, earnings per share, cost reduction, market share, and sales volume	Focused on long-term growth in revenue, profitability, earnings per share, and cash flow
Orientation and functional background of CEO	Little or no marketing experience or acumen; focused on financial community	Deep understanding of the importance of marketing; compelling vision of customer value. Advocate for the customer.
Top-management priorities	Cost reduction and labour productivity	Customers, resellers, and key accounts. Market information and tracking data are key management tools.
Growth strategy	Achieved through mergers and acquisitions	Achieved through serious commitment to R&D, product innovation
Role of brands	Strong brands used as cash cows to fund acquisitions, growth strategy	Substantial investment to build and maintain brand equity
Focus on new product development	Product-focused and technology-focused	Customer analysis is hard-wired into product innovation and new business development
Portfolio strategy	Managed for cash flow; pricing used to achieve volume goals	Customer portfolio analyzed and managed for loyalty, profitability

FIGURE 1.7

Characteristics of organizations that are not marketing led

Source: Frederick E. Webster; Alan J. Malter, and Shankar Ganesan (2005), "The Decline and Dispersion of Marketing Competence," *MIT Sloan Management Review*, Summer, p. 42.

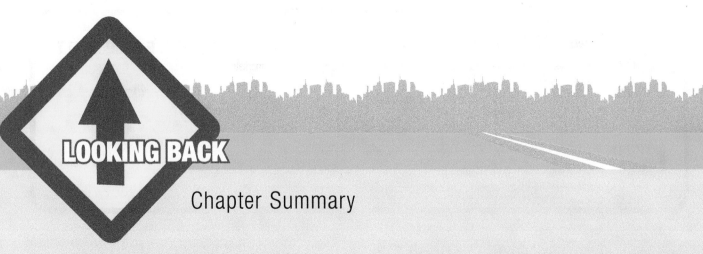

Chapter Summary

1. **Be primed for success by understanding what winning organizations do well.**

   Repeatedly, the research is clear on what separates winning organizations from their not-so-successful counterparts: (1) they develop superior marketing strategies and (2) they implement the strategy by engaging the rest of the organization.

2. **Learn the discipline of marketing that will lead you to success over your competitors.**

   Marketing is a disciplined process followed by organizations to solve business problems such as increased competition, commoditization of goods and services, and increasing customer price sensitivity. The four steps in the marketing process are understand-create-deliver-manage customer value. The end goal of the first step is to segment and target customers. Customer value is created by using the marketing mix elements of product, price, channels, and marketing communications strategies.

   Marketing strategies are implemented by the marketing area and, importantly, also by the sales force and other functions. The final step in the marketing process is to evaluate marketing strategies to assess customer satisfaction and to make adjustments to segmentation, customers served, and product mix.

3. **Get on the roadmap to success by learning how to use this book.**

   If you follow the recommendations in this book, you will have accounted for 90% of the factors that determine business

   success. To fully appreciate this book, start at the beginning and work your way through the chapters. Periodically, you will be asked to take a pause in each chapter to think about the material and assess if you are on the right track. Do not skip these Chapter Challenges.

4. **Master the 10 secrets of successful marketing organizations.**

   Successful marketing organizations live the 10 secrets every day. While these secrets may seem obvious, organizations stumble because they do not know how to implement them. However, successful marketers know that they have to go beyond the fundamental tasks of strategy formulation and implementation—they have to champion the customer, demonstrate the value of marketing, and be the change agent in their business organizations.

5. **Learn to avoid mistakes made by organizations that are not marketing led.**

   To begin with, these organizations do not have a clear agreement on what marketing is and what its role should be in the firm. Typically, such organizations are led by CEOs who are solely focused on the financial community. Lacking a customer focus, the business is focused on cost reduction and market share, not on long-term revenue growth and profitability driven by the development of a stable of strong brands.

CRITICAL THINKING QUESTIONS

1. Peter Drucker, one of the best management thinkers of our time, wrote: "The business enterprise has two and only two basic functions: marketing and innovation. Marketing and innovation produce results; all the rest are costs."[12] Explain this statement.

2. Visit the websites www.homemadesimple.com and www.vocalpoint.com. What insights do you think Procter & Gamble gains from these sites? How do you think it uses the information?

3. Your friend wants to start a business. When you ask her who her target market is, she says, "Why, *everybody* is my customer." What advice will you give this entrepreneur?

4. We have seen that successful businesses use the marketing mix elements to create value for the customer. Pick one for-profit business and one non-profit business and explain how they create value for their customer using the marketing mix elements.

5. Marketing needs to work closely with other functions in an organization. We have seen how marketing and finance need to work together. Can you describe why marketing should work closely with (a) manufacturing, (b) sales, and (c) human resources?

6. One of your friends says, "If you want to succeed in marketing, you have to be creative." The other says, "If you want to succeed in marketing, you have to be analytical." What position do you take? Why?

RUNNING CASE

ARBOL INDUSTRIES DECIDES TO BECOME CUSTOMER FOCUSED

To help you further understand the material in this book, I have included a running case on Arbol Industries[13] at the end of each chapter. Each segment of the case will apply the material being discussed in the chapter. The case is based on a five-year consulting project I did with Arbol.[14] As a result of such deep engagement with the company, I became very familiar with it—from its initial start toward becoming a marketing-led business to the challenges and frustrations that ultimately led to its strong success.

Arbol Industries is a 100-year-old company operating in the forestry products industry. Their products include pulp, paper, lumber, engineered wood, and plywood. They sell to the home building industry and to end consumers through such retailers as Home Depot and specialized suppliers such as Dick's Lumber. Arbol is a very successful company, primarily because it is well run. Its management is composed mainly of engineers. These individuals are very good at getting the most from their assets (factories) and keeping their costs low. As a result, Arbol is very profitable.

A few years ago, a new CEO was brought in. He realized that, although Arbol was successful, it was not going to last. This was because competitors from Eastern Europe and Asia were flooding the market with their cheaper goods. He knew the way forward was to transform Arbol from a cost-focused company to a marketing-led company. He knew the solution lay in differentiating Arbol's products and charging a higher price for them. So, he started asking questions. "Why can't we charge more for our lumber and plywood?" "Because," came the reply, "they are commodities. Commodities are not brands, they cannot be differentiated. How can you charge more for commodities such as lumber and plywood? Their price is quoted on the Mercantile Exchange."

But the CEO was not satisfied with these answers. He persisted. One of his first steps was to hire a marketing manager from outside the industry and develop the first marketing function in the organization's 100-year history! The marketing manager was shocked that a company that did not think about customers or marketing could actually make money. But just like the CEO, he too realized that Arbol could be a lot more successful if it began developing and implementing marketing strategies.

Let us reveal the ending first. When Arbol began its marketing journey, it was successful. At that time, its **return on investment** (ROI) was in the top 25% of competitors in the industry, a very creditable fact indeed. Five years later, Arbol's ROI had jumped to the top of the competitor list, and the gap between Arbol and its competitors was growing. Arbol was making money in an industry that, five years later, was losing money.

When Arbol began its marketing journey, people laughed. "How can you apply marketing principles to pulp, lumber, and plywood?" they would ask. "Marketing is for consumer goods only. What do you think we are selling, Gucci handbags?" Five years later, they were no longer laughing, as cheaper imports had eaten into their business. In fact, at industry conferences, Arbol's employees were being offered jobs at competitor firms. This is because the competition wanted to replicate Arbol's success.

What follows in each case at the end of each chapter is how Arbol did it. I hope you enjoy the marketing journey along with them!

Case Assignment

Many years ago, a famous professor said, "There is no such thing as a commodity. All goods and services can be differentiated and usually are." Do you agree with this statement? Why or why not? Be sure to provide examples in support of your arguments.

SUGGESTED READINGS
If You Want to Become a Brilliant Marketer, Do Not Miss These Publications

George Harter, Edward Landry, and Andrew Tipping, "The New Complete Marketer," *Strategy + Business*, Issue 48, Autumn 2007, pp. 78–87.

Nitin Nohria, William Joyce, and Bruce Roberson, "What Really Works?" *Harvard Business Review*, July 2003, pp. 42–52.

Ajay Sirsi, *Marketing Led–Sales Driven: How Successful Businesses Use the Power of Marketing Plans and Sales Execution to Win in the Marketplace* (Victoria, BC: Trafford Publishing, 2005).

NOTES

1. Nitin Nohria, William Joyce, and Bruce Roberson, "What Really Works?" *Harvard Business Review*, July 2003, pp. 42–52.

2. Based on Brian Grow and Susan McMillan, "Home Depot: Last among Shoppers," *Business Week*, June 19, 2006, p. 34; Gene G. Marcial, "Remodeling Home Depot," *Business Week*, March 19, 2007, p. 104; Jia Lynn Yang, "Consulting Past CEOs Wise Guys," *Fortune*, June 25, 2007, p. 95.

3. Grow and McMillan, *ibid.*

4. Initial idea provided by Glenn Rifkin in "How Snap-On Tools Ratchets Its Brand," *Strategy and Business*, First Quarter, 1998, pp. 51–58, and research done on the Snap-on website.

5. For additional details read Ajay Sirsi, *Marketing Led—Sales Driven: How Successful Businesses Use the Power of Marketing Plans and Sales Execution to Win in the Marketplace* (Victoria, BC: Trafford Publishing, 2005).

6. Based on Siemens.com, press release of October 2007, and conversations with my ex-students who work for Siemens.

7. See Chapter 5 for another example of how failure to pay attention to changing market conditions can catch a business unawares.

8. Material for this section is from: George Anders, "Drucker's Teachings Find Following in Asia," *The Wall Street Journal*, June 18, 2008, B2; George Harter, Edward Landry, and Andrew Tipping, "The New Complete Marketer," *Strategy + Business*, Issue 48, Autumn 2007, pp. 78–87; Nirmalya Kumar, *Marketing as Strategy*, Harvard Business School Publishing, 2004.

9. In my experience, strategic planning departments that are not being advised by marketing often work away in some part of the organization, and nobody knows what they really do. They tend to equate strategy with mergers and acquisitions efforts (see Figure 1.7 on page 19 for more details).

10. Example provided by a student of mine in the executive program.

11. In Geoffrey Precourt, ed., *CMO Thought Leaders: The Rise of the Strategic Marketer*, strategy + business books, 2007 and reported in Harter et al., *ibid.*

12. Peter F. Drucker, *The Practice of Management* (New York: Harper Collins, 1954).

13. I have disguised the name of the company.

14. I was initially brought in to teach marketing to a group of sales professionals. From there, my relationship with Arbol deepened: helping write and implement marketing plans, furthering education to all levels within the company, improving cross-functional alignment, and having a regular seat on the Operating Committee.

CHAPTER 2
Understanding Customer Needs

CHAPTER INTRODUCTION

In this chapter you will

Companies that try to push a good or a service on customers, without a proper understanding of their needs, are destined to fail. This is a proven fact in the history of business. Winning companies develop a deep understanding of their customers' needs. The really smart companies do not merely understand customer needs, they "create" needs. And finally, the really, really smart companies succeed by not doing any formal market research at all.

1. Learn to avoid mistakes made by companies that do not understand customer needs.

2. Meet companies that win by developing a deep understanding of customer needs, and learn the valuable lessons they offer.

3. Learn that smart companies are not happy to merely understand customer needs: they create them.

4. Learn practical tools and techniques of marketing research to understand customer needs.

5. Learn the secrets of smart companies that succeed by not doing any formal marketing research.

OBJECTIVE 1

Avoid Mistakes Made by Companies That Do Not Understand Customer Needs

> *The consumer is not an idiot; she is your boss.*
>
> ROTHENBERG AND LIODICE

Companies that do not base their decisions on customer needs make some common mistakes that cost them time, money, and resources. Of course, many of these companies eventually go out of business. Let us take a few examples.[2]

Example 1   Susan is a marketing manager for a mobile phone company. She laments all the time, "I cannot compete with my competitors. They are bigger and have bigger marketing [communications] dollars. You see their ads at soccer tournaments, cultural events, everywhere. If only I had more money, I could do a better job."

She is missing the point. Her marketing strategy is essentially to outgun the competition by spending even more on advertising. This approach just does not make sense. She is going after the 18- to 34-year-old segment, notorious for being price-sensitive and brand disloyal. "They change cell phones like you and I change underwear," she says. Yet she continues to stick to her position of wanting more money for advertising.

Susan typifies business people who do not understand the needs of their customers. Because they lack such understanding, their marketing strategies are superficial—mainly limited to bribing the customer with attractive advertising and promotional efforts. We know such an approach does not succeed.

General Motors (GM) is struggling with bloated inventories of unsold SUVs and trucks. A few years ago, it continued to insist that consumers would buy large, gas-guzzling vehicles, even though gas prices were going up and all indicators pointed in another direction. Its competitor, Toyota, on the other hand, has quietly continued to sell passenger cars and, in 2008, is on the verge of catching up to GM as the number one car company in the U.S. market. In order to entice customers to buy its larger vehicles, GM is desperately launching a last-ditch effort: 0% loans for up to six years or cash rebates of $7000.[3]

> *If you have to push advertising to consumers, you are out of business.*
>
> KEITH PARDY, NOKIA CORPORATION

Example 2   A sales organization waits for customers to call them and place an order. They constantly complain to the marketing managers: "The only reason we don't secure orders is because we are too expensive." Lacking any clear direction from the marketing function, the sales organization will do anything to secure a contract. This involves dropping the price. The end result? While marketing is busy trying to build a strong brand and maintain price premiums, the sales function is devaluing the brand in the marketplace.

Example 3   Engineering makes a wonderful gizmo that customers do not want. "Our product lets patients self-titrate!" they proclaim. Self-titration means the patient determines the level of dosage for the medication. For example, for pain medication, the patient can turn the dial up (more medication) or down (less medication) depending on the level of pain. However, neither patients nor physicians like the product for the same reason—patients are not sure exactly how much medication they should give themselves. They either over- or under-medicate themselves. The business is now stuck with the product and the sales function has the burden of trying to sell inventory.

Example 4   In organizations where there is no clear and widely shared understanding of customer needs, organizational silos exist.[4] In these businesses, each function does its own thing, often with negative consequences.

KEYPOINT

Many organizations have a magician they rely upon to get rid of products customers don't want—the salesperson.

A courier company has unused capacity (their transportation and package sorting facilities can handle more customers than they are currently serving). Without consulting the marketing function on the organization's strategy, the operations group signs up customers on its own. The problem? These are not the kind of customers the organization wants to serve. These customers are price-sensitive and do not want to pay a lot. As a result, they are unattractive to the organization. But the damage has been done, and contracts have been signed.

This situation exists because there is no "glue" to hold this business together. A deep and widely shared understanding of customer needs and target customer segments is one such glue. Very few organizations collect and share customer needs information throughout the business. We will profile these rare businesses (like Hagen) throughout this book.

> *The consumer is moving faster*
> *than most companies.*
>
> JOHN HAYES, AMERICAN EXPRESS

Travelling with your pet?
Get him there safely and comfortably.

A harmony of design, aesthetics and function, Pet Cargo responds to the needs of you and your pet. With Pet Cargo, your pet goes where you go. Via plane, train, boat or automobile.

Divider Grill and Castors sold separately.

For more information about Pet Cargo Carriers, visit **www.hagen.com**

Pet Cargo is a registered trademark of Rolf C. Hagen Inc © 2008

HAGEN.

An accurate understanding of customer needs enables Hagen to create customer value.

CHECKPOINT

Where We've Been

- We have seen that companies that do not understand their customers fall into predictable traps.
- They waste money on advertising, they drop their price to sell the product, they focus on the technology, or they behave like a dysfunctional family.

Where We're Going

- We will meet and learn from companies that win by understanding their customers.

Susan Abbott of Abbott Research talks about what can happen when firms do not understand customer needs.

OBJECTIVE 2 — Meet Companies That Win by Developing a Deep Understanding of Customer Needs, and Learn the Valuable Lessons They Offer

MARKETING DRIVES SUCCESS

2.1 TESCO

Objective: Understanding Customer Needs Is Crucial for Success

European grocer Tesco has four store formats: Express, Metro, Extra, and supermarkets. It undertook research on customers to understand what they were buying (or not buying) and why. Its loyalty card data showed them what customers were buying. **Survey research** with customers showed them what customers were not buying and why. Tesco found that, in some store formats, young mothers bought fewer baby products in its stores because they trusted pharmacies more. So Tesco launched Baby & Toddler Club to provide expert advice to parents and provide them with targeted promotional materials (like coupons for products). The program was a success—its share of baby products sales in the United Kingdom grew from 16% to 24% in just three years.[5]

Tesco understands its customers—and succeeds.

2.2 SOUTHWEST AIRLINES

Objective: Accurate Understanding of Customer Needs Helps in Target Marketing

In an industry characterized by wrenching changes, massive losses, and employee layoffs on a grand scale, there is one shining exception—Southwest Airlines. In January 2008, Southwest celebrated 35 years of consecutive profitability.[6] Even with the price of a barrel of oil at $130, Southwest carried almost 8% more passengers in the first quarter of 2008, while other airlines saw declines ranging from 0.5% to 8.5%.[7] Every other major airline company in the world has tried to duplicate Southwest's strategy and success, and has failed.

The secret to Southwest's success is an open book and is based on a deep understanding of customer needs. Herb Kelleher, co-founder of Southwest, has

An accurate understanding of customer needs enables Southwest Airlines to focus its customer strategy.

said that the firm's success is based on an understanding that

■ customers do not like paying high fares
■ customers do not like to spend time in airports, waiting for a plane
■ customers like to get to their destinations on time

Of course, all airlines understand these customer needs, but the difference is that Southwest has deeply ingrained its understanding of customers into its strategy:

■ It does not use the "hub and spoke" system used by other airlines; it only flies point-to-point.
■ It focuses on the customer segment that does not want frills, only low fares. So it does not offer pre-assigned seating and meals.
■ It only flies Boeing 737 aircraft, as they are low maintenance and any pilot can fly any plane, like a fleet of cars.
■ Customers can only buy tickets directly from the company.

Table 2.1 summarizes valuable lessons offered by companies that win by developing a deep understanding of customer needs.

TABLE 2.1 Lessons Offered by Companies That Develop a Deep Understanding of Customers

Lessons	What it means to you
Talk to your customers whenever and wherever you can.	While formal market research is useful, do not discount informal ways to listen to your customers.
Use data you already have.	There is a wealth of data within your company already. Use it. Some sources include sales professionals and customer care specialists.
Establish clear standards for research.	If you cannot answer these questions, do not do the research; save your money instead: ■ What is the value of the information? ■ What is the cost of incorrect information? ■ How will the data be used? ■ What criteria will be used to translate the results into action?

Where We've Been

■ We have learned that winning businesses have a deep understanding of customer needs.

■ Businesses that do not have a deep understanding of customer needs fall into predictable traps.

Where We're Going

■ We will see that smart companies are not happy to merely *understand* customer needs. They *create* them.

CHECKPOINT

CHAPTER CHALLENGE 2.1

ARE YOU ON THE RIGHT TRACK?

What do we mean when we say smart companies are not happy to merely understand customer needs, they create them?

(*Were you on the right track? Check your answers in Appendix 2.*)

OBJECTIVE 3

Smart Companies Are Not Happy to Merely Understand Customer Needs: They Create Them

> *You need to change at least as fast as consumer expectations. That's renovation. To maintain a leadership position, you also need to leapfrog, to move faster and go beyond what consumers will tell you. That's innovation.*
>
> PETER BRABECK-LETMATHE, CHAIRMAN AND CEO, NESTLÉ

Akio Morita, one of the founders of Sony, was walking the streets of Los Angeles when he saw a group of people doing something strange: they were listening to music.[8] But it did not appear to be a pleasant experience for them because on their shoulders they carried heavy "boom boxes" that pulsated music. Upon his return to Japan, Morita asked his engineers to solve this problem. And so was born the legendary Sony Walkman, a small device that let consumers listen to music outside their homes, a precursor to today's MP3 players.

Sony then conducted market research to ask consumers what they thought of this innovation, and whether they would use it. What do you think the reply was? "No." Intrigued, Sony asked consumers why they would not use the product, which obviously was a great innovation. The reply given was classic: "Why would we want to listen to music outside our homes? We only listen to music inside the home."

Thankfully for all of us, Sony decided not to believe the research. They realized that consumers could not imagine their lives with this innovation. Sony solved the problem by initially targeting the innovation to a group of customers who did appreciate a break from a tedious activity—joggers.

The Sony example teaches us a valuable lesson. Smart companies are not happy with merely understanding customer needs: they create them. Creating customer needs is not a sinister act. Instead, it is the act of giving shape to a need the consumer has a hard time articulating. We will have more to say on this topic in the last section of this chapter.

If I had listened to my customers, I would have given them a faster horse.

HENRY FORD

MARKETING DRIVES SUCCESS

2.3 DANONE

Objective: Smart Companies Create Customer Needs

French company Groupe Danone saw an opportunity in Ireland.[9] Its research showed that people in Ireland saw yogurt as a healthy snack and did not perceive a difference in competing products (Figures 2.1 and 2.2). No product really stood out in consumers' minds. Within the health market, yogurts were mainly natural, but their taste did not appeal to everyone. Danone bet on the idea that health and taste could be combined.

And Danone was right. By combining these two concepts, Danone brought about a revolution in the yogurt market. In effect, it changed the paradigm, or the way accepted norms are developed for products. Danone *created* a market for a product that consumers recognized they wanted *once* it became available (Figure 2.3).

The results speak for themselves. Prior to Danone's entrance into the market, growth was stagnant at 2%. Danone revolutionized the Irish dairy market by increasing growth to 23%. It grew to become the number one dairy brand in Ireland, and in less than three years, Danone increased its market share from 4.9% to 14.8%.

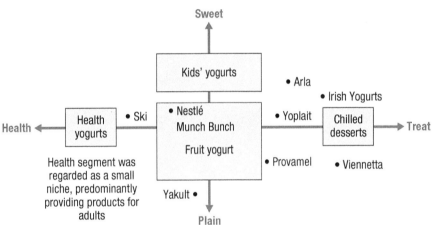

FIGURE 2.1

Yogurt market before Danone

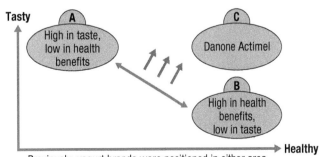

Previously, yogurt brands were positioned in either area A or area B; Danone Actimel created a new market with a brand combining health benefits and taste (area C)

FIGURE 2.2

Danone finds a gap.

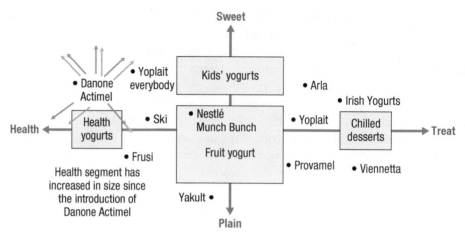

FIGURE 2.3

Danone creates a need.

An example of creating a customer need

Where We've Been

■ We have learned that if you conduct your business without an understanding of customer needs, you will fail.

■ Smart businesses do not just understand customers, they shape and create needs.

Where We're Going

■ We will learn practical tools and techniques for understanding customer needs.

CHECKPOINT

Practical Tools and Techniques for Understanding Customer Needs

OBJECTIVE 4

Some major marketing research techniques are shown in Table 2.2.

TABLE 2.2	**Marketing Research Techniques**
Technique	**Description**
Secondary research	Research that has already been conducted by someone else (available free of charge or for a fee)
Qualitative techniques	
Focus groups	A guided discussion with a group of respondents such as customers
Depth interviews	A one-on-one, in-depth discussion with a respondent
Ethnography	A technique where the researcher becomes a customer to learn more about customer needs and value drivers
Quantitative techniques	
Surveys	Quantitative method of data collection by questionnaires

Secondary Research

The very first step in conducting research to understand customers is to "go" to the library. Of course, these days going to the library can be a virtual trip. Thanks to the internet, you can search databases and gather insights about customers from research conducted by someone else. **Secondary research** data is available free of charge or for a fee, depending on the source. Common sources of secondary data are the government, academic institutions, think tanks, professional associations, consulting firms, and market research firms.

There are several advantages to conducting secondary research:

- You may find the answer to the question you are researching, thus making it unnecessary for you to do the research yourself.
- Even if you do need to conduct research yourself (this is called **primary research**), secondary research will give you tips on what has already been done (so you don't reinvent the wheel), what gaps exist in knowledge, and what traps to avoid.
- Secondary research is quicker than primary research and, depending on the source, could be free of charge.

Focus groups, **depth interviews**, and **ethnographies** are a class of techniques called **qualitative research** techniques or **exploratory research** techniques. The main goal of these techniques is to explore the dimensions of a problem and generate ideas. Details are provided here for each technique.

KEY POINT

Go to www.secondarydata.com for tips on secondary research data.

CHAPTER CHALLENGE 2.2

ARE YOU ON THE RIGHT TRACK?

Name at least three cautions you should heed when conducting secondary research.
(*Were you on the right track? Check your answers in Appendix 2.*)

Focus Groups

Tammy is sitting in her study when the phone rings. A marketing research firm is on the other line. The following dialogue takes place (I have abbreviated the conversation).

MARKETING RESEARCHER: "Hello, may I speak to the person in charge of making decisions about the internet in your household?"

TAMMY: "Speaking."

MARKETING RESEARCHER: "Would you be interested in attending a focus group session about the internet? The session will be held downtown on Wednesday at 6:00 p.m. We will pay you $100 for the 1½ hour session."

On Wednesday Tammy arrives at the focus group location. A receptionist greets her and directs her to the waiting room. She realizes that, besides the internet session, there are two other focus groups taking place that evening—one for cola drinks and the other for pet food. In the waiting room, she chats with the other focus group participants while nibbling on snacks provided by the facility. In a while, the receptionist arrives and directs the participants to the main focus group room. Tammy notices that there is a long table in the middle, with chairs for 12 people. She is curious as to why there is a mirror covering one entire wall. "Strange way to decorate a room," she thinks to herself.

A person arrives and sits at the head of the table. "I am the focus group moderator," she says. "The 10 of you are going to spend the next 90 minutes talking about the internet. But first, you will notice the mirror on the wall. It is a one-way mirror. Behind it is a room where the internet client is watching this session. The session will also be videotaped so I can review the session later to analyze the data. There are no right and wrong answers; I am only interested in your opinions."

For the next 80 minutes, Tammy and the other participants respond to questions posed by the moderator. Tammy notices that the moderator hardly speaks; all the discussion is taking place among the participants. The moderator ensures that all participants have a chance to provide their opinions. They take two short breaks, one in the middle and one at the end of the focus group session. Tammy notices that each time, the moderator disappears for a few minutes to the room behind the one-way mirror to converse with the client.

Finally, the moderator divides the larger group into groups of two and gives them a task—each group is asked to evaluate three internet packages and rank them from the most liked to the least liked. Each group is given a chance to explain what they like and dislike about each option. The moderator thanks them at the end of the session. Tammy collects her money at the front desk and goes home.

The salient points about focus groups are as follows:

- It is a very flexible technique. The moderator has a guide she follows, but she has the flexibility to change course depending on the answers being given by the respondents.
- Clients can see their customers (and non-customers) in action from behind the one-way mirror.

KEYPOINT

Go to www.managementhelp.org to get tips on how to conduct focus groups.

CHAPTER CHALLENGE 2.3

ARE YOU ON THE RIGHT TRACK?

What type of research situations would focus groups *not* be appropriate for?

(*Were you on the right track? Check your answers in Appendix 2.*)

- A focus group is a great way to explore the dimensions of a problem—generate ideas, test product concepts, and test marketing communications messages.

Depth Interviews

A depth interview is a data collection method where the moderator engages *one* respondent in a conversation for at least 60 minutes.[10] Depth interviews are a great data collection method when you want to know (a) how customers make decisions between competing alternatives and (b) the sources of influences on those decisions. Let us take an example.

A company that sells medical diagnostic equipment costing millions of dollars wants to train its sales force on strategic selling. It hires a researcher to collect data from hospitals. The researcher schedules 60-minute one-on-one depth interviews with the following individuals in the hospital: physicians, nurses, administrators, and technical staff.

The researcher wants to know the following: How is the decision made on which brand of medical diagnostic machine to buy? Who is involved in the decision? (The group of customers involved in the decision making is called a **buying centre**.) What roles do these individuals play? Are some individuals more important than others? What factors do they consider when making the decision?

The researcher uses a depth interview guide to help him with his effort. Table 2.3 on the next page illustrates a generic depth interview guide.

Ethnography

Unlike other research techniques where the researcher keeps at a distance from the respondents, in ethnographies the researcher becomes the customer. The hallmark of ethnographic research is **participant observation**, a process where the researcher actively participates with the customer to gain insights that other techniques may not be able to generate. Let us take some examples.

Example 1   DeWalt is a brand of tools aimed at the professional market. Forsaking traditional research methods such as focus groups, DeWalt understands customer needs by sending researchers to work alongside professionals. DeWalt believes its approach gives it superior, real-time insight into customer needs. Also, it demonstrates a commitment to its customers by employing this research method.

Example 2   What inspires customers to tattoo a brand name on their bodies? What is the relationship between the brand and the customer? What is the emotional connection? To answer such questions, Harley Davidson, the popular brand of motorcycles, might turn to ethnography. A researcher might spend the weekend with a group of Harley enthusiasts (white-collar professionals, not gang members), wearing the proper gear and participating in a long bike ride. During breaks she might ask questions to understand the strength of the brand. Her participant observation would generate insights she would not get with a more "sterile" technique such as a focus group.

Surveys

Survey research involves quantitative data collection by means of a questionnaire. If you have ever filled out a questionnaire, you probably were asked three classes of

KEYPOINT

Go to www.questionpro.com for free questionnaire design tips and templates.

TABLE 2.3   Depth Interview Guide

Note on using depth interview guide: questions under each heading are to be used as general guides to the interview. Use them to explore the topic, but do not treat them as a checklist. Schedule an hour with your customer to complete the interview. You may have to interview more than one participant within your customer's business to fully gather the necessary data.

Introduction
Thank you for agreeing to participate in this depth interview. Your input will go a long way in helping us understand your needs better.

Customer buying process
1. Specifically with regards to _____ (your product), how are buying decisions made within your company?
2. What buying process is used? Can you walk me through the process?
3. Who are the key members of the buying centre? What roles do they play?

Relationships with suppliers
1. What, in your opinion, are minimum requirements a supplier must meet?
2. What makes a preferred supplier?
3. What goods and services should a supplier offer to be considered a preferred supplier?
4. What are some best practices you have observed by suppliers, either in this industry or outside the industry?

Customer needs
1. What market segments (customers) are you serving today?
2. How might this change in the future?
3. How do you create value for *your* customers? In other words, how do you create solutions for your customers?
4. What needs do your customers have that are not being met currently?
5. Who are your direct and indirect competitors?
6. What are they doing to take business away from you?
7. What are you doing to differentiate yourself in the eyes of your customers?
8. When you think of the activities you have to pursue in order to purchase a product from us and use the product, is there any area you can think of where we can help you purchase and use the product better? [After the interview, try to affix a dollar value, as far as possible, to these activities. This will enable you to discover areas where you may be able to help your customer cut costs. See Chapter 6 for details on a technique called **Total Cost of Ownership analysis**.]
9. Is there anyone else in your company I can talk to who might give me more details on product purchase and usage activities?
10. How can a supplier help you to compete more effectively in the marketplace?
11. What can a supplier do to increase your revenues, or decrease your costs?

Customer's business
1. What is the one thing about your business that keeps you awake at night?
2. What are the top three opportunities you face within the next five years in your business?
3. What are the top three threats you face in your business within the next five years?
4. Examining your firm with a clear eye, how well poised are you to take advantage of these opportunities or mitigate threats? In other words, what do you think are your key strengths and weaknesses to take advantage of opportunities or minimize threats?
5. What strategic direction is your firm pursuing? Why?
6. How can a supplier help you in implementing your strategy?

Exit
1. Do you have any other comments on the areas we have covered, or any areas I may not have touched upon?
2. Thank you for your participation. We sincerely appreciate the time you have taken from your busy schedule to talk to me.

Joseph Amati of Loblaw Companies talks about the importance of marketing research to business success.

questions: What do you think (attitudes and feelings), what do you do (behaviour), and who are you (demographic variables). All questionnaires contain these three classes of questions.

Unlike the qualitative methods discussed so far, survey research is used to collect data from a larger sample of respondents, and it is used not so much to generate ideas, but to validate them. Questionnaires are good for counting and summarizing the results. You will find an example of a questionnaire to measure customer satisfaction in Chapter 11.

CHECKPOINT

Where We've Been

- ■ We have seen that smart businesses use the tools of marketing research to understand the needs of their customers.

- ■ They also do not merely accept an understanding of customer needs; they shape and create customer needs.

Where We're Going

- ■ In the final section of this chapter, we will see how some companies succeed by not doing any formal marketing research.

Secrets of Smart Companies That Succeed by Not Doing Any Formal Marketing Research

OBJECTIVE 5

The problem with using marketing research tools to understand customer needs is that customers may not know what their needs are, or they may not be able to articulate them. Certainly, customers are always able to articulate their needs in terms of **basic care variables**, but this insight will not help a business to develop a competitive edge over its rivals. Let us take an example.[11]

A bank conducts market research to understand its customers' needs. It finds out that customers

- ■ do not like waiting in lines
- ■ want friendly tellers
- ■ like longer bank hours
- ■ want convenient bank locations
- ■ want a variety of financial products to choose from

Admittedly, these are genuine customer needs. But, they are "basic care" variables—the price of entry in any industry, or "table stakes." Any bank that thinks it is going to develop a superior offering just on the basis of these factors is only fooling itself. (The fact that many banks cannot even deliver on these basic care variables is a different story!)

The really smart companies understand this. That is why they use marketing research, but not in the traditional, orthodox way. Here are the strategies they use.

Strategy #1: Ready, Fire, Aim

According to Herb Kelleher, the co-founder of Southwest Airlines, the approach most companies take is "Ready, aim, fire." The problem with this approach is that, by the time the research has been undertaken, the market opportunity may have passed. Instead, the approach taken by Southwest is "Ready, fire, aim." Accordingly, when an idea crops up, Southwest does not spend an inordinate amount of time conducting focus group sessions asking customers what they think about the idea.

Instead, Southwest launches the idea and tweaks it along the way. Southwest Airlines was one of the first to introduce self-serve check-in counters at airports, where passengers can get a boarding pass and check in their luggage. It introduced this concept based on two observations: (1) traditional check-in counters generate long lines and people do not like waiting in lines; and (2) airline personnel are not allowed (due to insurance requirements) to heft a passenger's suitcase on to the weighing machine for labelling.

KEYPOINT

Smart companies do not just understand customer needs; they create them.

Treat market research results with caution, especially when introducing a new product concept.

So Southwest decided to let passengers check themselves in. What would have happened if they had first conducted focus groups to assess customer dissatisfaction with current arrangements? Perhaps they would not have had the insight or the courage to launch the new product concept. Remember the Sony example?

Strategy #2: Co-create Value with the Customer

Smart companies are embracing a method whereby they are co-creating unique value with their customers.[12] In essence, these companies are getting the customer to do the research for them. This concept challenges two widely practised business approaches: first, that firms alone know what is good for the customer (the firm-centric view), and second, that firms typically take a product-centric approach to marketing (this was discussed in Chapter 1 and at the beginning of this chapter).

MARKETING DRIVES SUCCESS

2.4 BUILD-A-BEAR

Objective: Smart Companies Involve the Customer in the Innovation Process

At a company called Build-A-Bear (www.buildabear.com), children get a basic fabric shell to build a teddy bear. From there, they can customize the bear to suit their preferences. The bear can be made fat or thin (as if there are any thin bears!) using more or less stuffing. The bear can be given a heart, a sound, and accessories.

Build-A-Bear lets kids (and their parents) experience an intense association with childhood—the teddy bear. Children can build their own bear, discuss their choice with their parents, and join a thematic community of other like-minded consumers. Instead of taking the traditional approach to creating value for customers by giving customers a set of bears to choose from, Build-A-Bear lets customers customize their experiences. Essentially, this means that customers can have an unlimited set of needs, and the firm can accommodate each and every one of them!

Build-A-Bear lets customers do the innovating.

The co-creation concept challenges this dominant model because, thanks to the internet, consumers are no longer isolated from each other. Instead, like-minded people can form communities using chat rooms, blogs, and social networking tools. This allows smart companies to involve the customer in the innovation process.

Strategy #3: Treat the Whole World as Your Research Firm

Smart companies recognize that ideas can come from anywhere, not just customers. So they tap into a global network of employees, suppliers, institutions, academics, trend spotters (trendwatching.com, thecoolhunter.net, joshspear.com), entrepreneurs, and even competitors. Let us take an example.

In 2004, Procter & Gamble (P&G) launched a new product—Pringles potato chips printed with trivia questions. Under the old P&G model, the idea would have been hatched and developed in house. This would have taken a couple of years because P&G scientists would have to come up with a way to inject a potato chip with edible ink as it was being fried—no easy task.

Under a new market research model called Connect + Develop, P&G introduced the new product concept in less than one year.[13] How they did it has revolutionized the way marketing research will be conducted in years to come. Through their global network of connections, they found a baker in Bologna, Italy, who had perfected the technology of injecting loaves of bread with edible ink. As a result of this pioneering approach, P&G's research and development productivity has increased by more than 60%, and its innovation rate has doubled, while the cost of innovation has gone down from 4.8% of sales to 3.4%.[14]

Table 2.4 provides a partial list of global networks that let business organizations use the world as their market research firm.

Strategy #4: Create New Market Space

Companies know that, in order to win against their competitors, they have to innovate. But how? We have seen previously that merely asking customers what their needs are may not generate that hidden nugget of insight that can lead to a breakthrough innovation. That is why some companies create new and superior customer value by creating new market spaces.[15] Let us see how.

Look Across Substitute Industries   If you are in the mood for a snack, you might choose between an apple, a candy bar, a bag of chips, a glass of milk, a glass of orange juice, a handful of almonds, or a piece of cheese. However, most businesses view as their

TABLE 2.4	How to Use the Whole World as Your Market Research Firm
Network	**Description**
NineSigma (ninesigma.com)	NineSigma enables clients to source innovative ideas, technologies, products, and services from outside their organizations quickly and inexpensively by connecting them to the best innovators and solution providers from around the world.
InnoCentive (innocentive.com)	Founded in 2001, InnoCentive connects companies, academic institutions, and public sector and non-profit organizations, all hungry for breakthrough innovation, with a global network of more than 145 000 of the world's brightest minds.
YourEncore (yourencore.com)	YourEncore is a network of retired and veteran scientists and engineers providing clients with proven experience to help accelerate their pace of innovation.
Yet2.com	Founded in 1999, yet2.com is focused on bringing buyers and sellers of technologies together so that all parties maximize the return on their investments. It brokers technology transfer into and out of companies, universities, and government labs.

competitors a narrowly defined set of firms within their own industry. So candy manufacturers naively believe that their only competitors are within the candy sector. Of course, the customer does not see it that way. In reality, looking across substitute industries provides many opportunities for innovation.

Home Depot, the do-it-yourself warehouse store, started with the recognition that customers had two basic choices when confronted with a repair and remodelling project—they could buy tools at a hardware store and do the job themselves, or they could hire a contractor. The problem with the first option was that the customer might not have the expertise for the job. The problem with the second option was that contractors were expensive, and finding a reliable contractor who could do the job on time and within budget was difficult.

Home Depot's founders astutely recognized that, by looking across two substitute industries, they could create a winning business. So Home Depot was founded on the premise that customers could not only buy a can of paint and brushes, but also talk to an expert who would walk them step by step through the process.

Look at Different Customer Roles

The reason we see the "same old, same old" way of competing in most industries is because most firms define their customer very narrowly. For example, pharmaceutical companies focus their sales attention on doctors and ignore influencers such as nurses and pharmacists. Or, in business-to-business markets, most firms focus their efforts on the corporate purchasing department. However, smart companies win by recognizing that, in reality, there is not one customer, but different customers who play different roles—influencers, decision makers, purchasers, users, etc.

FedEx, the overnight package delivery company, bought Kinko's, the document printing company. Why? Because, while most package delivery companies focus on securing corporate contracts by appealing to the purchasing department, FedEx knows that it is often the front office manager who is ultimately responsible for ensuring not only that the documents get printed on time, but also that they get shipped to their destinations. So by focusing on the needs of a different customer, FedEx wins.

Look Across Complementary Goods and Services

Most businesses only focus on the good or service they are offering. They rarely think outside their business. But smart companies know that consumption does not take place in a vacuum—customers need a set of complementary goods and services to complete the experience.

Movie theatre companies used to only think about movies. They did not care that their customers had to perform many complementary tasks simply to watch a movie—get a babysitter, park (or take a taxi), and eat a meal. These days, movie theatre companies recognize this fact. Now, at many complexes, a customer can get a meal before going to the movies. Of course, these businesses have a long way to go because they are not yet thinking about the other activities such as babysitting and parking, but they should if they want to create value for the customer.

On the other hand, vacuum cleaner manufacturer Dyson wins by recognizing that consumers do not like to buy, attach, and dispose of vacuum cleaner bags. So its vacuum cleaners do not use bags. Dyson creates

FedEx Kinko's appeals to a different customer.

Core separator technology inside the new DC23 Stowaway.

The Dyson DC23 has our new core separator technology which helps remove even more microscopic dust particles than any other cyclone. Nothing else works like it and you'll only find it in a Dyson.

For more information please visit www.dyson.com or call 1-877-397-6622 six days a week.

root cyclone **+ core separator**

dyson

5 year warranty

The vacuum cleaner that doesn't lose suction.

Dyson creates customer value by looking across complementary products.

customer value by looking across the set of complementary products customers have to use to get the job done.

Appeal to a Customer Need Your Competitors Have Not Thought About

Most competitors compete in the same old way—they focus on a common set of appeals. As a result, all competitors look the same, offer the same value, and commoditize the industry, driving down prices. Winning companies, on the other hand, create new markets by broadening the appeal to customers.

Before Starbucks came on the scene, what would you have said if someone told you that, one day, customers would willingly spend $5 on a drink made with coffee and steamed milk? You would have thought such an idea to be crazy. Howard Schultz, the founder of Starbucks, examined how the coffee industry currently appealed to customers. Not surprisingly, he found that competitors (Nestlé, P&G, and General Foods) viewed coffee as a commodity. As a result, consumers also viewed coffee as an item to be consumed as part of a daily routine. The entire industry was awash in price cutting and promotions.

Starbucks changed all this by appealing to an emotional benefit, the café experience, common to most Europeans but unfamiliar to North Americans. As a result, Starbucks has revolutionized the entire industry. Now, Starbucks is broadening its appeal by encouraging customers to take the café experience home.

Starbucks is broadening its appeal by encouraging customers to take the café experience home.

Chapter Summary

1. Avoid mistakes made by companies that do not understand customer needs.

Companies that do not understand customer needs fall into some predictable traps. They try to buy customers by outspending their competitors on marketing communications vehicles like advertising, thus wasting resources. They build products that customers do not want, they drop their price to secure a customer's business, or they chase unattractive customers.

2. Meet companies that win by developing a deep understanding of customer needs, and learn the valuable lessons they offer.

Companies that win by developing a deep understanding of customer needs teach us some valuable lessons. They talk to their customers whenever and wherever they can. They use data and resources they already have. Finally, they establish standards for how the research is going to be used. If they cannot establish such standards, they do not conduct the research.

3. Understand that smart companies are not happy to merely understand customer needs: they create them.

Creating customer needs should not be viewed as a sinister, manipulative task. It merely means that smart companies know that often customers do not know what their needs are, or they

express them in basic care variables, or they cannot articulate their needs. These companies are taking a latent (hidden) need, giving it shape, and offering it to the marketplace. Invariably, the customers' response is, "Why didn't someone think of this sooner?"

4. Use practical tools and techniques of market research to understand customer needs.

Always start data collection with secondary research. This is research conducted by someone else that is available free of charge or for a fee. Qualitative techniques (or exploratory techniques) such as focus groups, depth interviews, and ethnographies are useful to generate ideas. Quantitative techniques such as surveys help quantify and validate ideas.

5. Learn the secrets of smart companies that succeed by not doing any formal marketing research.

Smart companies do not always rely on marketing research. Instead, they employ several strategies to create customer value: they introduce an idea and then tweak it based on customer feedback, they co-create value with customers, they use the entire world as their market research firm, and they create new market space. New market space is created by looking across substitute industries, the chain of buyers, customer benefits, and complementary products.

CRITICAL THINKING QUESTIONS

1. You have been hired to do a consulting project for an entrepreneur who sells office furniture. He complains to you, "I cannot succeed because my competitors are bigger than I am and they spend a lot of money on advertising." Write him a letter advising how you would approach the problem.

2. Provide three examples of companies that have succeeded by "creating" needs in the marketplace.

3. A pharmaceutical company that sells renal dialysis units to hospitals wants to understand how customers make decisions on what equipment to buy. Accordingly, they want to send out a survey to their customers and non-customers. Advise them on the merits of this approach.

4. Provide one example each of companies that have succeeded by (a) looking across substitute industries, (b) looking across the chain of buyers, and (c) looking across functional or emotional appeal to buyers.

5. We made a very provocative statement at the beginning of this chapter: some companies succeed by not doing any market research at all. What is your evaluation of this claim? Can companies succeed by not doing any research on their customers?

RUNNING CASE

ARBOL INDUSTRIES GETS A SHOCK

One of the very first tasks the new marketing manager at Arbol Industries did was to organize a seminar to teach sales professionals the fundamentals of marketing. His reasoning was simple: if a salesperson did not know the discipline and power of marketing, he could not create value for his customers.

With the help of the new CEO and Arbol's sales manager, the marketing manager instituted some sorely needed changes to the organization's culture. For one thing, Arbol now required sales professionals to go and meet customers at their place of work. While this may sound obvious, it was a radical change from the old practice. Previously, Arbol sales professionals would sit behind a desk all day long and wait for the phone to ring from customers wanting a product (lumber, plywood, or paper). Or, they would pick up the phone themselves and try to sell the customer something. It was the classic case of "push" marketing, emblematic of companies that do not understand their customers' needs.

When sales professionals visited their customers, they got a shock, albeit a pleasant one. They learned amazing things and uncovered tremendous opportunities to differentiate Arbol's commodity products from their competitors' products. What follows are some typical examples.

A team from Arbol visited a customer who makes heated flooring systems for homes. Those of you who live in cold climates perhaps know the joys of walking barefoot on a heated floor in the winter time! This customer bought plywood from Arbol, drilled a groove through it, passed a pipe through the groove, and ran hot water through the pipe to make a heated flooring system.

"So, *that's* what you do with our plywood," said an Arbol sales person to the customer. "You know, we could pre-drill that groove for you at our factories. Would that be worth something to you?"

Customer: "Are you kidding? I would be willing to pay more for plywood pre-drilled to my specifications because it would save

me time, effort, and wasted material drilling the groove here in my factory."

At another customer site, an Arbol team was walking through the factory and the warehouse. The place was a hive of activity and chaos. Raw material was piled up in a disorganized fashion everywhere. "Is it always like this here?" asked an Arbol employee to the customer.

Customer: "Yes, it's always like this here, total chaos. I don't have any place to put all the raw material you people send me. You ship material to me like clockwork once every week. You know what would really help me? It would help me tremendously if you shipped once in *two* weeks instead."

I hope you are chuckling at this point. Arbol was shipping material to the customer every week, incurring expenses and additional paperwork. This was actually causing problems at the customer's factory. Arbol's practice was not creating any value for him. By shipping every *two* weeks, Arbol would save money *and* satisfy the customer.

Examples such as these continued to pile up. Each instance brought with it a way to make the customer money or save the customer on cost. And, in each case, Arbol managed to charge more for its "commodity" goods. This would not have been possible without a deep understanding of its customers' needs.

Arbol was on a marketing journey. The successes continued to accumulate; you will read about them at the end of each chapter. That is the reason Arbol was able to de-commoditize their products, build strong brands, and beat their competitors. In pursuing the marketing journey, they were the first in their industry to try something bold.

Case Assignment

Through your research, identify another company that became "marketing led." Write a brief summary of what it did and what the end outcome was.

SUGGESTED READINGS

If You Want to Sell Coal in Newcastle,* Do Not Miss These Publications

Amar Bhide, "How Entrepreneurs Craft Strategy," *Harvard Business Review*, March–April 1994, pp. 150–161.

Larry Huston and Nabil Sakkab, "Connect and Develop: Inside Procter & Gamble's New Model for Innovation," *Harvard Business Review*, March 2006, pp. 58–66.

W. Chan Kim and Renée Mauborgne, "Creating New Market Space," *Harvard Business Review*, January–February 1999, pp. 83–93.

Brian Leavy and Deependra Moitra, "The Practice of Co-creating Unique Value with Customers: An Interview with C.K. Prahalad," *Strategy & Leadership*, Vol. 34, No. 2, 2006, pp. 4–9.

* Newcastle is a coal-mining town, so selling coal in Newcastle is quite a feat. In this context, this idiomatic expression means that if you understand your customers, you can accomplish anything.

NOTES

1. This is, of course, a bold statement designed to provoke you and make you curious.

2. All these examples are from my consulting projects and, therefore, are situations I have witnessed first-hand.

3. Jeff Bennett, Neal E. Boudette, and Serena Ng, "GM Slates Sweeping Rebates as Toyota Closes In on No. 1," *The Wall Street Journal*, June 24, 2008, pp. A1, A15.

4. A silo is a tall, cylindrical container found on farms that holds grain.

5. John E. Forsyth, Nicoló Galante, and Todd Guild, "Capitalizing on Customer Insights," *The McKinsey Quarterly*, 2006, No. 3, pp. 42–53.

6. CNN.com, January 23, 2008.

7. George Anders, "In Hard Times, Some Firms Go for The Jugular," *The Wall Street Journal*, June 25, 2008, p. B2.

8. While the veracity of this anecdote cannot be verified, under Morita's guidance, Sony invented the Walkman (and rejected marketing research).

9. MBA students Damon Hanna, Aleya Esmail, Marina Pakhomova, Ria Goculdas, and William Vargas presented this case in class. It can be found at business2000.ie/cases/cases_7th/case12.htm.

10. This is my recommendation. Of course, the depth interview can be shorter. However, with shorter depth interviews you are giving up the prime advantage of this method—the ability to drill down deep into a topic. For additional information on this topic, read John W. Mullins, "Discovering Unk-Unks," *MIT Sloan Management Review*, Summer 2007, Vol. 48, No. 4, pp. 16–21; Grant McCracken, *The Long Interview* (Newbury Park, CA: Sage Publications, Inc., 1988).

11. This point is discussed more fully in Ajay Sirsi, *Marketing Led—Sales Driven: How Successful Businesses Use the Power of Marketing Plans and Sales Execution to Win in the Marketplace* (Victoria, BC: Trafford Publishing, 2005).

12. Brian Leavy and Deependra Moitra, "The Practice of Co-creating Unique Value with Customers: An Interview with C.K. Prahalad," *Strategy & Leadership*, Vol. 34, No. 2, 2006, pp. 4–9.

13. Larry Huston and Nabil Sakkab, "Connect and Develop: Inside Procter & Gamble's New Model for Innovation," *Harvard Business Review*, March 2006, pp. 58–66.

14. Huston and Sakkab, *ibid.*

15. This section is based on W. Chan Kim and Renée Mauborgne, "Creating New Market Space," *Harvard Business Review*, January–February 1999, pp. 83–93.

CHAPTER 3

Choosing Which Customers to Serve

CHECKPOINT

Where We've Been

- We have learned that the roadmap to business success follows a marketing discipline of understand-create-deliver-manage customer value.

- To create superior customer value, a business needs a superior understanding of customer needs.

Where We're Going

- Smart businesses recognize that they cannot serve all customer needs; they have to select their target customer. Therefore, this chapter will focus on customer segmentation and targeting.

CHAPTER INTRODUCTION

The business world has seen an explosion of customer segments, products, channels, and media. This has made marketing more complex, more costly, and less effective.[1] Although customers will still come first, no marketer can meet their every need. It will be necessary to focus on fewer customer segments and to serve them well with fewer brands. If a business fails to heed this important lesson, it faces the prospect of escalating complexity costs—from product development to marketing communications. In the end, such a business will amount to nothing. It will not have given its customers a compelling reason to do business with it. And it will eventually bleed (costs) to death.

1. Understand the importance of segmenting customers and the dangers of not segmenting customers.

2. Avoid mistakes made by your competitors by learning how to segment effectively.

3. Learn to avoid common pitfalls in market segmentation.

4. Develop a simple checklist to segment customers successfully.

5. Learn how to confidently select target customers for maximum business success.

OBJECTIVE 1

Segmenting Customers Is Important to Business Success

Henry Ford famously said customers could have any car they wanted, as long as it was a black Model T. Ford was practising the opposite of **market segmentation—mass marketing**, a concept that ignores customer needs. A mass marketer decides not to recognize customer needs by providing all customers with only one offer.

> *If you want to succeed in business, find a need and fill it.*
>
> J.P. GETTY

Ford could get away with mass marketing because he had perfected the assembly line and could build and sell cars very cheaply. Today, there is no such a thing as a mass market. No legitimate business can hope to ignore customer needs. In fact, today there is an explosion of segments. In addition, business success depends on segmenting markets in a way that is different from competitors and then selecting the best target segments to serve.

MARKETING DRIVES SUCCESS

3.1 GLIDE

Objective: Segmenting and Targeting Customers Is the Key to Business Success

W. L. Gore & Associates is better known for manufacturing a waterproof and breathable fabric called Gore-Tex, used in making such products as jackets and shoes that keep consumers' bodies and feet warm and dry in cold or wet conditions.

The company identified an opportunity to serve a market segment that previously had been overlooked by other businesses—the user of dental floss. Readers who floss will appreciate one point: dental floss tends to shred and get stuck between teeth, making the flossing process very uncomfortable. W. L. Gore & Associates invented a dental floss that was shred proof. They named it Glide. There was only one problem: How could they distribute the product? After all, they were small compared to other manufacturers of dental hygiene products such as Colgate Palmolive and Procter & Gamble (P&G). And supermarkets and drug stores require manufacturers to pay for putting products on the shelf—a process known as **listing fees**—which can get very expensive for a smaller player.

The company hit upon a creative solution. They decided to target their innovation at dentists. Dentists are very important influencers in dental hygiene decisions because they often recommend which brands to purchase. They also give free samples of floss to their patients. The strategy worked! Glide became a very popular brand, eventually being bought by P&G, which placed it under the Crest brand umbrella.

Market segmentation and targeting led to Glide's success.

Dangers of Not Segmenting Customers

To put it bluntly, a business has no choice—it has to segment its markets. There are several dangers facing any business that does not segment its customers.

Danger 1: The Business Ignores Customer Needs and Treats All Customers the Same
Not segmenting customers means that the business chooses to ignore the fact that different customers have different needs. As a result, the business tries to become a mass marketer—offering all customers the same value proposition. By trying to be all things to all people, the business ends up satisfying no one. This leaves room for a competitor to enter the market and satisfy pockets of unmet needs.

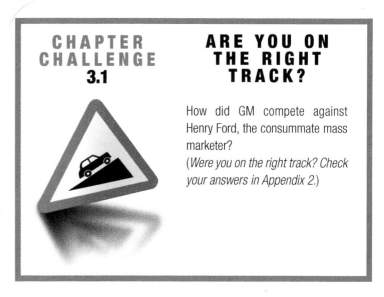

CHAPTER CHALLENGE 3.1

ARE YOU ON THE RIGHT TRACK?

How did GM compete against Henry Ford, the consummate mass marketer?
(*Were you on the right track? Check your answers in Appendix 2.*)

Danger 2: The Business Wastes Resources
If a business offers all its customers only one value proposition, it is wasting its resources. Why? Because it will be either over-serving or under-serving customer needs. Let us take an example.[2]

A health clinic offers prenatal counselling to expectant parents. Let us say that it decides to provide one-on-one counselling to *all* couples who walk through the door. Couple A is very happy with this service—they are in their early twenties, inexperienced, and nervous about their first child. Couple B, on the other hand, is dissatisfied because they are more mature—in their mid-forties—and find the personal counselling too suffocating.

So the clinic retreats and only provides a brochure on prenatal advice. The end result? Dissatisfied customers. Only this time, Couple A is dissatisfied, while Couple B is satisfied. The lesson is clear—with only one value proposition (mass marketing), the business wastes resources because it is either over-serving or under-serving customer needs.

Danger 3: The Business Tries to Be All Things to All People
A business that does not segment its customers tries to be all things to all people. This does not give it a unique or differentiated position in the marketplace. Essentially, the business does not give its customers a reason to want to do business with it. As we will see in Chapter 5, which discusses product and brand strategies, such a go-to-market approach is untenable. Cessna, the aircraft manufacturer, knows this only too well. That is why it focuses its efforts on serving the needs of the corporate customer.

Danger 4: The Business Is Not Giving the Sales Force Any Direction
Market segmentation has a profound impact on the rest of the organization. Smart businesses use their segmentation to direct *every* business activity. Segmentation forms the core of their strategy.

Without customer segmentation, salespeople do not know which customers to target. Even worse, lacking proper direction, salespeople do not know what to offer and what to withhold from a customer (what value propositions to deliver). As a result, they often give the customer too much without charging for the value they create, or they drop the price to secure the contract. We saw this in Chapter 2 and we will encounter it again in this chapter, in Chapter 4, and in Chapter 9.

KEYPOINT

Imagine a world where the only ice cream available was vanilla.

KEYPOINT

One of the fastest ways to increase profits is to segment and target your customer.

Cessna is successful because it does not try to be all things to all people.

3.2 RITZ-CARLTON

Objective: Segmentation Impacts Every Part of the Organization

Ritz-Carlton is a hotel that serves the needs of a specific market segment—upmarket travellers. These individuals, travelling either for business or for pleasure, demand the best and are willing to pay for the service. Every aspect of Ritz-Carlton's strategy is predicated on its segmentation strategy.

The hotel is famous for training its staff to accommodate any need a guest may have. All guest requests and needs are put into a database. So Ritz-Carlton knows, for example, that a particular guest has certain types of allergies, or another guest likes to play tennis. This enables the sales organization to do a much better job of catering to the customer's needs.

Let us say you are visiting San Francisco and call the Ritz-Carlton toll-free number. The operator (essentially a salesperson) knows that you like to play tennis. She will remind you that the San Francisco property has excellent tennis facilities and offer to book you a lesson with their tennis pro (an extra paid service, of course). Such sales efforts are not pushy; they are designed to create added value for the customer who otherwise may have forgotten to plan a game of tennis.

Over time, the Ritz-Carlton brand has expanded to serve additional needs of the well-heeled traveller: the brand has residences for ownership in exotic places where people can enjoy the beach or skiing opportunities.

Segmentation impacts every aspect of Ritz-Carlton's strategy.

Where We've Been

- A business has no choice; it has to segment its customers.
- Businesses that fail to heed this advice face many dangers: they try to be all things to everybody, they waste resources, they are not profitable, and they do not give their sales force any direction.

Where We're Going

- We will see how to segment markets for maximum impact.

CHECKPOINT

OBJECTIVE 2

The Right and Wrong Way to Segment Customers

Segmentation is not a hard concept to grasp intuitively, but it is a very hard concept to implement successfully. In one survey of executives at 200 large firms, 59% reported they had conducted a major segmentation exercise during the previous two years. However, only 14% said they derived any real value from the exercise.[3]

Such findings are not surprising because if you approach segmentation the wrong way, the benefits will not materialize. If you want to learn how to segment your markets, you must first learn the basic principles of market segmentation.

> *The social responsibility of business is to increase its profits.*
>
> MILTON FRIEDMAN, NOBEL PRIZE–WINNING ECONOMIST

KEYPOINT

Every business needs to decide whether it wants to chase customers or chase profitability. It usually cannot have both.

Basic Principles of Market Segmentation

There are three basic principles of market segmentation.

Segmentation Principle 1: A Business Exists to Be Profitable
In my consulting work, I will often have the following dialogue with a client:

ME: "What is your business' greatest strength?"

CLIENT: "We are big."

ME: "What strategy are you pursuing in the marketplace? What do you want to be when you grow up?"

CLIENT: "We want to become bigger."

Do you notice what is happening here? First, the client thinks that the size of the business should somehow matter to customers (it doesn't). Further, the business does not really have a strategy in place; it just wants to gorge on customers, regardless of whether those customers are attractive or unattractive (Chapter 6 discusses the dangers of this in more detail). This business wants to gain **market share** at the expense of profitability.

In reality, segmenting and targeting customers enables a business to dramatically improve its profitability.[4]

Segmentation Principle 2: All Customers Are Not Created Equal
Customers differ based on four factors:

- their needs
- your cost to serve them
- their appreciation of your value creation
- their propensity (willingness) to pay

A casual glance at customers will reveal that different customers have different needs. Some customers only want the basic product, while others are willing to pay for the extra frills. Finally, some customers are more expensive to serve than others. Remember what Tim said in Chapter 1? Some customers are more expensive to serve because they complain a lot and put increased demands on sales professionals.

CHAPTER CHALLENGE 3.2

ARE YOU ON THE RIGHT TRACK?

What does Milton Friedman mean when he says that it is the social responsibility of every business to make a profit?
(*Were you on the right track? Check your answers in Appendix 2.*)

Segmentation Principle 3: We Cannot Be All Things to All Customers   Because all customers are not created equal based on their *needs* and their *attractiveness* to you, it makes no sense for a business to treat all customers the same. This is where the logic of segmentation and targeting enters.

How to Segment: The Wrong Way

The easiest way to segment customers is by geography or demographic variables. In business-to-consumer (B2C) markets, this would imply segmentation by factors such as where the customer lives, age, income, or gender. In business-to-business (B2B) markets, this would imply segmenting customers by where their business is located, size of the firm, or industry. Although segmenting by demographic variables is easy, it is rarely effective. Let us take some examples.

Two consumers may make the same amount of money each year, but given their attitudes and beliefs, they may spend their money in different ways. Therefore, segmenting by income (a demographic variable) will not enable a business to group customers in any meaningful fashion.

A supplier of telecommunications services to businesses in the financial services industry segmented its customers by firm size (a demographic variable), thinking that bigger customers (as measured by number of employees) would have more sophisticated needs than smaller customers. To its surprise, it found there was no such correlation between size and needs. A 2-person firm, operating in the basement of a house, might be doing very advanced financial modelling (requiring heavy access to telecommunications services such as data services) for the hedge fund industry, similar to a 100-person firm.[5]

Most banks have two distinct divisions serving two distinct types of customers: business banking (serving business customers) and retail banking (serving general consumers). Where would a bank put a new type of customer—the SOHO customer? SOHO (Small Office Home Office) customers are small businesses run by entrepreneurs who operate their business from their home. Demographics would dictate that these customers belong in the business banking division. But when we examine the customer group's *needs*, they more closely resemble general consumers. Therefore, they ideally belong in the retail banking division.

To overcome the limitations of demographics as a segmentation variable, researchers turned to **psychographic segmentation**. In 1978, Arnold Mitchell and colleagues launched the Values and Lifestyles (VALS) program, a method of classifying individuals into nine psychological types based on their lifestyles, attitudes, interests, and personality. Although VALS and other psychographic techniques have become very popular, their efficacy is limited to advertising and brand reinforcement.[6] Although psychographics are good at moving viewers emotionally, the characteristics and attitudes such ads invoke are not drivers of buying behaviours. Finally, psychographics do not tell companies what markets to enter, what products to introduce, and how to price these products.[7]

How to Segment: The Right Way

Professor Theodore Levitt used to tell his students, "People don't want to buy a quarter-inch drill. They want a quarter-inch hole!" He was urging businesses to focus their efforts on customer needs. Although nobody would argue with Levitt, many businesses do not heed his message

> *The Miller Lite ads featuring mud-wrestling supermodels certainly impressed the young, male segment they were intended to reach, but sales did not increase.*
>
> Yankelovich and Meer

when they segment their customers. But smart businesses know that the best way to segment customers is by examining their needs. Let us take examples from B2C and B2B markets.

A fast food restaurant chain wanted to improve sales of milkshakes. So it profiled heavy consumers of milkshakes using demographic and psychological variables. It invited customers who fit the profile to focus group sessions and asked for feedback on how to improve the product (by making it thicker or more chocolatey, for example). The restaurant chain received great feedback from customers. It made improvements to the product, but sales did not increase.[8]

Another researcher hired to do the job focused on understanding customer needs. He spent time observing customers in the restaurant (remember **ethnographies** from the previous chapter?). He noticed that most milkshakes were purchased during the morning by people who were wearing business attire, and the customers left without consuming the shakes on the premises. So he interviewed a few of them to develop a deeper understanding. This is what he found.

Milkshakes were purchased by customers on their way to work. The product fulfilled the following needs:

- It could be consumed with one hand.
- It lasted the entire, boring commute.
- It held them until lunchtime. Otherwise, they would have a hunger attack by 10:00 a.m.
- It was easier to consume than substitutes such as bagels, which were dry and cumbersome to eat, and the jam made their fingers sticky.
- It was more filling than donuts, which left them hungry by 10:00 a.m.

Armed with these insights on customers, the restaurant chain could make improvements to satisfy the needs of this segment: it made the shake thicker (so it would last longer), it added bits of fruit (to alleviate the boredom of commuting), and it moved the dispensing machine up front to get customers in and out as quickly as possible.

The researcher noticed that another segment consumed milkshakes at a different time of day: parents who would buy the product for their children. What needs did the product fulfill? Exhausted by constantly saying no to their children, parents bought the product to placate their children and feel good about themselves at the same time (for giving their children a healthy "dessert").

In each case, customers were using the product to fulfill a different set of needs, enabling the restaurant chain to deliver differentiated value propositions to each group.

The previous example used the customers' needs to segment markets. But, there is one set of needs that it ignored—the needs of the business. As we said previously, all customers are not created equal. They differ not only in terms of their needs, but also in their willingness to pay for your goods and services. Any business that thinks it can satisfy all needs without getting paid is eventually going to go out of business. Therefore, another dimension of "need" we must add to the segmentation effort is customer attractiveness.

A manufacturer of packaging material segmented customers using these variables:[9]

- customer needs
- cost to serve the customer
- customer willingness to pay extra for value propositions
- customer strategic fit (to what extent the customer fits with the organization's strategic direction)

Chen Yongjian of Hillsdale Investments talks about how his firm wins by segmenting customers based on needs.

KEY POINT

All customers are not created equal. They differ in terms of needs and willingness to pay for your goods and services.

- potential for revenue growth
- profit potential

The end segmentation resulted in three groups of customers, shown in Table 3.1.

The packaging materials supplier did not stop there. It also segmented markets (industries) it operated in. The end result was the segmentation matrix shown in Table 3.2.

The segmentation in Table 3.2 enabled the business to develop a profile of customers in each of the nine cells based on their needs. We will see in Chapter 9 why this segmentation matrix is so important, how to use it, and how it forms the basis for translating marketing planning into sales action.

How to Segment on the Internet

A study by the Digital Customer Project[10] has found that demographics and psychographics are *poor* variables for segmenting customers on the internet. In fact, the research shows that a variant of need-based segmentation, called **usage segmentation**, is very useful in segmenting customers on the internet.[11]

Usage segmentation first groups customers by their individual behaviour at a point in time, not by demographics or psychographics, and not by aggregate online behavior. The researchers call this form of segmentation "occasionalization," as it is based on what people do on the internet on different occasions. The resulting segmentation is shown in Table 3.3. Unlike traditional online segmentation schemes, which rigidly define consumers as emailers or surfers, occasionalization recognizes that customers have different moods and use the internet for different reasons at different points in time.

KEYPOINT

In B2B markets, it is important to make a distinction between a customer segment and a market (industry) segment.

KEYPOINT

The ideal segmentation method takes into account not only the customers' needs, but also the needs of the business by examining customer attractiveness.

TABLE 3.1	Customer Segmentation

Premium customers	Performance customers	Value customers
- Are price-insensitive	- Are price-sensitive	- Are price-sensitive
- Want the highest quality product	- Want adequate product performance	- Want the basic product
- Will pay price premiums	- Will pay price premiums if case can be made	- Will not pay price premiums
- Value relationship with us; will not switch suppliers	- Are generally loyal, but can switch to competitors	- Will do business with any supplier that can offer the cheapest price

TABLE 3.2	Market X Customer Segmentation

Market	Premium customers	Performance customers	Value customers
Fast food industry	Premium fast food customers are different from the other type of fast food customers.	—	—
Music industry	—	In Chapter 9 we will see how to use this matrix.	—
Automotive industry	—	—	Such a matrix enables a business to select target customers. For example, the business may decide to get out of this segment as it is not profitable.

How can we use the occasionalization segmentation method? You will find the answer in Chapter 11, which describes how to attract and keep customers.

TABLE 3.3	**Traditional Segmentation Does Not Work on the Web**		
Segment	**Session length**	**Number of sites**	**Example**
Quickies	1 min.	1.8	Daily check of the weather forecast
Just the facts	9 min.	10.5	Visiting online stores to buy hard-to-find foreign movies
Single mission	10 min.	2.0	Longer visits to research a single topic, for example, recommended restaurants in a city
Do it again	14 min.	2.1	Lingering visits to a few familiar sites, for example, paying bills online
Loitering	33 min.	8.5	Leisurely visits to a few "sticky" or time-consuming sites, for example, reading the daily news
Information please	37 min.	19.7	In-depth information gathering on a particular topic by visiting many related sites; for example, researching what car to buy and financing options
Surfing	70 min.	44.6	Aimless wandering around the web

Source: Adapted from Horacio D. Rozanski, Gerry Bollman, and Martin Lipman, "Seize the Occasion! The Seven-segment System for Online Marketing," *Strategy + Business*, Issue 24, Third Quarter, 2001, pp. 42–51.

CHAPTER CHALLENGE 3.3

ARE YOU ON THE RIGHT TRACK?

Why wait for Chapter 9? Can you comment on why developing the segmentation matrix in Table 3.2 is so crucial for business success? (Hint: we discussed this earlier in this chapter.)

(Were you on the right track? Check your answers in Appendix 2.)

CHECKPOINT

Where We've Been

- ■ We have learned that segmenting customers is crucial to business success.
- ■ Segmenting using easy factors such as demographics is rarely effective.
- ■ The best way to segment customers is by examining their needs and their attractiveness to you.

Where We're Going

- ■ We will see some common pitfalls that you should avoid when segmenting customers.

Common Pitfalls in Market Segmentation

OBJECTIVE 3

Table 3.4 captures the common pitfalls in segmenting customers. While some pitfalls are self-explanatory, others merit more discussion.

TABLE 3.4	**Common Pitfalls in Segmenting Customers**
Over-segmenting	Having too many market segments makes it hard for a business to satisfy the needs of each segment in a unique fashion. Over-segmentation puts enormous resource burdens on the firm.
Targeting too many customers with one offering	The opposite of over-segmenting, targeting too many customers with one offering means certain customers' needs are not being met.
Relying on the easiest segmentation methods	Segmentation methods based on geography or demographic variables (such as age, income, or firm size) are not effective.
Relying on complex segmentation approaches	Segmentation should be understood by all within a business, and it should form the basis from which all business decisions follow. Complex segmentation approaches are usually abandoned.
Segmenting by product, not by market	A common mistake, segmenting by product does not take into account customer needs.
Using the same segmentation as competitors	Imitating the competition will not let your business differentiate itself in the marketplace.
Always targeting the largest segment	The largest customers may not be the most profitable. Targeting the largest segment puts blinders on a business.
Forgetting that segments change	Customer needs change over time; this is a given. Consequently, segments change over time as well.
Not investing in emerging segments	Emerging segments are often the source of new revenue growth.
Always using the same segmentation approach	A static segmentation scheme gets stale over time. Segmentation has to evolve. Arbol Industries demonstrates this point very well at the end of this chapter.

Over-Segmenting

A business first segmented its customers by geography (east, central, west). It then segmented its customers by size of firm (small, medium, large). Next, it used customer needs data and divided customers into three groups (gold, silver, bronze). Finally, it divided customers into three groups based on potential for revenue growth. In the end, the firm realized it had segmented its customers into 81 segments ($3 \times 3 \times 3 \times 3 = 81$)! Clearly, it could not possibly serve the needs of 81 distinct segments. Imagine the burden this would impose on the organization!

Segmenting by Product, Not by Market

A marketing communications firm had three product lines: developing corporate videos, organizing sales conferences, and helping customers with ecommerce solutions. When asked how it segmented its customers, the reply was, "That's easy. We segment customers by those who want corporate videos developed, those who want sales conferences organized, and those who want ecommerce solutions."

CHAPTER CHALLENGE 3.4

ARE YOU ON THE RIGHT TRACK?

What problems do you see facing the marketing communications firm that segmented its customers by product, and not by market?
(*Were you on the right track? Check your answers in Appendix 2.*)

Using the Same Segmentation as Competitors

Business history is full of entrepreneurs who succeeded by viewing the world differently from their competitors. In other words, these business leaders segmented customers differently from their competitors. We saw this in the previous chapter on developing new market space as well. Some examples of successful businesses are shown in Table 3.5. If a business is using the same segmentation approach as its competitors, it is not garnering a competitive advantage for itself.

> *Good segmentations identify the groups most worth pursuing— the underserved, the dissatisfied, and those likely to make a first-time purchase.*
>
> YANKELOVICH AND MEER

> *Effective segmentations focus on just one or two issues, and they need to be redrawn as soon as they have lost their relevance.*
>
> YANKELOVICH AND MEER

Not Investing in Emerging Segments

The problem with many businesses is that, having undertaken the segmentation exercise, they say, "Our job is done." Actually, their job is just starting because, as customer needs change over time, segments that have lost their relevance need to be rethought, and the business has to be on the lookout for new segments to serve.

The problem is, these new segments are small initially; therefore, firms tend to ignore them. This is a mistake as these segments can grow and become very important. When Sony introduced the transistor radio almost 60 years ago, consumer electronics manufacturers in North America sneered at the new product because the sound was "tinny." But the transistor radio gave a segment of customers—teenagers—the freedom to listen to music on the beach. We may think of the humble transistor radio as the original MP3 player!

TABLE 3.5	**Businesses That Succeeded by Segmenting Differently from Competitors**
The Body Shop	Is The Body Shop really a cosmetics company? Its segmentation efforts uncovered a customer need—profits with ethics.
Starbucks	It segmented the market based on where coffee was consumed and how it was viewed.
Dell	It segmented the market based on where computers were bought—it pioneered the direct-to-customer model.
Cirque du Soleil	Is Cirque a circus or an acrobatic performance? Actually, it is both. Cirque removed what customers do not like about a circus (animal acts) and added what customers like (street entertainment).
salesforce.com	It recognized that business customers do not want to spend millions of dollars up front on costly hardware and software.
Arbol Industries	Read the case at the end of the chapter to see how Arbol cleverly segmented the market in a different way from its competitors, gaining a huge competitive advantage in the process.

MARKETING DRIVES SUCCESS

3.3 APPLE

Objective: Avoiding Common Pitfalls in Market Segmentation Is Important

Steve Jobs and Steve Wozniak founded a different kind of computer firm in 1977. The market for their Macintosh computers was not very big initially (and it still is not as big as the market for PCs), but they were determined to serve the needs of the customer who wanted the computer to be fun and easy to use. Apple pioneered the use of "drag and drop" icon-based computing with an external mouse.

The founders of Apple avoided the classic pitfalls in market segmentation. For example, they doggedly pursued their market segment, which engendered tremendous loyalty on the part of their customers. They did not imitate their competitors. And, they did not attempt to satisfy all needs by becoming big. In fact, for many years, business commentators speculated that Apple would not survive.[12]

But Apple's focus on making products fun and easy to use has paid off handsomely. Today, Apple makes much more than computers; they make such iconic products as the iPod and iPhone. Apple ushered in a brand new way of listening to music by not only inventing the iPod, but also making it easy to use by introducing a service called iTunes, where customers can download music for a small price.

Apple's focused segmentation strategy enables it to innovate consistently.

CHECKPOINT

Where We've Been

- We have learned that segmenting customers is crucial to business success.
- The best way to segment customers is by examining their needs and their attractiveness to you.
- There are common pitfalls in segmentation you should avoid.

Where We're Going

- The next section provides a simple-to-use checklist to ensure your segmentation efforts are on the right track.

Simple Checklist for Market Segmentation

OBJECTIVE 4

Based on the common pitfalls to avoid in segmentation, the checklist in Table 3.6 will guide your segmentation efforts.

TABLE 3.6 Checklist for Market Segmentation

Are we starting small, but starting now?	■ Do not wait to start segmentation efforts after you have done market research. ■ Start with the data you have today.
Have we based our segmentation on customer needs and customer attractiveness?	■ Are we falling into the same trap as our competitors by segmenting customers using easy-to-access data such as demographics? ■ Have we used both customer needs and our needs (how attractive a customer is to us) to segment customers?
Is our segmentation simple?	■ Will our people understand and use the segmentation? ■ Complex segmentation schemes collapse under their own weight.
Is our segmentation actionable?	■ Will our sales force use the segmentation to guide their efforts? ■ Have we over-segmented the market?
Will our segmentation give us a competitive advantage?	■ Is our segmentation different from our competitors'? ■ Is our segmentation going to enable us to develop and implement differentiated value propositions?
Do we have mechanisms to evolve our segmentation over time?	■ How will we ensure that our segmentation does not stagnate? ■ Have we assigned responsibilities and provided resources to evolve our segmentation?
Will our segmentation enable us to be better business operators?	■ Will our segmentation enable us to work together as one? ■ Will our segmentation, acting as glue, align all our functions so we are all focused on the same thing?

Where We've Been

■ We have seen how to segment customers effectively.

■ We have learned to avoid common pitfalls in segmentation.

■ We have seen how a checklist can help ensure our segmentation efforts are on the right track.

Where We're Going

■ In the last section of this chapter, we will see how to select target customer segments.

CHECKPOINT

OBJECTIVE 5

How to Select Target Customers

Once the segmentation is complete, how does a business select customers to target? The temptation might be to say, "That's easy, just pick the largest customer by sales volume." But this simplistic reasoning could be problematic. Research has shown that large customers may actually be unprofitable, and small customers may be profitable.[13] This is because large customers, in spite of their higher sales volume, may be more expensive to serve, thus wiping out their profitability to us.

If large customers may not be profitable, and small customers may be profitable, why do companies intuitively focus on large customers? They do so because firms typically spend little time analyzing customer profitability, attractiveness, and customer selection.[14] Selecting the right target customer takes effort, but the benefits are tremendous. Let us take some examples.

A large grocery chain analyzed its customers and segmented them into three categories: primary shoppers (give the store 80% or more of their business), secondary shoppers (spend more than 10% but less than 50% of their grocery budget at the store), and non-shoppers.[15] The analysis showed that even making small changes to customers' behaviours would make a significant impact on profitability. For example, increasing primary shoppers by 2% would increase profitability by 45%. Converting just 200 secondary customers into primary shoppers would increase profitability by 20%.

While the analysis might have tempted them to focus on the secondary shoppers, as they represented a greater potential to impact revenues, further analysis found that it would be cost prohibitive to attract them. This is because this customer segment wanted longer store hours and more promotional offers (like coupons). Therefore, the company decided to focus on increasing business from their primary customers.

A division of ACNielsen, the marketing research company, uses the grid shown in Figure 3.1 to segment and target customers.[16]

There are two dimensions to the segmentation grid—the amount of money spent by customers every year (this dimension has two levels: less than $1 million and greater than $1 million) and their level of sophistication (this dimension also has two levels: sophisticated users of data and unsophisticated users). In the upper-right quadrant we have sophisticated users of data who spend a lot of money. This is a prime target customer that ACNielsen wants to keep happy.

Diagonally opposite, we have unsophisticated customers who do not spend much money. These are customers who should not be targeted. The other two groups of customers are interesting. Unsophisticated customers who spend a lot of money will leave unless they are taught how to use data, and sophisticated customers who do not spend much money must be educated on the value of data to get them to spend more.

	< $1 million	> $1 million
Sophisticated	**Sophisticated users of data (want business expertise from ACNielsen):** • These customers are not buying much currently, but they can be educated to buy more. • How much time am I spending on these customers? • How do they answer our customer satisfaction survey?	**Sophisticated users of data (want business expertise from ACNielsen):** • These customers are buying a lot, and I need to keep them happy. • How much time am I spending on these customers? • How do they answer our customer satisfaction survey?
Unsophisticated	**Unsophisticated users of data (only want market share data):** • These customers are not buying a lot. • Am I spending too much time on these customers? • How do they answer our customer satisfaction survey?	**Unsophisticated users of data:** • These customers are buying a lot, but they will leave unless I work with them. • How much time am I spending on these customers? • How do they answer our customer satisfaction survey?

FIGURE 3.1

Good segmentation provides direction on choosing target customers.

MARKETING DRIVES SUCCESS

3.4 MASTERCARD

Objective: Targeting Customers Is Crucial for Business Success

MasterCard Worldwide is a multinational corporation whose business is to process payments between the banks of merchants and the banks of customers who use the MasterCard brand of credit and debit cards to make purchases. The problem with this industry is that there are many card issuers (Visa, American Express, Discover, and Diners, to name a few), and all of them are trying to target the same type of customer.

So MasterCard decided to try a new approach by targeting the customer who feels that everything is becoming commoditized and companies treat customers as mere numbers on a credit card. MasterCard began an advertising campaign: "There are some things money can't buy. For everything else, there's MasterCard." The first of these *priceless* ads ran in 1997.

The targeting has proved to be successful. Initially, MasterCard's intention was to target the end consumer. However, the success of the message has given it the base to target another segment—the small business owner. A visit to MasterCard's website (www.mastercard.com) reveals that small business owners can access a wealth of resources, from financing solutions to ideas on how to run a successful business.

MasterCard's targeting efforts have been successful.

Chapter Summary

1. Understand the importance of segmenting customers and the dangers of not segmenting customers.

Market segmentation is a pillar of any business' success or failure. If a business does not segment its customers, it is ignoring customer needs. This opens the door for competitors. When a business treats all customers in the same manner, it is wasting its resources because it is either under-serving or over-serving customers.

2. Avoid mistakes made by your competitors by learning how to segment effectively.

A common mistake businesses make in segmenting their customers is to use readily available data such as geography and demographics. Although these variables are easy to use, the resulting segmentation is rarely effective. Psychographic segmentation has rather limited uses, mainly in advertising and brand coherence. The best way to segment customers is to examine their needs and their attractiveness to the business.

3. Learn to avoid common pitfalls in market segmentation.

Common pitfalls in market segmentation include segmenting using demographics, over-segmenting, targeting too many customer groups with one offering, using complex segmentation methods, segmenting by product, always targeting the largest segment, not understanding that segments change, failing to invest in emerging segments, following the same segmentation as competitors, and using stagnant segmentation schemes that are past their expiry dates.

4. Develop a simple checklist to follow in segmenting customers successfully.

A segmentation checklist is useful to ensure that segmentation efforts are on the right track. The checklist has seven items on it: Are we starting small, but starting now; are we segmenting customers based on their needs and attractiveness; is our segmentation simple; is our segmentation actionable; will our segmentation give us a competitive advantage; do we have mechanisms to evolve our segmentation; and will our segmentation enable us to be better business operators?

5. Learn how to confidently select target customers for maximum business success.

Many businesses do not spend enough time thinking about which customers to target. They mistakenly believe that focusing on large customers is the smart thing to do. But research shows that large customers may in fact be unprofitable, while smaller customers may be profitable. The best way to select target customer segments is to use a set of criteria such as segment revenue, revenue potential, profitability, profit potential, fit with overall business strategy, and competitive concentration.

CRITICAL THINKING QUESTIONS

1. All successful business start-ups have relied on market segmentation. Provide a detailed example of one successful company and explain how it used market segmentation to achieve its success.

2. You tell your business colleague that mass markets do not exist. He disagrees. "Electricity, oil, and steel are mass marketed. There is no segmentation in these industries," he says. What is your response?

3. Psychographic segmentation is a way to segment customers based on their activities, interests, and opinions. Do some research on psychographic segmentation and write a brief report outlining the method and pros and cons of this approach.

4. Why should segmentation be an evolutionary exercise? Why can't a firm be done with its segmentation efforts, once and for all?

5. In Chapter 1 we saw that Snap-on Tools targets the automobile professional. Let us say that Snap-on wants to also target the general consumer market. What factors should it keep in mind when making this strategic move?

RUNNING CASE

ARBOL INDUSTRIES LEARNS AN IMPORTANT BUSINESS LESSON

By asking a fundamental question, "Why can't we differentiate commodity products?" Arbol's new CEO set in motion a total transformation of the business. Getting sales professionals to visit customers, understand their needs, develop superior value propositions and charge premiums for their products proved to be a huge boost not only to the bottom line, but also to the culture of the company.

One day, a sales professional hesitantly approached the marketing manager. "I don't know much about marketing, but I want to ask you a question. I notice that I serve all my customers the same way. Regardless of whether they are big or small, or what industry they are in, I offer them the same mix of products. Is this the right way to do business?"

The marketing manager was delighted with this question. It showed that the rest of the organization was starting to "get" the power of marketing. "As a matter of fact," he replied, "we are in the process of segmenting our markets. I will be asking your views on this topic. Once we are done, you will see how radically different our go-to-market approach will be."

Working with the sales force and other functions, the marketing function developed the segmentation approach shown in Figure 3.2.

When Arbol started its marketing journey, it segmented its customers in the same way as its competitors—the entire industry divided customers into two categories based on geography: domestic customers (customers within North America) and export customers (customers outside North America). Let us call this Phase 1. As you can appreciate, Phase 1 is not based on customer needs. Importantly, it did not give Arbol a competitive edge over its rivals.

In Phase 2, Arbol did not touch the export segment (because of lack of resources), but it further segmented domestic customers into three groups—home builders, industrial customers, and repair and remodelling customers. Industrial customers use wood to make products (pallets used in supermarkets; stakes used in a vineyard to grow vines). Repair and remodelling customers, as the name implies, are engaged in repairing and refurbishing homes.

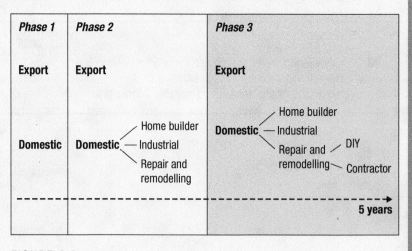

FIGURE 3.2

Arbol Industries' segmentation approach

Using the segmentation scheme in Phase 2, Arbol began developing differentiated value propositions for each segment. For example, for the home builder segment, it started offering a product called Engineered Wood (designed to compete with steel beams), guaranteed shipping schedules (in partnership with lumber wholesalers), and guaranteed pricing schemes. Recognizing that the industrial segment had unique needs, Arbol offered this segment advice on how to cut manufacturing costs. Finally, for the repair and remodelling segment, it began offering such innovations as decking material with no splinters (so the end consumer can walk on a wooden deck in bare feet).

And, of course, in each case Arbol either sold more quantity to the customer over its competitors or charged more for the value propositions it was offering.

In Phase 3, Arbol sub-segmented the repair and remodelling segment into two segments—the do-it-yourself (DIY) customer and the contractor. DIY customers buy products from retailers such as Home Depot, and they prefer to work on a project themselves. Contractors, of course, are professional repair and remodelling customers.

Arbol began offering differentiated value propositions to these segments based on their needs. DIY customers, for example, loved a new product introduced by Arbol—the Total Kit. Essentially, a DIY customer who wanted to build a deck or a shed, for example, could buy an entire kit consisting of wood, plywood, tools, nails, and glue and finish the job in less time than sourcing each component separately.

For the contractor segment, Arbol introduced services on its website and at retail stores where a contractor could specify the dimensions of a job and obtain a printout of the quantity of material needed and the number of hours it would take to do the job. This helped contractors provide better estimates to their customers.

The best part about all the segmentation work Arbol undertook is that it did not cost a single penny. All the market research data it needed on customer needs was available free of charge from the National Association of Home Builders. The data was always there, but Arbol was the first organization in the industry to actually do something with it.

It took Arbol five years to go from Phase 1 to Phase 3. This is because it took the time to thoroughly implement each phase across all functions before undertaking the next phase. For example, going from Phase 1 to Phase 2 required refocusing, reorganizing, and retraining the sales force. Previously, a sales professional would serve any customer, in any industry. Under the new segmentation model, sales professionals began to focus on specific customer segments to enable them to develop expertise and build deep customer relationships.

Arbol Industries exemplifies a comment made earlier in this chapter: segmentation has to be an evolutionary exercise.

Case Assignment

Arbol Industries went from Phase 1 to Phase 3. Can you picture Phase 27? What comments would you have for an organization that went from Phase 1 to Phase 27 in its segmentation efforts?

SUGGESTED READINGS
If You Want to Segment and Target Your Customers, Do Not Miss These Publications

Clayton M. Christensen, Scott Cook, and Taddy Hall, "Marketing Malpractice: The Cause and the Cure," *Harvard Business Review*, December 2005, pp. 74–83.

Alan W. H. Grant and Leonard A. Schlesinger, "Realizing Your Customers' Full Profit Potential," *Harvard Business Review*, September–October 1995, pp. 59–72.

Benson P. Shapiro et al., "Manage Customers for Profits (Not Just Sales)," *Harvard Business Review*, September–October 1987, pp. 101–108.

NOTES

1. David Court, "A new model for marketing," McKinsey Quarterly 2004, No. 4, pp. 4–5.

2. This example was provided to me by a participant in one of my executive classes.

3. Marakon Associates and Economist Intelligence Unit (2004).

4. I know of examples where the business' profitability increased dramatically after it let go of its unattractive customers. This point is made very well in Susan Bishop, "The Strategic Power of Saying No," *Harvard Business Review*, November–December 1999, pp. 50–61.

5. This example was given to me by one of my clients that supplies telecommunications services to the financial services industry.

6. Daniel Yankelovich and David Meer, "Rediscovering Market Segmentation," *Harvard Business Review*, February 2006, pp. 122–131.

7. Yankelovich and Meer, *ibid.*

8. This example is provided in Clayton M. Christensen, Scott Cook, and Taddy Hall, "Marketing Malpractice: The Cause and the Cure," *Harvard Business Review*, December 2005, pp. 74–83.

9. This is an example from one of my consulting projects.

10. An alliance between the consulting firm Booz and Nielsen// NetRatings Inc.

11. This section is based on Horacio D. Rozanski, Gerry Bollman, and Martin Lipman, "Seize the Occasion! The Seven-segment System for Online Marketing," *Strategy + Business*, Issue 24, Third Quarter, 2001, pp. 42–51.

12. Even business "gurus" like Gary Hamel predicted Apple's demise.

13. Bristol Lane Voss, "Angel Customers & Demon Customers: Discover Which is Which and Turbo-charge Your Stock," *Journal of Business Strategy*, 2003, Vol. 24, No. 5, p. 44.

14. Benson P. Shapiro et al., "Manage Customers for Profits (Not Just Sales)," *Harvard Business Review*, September–October 1987, pp. 101–108.

15. This example is based on Alan W. H. Grant and Leonard A. Schlesinger, "Realizing Your Customers' Full Profit Potential," *Harvard Business Review*, September–October 1995, pp. 59–72.

16. This example was given to me by a student of mine in an executive class.

PART 2

Creating Customer Value

provides tools to create winning marketing strategies.

CHAPTER 4   Provides an easy-to-use template, tips, and techniques to develop and implement a strong marketing plan.

CHAPTER 5   Describes how to build a strong brand to differentiate a business from competitors.

CHAPTER 6   Provides strategies on how to price effectively for maximum business success.

CHAPTER 7   Provides tools and techniques to confidently make channel decisions.

CHAPTER 8   Provides cutting-edge tools for communicating effectively with customers.

Understanding Customers
PART 1, P. 1

Creating Customer Value
PART 2, P. 67

Delivering Customer Value
PART 3, P. 195

Managing Customer Value
PART 4, P. 231

CHAPTER 4

Developing a Strong Marketing Plan

CHECKPOINT

Where We've Been

- We have seen that the research is clear: all winning businesses *develop* and *implement* strong marketing strategies.

- These businesses understand customer needs, segment their customers, and select attractive target customers to serve.

- For each target customer segment, successful businesses craft a winning marketing strategy based on the marketing mix elements of product, price, channel, and marketing communications strategies.

Where We're Going

- We will learn how winning businesses capture their superior marketing strategies and implementation actions in a document called the marketing plan.

CHAPTER INTRODUCTION

Imagine the fate that would befall a sports team that did not have a playbook. There would be total chaos on the field. The team would not know what weaknesses its opponent had, what plays to execute, what actions to take in case of unexpected events, and what the role of each player should be in ensuring success. Such a team would be certain to lose against an opponent who had a well thought-out, disciplined approach to the game.

Organizations, whether **for-profit** or **non-profit**, are no different. Without a well thought-out go-to-market strategy, such a firm is bound to lose. As we saw in Chapter 1, the research is crystal clear on one point: firms that succeed do so because they are capable of developing and implementing a superior **marketing strategy**. And as we also saw in Chapter 1, the firm's marketing strategy is encapsulated in a document called the **marketing plan**, which is essentially the organization's "playbook" for success.

In this chapter you will

1. Learn the key role a marketing plan plays in determining the success of any business.

2. See what happens if a firm does not develop a marketing plan.

3. Learn the steps in developing a strong marketing plan.

4. Learn to avoid common mistakes made in developing a marketing plan.

OBJECTIVE 1

The Key Role a Marketing Plan Plays in Determining the Success of Any Business

Take the quiz in Figure 4.1. Assume you want to run a business someday (or work for a profit or non-profit firm). If you answer "yes" to at least five out of the seven statements, you have no choice but to develop a strong marketing plan.

In fact, most businesses would probably answer "yes" to all seven statements. This is because the business environment facing businesses has become more, not less, complex and competitive due to many forces conspiring to create the "perfect storm." Businesses face the following challenges:

- Goods and services are becoming increasingly **commoditized** as firms introduce similar new products every year.

- It is becoming increasingly difficult for a business to sustain a position of **competitive differentiation**.

- Customers are more price-sensitive as they cannot perceive the differences between competing goods and services.

- Customer loyalty is eroding.

- There is an explosion of media and channels facing a business, increasing the complexity of serving customers.

In the light of this reality, a business has no choice but to develop and implement superior go-to-market strategies. We saw in Chapter 1 that the research supports this argument. And as we have also seen, superior marketing strategies are captured in a document called the marketing plan.

	Yes	No
I want to run a successful business.	☐	☐
My customers are price-sensitive.	☐	☐
I want to beat the competition.	☐	☐
My goods and services have become commodities.	☐	☐
I want to develop superior strategies.	☐	☐
I want to implement strategies flawlessly.	☐	☐
I want different parts of my business to work together focusing on the customer.	☐	☐

FIGURE 4.1

A business needs a marketing plan if it answers "yes" to at least five out of seven statements.

MARKETING DRIVES SUCCESS

4.1 ARTEMIS PET FOOD CO.

Objective: Successful Businesses Design and Implement Superior Marketing Strategies

In 2007 many top brands of pet food were found to be tainted with melamine, an industrial chemical used to make plastic. The melamine was found in Chinese-made wheat gluten used as filler to raise protein levels in pet food. Its presence has been linked to the deaths of at least 13 cats and 1 dog, and is potentially the culprit in thousands of other pet deaths.[1]

continues...

Although Ken Park did not anticipate this devastating event, he wisely spotted the need for healthier pet food. In 1995 he started Artemis Pet Food Co. with $400 000 in savings. A pet store owner, Park accurately read the external environment facing his firm and saw an opportunity—people were spending a lot of money caring for their pets, and they wanted to feed them food that was as close to human quality as possible. Accordingly, his pet food includes turkey, lamb, chicken, peas, carrots, cranberries, and apples, all sourced mostly from North America. Artemis' super-premium dog food runs about $40 for a 15.88 kg (35-lb) bag, compared to $15 for a grocery store brand.

The problem facing smaller pet food companies is that they cannot afford their own production facilities, so they outsource their production. But Park realized that if he chose this option, he would lose his point of distinction from his competitors. Although keeping production in-house raises his costs, Park chose to go this route. The melamine scandal has highlighted the wisdom of this approach—his sales have increased by as much as 50%.

Tammy is typical of consumers who spend money on all-natural, premium food for their pets.

Where We've Been

- We have learned that all winning businesses develop a strong marketing plan.

Where We're Going

- We will see what happens if a business does not develop a marketing plan.

CHECKPOINT

Negative Consequences of Not Developing a Marketing Plan

OBJECTIVE 2

Without a marketing plan, a business tends to shuffle along without a clear point of view of what's next. Let us take two examples.[2] Joe Merino and his partner saw an opportunity in the marketplace and they started a business helping institutions (schools and government buildings) get rid of contaminants such as mould and asbestos. They quickly reached sales of $1 million. But Joe noticed that their business had reached a plateau; sales were not increasing. These are the questions the partners were struggling with: What do we do next? How do we jump from the present sales curve to the next? They knew that without a strong marketing plan, their business would shuffle along and perhaps die.

Sebastian Cassavetes started a graphic design firm. He quickly secured a lucrative contract with a business. Today, his firm enjoys sales of $10 million. The problem? About 80% of his business comes from one single customer. Over time, to keep the customer happy, Sebastian has provided the customer with free services at no extra charge. Now, the customer is expecting even more from him, all for no charge. Sebastian is afraid that if he refuses, the customer will simply take the business elsewhere. But he is stuck because he has not developed a marketing plan to secure other customers.

A marketing plan provides focus and discipline to a business. Without a marketing plan, a business has a tendency to drift from one attractive opportunity to another. Also, as we saw in Chapter 1, the marketing plan needs to be translated into other **functional plans**. In this way, the marketing plan plays a crucial role in contextualizing the market for the other functions. In other words, the marketing plan provides all functions with a common understanding of the organization's go-to-market strategy: which customer segments are being targeted, how value will be created for these customers, and how the business will secure an advantage over competitors. Read the case on Arbol Industries at the end of this chapter to understand more about this topic.

KEYPOINT

A strong marketing plan acts as a glue that unites all functions of a business.

CHAPTER CHALLENGE 4.1

ARE YOU ON THE RIGHT TRACK?

Why is it necessary to translate marketing plans into functional plans?

(*Were you on the right track? Check your answers in Appendix 2.*)

MARKETING DRIVES SUCCESS

4.2 XEROX

Objective: A Marketing Plan Provides Focus and Discipline to a Business

Xerox began by making photocopiers. As you will see in Chapter 5, a business cannot succeed in the long run if it defines its marketing strategy in terms of what is called the **core product**—photocopiers in this case. Why? Because over time, as more competitors enter the market, photocopiers become commodities, driving down prices. As we saw in Chapter 1, a prime task of marketing is to help the business *differentiate* its goods and services from its competitors.

As a result, Xerox has evolved its marketing strategy over time to constantly look for a competitive edge. We can distinguish three phases in its marketing strategy.

PHASE 1:   The marketing strategy is defined in terms of making and selling photocopiers.

PHASE 2:   The marketing strategy is defined in terms of documents. Xerox realized that photocopiers were only a means to a certain end—organizations use photocopiers to create and distribute documents.

PHASE 3:   The marketing strategy is defined in terms of helping organizations manage *knowledge* created by documents (this is shown in their advertisement). As documents have become increasingly electronic, Xerox realized that it could

continues

no longer sustain a business built on photocopiers. Simultaneously, it realized that documents too are a means to an end—successful organizations create and share knowledge (about customers, competitors, and markets) among different parts of the business (featured as "work-flow" in the Xerox advertisement).

What you should recognize is the focus and discipline with which this organization has evolved its marketing strategy over time.

Xerox Global Services helps organizations find, modify and manage documents instantly. Result? Service levels up. Processing costs down. There's a new way to look at it.

Where are mission-critical documents when you need them? In a file cabinet? A computer? Our professional and document outsourcing services digitize and manage critical business processes, taking paper and manual steps out. The results are a dramatic reduction in processing costs, a significant improvement in workflow, and a distinct competitive edge that comes from working faster and more efficiently than your competition. Who do we retrieve for? JPMorgan Chase & Co. and Enterprise Rent-A-Car Company. We can do the same for you. To see how we handle everything from accounting and contracts to HR and legal, visit us today at xerox.com/retrieve.

xerox.com/retrieve **1-800-ASK-XEROX**

xerox

Xerox has evolved its marketing strategy over time with focus and discipline.

Where We've Been

- We have learned that all winning businesses develop a strong marketing plan.
- Without a marketing plan, a business lacks a sense of "what's next"—it tends to drift, and other functions do not share a common understanding of the business's go-to-market approach.

Where We're Going

- We will see how to construct a strong marketing plan.

CHECKPOINT

OBJECTIVE 3

The Steps in Developing a Strong Marketing Plan

Table 4.1 presents a practical template you can use to develop a strong marketing plan. Spend a few minutes familiarizing yourself with it. The template has 13 sections (excluding the appendix), and although it may look complicated, it really is not. As shown in Figure 4.2, the marketing plan sections fall into four *major* areas.

TABLE 4.1   Marketing Plan Template

1. Executive Summary
- Key issues to be addressed by the marketing plan
- Key strategies in place to address key issues
- Key expected outcomes for the business

2. Table of Contents

3. Market Analysis
- How attractive is the market?
  - Description of market segments we currently serve (or want to serve, for a new business)
  - Size of market and rate of growth
  - Market share of key players
- Analysis of the macroenvironment that could impact the business
  - Demographic factors
  - Socio-cultural factors
  - Economic factors
  - Technological factors
  - Political and regulatory factors

4. Competitor Analysis
Format: In the main body of the marketing plan, 1 or 2 pages of competitive analysis summary indicating what we need to do to become a better competitor. In the Appendix, 1 page profiling each major competitor on these factors:
- Size
- Market share
- Goals
- Products currently offered
- Product quality/capability
- Strengths
- Weaknesses
- How they currently serve our customer segments
- Likely future moves
- Other competitors planning entry into this market

5. Customer Analysis
- Customer segments we serve
- Customer needs—current and future
- Key decision-making criteria used by customers
- Customer satisfaction levels

6. Key Issues Analysis
- Opportunities and threats analysis (OT)
- Strengths and weaknesses of business to respond to opportunities and threats (SW)
- Analysis of past marketing effort
  - What we did right last year
  - What we did wrong
  - Key lessons learned and implications for this year's plan
  - Analysis of last year's marketing strategy: what gaps exist in our strategy and implementation?
  - Which marketing strategies from last year should we keep?
- Key issues to be addressed by the business based on OTSW analysis
  - Next year
  - Years 1–5 (prioritize by year, if necessary)

7. Objectives to Be Achieved
- Financial objectives
  - Sales volume
  - Revenue
  - Profitability
- Marketing objectives
  - Market share
  - Product innovation objectives
  - Development of new markets
  - Customer service objectives
  - Sales training objectives
  - Channel objectives

7. Objectives to Be Achieved (cont'd)
- Marketing communications objectives
- Pricing objectives
- Marketing research objectives
- Other objectives

8. Marketing Strategies
- Product strategy
  - Market segments selected and targeted
  - Product benefits and customer value created
  - Product positioning (how different from competition)
  - Brand strategies
  - Service strategy
  - Product innovation strategies
  - Development of new markets
- Pricing strategy
- Channel strategy
- Marketing communications strategy
- Other strategies needed to make marketing plan a success
  - Sales strategy
  - Marketing research strategy
  - Supply chain strategy
  - Operations
  - Human resources
  - Cross-functional implications of marketing strategy

9. Marketing Plan Implementation
For each item identified in the previous section, outline:
- What will be done (tactics)
- When will it be done (timeline)

9. Marketing Plan Implementation (cont'd)
- Who will do it (person or functional responsibility)
- What help will be needed (resources)
- Contingency plans in event of blockage of marketing plan

10. Marketing–Sales Linkage
- Identify how the sales function will be engaged

11. Key Outcomes for the Business
- Revenue and profit impact of strategies
- Sales volume
- Market share
- Return on investment (ROI)

12. Marketing Plan Budget
- Cost of marketing plan elements

13. Marketing Plan Control
For key marketing and financial objectives, identify:
- Goals to be achieved by period
- Information needed to track goals
- What mechanisms will be in place to test marketing plan assumptions, track progress toward goals, and make corrective changes?

14. Appendix
- Supporting documentation

Source: Ajay Sirsi, Marketing Led—Sales Driven: How Successful Businesses Use the Power of Marketing Plans and Sales Execution to Win in the Marketplace (Victoria, BC: Trafford Publishing, 2005).

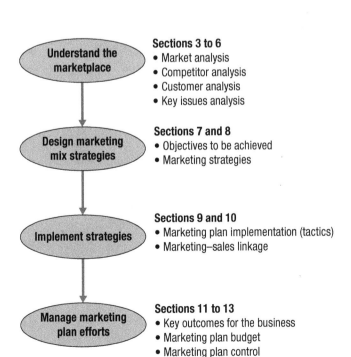

Understand the marketplace

Sections 3 to 6
- Market analysis
- Competitor analysis
- Customer analysis
- Key issues analysis

Design marketing mix strategies

Sections 7 and 8
- Objectives to be achieved
- Marketing strategies

Implement strategies

Sections 9 and 10
- Marketing plan implementation (tactics)
- Marketing–sales linkage

Manage marketing plan efforts

Sections 11 to 13
- Key outcomes for the business
- Marketing plan budget
- Marketing plan control

CHAPTER CHALLENGE 4.2

ARE YOU ON THE RIGHT TRACK?

What do the four major areas in Figure 4.2 remind you of? (Were you on the right track? Check your answers in Appendix 2.)

FIGURE 4.2
The sections of a marketing plan fall into four major areas.

Details of the Marketing Plan Template

Let us examine the marketing plan template in Table 4.1 in more detail.

Section 1: Executive Summary

The purpose of writing an executive summary is to enable the reader to know the core of the marketing plan. A good executive summary should be written last, should not exceed one or two pages, and should contain three sections:

- key issues to be addressed by the marketing plan
- key strategies in place to address key issues
- key expected outcomes for the business

Section 2: Table of Contents

The Table of Contents shows, at a glance, what sections the marketing plan covers and on what page each section can be found. In this way the reader can navigate easily through the marketing plan.

Section 3: Market Analysis

This section shows how attractive the market is (the one in which we operate or the one we want to get into) and **macroenvironmental trends** that could have an impact on the business. Without an assessment of the market, a business could ignore opportunities or be unaware of looming danger. Let us take an example.

Between 2001 and 2004, Mattel lost 20% of its share of the worldwide fashion doll segment to smaller rivals such as MGA Entertainment, creator of a hip new line of dolls called Bratz.[3] Mattel had failed to notice a shift in demographic and socio-cultural factors—that preteen girls were becoming more sophisticated and maturing more quickly. These girls were outgrowing their Barbie dolls at a younger age. They were, instead, more interested in emulating their teenage sisters and the pop stars they idolized. The target market for Barbie had narrowed from girls aged 3 to 11 to girls aged 3 to 5, but Mattel was oblivious to these shifts in the macroenvironment. Although Mattel reacted with a line of hip dolls of its own, the damage was done—Barbie had lost a fifth of her seemingly incontestable market share.

> *The biggest dangers to a company are the ones you don't see coming.*
>
> DAY AND SCHOEMAKER

Section 4: Competitor Analysis

No business operates in a vacuum. For any given product category, a group of competitors vie for the customer's business. In this section it is important to develop a profile of each competitor in terms of size, strengths, weaknesses, strategies, likely future moves, and so forth.

But developing detailed competitor profiles is not going to help much unless the marketing strategist synthesizes this information to ask one question: What are my competitors doing to take business away from me, and what should I be doing to serve my customers in a fashion that will differentiate my business from my competitors? Unfortunately, many marketing plans contain detailed competitor profiles, but the author fails to take this extra step, weakening the power of this section.

Section 5: Customer Analysis

The ultimate focus of our value creation efforts is the customer. Therefore, in this section we examine the needs of our customers, the decision-making criteria they use, and how those needs may be changing. Without an accurate understanding of customer needs, a business has no hope of ever satisfying them. Finally,

KEYPOINT

The only sustainable competitive advantage an organization has is its ability to understand the needs of its customers faster and in a superior fashion to its competitors.

Quaker has accurately embraced the trend toward healthy eating.

4.3 DISNEY

MARKETING DRIVES SUCCESS

Objective: Market Analysis Reveals Opportunities

Karen Gammiere was skeptical. She had heard that the Walt Disney Company was offering guided tours to exotic places like Peru, but she didn't want to arrive at her destination to find Winnie the Pooh shaking her hand.[4] Nevertheless, based on rave reviews, she ended up on a Disney guided tour of Italy and had a great time, not once seeing a costumed character.

Keeping a sharp eye on the market and evolving with the travelling public has always been Disney's strong point. In the 1950s, Disneyland (in California) satisfied the needs of families on vacation in their new cars. Florida's Walt Disney World, built in the 1970s and 1980s, satisfied the needs of families flying to a vacation destination. And in the 1990s, Disney launched a successful cruise vacation business.

Disney noticed that "participatory" vacations were on the rise. These are vacations where tourists participate in activities such as hiking, wine tasting, and cooking. But instead of merely imitating its competitors, Disney launched a new market for participatory vacations the whole family can enjoy. So Adventures by Disney is designed to take families to places they might be too reluctant to visit on their own.

Although Disney has not advertised the new product line, relying instead on word-of-mouth, the public's response has been beyond Disney's expectations. It started the new business in 2005 with just two itineraries. In 2008 it booked 17 itineraries in 13 countries, with a total of 370 scheduled tours of up to 40 people each.

Accurate market analysis has enabled Disney to go beyond theme parks.

CHAPTER CHALLENGE 4.3

ARE YOU ON THE RIGHT TRACK?

Compared to Disney's other product lines, such as theme parks and cruise ships, what key challenges do you think Disney will face with the new venture?

(*Were you on the right track? Check your answers in Appendix 2.*)

remember our discussion in Chapter 2 that winning businesses not only understand customer needs, they *create* them.

Section 6: Key Issues Analysis   Up to this point, the marketing plan template has focused for the most part on data collection. Therefore, in this section it is time to take a deep breath and reflect on what the data actually means. To do this, a business has to identify a set of key issues that must be addressed by the marketing plan. To identify key issues, we first start by identifying some opportunities or threats faced by the business. We then examine the business' strengths and weaknesses to respond to these opportunities and threats.

This process is commonly called a SWOT analysis (Strengths, Weaknesses, Opportunities, Threats); however, a traditional SWOT analysis often leads to wrong conclusions. That is why it is better to do an OTSW analysis (some people call this a TOWS analysis, as it is easier to pronounce). Let us take two examples to justify this point.[5]

"Our strength is that we have great relations with wholesalers," reads the marketing plan. Indeed, having strong relations with a channel-of-distribution member is admirable. However, upon further reading of the marketing plan, it becomes evident that wholesalers in this industry are going out of business. Instead, a new form of channel is emerging—the internet. And, the business has no presence in this channel. So, the identified strength is not a strength, but a severe liability. This business is headed for trouble, but managers cannot see it coming because of their internal focus.

"Our customer service platform is not as good as our nearest competitor," reads the marketing plan. The immediate reaction taken by the business? Raise customer service standards, of course. However, by the time the business raises and successfully implements its customer service standards to equal its competitor's, the competitor has moved on by setting a higher benchmark.

KEYPOINT

Starting with strengths and weaknesses could lead a business to wrong conclusions.

Nokia understands that its customers want to increase productivity and cut operating costs.

Based on the OTSW analysis, a set of key issues to be addressed by the marketing plan become obvious. Here are some examples of key issues:

- We must take advantage of the increased popularity of participatory vacations. (Disney)
- Preteen girls' needs have dramatically shifted, and we must address this situation right now. (Mattel)
- Customers are demanding greater corporate social responsibility; what are we doing to address this? (Suncor)
- Golf is becoming a popular sport: we need to develop products to maintain golf courses. (John Deere)
- We need to respond to a competitor (Geox) who has introduced a new product— breathable shoes. (Clarks)

The key issues set the stage for delineation of strategies. Table 4.2 summarizes the arguments for conducting an OTSW analysis, not a SWOT analysis.

Section 7: Objectives to Be Achieved   While the previous section enabled the business to identify a set of key issues that must be addressed by the marketing plan, specific guidelines are needed. It is for this reason that we use this section to define objectives (financial, marketing, and other) that we should achieve. For example, if a business wants to develop a new market (participatory vacations), it will need to set objectives related to revenue, market share, pricing, profitability, and social responsibility.

Section 8: Marketing Strategies   To successfully realize the key issues identified in Section 6 and the objectives specified in Section 7, a set of marketing strategies has to be crafted. As we saw in Chapter 1, marketing strategies are developed using the marketing mix elements of product, price, channel, and marketing communications.

However, as we also realized in Chapter 1, many parts of an organization's marketing strategy are actually implemented by other functions. Remember the example of Travelers from Chapter 1? Although Travelers wants to build and project a brand of "customer focus," its go-to-market strategy will fail if the sales force lacks product knowledge or the customer service employee is not friendly.

It is for this reason that, in this section, an astute marketing strategist considers *cross-functional* implications of marketing strategies. In other words, the marketing plan author must think about what other functions need to do to successfully implement marketing strategies. The marketing plan example in Appendix 1 provides an example.

TABLE 4.2   OTSW vs. SWOT
1. SWOT leads to the wrong conclusions.
2. SWOT leads to an internal focus.
3. OTSW leads to an external focus.
4. OTSW enables a business to first take an unconstrained view of its business; then constraints can be added.
5. Opportunities and threats are external, while strengths and weaknesses are internal.
6. A strength is not a strength unless it enables the business to capture an opportunity or minimize a threat, regardless of how well loved the strength is within the business.
7. Theoretically, all opportunities and threats must be responded to. Practically, a business should examine its resources (strengths and weaknesses) and then decide which opportunities and threats it should focus on. These become the key issues to be addressed by the marketing plan.

John Deere has identified a key issue—seizing an opportunity to capitalize on the popularity of golf.

Section 9: Marketing Plan Implementation   Developing marketing strategies is admirable, but without an action plan, strategies will not get implemented. Therefore, in this section we specify a set of tactics, person and timeline responsibilities, and resources necessary to successfully implement the marketing strategies. There is yet another reason why an action plan is key: without a plan to implement strategies, there is a tendency to want to take on too much. It is better to take on fewer strategies and implement them well than to take on too much and botch the implementation.

Section 10: Marketing–Sales Linkage   Chapter 9 is devoted to the important topic of achieving marketing–sales linkage. In many organizations, marketing and sales do not work well together.[6] As we saw in Chapter 1, the sales force is a key component of marketing strategy implementation. No wonder, then, that the American Marketing Association (AMA) has identified achieving marketing–sales linkage as a crucial topic for any business to tackle. Therefore, in this section we outline how marketing is going to engage the sales function. More details on this can be found in Chapter 9, as well as in the marketing plan example in Appendix 1.

Section 11: Key Outcomes for the Business   In this section, we outline what rewards we hope to attain if we design and implement our strategies properly. So we examine what share, volume, and revenues our strategies will generate and what levels of profitability and return on investment (ROI) we can look forward to.

Section 12: Marketing Plan Budget   There are costs associated with designing and implementing strategies. Therefore, in this section we calculate a budget for the marketing plan.

Section 13: Marketing Plan Control   Markets are dynamic entities, and change is a constant: marketing plan assumptions are no longer valid, a new competitor emerges from nowhere, the economy sours, customers stop spending, or new opportunities arise. For this reason, the marketing plan must be constantly revisited to check for assumptions, track progress against goals, and make any necessary adjustments. While it is true that without a marketing plan a business tends to drift, it does not necessarily follow that the marketing plan should be set in stone, making the organization inflexible.

KEY POINT

An action plan to implement marketing strategies grounds the organization in reality. Without this, there is a tendency to want to take on too much.

If you do not build a system for marketing and sales to work together, you are not harnessing the power and unique capabilities of each function.

AJAY SIRSI

4.4 GREYSTONE PROPERTY MANAGEMENT

Objective: A Marketing Plan Is a Living, Breathing Document

Greystone Property Management manages high-rise residential buildings for landlords (wealthy individuals and institutional investors such as pension funds).[7] Although the marketing function had developed a one-year marketing plan and the organization was in the middle of implementing it, something interesting happened—an opportunity presented itself.

The city government was interested in rejuvenating a neighbourhood notorious for crime, drugs, and other nefarious activities. It felt that by building such things as parks and recreation centers, residents would take more pride in their neighbourhood, and this would lead to a reduction in crime. It asked Greystone if it would be interested in taking on a role that would propel it beyond just property management to community development.

What was Greystone to do? On the one hand, it could be argued that this opportunity was not part of the marketing plan and, therefore, it would be wise to not grab it. "Stay the course," one executive said. "We should stick to the strategy we have developed." On the other hand, it could be argued that such an opportunity was not likely to fall into Greystone's lap again. Developing communities was a much more lucrative option than property management—one that could open doors to other opportunities.

Greystone changed its marketing strategy when it saw an opportunity to move beyond property management.

Florence Furlong of Solo Cup shares the discipline needed to develop a marketing plan.

CHAPTER CHALLENGE 4.4

ARE YOU ON THE RIGHT TRACK?

What would you do if you were in Greystone's shoes? (*Were you on the right track? Check your answers in Appendix 2.*)

Section 14: Appendix This section should contain all the backup material to support the marketing plan. We will have more to say on this topic in the next section.

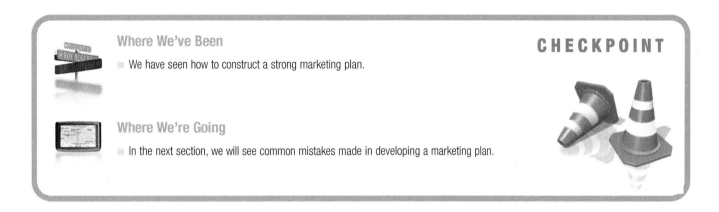

Where We've Been

■ We have seen how to construct a strong marketing plan.

Where We're Going

■ In the next section, we will see common mistakes made in developing a marketing plan.

CHECKPOINT

Avoid Common Mistakes Made in Developing a Marketing Plan

OBJECTIVE 4

There are some common mistakes made by creators of marketing plans. Learn from their mistakes.

Mistake 1: Forgetting That the Marketing Plan Template Is Directional

It is unwise to treat the marketing plan template as a checklist. "I don't have data on market share of key players!" says a panic-stricken manager. "So I cannot complete Section 3." This is a mistake because the template is directional. This means you should look at what Section 3 is asking of you—how attractive is the market and what are some trends within it?

Mistake 2: Feeding the Data Monster

The data monster has an insatiable appetite for data; the more you feed it, the more it wants. So when developing a marketing plan, keep in mind that data is not important, the insight is. Always ask, "What does the data mean? What implications does this have for my business?" If you cannot answer these questions, question the need for the data. Let us take an example.

"The local economy is growing at 9% per annum," says a marketing plan, without going further. Why is this piece of data important? By itself it says nothing, but when we ask the question "What does the data mean?" the following logic is revealed. The hot local economy (an oil boom) means that there are more jobs than job seekers. Anecdotal evidence reveals that employees are routinely lured away by competitors offering higher salaries and more attractive benefits.

Therefore, employee retention is a key issue the marketing plan must address (through the human resources function). This is a key issue because, without a stable cadre of employees, the business will fail to satisfy and keep its customers.

KEYPOINT

In the main body of the marketing plan, put the implications of the data. All backup material (data) should be put in the appendix to the marketing plan.

Mistake 3: Not Spending Enough Time on Section 6

Section 6, on identifying the key issues the marketing plan must address, is guaranteed to give any manager a headache. Sections 3–5 are relatively easy; they involve data collection, an activity facilitated by copious downloading from the internet. But Section 6 is very demanding; it asks the manager to distill the data to a set of "so whats." This requires discipline and hard work. But if Section 6 is weak, the marketing plan will also be weak as it sets out what key issues or challenges the business must address.

Mistake 4: Trying to Take on Too Much

Without a marketing plan, a business tends to drift because it lacks focus. However, simply having a marketing plan does not bestow focus on a business. This is because the business can be trying to implement too many strategies in a given year. It is better to focus on a few key strategies and implement them well, and then tackle the next set. Prioritizing key issues by year is a way to facilitate this.

Mistake 5: Forgetting That the Marketing Plan Is a Living, Breathing Document

Although a marketing plan is developed for a time period of one year, a business does not discard the previous year's marketing plan to start fresh for the current year. Rather, the marketing plan is updated. In this way, it becomes a living, breathing document. There are two sections in the marketing plan that accomplish this: Sections 6 and 13.

As shown in the marketing plan template in Table 4.1, in Section 6 we analyze our marketing effort from last year to determine what worked, what didn't work, and what strategies we must keep (or update). In Section 13, the marketing plan is revisited throughout the year to evaluate the assumptions that went into plan development, track progress, and make any changes.

Lisa Shepherd from Mezzanine Consulting discusses how to successfully implement a marketing plan.

Chapter Summary

1. Learn the key role a marketing plan plays in determining the success of any business.

A marketing plan is like a playbook for a sports team; it outlines the organization's go-to-market approach. Without a playbook, a sports team does not know what strategies and tactics to employ against a rival. Similarly, without a marketing plan, a business does not know what to do in the face of increasing competition, commoditization of goods and services, increasing price sensitivity among customers, and explosion of media and channels.

2. See what happens if a firm does not develop a marketing plan.

Lacking a marketing plan, a business does not know what to do to succeed. As a result, it drifts without any focus, opportunistically going down a path, only to retreat and try another "exciting" opportunity.

3. Learn the steps in developing a strong marketing plan.

To develop a strong marketing plan, use the template shown in Table 4.1. The template has 13 sections (excluding the appendix) that can be divided into seven main categories: data (Sections 3–5), OTSW analysis (Section 6), strategies (Sections 7–8), action plan (Sections 9–10), outcomes (Section 11), cost (Section 12), and control (Section 13).

The front end of the marketing plan is focused on data collection, which does not amount to much if it is not subject to an analysis to determine key issues that the business must address. The strategies and action plan sections enable successful implementation of strategies. The outcomes and cost sections determine the level of success. Finally, the control section acts like a rudder on a boat, controlling and making adjustments to the organization's strategies.

4. Learn to avoid common mistakes made in developing a marketing plan.

There are five main mistakes made in developing a marketing plan. The first mistake is to treat the marketing plan template like a checklist and panic over the lack of a piece of data. Focusing exclusively on data (mistake 2), without asking the question "What does the data mean?" leads to the next mistake (not spending enough time on Section 6, outlining the key issues the marketing plan must address). If a business tries to implement too many strategies (mistake 4), it spreads itself too thin. It is better to take on fewer strategies and implement them flawlessly. Finally, it is important to remember that the marketing plan is a living, breathing document. This means that business strategies must evolve over time, providing the business with discipline and focus.

CRITICAL THINKING QUESTIONS

1. The only sustainable competitive advantage an organization has is its ability to understand the needs of its customers faster than and in a superior fashion to its competitors. Explain what this key point means. Provide an example of a business that enjoys greater success than its competitors because its leaders believe in this key point.

2. Does the marketing plan template in Table 4.1 (pages 74 and 75) apply equally to a business that manufactures a good as well as a firm that provides a service? Why or why not? Be sure to justify your answer with examples.

3. A business colleague tells you, "I don't have time to develop a marketing plan. I am so busy with day-to-day activities." How would you respond?

4. A famous professor once said, "Marketing is everyone's job." What does this mean?

5. Joe Merino and his partner (see "Negative Consequences of Not Developing a Marketing Plan") have asked you to develop a marketing plan for them. Outline the *process* you will use to develop a marketing plan.

RUNNING CASE

ARBOL INDUSTRIES DEVELOPS A MARKETING PLAN

Arbol's marketing manager was happy with the progress his company had made since his arrival: Arbol was transforming itself from a cost- and product-focused company to a customer-focused company, it was conducting research to understand customer needs, and it was segmenting and targeting customers. The marketing manager knew exactly what the next step ought to be—developing a marketing plan.

Although Arbol's senior management developed a rolling five-year **strategic plan**, it was, as many strategic plans are, at a very high level. Besides, it really was not developed based on a thorough understanding of customer needs; it was a plan that essentially set financial targets that functions were required to achieve. The marketing manager noticed that there was little cohesion among the various functions in the organization. Each seemed to do its own thing. He knew the reason why—Arbol lacked a marketing plan.

The marketing manager knew that besides providing discipline and focus to a business, a strong marketing plan plays another very important role—it contextualizes the market for other functions by outlining what segments the business is going to serve and how customer value is going to be created. The reason Arbol's functions were doing their own thing and working independent of one another was because they lacked a "glue" that bound them together. This "glue" is provided by the marketing plan in its crucial role of contextualizing the market.

The marketing manager knew from previous experience that in many organizations, the marketing function develops a marketing plan, hands it over to the other functions, and says, "Implement this." The functions take the marketing plan and put it on a shelf, where it gathers dust. Developing and implementing a strong marketing plan requires input and buy-in from the other functions.

So Arbol put in place a planning approach where, at the beginning of the fiscal year, the marketing function would present to all functional heads market research data on customers, segments, competitors, and general market trends. The group would determine what the key issues were the marketing plan should address. At this point, armed with a knowledge of the key issues the business was going to tackle for the upcoming year, functions could begin to develop their functional plans.

In this way, the marketing plan is "translated" into functional plans. The end result? The entire organization is focused on the customer (Chapters 9 and 10 have more details on this topic). Without this crucial step, functions tend to do their own thing.

Case Assignment

The marketing plan sets the context for the development of functional plans. Assume you are in charge of developing a marketing plan for the Four Seasons hotel: (1) develop three key issues it must address in its marketing plan and (2) outline a maximum of three implications for the sales, operations, and human resources functions.

SUGGESTED READINGS

If You Want to Develop and Implement Winning Marketing Plans, Do Not Miss These Publications

George S. Day and Paul J.H. Schoemaker, "Scanning the Periphery," *Harvard Business Review*, November 2005, pp. 135–148.

Ajay Sirsi, *Marketing Led—Sales Driven: How Successful Businesses Use the Power of Marketing Plans and Sales Execution to Win in the Marketplace* (Victoria, BC: Trafford Publishing, 2005).

NOTES

1. Jeremy Quittner, "Selling Pet Owners Peace of Mind," *Business Week*, May 28, 2007, p. 48.

2. Both examples are from businesses I have come in contact with. The names have been disguised.

3. George S. Day and Paul J.H. Schoemaker, "Scanning the Periphery," *Harvard Business Review*, November 2005, pp. 135–148.

4. This example is from Brooks Barnes, "Disney Ventures Far from the Parks," *The New York Times*, Travel, August 3, 2008, p. 3.

5. Both examples are from my consulting work.

6. For example, see Christian Homburg and Ove Jensen, "The Thought Worlds of Marketing and Sales: Which Differences Make a Difference?" *Journal of Marketing*, Volume 71, July 2007, pp. 124–142; Philip Kotler et al., "Ending the War between Sales and Marketing," *Harvard Business Review*, July–August 2006, pp. 68–78.

7. This example is taken from my consulting work. I have disguised the name of the business. We will meet Greystone again in Chapter 10.

PEARSON **mymarketinglab**™

Visit the MyMarketingLab website at **www.pearsoned.ca/mymarketinglab**. This online homework and tutorial system puts you in control of your own learning with study and practice tools directly correlated to this chapter's content.

CHAPTER 5

Product and Brand Strategies

CHECKPOINT

Where We've Been

- We have learned that a crucial marketing task is to determine which customers to serve and to assess their needs.

- Successful businesses serve customers by utilizing all elements of the marketing mix—product, price, channel, and marketing communications strategies.

- Marketing strategies are "packaged" in the form of a marketing plan.

Where We're Going

- We will start by examining the first marketing mix element in this chapter—product.

- Other chapters in this part of the book will discuss price, channel, and marketing communications strategies.

Before you begin, visit your MyMarketingLab to hear the author's **Audio Chapter Intro**.

CHAPTER INTRODUCTION

Every person reading this book is concerned (or soon will be concerned) with one paramount challenge: "How can I get customers to buy more of my goods or services than my competitors'?" It does not matter what kind of firm you work for or if you work in a function other than marketing—the concerns of *any* enterprise are the same: getting a customer to choose your "offering" while rejecting others. Here are a few scenarios:

"How can I get farmers to prefer my tractors over my competitors'?" (Business-to-business organization)

"How can I get parents to choose my brand of shoes versus my competitors' for their children?" (Business-to-consumer organization)

"How can I get people to donate more to my charity than other causes?" (Non-profit organization)

"How can I get the Federal Government to give my department more monies than other departments?" (Governmental organization)

"How can I get people to wear seatbelts?" (Public service message)
(The competing alternative is for drivers to not wear seatbelts. As we know, many drivers choose the alternative, resulting in many preventable deaths on the roads each year.)

Regardless of orientation, each person is essentially struggling with one question: "How can I build an offering that is more attractive than other options?" If we recast this struggle in the language of marketing, each person is essentially grappling with how to build a *brand*. This is because, as you will see in this chapter, a **brand** is an option that is attractively different from other options in the category.

But if you want to build strong brands, you must first understand the concept of "**product**"—the core material of this chapter.

OBJECTIVE 1

If You Want to Successfully Build Brands, You Must First Understand the Strategic Definition of "Product"

KEYPOINT

Many managers mistakenly equate "products" with "goods."

The word *product* is misunderstood widely. Even seasoned marketing managers tend to use "products" synonymously with "goods." Pick up any newspaper or business magazine and you will read about a company's "products and services." What are being referred to, of course, are a company's "goods and services." To fully understand the concept of product, let us start with an example.

5.1 STARBUCKS

Objective: To Help You Understand the Strategic Concept of "Product"

Named after a character in the novel *Moby Dick*, Starbucks is the largest coffee house chain in the world[1] with 7521 self-operated and 5647 licensed stores in 40 countries.[2] Starbucks serves drip-brewed coffee, espresso and non-espresso-based hot beverages, tea, and ice-blended drinks. It supplements these offerings with pastries, salads, and sandwiches. It also sells coffee mugs, brewing equipment, coffee beans, and other products. Through its Starbucks Entertainment division and Hear Music brand, the company has ventured beyond refreshments into books, music, and film.

Let us follow Tammy, a loyal Starbucks customer, as she goes to the store and witness what she experiences. Tammy is first greeted by the familiar and prominent green and white Starbucks logo outside the store. Her little white poodle, Belle, is not allowed into the store, but Tammy finds that Starbucks has thoughtfully provided a hitching post and a bowl of water outside for her. As she enters the store, she experiences the ambience created by vibrant colours and textures, comfortable chairs, and merchandise for sale. Jazz music is playing, and as Tammy approaches the counter, she realizes she is listening to a CD that can be purchased in the store.

The person behind the counter, a "barista" in Starbucks lingo, greets her warmly and asks how he can assist her today. Tammy knows exactly what she wants—a no-foam latte made with soy milk and a slice of lemon poppy seed cake. As she is waiting for her drink to be prepared, she glances at the other patrons to see what they are doing. Over in the corner a group of friends are enjoying coffee drinks and laughing over a joke. Another customer is reading a newspaper while sipping on a cold drink, while yet another customer is working online, taking advantage of the "hotspot" Starbucks offers. Tammy overhears the following conversation between the barista and the next customer.

CUSTOMER: "I would like a cup of Irish Cream coffee please."

BARISTA: "I'm sorry, but we don't carry flavoured coffee. We can add a shot of flavouring if you like."

Tammy and Belle enjoying a latte at Starbucks

CUSTOMER: "Oh, you don't carry flavoured coffee? What kind of a coffee shop *are* you?"

As Tammy goes to the station to pour some sugar into her latte, the barista offers her a doggy biscuit for Belle. On her way out, she glances through some pamphlets on the counter. The first one talks about the great effort Starbucks makes to procure the highest quality coffee beans from throughout the world, while paying farmers a fair price for their produce. The second pamphlet teaches consumers how to brew the perfect cup of coffee at home.

The third pamphlet discusses Starbucks' corporate social responsibility efforts. On August 19, 2005, Starbucks opened its first "green store" built to the U.S. Green Building Council's LEED (Leadership in Energy and Environmental Design) Green Building Rating System. Located in

continues..

Hillsboro, Oregon, the store is part of the Hillsboro Civic Center, which was built according to LEED specifications.[3] These standards include the use of building materials and practices that have a minimal effect on the environment, as well as energy- and water-efficient equipment.

Although this is Starbucks' first LEED-certified store, the components that make up the store are very similar to the company's existing stores. Starbucks has a strong commitment to environmentally friendly store design and construction, which includes the use of sustainable wood products, energy-efficient lighting, and reduced-flow water fixtures. As an active member of the U.S. Green Building Council, Starbucks is helping to develop LEED retail standards that all industries will adopt.

As Tammy is sipping her latte outside the store, enjoying the fine weather, two Starbucks employees ("partners" in Starbucks' corporate-speak) on break are conversing with each other.

EMPLOYEE 1:	"I just returned from Costa Rica."
EMPLOYEE 2:	"Costa Rica! Wow! Were you on vacation?"
EMPLOYEE 1:	"No, I was selected by Starbucks to participate in an Earthwatch Institute expedition. I travelled with 20 customers and 10 partners. We were chosen based on essays we had written to express our passion and views on Starbucks and the company's fifth guiding principal: contributing positively to the community and environment."
EMPLOYEE 2:	"What is Earthwatch Institute?"
EMPLOYEE 1:	"Earthwatch Institute is the world's oldest, largest, and most respected international non-profit organization. It directly involves the public in scientific research. Starbucks and Earthwatch Institute have been working together since 2002 on 15 different conservation projects and/or expeditions. These expeditions have taken place all over the world."

CHAPTER CHALLENGE 5.1

ARE YOU ON THE RIGHT TRACK?

Before you read further, see if you can answer this question: Can you develop a one-line definition of "product"? (Hint: as the Starbucks example shows, "product" is more than "goods.")

(*Were you on the right track? Check your answers in Appendix 2.*)

You have now gone to a Starbucks location with Tammy and, except for her delicious latte, have experienced all she has experienced.

A partial list of Tammy's experiences at Starbucks would include

- Starbucks' green and white logo
- hitching post and water bowl for dogs
- comfortable chairs
- coffee-related goods
- sandwiches, pastries, and drinks
- latte
- friendly Starbucks employee
- Starbucks' unwillingness to serve flavoured coffee (this demonstrates that they are serious about coffee; a customer wanting flavoured coffee has to go down the street to the "ordinary" coffee purveyor)
- internet hotspot
- Starbucks' corporate social responsibility efforts like environmentally friendly stores, their partnership with the Earthwatch Institute, and their participation in fair trade—paying farmers fair prices for their produce

So what is a product? It is *everything* the customer experiences from your offering. It is the totality of the customer's experiences.

In marketing, the term *product* refers to a combination of

- a tangible good (cup of coffee)
- a service (hitching post for dogs)
- a person (friendly employee)
- a company (Starbucks)
- an idea (corporate social responsibility)

We have said something very important, so it is worth revisiting.

A product is not just a tangible good, a service, what is on the order form, what you make in the factory, or what you ship or sell. A product is the totality of the customer's experiences.

MARKETING DRIVES SUCCESS

5.2 D-BASE TRANSFORMERS INC.

Objective: Not Thinking about Products from the Customer's Viewpoint Prevents a Business from Differentiating Itself from Its Competitors

Harry Walker started D-Base Transformers[4] in 1980, a manufacturer of toroidal transformers. These are donut-shaped devices (pictured) with a coil of wire wrapped around them; they are used in such applications as medical diagnostic machines, audio components, and utility generation. Harry, an engineer by training, started his company in his garage and supplied his transformers to other businesses by making cold calls. He was successful. Business was so good that he built a factory in the industrial zone of the city. His annual sales reached $20 million by 1990. Life was all that he could ask for.

Harry was devoted to making the best quality transformers on the market. Whenever a customer would call with a problem (for example, a delayed shipment), Harry would personally get involved and resolve the issue. Harry's customers loved him.

But even though Harry was successful, his business was headed for trouble. One day Harry received a call from Frank, one of his best customers. "Harry," Frank said, "I've just finished a meeting with a salesperson from one of your competitors. They are sourcing toroidal transformers from China, and they can sell me one for less than half what you are charging me. And I must say their quality is just as good."

Harry was stunned! He did the math. The customer was right. Even after factoring in shipping costs from China, his competitor could sell for less than half what it cost Harry to manufacture his transformers. "Who are these competitors, and where did they suddenly appear from?" he thought. He was through.

In desperation, he called the local business school. A group of students studied his business and gave him some painful advice: he had to segment his customer base and focus only on those

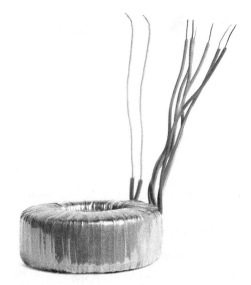

Donut-shaped toroidal transformer

customers who needed an offering that went beyond the core transformer. These customers (like manufacturers of high-end audio equipment or medical diagnostic machines) wanted custom orders, short production runs, and on-site technical advice that his Chinese competitors could not offer. In other words, these customers viewed Harry's transformer merely as a means to achieving *their* end goals of serving *their* customers. Harry had forgotten the key point about products—they are the totality of the customer's experiences.

CHAPTER CHALLENGE 5.2

ARE YOU ON THE RIGHT TRACK?

Business leaders like Harry are common. Why do such businesses not see an external threat (such as low-cost manufacturers) before it is too late?

(*Were you on the right track? Check your answers in Appendix 2.*)

KEYPOINT

Harry had been so busy making transformers, he had forgotten there was an actual customer with real needs buying his product.

We have seen that, in order to set yourself apart from your competitors, you have to think of products from the customer's viewpoint. To understand how to use this strategic definition of product, we need to delve deeper into the concept of product.[5] Any product (offering) is actually made up of four levels as shown in Figure 5.1: **core product**, **functional product**, **augmented product**, and **potential product**.

Using D-Base Transformers and Starbucks as a backdrop, Table 5.1 shows what these four levels refer to.

Perhaps you are beginning to see why Starbucks achieved brand status, while D-Base Transformers did

> *The organization must learn to think of itself not as producing goods or services but as buying customers, as doing the things that will make people want to do business with it.*
>
> THEODORE LEVITT

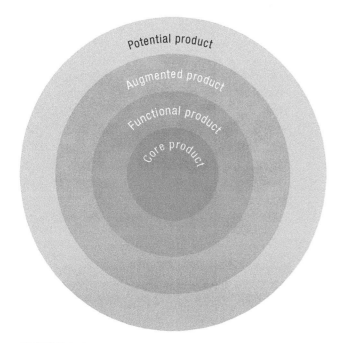

FIGURE 5.1
A product is actually made up of four levels.

TABLE 5.1	The Four Levels of Product		
Term	**What it means**	**D-Base Transformers application**	**Starbucks application**
Core product	Core product features or attributes	The material used in making the transformer	Coffee drinks, coffee-making equipment, sandwiches
Functional product	How the product functions or performs	■ How the actual transformer performs ■ Sales force knowledge ■ Responsiveness to the customer	■ Friendliness of staff ■ Speed of service ■ Quality of coffee drinks
Augmented product	All the "augmentations" or additions to the basic product	■ D-Base Transformers Inc. logo ■ Warranties ■ Product guarantees ■ Call centre	■ Starbucks logo ■ Product guarantees ■ Starbucks website ■ Corporate social responsibility efforts
Potential product	The "true" solution the customer wants or seeks from the offering	■ Hospital buying medical diagnostic equipment wants to enhance patient satisfaction and hospital efficiency ■ High-end audio equipment manufacturer wants to compete with Japanese brands	■ Coffee consumer wants to relax in a "third place" (home and office being the first two) ■ Coffee equipment buyer wants to give the perfect gift without spending too much

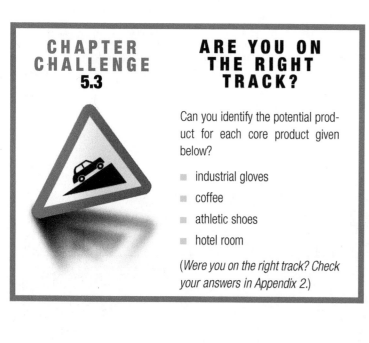

CHAPTER CHALLENGE 5.3

ARE YOU ON THE RIGHT TRACK?

Can you identify the potential product for each core product given below?

■ industrial gloves
■ coffee
■ athletic shoes
■ hotel room

(Were you on the right track? Check your answers in Appendix 2.)

> *People buy expectations, not things.*
>
> THEODORE LEVITT

A Starbucks manager provides powerful lessons on how to build a strong brand.

not—Starbucks correctly recognized that customers do not buy the core product; they buy the potential product.[6] Customers go to Starbucks to relax, read a newspaper, chat with friends, and, incidentally, drink coffee. As we saw with D-Base Transformers, Harry Walker missed this crucial point—he focused exclusively on making the best core product, ignoring customer needs (such as increasing hospital efficiency) in the process.

This powerful product model offers us these lessons:

1. Customers do not buy product features or attributes (the core product); they buy the potential product—what the product can do for them—so do not fall into the "attribute trap."

2. Build your brand from the inside out, but always communicate (focus) from the outside in. This is because, while you need a decent core product, over time all core products become commodities. (Remember Harry Walker's transformers?)

3. If you focus on the potential product, you will have infinite opportunities to differentiate because, as we have seen throughout this book, customer needs are infinite.

4. Customer needs are not only are infinite, they are constantly changing. Therefore, even if your competitor imitates your potential product, there will always be another potential product on the horizon. This is because, by definition, a potential product is the "true" solution the customer seeks from the basic product.

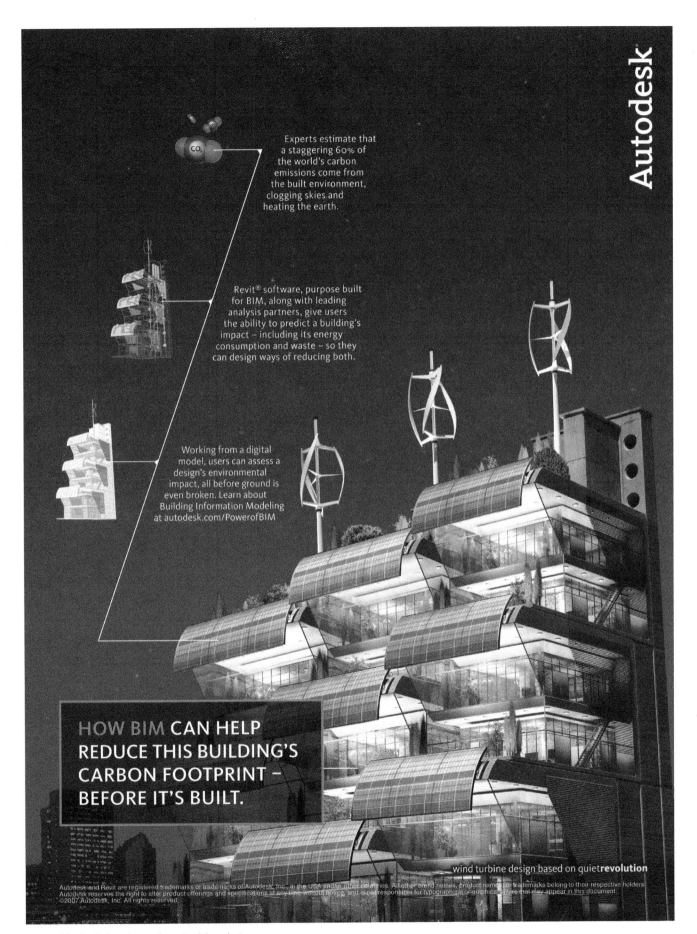

Experts estimate that a staggering 60% of the world's carbon emissions come from the built environment, clogging skies and heating the earth.

Revit® software, purpose built for BIM, along with leading analysis partners, give users the ability to predict a building's impact – including its energy consumption and waste – so they can design ways of reducing both.

Working from a digital model, users can assess a design's environmental impact, all before ground is even broken. Learn about Building Information Modeling at autodesk.com/PowerofBIM

HOW BIM CAN HELP REDUCE THIS BUILDING'S CARBON FOOTPRINT – BEFORE IT'S BUILT.

wind turbine design based on quiet**revolution**

Autodesk

Autodesk is clearly focusing on the potential product.

Where We've Been

■ Understanding the four levels of "product" has given us the foundation to think about building brands.

Where We're Going

■ We will learn a step-by-step framework to build and manage strong brands.

OBJECTIVE 2

Strategies and Tactics to Build a Strong Brand and Differentiate Yourself from Your Competitors

KEYPOINT

There is no such a thing as a commodity. Anything can, and should, be differentiated. There is only commodity thinking.

KEYPOINT

At the end of this section, you will have the confidence to say, "If you can brand cement, you can brand anything."

KEYPOINT

A brand is a differentiated offering in the marketplace.

Many managers moan, "I'm in a commodity business." What they are really saying is "I cannot build a brand because my product cannot be differentiated." In this section we will see how you can build a strong brand, regardless of what industry you are in. You will see how even organizations in so-called commodity industries such as cement have been successful in branding themselves.

CHAPTER CHALLENGE 5.4

ARE YOU ON THE RIGHT TRACK?

Can you describe the opposite of "brand" in a single word? (*Were you on the right track? Check your answers in Appendix 2.*)

Perhaps you have already figured out that successful brands are built by thinking not in terms of the core product, but in terms of the potential product. This is because potential products are the "true" solution the customer seeks. And strong brands are successful in offering their target market true solutions to satisfy their needs. Table 5.2 shows a few examples.

TABLE 5.2	Brands That Succeed by Providing the Potential Product to Customers	
Brand	**Product category**	**Solution the brand offers**
Nike	Athletic shoes	Providing the ability to be your best, regardless of what level of athlete you are
Apple	Electronics	Making technology fun and hassle free
Cemex	Cement	Making it easy for construction sites to go about their business, eliminating worries about delays in construction

Nike makes athletic shoes, just like its competitors. In other words, the core products are the same—pieces of rubber, fabric, air bubbles, and gels. However, when we look at Interbrand's[7] list of the top 100 global brands, Nike's competitors do not show up in the list (Nike is ranked 29). We can easily attribute this to Nike's relentless focus on customers, from memorable marketing communications such as the "Just Do It" campaign to the current Nike+ website, where you can connect with other enthusiasts, buy goods, keep track of your workout progress, and constantly challenge yourself to achieve more.

MARKETING DRIVES SUCCESS

5.3 CEMEX

Objective: Anything, Even Commodities, Can Be Branded if You Think About the Potential Product

How do you brand cement? Easy: think about customer needs. Based in Mexico, Cemex is the world's largest building materials supplier and the world's third largest cement company. In order to differentiate itself from its competitors, Cemex wisely focuses on the potential product. The *core* product, cement, does not differ from company to company. In this endeavor, Cemex is always thinking about customers, their needs, and the challenges they face.

Cemex supplies different grades of cement to construction sites, which are noted for one major industry problem—delays. Construction sites are usually behind schedule. This means that their suppliers have to waste resources while waiting for the construction site to be ready to receive supplies. Let us say a cement supplier has a delivery to a construction site at noon. The supplier receives a call at 10:00 a.m. saying that, due to delays, the shipment is now needed at 3:00 p.m. instead. What is the supplier to do? After all, the cement trucks are filled with the order and the drivers are waiting. The standard industry practice, acceptable to all, is to simply fine the customer for the delay.

Cemex managers asked, "Why do we penalize customers for the delay? After all, they do not delay us on purpose. It is the nature of their business." Cemex set about trying to find a solution to this problem and, in the process, to build a competitive advantage for itself.

It looked in an unlikely place: The 911 (emergency) system in Houston, Texas. Apparently, in Houston, 911 vehicles do not sit in one place waiting for an emergency to take place. They are in constant motion around the city and in constant contact with a central dispatcher, much like a fleet of taxis. Cemex managers asked, "If they can do this with 911 vehicles, can we do this with cement trucks?"

They equipped each truck with a communication system and devised a central dispatch office. Each day, trucks would be loaded with different grades of cement (based on placed orders). These trucks would then be on the move, waiting for the dispatcher to match each truck with a construction site ready to accept an order. Customers would be guaranteed to receive the grade of cement they ordered, or a higher grade, at no extra charge.

The end result: happy customers and a way to differentiate a "commodity" from competitors!

Cemex has built a global brand by focusing on the customer's needs.

Apple, with a brand value just over $11 billion (2007 Interbrand figures), has seen its brand value jump 21% since 2006. How does it do it? Its secret lies in making technology fun and easily accessible to the ordinary consumer. Take its popular iTunes, for example. Instead of buying hardware from one location, software from another, and music from a third source, Apple provides consumers with a simple, end-to-end solution. All you need is an MP3 player and a visit to the iTunes website, and you can download (and own) music for as little as 99¢ a song.

How to Build a Strong Brand: A Step-by-Step Guide

By now you are perhaps saying, "Okay, I understand that in order to build a strong brand I need to focus on the potential product and not on the core product. But what I'd really like is a step-by-step process to help me build a strong brand."

Well, here it is.

The brand-building process[8] starts with thinking about what business you are in. It ends with refreshing the brand (making changes to it), which essentially takes you back to step 1. Let us examine these steps, shown in Figure 5.2, in detail.

Step 1: Ask "What Business Am I In?"

Let us travel through time. We are going to the mid-1800s, to a small town where two manufacturers of buggy whips have set up shop. For city dwellers who don't know what a buggy whip is, it is a length of leather or rope tied to a stick that makes a horse "go."

Now we are going to fast-forward to the early 1900s. While one of the buggy whip manufacturers has gone out of business, the other one is still in business. If we fast-forward yet again to the present year, you will discover that our buggy whip manufacturer is still in business.

If you said that our buggy whip manufacturer is making car parts like starters, or even assembling entire cars, you would be right. To understand why, let us go back to the mid-1800s. If we were to ask both manufacturers a basic question, "What business are you in?" these are the replies we would get.

MANUFACTURER #1:   "What kind of a silly question is that? I am in the buggy whip business."

MANUFACTURER #2:   "Well, I make buggy whips, but that is not the business I am in. I'm in the transportation accessory business." (Of course, he may not have been as sophisticated in his answer, but you get the idea.)

It is easy to surmise that the first manufacturer went out of business in the early 1900s. Why? That is when the automobile was invented. Manufacturer #1 focused on making the best core product (buggy whips) and could not adapt to this new environment. He probably even looked at the automobile with derision, thinking that nothing could replace the current transportation mode of horse and buggy.

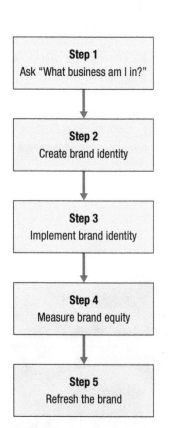

KEYPOINT

Building a brand is a *process*, not an *act*.

Step 1
Ask "What business am I in?"

↓

Step 2
Create brand identity

↓

Step 3
Implement brand identity

↓

Step 4
Measure brand equity

↓

Step 5
Refresh the brand

FIGURE 5.2
Building a brand is a process.

CHAPTER CHALLENGE 5.5

ARE YOU ON THE RIGHT TRACK?

Before reading further, can you guess what our buggy whip manufacturer is making today? (Hint: it is not buggy whips!)
(*Were you on the right track? Check your answers in Appendix 2.*)

Given his broad definition of what business he was in, Manufacturer #2 looked upon the innovation (the automobile) and asked, "What makes it go? What does it need?" So, he started making "buggy whips" for the "horseless carriage" (as automobiles used to be called in the early days). As you recall from black-and-white movies, early automobiles needed to be started by inserting a z-shaped iron rod into their fender. This is what our manufacturer started making; he gradually phased out his buggy whip business as the horse-and-buggy mode of transport gave way to the automobile.

A buggy whip makes the horse "go."

As the automobile evolved, so did Manufacturer #2. Over time, the z-shaped rod gave way to self-starters. This is what he started making. Then, he started making remote-controlled starters. Today, he is making starters that read a fingerprint to start the engine, without the need for a key. He is also looking into not just manufacturing other automobile accessories, but also assembling cars for brands such as Mercedes Benz.

As we have seen, building a strong brand starts with thinking carefully about what business you are in. If you adopt this approach, you will take a strategic view of brand building. Businesses that do not adopt this approach take a tactical view of brand building. As a result, their brands are not true innovations that create value for their customers. Instead, their brands tend to evolve by making minor changes to their existing product offerings (for example, adding a new scent to a laundry detergent). A narrow business definition based on the core product does not allow the business to build and evolve its brand in bold ways that resonate with customers.

KEYPOINT

Never define your brand in terms of what you do. If you want your business to grow and succeed, always define your brand in terms of the outcomes of what you do.

There is another reason to start building your brand by first thinking about what business you are in. As we saw earlier, the buggy whip manufacturer who adopted a broad view of his business definition (transportation accessories) is still in business today. Although he is no longer making buggy whips with wood, rope, and leather, he is still making "buggy whips" that enable modern cars to "go." This manufacturer will never fall victim to a concept called the **product life cycle**. This concept states that products predictably go through four stages—introduction, growth, maturity, and decline. So, while product categories may eventually die (we no longer use buggy whips or typewriters), brand life cycles can go on forever if the strategist carefully thinks about the answer to the question, "What business am I in?"[9]

KEYPOINT

Brand identity is the set of **brand associations** the marketing strategist wants to create or maintain in the minds of customers. These associations represent a promise from the brand to the customer.

Step 2: Build Brand Identity The second step in building a strong brand is to use the business definition in Step 1 to create the identity of the brand.

Let us take an example. In Figure 5.3, we see the brand identity of McDonald's: a set of associations McDonald's wants to develop or maintain. You will also notice a brand association McDonald's does not want to make widely known—it is part owner of an upscale chain of sandwich stores in the United Kingdom and New York called Pret A Manger.

McDonald's is very careful to build its brand identity in terms of the core, functional, augmented, and potential products as shown in Table 5.3.

Why is it important to think about a brand's identity so carefully? A brand's identity (or set of associations) is responsible for a customer's behaviour toward the brand. If I like what the McDonald's brand represents, I eat at McDonald's. If I don't like the brand's identity, I do not patronize McDonald's.

"Whenever a clear and strong brand identity is lacking, a brand is like a ship without a rudder."

JOACHIMSTHALER AND AAKER

In the set of associations depicted for McDonald's, we have assumed each association plays an equal role. In reality, this is not the case. Different associations weigh differently with different customer segments. Children, for example, pay more attention to the food and play aspect of McDonald's. A student

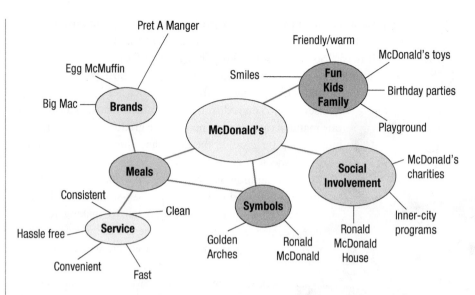

FIGURE 5.3

McDonald's builds its brand identity.

might pay more attention to the fast, cheap, and convenient aspect of McDonald's. Finally, for a non-customer, even though the brand's social involvement may earn it high marks, the fast food aspect of the brand may negatively overshadow everything else.

Let us close this section by understanding the negative consequences that accrue to a company if it fails to build a clear brand identity. Why, when a clear and strong brand identity is lacking, is a brand like a ship without a rudder?

Kun-Hee Lee, chairman of Samsung Electronics, a Korean manufacturer, sent each of his closest friends and key employees a wireless phone as a New Year's present. He soon found out that the phones did not work properly. Horrified, he went to the factory in Gumi, South Korea, and ordered that the entire inventory, $15 million worth, be set on fire.[10]

This incident marked a turning point in Samsung's history. Before 1995, it was known mainly as a manufacturer of cheap knock-offs. After the Gumi incident, Samsung resolved to change its brand identity. It increased investment in research and development and product quality. The strategic turnaround worked. Samsung has produced the world's first MP3 phone, the world's thinnest phones, the highest megapixel camera phone, and the first WiMAX phone.

And yet, its brand image in North America remains fuzzy and rooted in the past—a situation Nokia and Motorola do not face.

Why is Samsung in the clutches of an identity crisis? "Samsung always has the newest, most advanced products," says Tina Teng, a wireless analyst at iSuppli, a research firm. "But it needs a signature product—something that will make its brand stick in consumers' minds."

How is Samsung planning to resolve its brand identity crisis? Let us find out in the discussion of Step 3.

TABLE 5.3	**How McDonald's Builds Its Brand Identity**		
Core product	**Functional product**	**Augmented product**	**Potential product**
■ Meals	■ Quality service	■ Ronald McDonald	■ Smiles
	■ Consistency of food and service	■ Corporate social responsibility efforts	■ Forever young
			■ Families
		■ Golden Arches	

Step 3: Implement Brand Identity Thinking about "What business am I in?" helps to develop a brand's identity. Samsung, for example, used to define its business as a manufacturer of consumer electronics. Today, its business definition (and brand identity) is couched in terms of building an emotional connection with consumers. In other words, it has adopted more of a customer focus, rather than a narrow product focus.

But as we saw in the previous section, building a brand identity is not enough. That identity has to be carefully implemented. How do business organizations implement brand identity?

5.4 SAMSUNG

Objective: Samsung Is Fighting Weak Brand Perception by Developing an Emotional Connection with Customers

Samsung's identity in its native Korea is very strong. It has succeeded in building a leading brand that has an emotional connection with its customers. Its Anycall phones are as popular as iPods are in North America. In Seoul, Samsung's Anycall Studio has become a fashionable after-school hangout, where customers can try Samsung's latest gadgets. So unlike in North America, Samsung has successfully implemented its brand identity in Korea. What does Samsung plan to do to implement its brand identity successfully elsewhere?

Samsung's first move was to put Geesung Choi, a marketer, in charge of reviving Samsung's brand identity in cell phones in North America. Choi is the first executive without a background in technology to be put in charge of the mobile phone division. Choi's strategy is to reconnect with customers by building an emotional attachment between them and the brand.

Samsung has brought in industrial artists, cognitive scientists, and sound engineers to compose ringtones and design colour palettes that include hues like "glazed chocolate" and "chic silver." By paying close attention to form and function, Samsung hopes to differentiate its cell phones. This strategy has spilled over into thinking about brand names also. Previously, Samsung used forgettable brand names like VM-A680 and SGH-S307. These names have given way to more consumer-centric names such as BlackJack and UpStage.

Samsung is trying to build an emotional connection with customers.

Brand identity	Brand identity implementation	Brand image
• Strategic • A set of brand associations • The brand's promise • The brand concept as the strategist *intends* it to be	• Accomplished by using all elements of the marketing mix	• The set of brand associations actually received in the marketplace • Strategist has no control over brand image, can only measure it

FIGURE 5.4

Difference between brand identity and brand image

KEYPOINT

Successful brand identity implementation requires a strategist to use all elements of the marketing mix—product, price, channel, and marketing communications strategies—in a cohesive way.

Samsung plans to implement its brand's identity not just with its **product** (distinctive forms, colours, and brand names), channel (studios where consumers can try new gadgets), and marketing communications strategies (TV ads), but also with its pricing strategy. Just like Nokia and Motorola, it is entering emerging markets in India and Latin America, from which 85% of all handset shipment growth is expected to come in the next three years (in India alone, six million people buy their first handset each month).[11] But unlike these competitors, who are flooding the market with cheap cell phones, Samsung plans to cater to the "high end" of the market in these countries, selling phones with distinctive designs and colours in the $50 to $70 range.

Step 4: Measure Brand Equity[12]   The brand's identity is the set of associations (brand promise) that the marketing strategist wants to create or maintain in the mind of the customer. But as we saw with the Samsung example, this is not always achieved. While Samsung wants to portray an identity of technological sophistication, its brand is fuzzy compared with Nokia and Motorola. This end result in the marketplace is called **brand image**.

In other words, while brand identity is strategic, brand image is what actually gets achieved in the marketplace. This is shown in Figure 5.4.

As shown in the figure, marketing strategists have no control over what brand associations actually develop in the marketplace. However, they have control over what brand associations they *want* to convey, and they have control over implementation of brand identity by using the marketing mix elements.

The only thing marketing strategists can do is *measure* brand image to learn from actual associations customers have formed of the brand, and then use this information to make changes to the brand ("refresh" the brand, as discussed in the next step). We call this **brand equity** measurement.

To understand the concept of brand equity, consider this: if you put a few cell phones made by Nokia, Motorola, and Samsung side by side, stripped them of their labels, and asked customers to identify the brands, they would pick out the Nokia and Motorola phones with ease, but not the Samsung phones.[13] As we have seen with the Samsung example, this is because consumers do not associate Samsung cell phones with any distinctive brand shapes. It is a fuzzy brand at the moment. In the language of branding, we say that Samsung's brand equity (brand strength) in cell phones is weak compared to its competitors.

Brand equity is measured on three dimensions: **brand awareness**, brand associations, and **brand loyalty**. While there are many methods available to measure brand equity,[14] let us consider the method shown in Table 5.4.

CHAPTER CHALLENGE 5.6

ARE YOU ON THE RIGHT TRACK?

A brand's image will never be equal to its brand identity. Can you guess why?

(*Were you on the right track? Check your answers in Appendix 2.*)

TABLE 5.4 Questionnaire-Based Method to Measure Brand Equity

Brand name _____

Brand awareness	Disagree						Agree
I have heard of this brand	1	2	3	4	5	6	7
I am familiar with this brand	1	2	3	4	5	6	7
I have an opinion on this brand	1	2	3	4	5	6	7
Brand associations							
This brand has very high quality	1	2	3	4	5	6	7
This brand is the best	1	2	3	4	5	6	7
I hold this brand in high esteem	1	2	3	4	5	6	7
This brand is a leading brand in its category	1	2	3	4	5	6	7
This brand is the only one I buy and use	1	2	3	4	5	6	7
This brand is growing in popularity	1	2	3	4	5	6	7
This brand has a personality	1	2	3	4	5	6	7
This is a brand I would trust	1	2	3	4	5	6	7
This brand is the same as the other brands	1	2	3	4	5	6	7
I admire this corporation	1	2	3	4	5	6	7
I am proud to be a customer of this brand	1	2	3	4	5	6	7
Brand loyalty							
This brand met my expectations the last time I used it	1	2	3	4	5	6	7
I will buy this brand next time	1	2	3	4	5	6	7
I would recommend this brand to others	1	2	3	4	5	6	7

Overall brand equity:

An important component of brand equity is brand awareness, which acts like a gate. If the gate is shut (the customer is unaware of the brand), we would not expect the customer to have any brand associations. Therefore, measuring brand awareness is a key component of measuring brand equity.

On the other hand, just because a brand has high brand awareness does not necessarily mean its brand equity is high as well. This is because the brand's associations are also an important component of brand equity. There are two types of brand associations that we need to measure: objective ("this brand has high quality") and subjective ("this brand has a personality"). Finally, brand loyalty measures to what extent the brand meets expectations, and whether the customer would repurchase the brand. The overall equity of the brand is measured by taking an average of the 17 items in the questionnaire.

The literature on brand equity is vast. In Table 5.5, you will find some key takeaways about this very important concept.

Step 5: Refresh the Brand   Even though a brand strategist has no control over what develops in the marketplace, measuring the brand's equity is a crucial step in building and managing strong brands because the diagnosis from the measurement leads to the final step—making changes to the brand (refreshing the brand). Refreshing the brand means many things. Let us examine a few examples.

Repositioning the Brand[15] Mouton Cadet was launched by Baron Philippe de Rothschild in 1931 as the first branded premium wine from Bordeaux, France, priced for the middle

TABLE 5.5 Brand Equity: Key Takeaways

1. Building a strong brand with high equity provides a host of possible benefits to the firm: greater customer loyalty, less vulnerability to competitive actions and crises, larger margins, more favourable customer response to price increases and decreases, greater channel of distribution support, increased marketing communications effectiveness, and licensing and brand extension opportunities.

2. Brands with high equity have high awareness levels, strong and positive brand associations, high perceived quality, and high levels of satisfaction and loyalty.

3. The equity in the brand resides in the mind of the customer, not in the brand itself. Therefore, brand equity measurement tools measure brand associations.

4. Once brand associations are formed in the customer's mind, they are not easy to dislodge. This is the foundation of brand loyalty. That is why it is so important to think about what associations we want to build or maintain.

5. Management of brand equity is primarily the management of brand associations.

6. Brand identity (brand concept as intended) is not the same thing as brand image (brand concept as received). We can only measure brand image (associations actually formed in the marketplace) via the brand equity measurement tool we choose.

class. By 2002, it was selling 15 million bottles worldwide. Then came competitors from Australia, South America, and the Napa Valley in California with catchy names like Yellow Tail, Little Penguin, Monkey Bay, and Funky Llama. The newcomers seemed to know exactly what customers wanted—fruitier wines with a modern appeal, not fussy wines from France. Mouton Cadet's sales in North America shrunk and hit a low point in 2004, when it only sold 2.9 million bottles.

Now, Mouton Cadet is attempting to regain its former status as a trusted and sophisticated budget brand. It is making wines to taste more like Australian and Napa Valley brands, recasting its labels, and entering into a new distribution arrangement with Constellation Brands Inc. On the packaging front, it is experimenting with screw caps and wine boxes. The wine itself has undergone changes. Both the red and white wines are fruitier (more Merlot and Sauvignon Blanc, and less Cabernet Sauvignon).

Extending the Brand A brand can be extended to new products, new markets, and new geographic areas. Consider the following example.

The Disney brand was launched in 1923 and followed by the first Mickey Mouse cartoon in 1928. Since then, the brand has been extended to films, network and cable television programs and studios, publishing, internet businesses, theme parks, hotels, stores, and merchandise. This is called extending the brand to *new products* (goods or services).

The Disney brand's initial focus (target market) was children. Today, the brand has been extended to the full range of age groups (young and old alike), reinforcing the "childhood at any age" core brand identity worldwide. We call this extending the brand to *new markets*.

Finally, Disney films and products are distributed worldwide. Their theme parks can be found in the United States, Europe, and Asia. This is called extending the brand to *new geographic areas*.

Repositioning the Corporate Brand Recently, Apple changed its name from Apple Computer Inc. to Apple Inc. Why? With the introduction of such devices as the iPod and iPhone, Apple has moved way beyond its initial foray into personal computers. In other

CHAPTER CHALLENGE 5.7

ARE YOU ON THE RIGHT TRACK?

Mouton Cadet is responding to changing market forces. If you were a marketing consultant advising the company, what cautions would you offer Mouton Cadet regarding its proposed changes?
(*Were you on the right track? Check your answers in Appendix 2.*)

words, it has broadened its business definition. Without a name change to reflect a broader business definition, Apple risks being pigeonholed as nothing more than a personal computer manufacturer, jeopardizing the sales of its consumer electronic products.

We will close this section by making one final observation.

Building a strong brand is a *process*, not an *act*. It starts with business definition and ends with brand refreshment. The process then starts all over again. It does not matter where you start—you will end up in the same place. So if you are an existing business, start by measuring your brand's equity. This will enable you to diagnose the health of your brand (what brand image you currently have in the marketplace). The diagnosis can help you to refresh your brand. If you are a new business, start by thinking about what business you are in and then follow the step-by-step process given in this chapter.

CHECKPOINT

Where We've Been

- We have learned that to understand how to build strong brands, it is important to first understand "product."
- Strong brands focus on the potential product.
- Building a strong brand is a *process*, not an *act*.
- The process starts with asking "What business am I in?" and ends with refreshing the brand.

Where We're Going

- We will see that the world's best companies do not just have one brand; they grow their business by innovating.
- We will study the importance and process of innovation.

Growing Your Business by Mastering the Secrets of Innovation

OBJECTIVE 3

No company wants to be a "one-trick pony." Smart companies know that building a portfolio of brands through innovation is key. And it pays. Since 1995, the world's most innovative companies have achieved median profit margin growth of 3.4%, compared with 0.4% for Standard & Poor's (S&P) Global 1200 companies.[16] The group's median annual stock return of 14.3% was also a full three points better than the S&P 1200 median.

What exactly is innovation? Even though this subject is foremost in the minds of most CEOs, many companies have a mistakenly narrow view of innovation, equating it with new product development or research and development (R&D).

But such a narrow view of innovation leads to an erosion of competitive advantage, because firms tend to innovate along similar dimensions by copying best practices. In technology-based industries, for example, most firms focus on product R&D. In consumer packaged goods companies, the focus tends to be on branding and distribution. In service-based industries, firms emphasize process innovations. Over time, such copycat behaviour leads to a disease called "isomorphism," where different firms within an industry tend to look

> *Innovation is allowing companies to grow faster [and] have a richer product mix.*
>
> JAMES P. ANDREW, BOSTON CONSULTING GROUP

> *Innovation is the only way that Microsoft can keep customers happy and competitors at bay.*
>
> STEVE BALLMER, CEO, MICROSOFT CORP.

The way you will thrive in this environment is by innovating— innovating in technologies, innovating in strategies, innovating in business models.

Samuel J. Palmisano, CEO, IBM

Hear a successful marketing consultant talk about how you can grow your business and beat your competitors by mastering the secrets of innovation.

increasingly alike, and they tend to offer similar things to customers.

In actuality, the term *innovation* should refer to "business" innovation, not just to product or technological innovation. The most successful innovators tend to use this definition to create value for their customers and beat their competitors. Let us see how in Table 5.6.

Finally, keep in mind that the innovation dimensions discussed in Table 5.6 are not mutually exclusive. Apple Inc., for example, used no fewer than seven types of innovation to launch the iPod. They included networking (a novel agreement among music companies to sell their music online), a new business model (songs sold for a buck each online), and branding (cool designs for the iPods).[17]

The Science and Art behind Innovation

As we've seen, innovation is about much more than developing new products. Let us see what lessons the world's best innovators offer on the science and art of innovation.[18]

TABLE 5.6	**The Dimensions of Business Innovation**	
Dimension	**Definition**	**Examples**
Offerings	Develop innovative new goods or services.	Research in Motion's BlackBerry has changed the way businesses communicate.
Platform	Use common components or building blocks to create derivative offerings.	Apple uses innovative software platforms to create unique but familiar user experiences for its products (iPod, iPhone, iMac).
Solutions	Create integrated and customized offerings that solve end-to-end customer problems.	Fedex logistics services help businesses with their supply chain challenges.
Customers	Discover unmet customer needs or identify under-served customer segments.	Enterprise Rent-A-Car focuses on replacement car renters.
Customer experience	Redesign customer interactions to include all touch points.	Southwest Airlines, WestJet, and Ryanair focus on a unique customer experience, from buying a ticket to taking the flight.
Value capture	Redefine how the company gets paid or create innovative revenue streams.	Google paid search—businesses pay Google a fee to have their names come up when a consumer searches the internet for a good or service.
Processes	Redesign core operating processes to improve efficiency and effectiveness.	Toyota Production System for operations is famous for empowering assembly line workers to detect and flag quality problems.
Organization	Change the form, function, or activity scope of the firm.	Procter & Gamble's Connect + Develop™ model calls for 50% of new products to come from outside the company. For example, the technology to print edible ink on potato chips (Pringles) came from a baker in Bologna, Italy.
Business model	Use core brand identity to venture into different areas.	Virgin Group Ltd. applies its hip lifestyle brand to mundane product categories such as airlines, financial services, and insurance.
Supply chain	Work differently with suppliers.	Toyota's Value Innovation Strategy means that rather than work with suppliers just to cut costs, it is working with them to generate innovation.
Networking	Work differently with industry players.	Apple had to get music companies to agree to sell their music online.
Presence	Create new distribution channels or innovative points of presence, including the places where offerings can be bought or used by customers.	Starbucks sells music CDs in stores.
Brand	Leverage a brand into new domains.	Disney has extended its brand into new offerings, markets, and geographies.

Source: Adapted from Mohanbir Sawhney et al., "The 12 Different Ways for Companies to Innovate," *MIT Sloan Management Review,* Spring 2006, pp. 75–81.

Innovation Lesson #1: Get Good Customer Insight   As we saw previously in the chapter on marketing research (Chapter 2), getting a handle on customer needs is critical, but it is not a simple task. Although blogs and online communities make it a lot easier to know what customers are thinking, identifying the "unmet need" of a customer remains elusive.

The world's best innovators believe in getting out of the office and observing customers directly. Starbucks recently started taking product development and other cross-company teams on "inspiration" field trips abroad to Starbucks and other restaurants to watch customers and get a sense of local cultures, behaviours, fashions, and trends.

Nokia faced an unusual problem when it began making low-cost phones for emerging markets in India, China, and Latin America—the illiterate customer. Nokia spent a long time in these markets observing users to understand how illiterate people live in a world full of numbers and letters. The insight enabled it to develop a new "iconic" menu that lets illiterate customers navigate contact lists made up of images.

> *You come back just full of different ideas and different ways to think about things than you would had you read about it in a magazine or email.*
> MICHELLE GASS, STARBUCKS' SENIOR VICE-PRESIDENT FOR CATEGORY MANAGEMENT, ON THE IMPORTANCE OF "INSPIRATION" FIELD TRIPS

Innovation Lesson #2: Get Customers and Others to Do the Work   The world's leading innovators have embraced an idea called "open innovation,"[19] which challenges the age-old notion of "If it isn't invented in-house, it is not worth anything." Google, for example, has opened its mapping technology to the public. Programmers can combine Google maps with just about anything, from real estate listings to local poker game sites. Such customer co-option of technology enables them to transform products into their own inventions. In turn, Google gets the opportunity to convert some of these innovations into commercial products.

Procter & Gamble has transformed its traditional in-house research and development process into an open-source innovation strategy it calls Connect + Develop™. The new method embraces the collective brain of the world to tap into networks of inventors, scientists, and suppliers to find ideas for new products. These networks include NineSigma (links companies with scientists at universities, private labs, and government); YourEncore (connects retired scientists and engineers with companies); and yet2.com (an online marketplace for intellectual property). As a result of this approach to innovation, P&G has managed to cut its R&D budget, while increasing the success rate of new products. This concept was discussed in detail in Chapter 2.

Innovation Lesson #3: Coordinate and Collaborate   Doing what is being suggested here requires a different mindset in an organization. According to the Boston Consulting Group (BCG) survey on the world's best innovators, the second biggest obstacle to innovation faced by firms is a lack of coordination and collaboration among different business units (the number one obstacle is slow development time). In other words, good old-fashioned organizational silos between functional units hamper new product development efforts.[20] (You will find more on this material in Chapters 9 and 10.)

Procter & Gamble, for example, found that its radical new approach couldn't be simply incorporated into managers' existing responsibilities. Rather, it had to tear apart and restitch much of its research organization. It created new job classifications, such as 70 worldwide "technology entrepreneurs" (TEs) who act as scouts, looking for the latest breakthroughs, regardless of where they may come from. For example, a TE in Japan was in a store and noticed a children's eraser; this became the genesis for the highly successful Tide eraser product.

Coordinating the efforts of TEs, suppliers, scientists, P&G managers, and even customers, is an enormous task. To enable this, P&G created the role of "Vice-President for Innovation and Knowledge." Each business unit, from household care to family health, added a new manager responsible for driving cultural change around the new innovation model.

These managers communicate directly with the vice-president, who acts as a hub to coordinate the efforts of the TEs and the managers running the external innovation networks.

Coordination and cross-functional cooperation does not have to last years, as in the case of P&G; it can last only a few weeks or months. At Southwest Airlines, a group of in-flight, ground, maintenance, and dispatch operations met for 10 hours a week for six months to brainstorm on what highest-impact changes they could make to their aircraft operations. The cross-functional diversity in the group was credited with 109 ideas presented to senior management.

Innovation Lesson #4: A Culture of Innovation Starts from the Top

The world's leading innovators recognize that, to change corporate culture, the CEO has to get personally involved. Alan G. Lafley, CEO of Procter & Gamble, sits in on all R&D review meetings that showcase new products. He also spends three full days a year with the company's Design Board, a group of outside designers who offer their perspective on P&G's upcoming products.

Innovation Lesson #5: Make a Seat at the Table

A familiar void in many organizations is the lack of voice given to employees at the edges—for example, front-line personnel or junior employees. But the world's leading innovators know that these employees often have great ideas that need to be captured. So they build mechanisms and structures to give these employees "a seat at the table."

Infosys Technologies Ltd., based in Bangalore, India, is a world leader in information technology services. Chairman and "chief mentor" N.R. Narayan Murthy introduced the company's "voice of youth" program seven years ago. Each year, the company selects nine top-performing employees (all under the age of 30) to participate in its eight yearly senior management council meetings to present their ideas.

Mike Lazaridis, president and co-CEO of Research In Motion (the company that gave the world the BlackBerry), hosts a "Vision Series" session at the company's headquarters in Waterloo, Ontario. These meetings focus on new research and future goals for the company.

Innovation Lesson #6: Preserve Oral Traditions

At innovative companies, innovation tends to become a habit, not an act. Under the leadership of the CEO, a culture of enthusiasm, entrepreneurship, and a sense of "can do" develops over time. At 3M, for example, employees are expected to hand down tales of the company's long innovation tradition to new engineers. Before long, every employee can quote the philosophies of former CEO William McKnight. A culture of innovation attracts talented employees and motivates current employees. Essentially, this culture becomes part of the corporation's core brand identity.[21]

Innovation Lesson #7: Use Proper Metrics (Measures)

Among the world's most innovative companies, there are wide differences in the kind of metrics they use to track the success of their innovation efforts. In spite of this variance, they do have some commonalities, as shown in Table 5.7.

KEYPOINT

The world's innovators know that the CEO determines the culture of the organization. The CEO has to be the "Chief Innovation Officer."

TABLE 5.7   Metrics to Evaluate Innovation Efforts: Lessons from the World's Best Innovators

■ Innovation is a murky process: it is very hard to measure success only with hard metrics.

■ Don't use too many metrics—between 8 and 12 is a good number.

■ Hard metrics include price premiums, customer delight, and speed to market of new products.

■ Only 30% of firms in BCG's survey use return on investment (ROI) on innovation investments.

■ Do not tie managers' incentives directly to specific innovation metrics, as this could lead to undesirable behaviours. For example, a metric such as percentage of revenue from new products can lead to incremental brand extensions, rather than true breakthroughs.

■ Besides numbers-driven metrics, add subjective assessments related to innovation, such as a manager's risk tolerance, external focus, and "imagination and courage." (GE uses this to evaluate managers.)

CHECKPOINT

Where We've Been

■ We have studied products, brands, and the importance and process of innovation for business success.

Where We're Going

■ In this final section, we will learn how companies manage portfolios of brands for optimum strategic and financial health.

Product Mix Review: Managing a Stable of Products (Brands) for the Long-Term Success of Your Business

OBJECTIVE 4

Innovation allows a company to grow by having a richer product mix, keeping customers happy, and keeping competitors at bay. However, such activity comes with a price. Over time, companies develop a stable of brands and, if not managed correctly, the collection becomes bloated with weak brands, or brands that overlap each other. If the collection is neglected, the company confuses its customers and invests in overlapping product development and marketing efforts. Killing off weaker or ill-fitting parts of the product range frees marketers to focus resources on the stronger remaining brands and to position them distinctively.[22] Table 5.8 highlights why brands should be managed as portfolios.

Smart companies know that they must manage their collection of brands as a *strategic* portfolio. Since 2000, Procter & Gamble has successfully phased out more than 1000 global brands. Disney has done similar pruning with its licensed brands. Several other consumer goods companies have achieved rates of revenue growth two to five times higher than their historic norms and saved 20% of their overall marketing expenditures by managing their brand portfolios more effectively.[23]

There is a strong link between portfolio strategy and profitability. In 1972, Richard Rumelt, a researcher, discovered that moderately diversified but focused companies outperform more diversified companies. This finding has held up after more than 35 years of research. This is because as companies diversify (add more brands and businesses to their portfolio), they become very complex and bloated. Within this complexity, weak brands tend to hide from scrutiny in nooks and crannies—bringing down the overall profitability of the company.[24]

TABLE 5.8	**Why Brands Should Be Managed as Portfolios**

■ An explosion of brands makes it harder to define customer segments and position objectives consistently. As we have seen in previous chapters, successful companies match offerings (goods and services) with segment needs.

■ Companies with too many brands suffer from increasing marketing and operational complexity. This leads to higher costs and diseconomies of scale.

■ Too many similar brands confuse customers. This erodes brand loyalty.

5.5 PROCTER & GAMBLE

Objective: To Show the Perils of Product Proliferation and How to Build a Synchronized Product Portfolio

Segments/Application	Price/Image		
	Premium	Mid-range	Value
Personal and beauty	Camay Zest Noxzema Pantene Always Tampax Scope Fixodent Crest toothpaste Crest toothbrushes	Old Spice Secret Sure CoverGirl Max Factor Olay Head & Shoulders	Ivory Zest Safeguard Pert Plus
House and home	Febreze Downy Charmin paper products Bounty Pampers Duracell Dawn Cascade Folgers Mr. Clean	Crisco Puritan Oil Sunny Delight Bounce Luvs	Oxydol Banner paper products Joy Ivory Bold High Point White Cloud
Health and wellness	Metamucil Pepto-Bismol		

Alan Lafley became CEO of P&G in 2000, a year in which the company's profits and share price had taken a big drop. Lafley knew exactly why: the company was bureaucratic and out of touch with its customers, its brand portfolio was filled with some weak and ill-positioned brands, there were gaps in the brand portfolio, and there was no clear strategy for growth.[25] Under his leadership, P&G's financial performance has improved tremendously: sales are over $100 billion, net profits have risen to over $10 billion, and the share price has gone from a low of under $30 to around $65. P&G's brand portfolio turnaround strategy has three steps as depicted in Figures 5.5, 5.6, and 5.7.

FIGURE 5.5

Step 1: Understand where current brands play.

Segments/Application	Price/Image		
	Premium	Mid-range	Value
Personal and beauty	• Each brand in this segment plays a unique role. • Hair care line is limited (only shampoos).	• Overlap between Secret and Sure leads to customer confusion.	• We have too many soaps in this category. • Does a value shampoo (Pert Plus) fit with our brand identity?
House and home	• This category is a hodgepodge of different products (coffee, paper products, and cleaners do not fit together). • Charmin paper towels, napkins, facial tissue, and bath tissue overlap with Bounty.	• Shortening and oil may not fit into our overall brand identity. • Sunny Delight (orange drink) has come under criticism from consumer groups for low nutritional value.	• Too many low-end paper products. • High Point (coffee) conflicts with Folgers.
Health and wellness	• We need to develop new products in this category.	• We do not have any products in this category.	• This may not be a category we want to be in.

FIGURE 5.6

Step 2: Diagnose and determine brand moves.

continues

Segments/Application	Price/Image		
	Premium	Mid-range	Value
Personal and beauty	Camay Zest Noxzema Pantene Always Tampax Scope Fixodent Crest toothpaste Crest toothbrushes Oral B Gillette M3Power Wella (haircare)	Old Spice Secret Sure CoverGirl Max Factor Olay Head & Shoulders	Ivory Zest Safeguard Pert Plus
House and home	Febreze Downy Charmin paper products Bounty Pampers Duracell Dawn Cascade Folgers (moved to coffee and snacks category) Mr. Clean Swiffer	Crisco Puritan Oil Sunny Delight Bounce Luvs	Oxydol Banner paper products Joy Ivory Bold High Point White Cloud
Coffee and snacks	Folgers Pringles		
Health and wellness	Metamucil Pepto-Bismol	Vicks Prilosec OTC	
Pet nutrition and care	Iams	Eukanuba	

Legend
■ Deleted product   ■ Product with questionable future   ■ New product   ■ New category

FIGURE 5.7

Step 3: Transform the brand portfolio.

So if businesses want to thrive, they must resist the temptation to add more and more new brands while stubbornly holding on to old brands. Instead, they should introduce fewer, stronger brands in a more synchronized way. Table 5.9 provides 10 key lessons for strategically managing brand portfolios.

As you can see, P&G has made its brand portfolio much tighter by

- eliminating brands that do not fit with the overall portfolio (Crisco and Puritan oil, and Sunny Delight)

- eliminating overlap by pruning brands such as Charmin paper products (only Charmin bath tissue remains), Banner paper products, High Point coffee, and Sure deodorant

- adding new categories such as pet nutrition and care

- dividing house and home into two categories (house and home, and coffee and snacks)

P&G grew its Beauty and Grooming categories with the acquisition of Gillette.

■ closing portfolio gaps by adding mid-range health and wellness brands (Vicks and Prilosec OTC)

■ strengthening categories by adding brands (Wella, a German hair care line was added to the personal and beauty category, as was the Gillette product range after P&G acquired Gillette)

TABLE 5.9	**Managing Brand Portfolios Strategically: 10 Lessons from the Best**
1.	Start with a deep understanding of customer needs in the product category.
2.	Acquire or develop brands based on customer needs.
3.	Establish clear roles (identities) for each brand.
4.	Establish goals for each brand.
5.	When expanding globally, adapt to local tastes.
6.	Establish the relationships and boundaries among different brands.
7.	Make sure new markets still serve your core customer and brand identity.
8.	Designate a portfolio manager to oversee the entire brand portfolio.
9.	Do not be afraid to prune brands or reposition brands as necessary.
10.	Don't think of yourself as a North American company with international operations; take the mindset of a truly global company.

Chapter Summary

1. **Understand the *strategic* definition of product and why you need to know this to successfully build brands.**

   A product is the totality of the customer's experiences. There are four layers of a product: core, functional, augmented, and potential. If you want to build strong brands, you must understand that customers do not buy the core product (product features or attributes); they buy the potential product (what the offering can do for them). Therefore, a focus on the potential product enables a business to successfully build a brand, which is essentially an offering that satisfies the customer's needs better than competing alternatives.

2. **Learn strategies and tactics that will help you build a strong brand and differentiate yourself from your competitors.**

   Building a strong brand is a process, not an act. It starts by asking, "What business am I in?" This definition allows a firm to build brand identity, a set of associations that represent a promise to the customer. The brand identity is implemented using the marketing mix elements (product, price, channel, and marketing communications strategies). What results is called brand image, which can be measured, and the results are used to refresh the brand, starting the process all over again.

3. **Learn how to grow your business by mastering the secrets of innovation.**

   Even though innovation is foremost in the minds of most CEOs, many companies have a mistakenly narrow view of innovation,

equating it with new product development or research and development (R&D). But such a narrow view of innovation leads to an erosion of competitive advantage, because firms tend to innovate along similar dimensions by copying best practices. Over time, such copycat behavior leads to "isomorphism," where different firms within an industry tend to look increasingly alike and provide similar offerings to customers.

In actuality, the term *innovation* should refer to "business" innovation (innovating along process or customer experience), not just to product or technological innovation. The most successful innovators tend to use this definition to create value for their customers and beat their competitors.

4. **Learn how to manage a stable of products (brands) for the long-term success of your business.**

   Innovation allows a company to grow by having a richer product mix, keeping customers happy and keeping competitors at bay. However, such activity comes with a price. Over time, companies develop a stable of brands and, if not managed correctly, the collection becomes bloated with weak brands or brands that overlap each other. If the collection is neglected, the company confuses its customers and invests in overlapping product development and marketing efforts.

   Smart companies know that they must manage their collection of brands as a *strategic* portfolio. So if businesses want to thrive, they must resist the temptation to add more and more new brands while stubbornly holding on to old brands. Instead, they should introduce fewer, stronger brands in a more synchronized way.

CRITICAL THINKING QUESTIONS

1. The year is 1990. Harry Walker's business (D-Base Transformers, page 92) is booming. You are trying to break into the marketing consulting business. Grudgingly, Harry has granted you 10 minutes of his time. Using your knowledge of core versus potential products, build an argument that will convince him that his business is headed for trouble. Show him how he can avoid future trouble by paying attention to your advice.

2. We said in this chapter that strong brands are built by thinking of the potential product, not the core product. Pick three product categories. In each product category, pick a strong brand and a weak brand. By looking at the core, functional, augmented, and potential products for each brand, demonstrate why the strong brands have achieved their superior status.

3. According to Interbrand, while brands like Apple gained in brand value during the last year (+21%), the biggest losers were Ford (−19%), GAP (−15%), and Kodak (−12%). Can you explain why?

4. As we have seen in this chapter, innovations should be broadly defined to include business innovation. Conduct research on Southwest Airlines, WestJet, and Ryanair and write a short report on how they innovate on the "customer experience" dimension.

RUNNING CASE

ARBOL INDUSTRIES SUCCEEDS IN BREAKING OUT OF THE COMMODITY MINDSET

Arbol Industries has taken a bold move in an orthodox industry where things are done today as they have always been done—it decided to "decommoditize" its products. That is, it decided to build a brand. As we have seen in previous chapters, Arbol made a commitment to customer focus and differentiation—managers did market research to deeply understand their customers' needs, they segmented their customer base, and they developed marketing plans.

The next step in their evolution was to brand their products. To do this, they used the concepts discussed in this chapter. They realized that the core product (lumber, plywood, or paper) could not be differentiated. After all, they are true commodities. Lumber, for example, has to have an engineering stamp on it. So, suppliers cannot make the claim that their offering is in any way different. But, Arbol shrewdly recognized that a business must focus on the potential product in order to differentiate its offering and build a brand. Let us take one example to demonstrate.

A common complaint of homeowners is the fact that, over time, their floors start to squeak. Arbol engineers came up with a unique solution to the problem. They glued together lumber and plywood to make a flooring system that was guaranteed never to squeak. They called it the Hush! Floor. They then partnered with home builders to offer this benefit to new home buyers. Their strategy was bold for this reason—you cannot really see your floor because it is hidden underneath the carpet. Even if you remove the carpet, what you see is not the actual floor, which is hidden one level below. So Arbol was successful in making the "invisible" visible!

Arbol succeeded in building a brand because its managers understood their customers' needs, and they put their efforts not into making incremental improvements to the core product, but into the potential product. *This is because they knew that customers do not buy the core product, they buy the potential product.* Their Hush! Floor became so popular that prospective new home buyers would walk out if the developer had not installed the Hush! Floor brand in his new homes.

Case Assignment

If you were working at Arbol Industries, how would you use the concepts in this chapter to brand other commodities such as plywood and paper? To provide a complete and specific answer, you will have to think about the needs of customers who buy plywood and paper.

SUGGESTED READINGS

If You Want to Build Winning Brands and Set Yourself Apart from Your Competitors, Do Not Miss These Publications

David A. Aaker, *Building Strong Brands* (New York: The Free Press 1996).

Theodore Levitt, "Marketing Myopia," *Harvard Business Review*, July–August 1960.

Theodore Levitt, "Marketing Success through Differentiation of Anything," *Harvard Business Review*, January–February 1980.

Erich Joachimsthaler and David A. Aaker, "Building Brands without Mass Media," *Harvard Business Review*, January–February 1997.

Michael Schrage, "The Myth of Commoditization," *MIT Sloan Management Review*, Winter 2007.

NOTES

1. Hoovers.com website.

2. Starbucks company fact sheet.

3. www.usgbc.org website.

4. My MBA students advised this company, while I acted as a faculty adviser. I have disguised the name of the company.

5. This material is based on Levitt's article, "Marketing Success through Differentiation of Anything," *Harvard Business Review*, January–February 1980.

6. The funny thing is, when Howard Schultz (one of the founders of Starbucks) initially suggested this idea to the original partners (who were selling the core product—coffee beans), they rejected the idea because it would mean deviating from the company's core business.

7. Interbrand, a brand consultancy firm, compiles a yearly list of the top 100 global brands based on brand value (financial worth of a brand, a concept we call brand equity later in the chapter). In 2007, Nike's brand was worth just over $12 billion.

8. This material is based on Theodore Levitt, "Marketing Myopia," *Harvard Business Review*, July–August 1960; Erich Joachimsthaler and David A. Aaker, "Building Brands Without Mass Media," *Harvard Business Review*, January–February 1997, pp. 39–50; David A. Aaker, *Building Strong Brands* (New York: The Free Press 1996).

9. Identifying "What business am I in?" is not easy, but it is a critical strategic skill to develop. When I ask students in my seminars what manufacturer #2 is making today, many answers focus on the core product or a variant of it. Students tend to say that manufacturer #2 is making "leather goods."

10. Michal Lev-Ram, "Samsung's Identity Crisis," *Business 2.0*, August 2007, p. 60.

11. *ibid.*

12. Based on David A. Aaker, *Managing Brand Equity* (New York: The Free Press 1991); Kevin L. Keller, "Conceptualizing, Measuring, and Managing Customer-Based Brand Equity," *Journal of Marketing*, Vol. 57, No. 1, pp. 1–22.

13. Michal Lev-Ram in "Samsung's Identity Crisis."

14. Keller's *Journal of Marketing* article provides a good set of brand equity measures.

15. David Kiley, "Winning Back Joe Corkscrew," *Business Week*, April 24, 2006, p. 82.

16. David Henry, "Creativity Pays, Here's how much," *Business Week*, April 24, 2006, p. 76.

17. Jena McGregor, "The World's Most Innovative Companies," *Business Week*, April 24, 2006, p. 63.

18. Based on Andrew Hargadon and Robert Sutton, "Building an Innovation Factory," *Harvard Business Review*, May–June 2000, pp. 157–166; and Jena McGregor, *ibid*.

19. This idea was first proposed by Henry W. Chesbrough in a 2003 book, *Open Innovation*.

20. As mentioned earlier, a "silo" is a tall, slim structure on a farm in which grain is stored. Here, it refers to functional units in business organizations that do not work co-operatively with each other.

21. For an interesting look at this topic, read Marvin Bower, "Company Philosophy: The Way We Do Things Around Here," *The McKinsey Quarterly*, 2003, No. 2, pp. 111–117.

22. This material is based on Stephen J. Carlotti Jr. et al., "Making Brand Portfolios Work," *The McKinsey Quarterly*, 2004, No. 4, pp. 25–35; David A. Aaker and Erich Joachimsthaler, *Brand Leadership* (New York: The Free Press, 2000).

23. *ibid.*

24. For a fascinating look at strategy, diversification, focus, the role of the CEO, and innovation, read "Strategy's Strategist: An Interview with Richard Rumelt," *The McKinsey Quarterly*, August 2007.

25. This case is based on "Will She, Won't She," *The Economist*, August 11, 2007, pp. 61–63, and Stephen J. Carlotti Jr. et al., *ibid*. The case is meant for illustrative purposes only and does not reflect all of P&G's products.

CHAPTER 6
Pricing Strategies

CHECKPOINT

Where We've Been

- We have seen how successful businesses serve their target customers by utilizing all elements in their marketing tool box—the marketing mix (product, price, channel, and marketing communications strategies).

- You have learned strategies and tactics that will help you build a strong brand and differentiate your business from competitors.

Where We're Going

- We will examine the second element of the marketing mix in this chapter—price.

- Other chapters in this part of the book will discuss channel and marketing communications strategies.

CHAPTER INTRODUCTION

In this chapter you will

By now you have learned how to target customers, use tools and techniques to understand their needs, and implement strategies to build a strong brand to set yourself apart from your competitors. You may think that all the hard work is behind you, but there is one task ahead of you that most business organizations find extremely difficult. And yet it is a task that has tremendous impact on their profits. That task is to arrive at a *price* for their goods and services. As will be shown in this chapter, most businesses leave money on the table—they undercharge for the value they offer their customers. In other words, price is an underutilized marketing mix element. If you want to run a successful and profitable business, you have to learn how to set a price for your goods and services.

Often, non-profit organizations will claim that this section on pricing does not apply to them. In reality, it does. Think of price as something a customer has to *give up* in order to receive a benefit (value), and you will clearly see how the term "price" is applicable to non-profits as well. In the non-profit environment, organizations are asking donors and funding entities (such as the government) to give something up (donations or funding) in order to receive something in exchange (the satisfaction of doing good deeds or providing necessary social services). These donors and funding bodies will not be forthcoming unless the "price is right" (the value they receive matches what they are giving up).

1. Learn why price is a *key* marketing decision you will have to make.

2. Learn why the majority of firms, in spite of knowing how critical the pricing decision is, set their prices too low, sapping their company of untold profits.

3. Learn the right and wrong way to approach pricing decisions.

4. Learn a pricing process to confidently make pricing decisions and avoid mistakes made by your competitors.

Price Is a *Key* Marketing Decision Any Business Has to Make

Pricing is a manager's biggest marketing headache. It is where most managers feel intense pressure to perform, yet most managers feel least confident that they are doing a good job in this arena. There are three main reasons why price is a key marketing decision you will have to make.

Why Price Is Important: Reason #1

Price Is Your Reward   Every business wants to differentiate itself from its competitors; it wants to build a strong brand. The price charged by a firm is like an instrument on the dashboard of a car—it tells you whether or not you have succeeded in differentiating yourself from your competitors. Strong brands command price premiums. "Me too" brands (undifferentiated offers) cannot command price premiums. Let us take an example.

MARKETING DRIVES SUCCESS

6.1 LULULEMON

Objective: Strong Brands Command Price Premiums

Ask any yoga enthusiast about lululemon, the Canadian brand that retails yoga-inspired apparel—stretchy pants and colourful tops—and you are going to hear nothing but "oohs" and "aahs." The brand has a devoted following. Since opening its first outlet in 1999, it has grown into a global presence. Its customers are not just yoga practitioners. The form-fitting garments appeal to fashionistas, soccer moms, and professionals of both genders.[1]

The brainchild of entrepreneur Chip Wilson, lululemon has built its strong brand by breaking rules:

- It does not advertise in the traditional way—no television commercials, no radio ads, no national newspaper campaigns.
- It relies heavily on word of mouth. It generates buzz by supplying free clothing to yoga teachers and fitness instructors, and encouraging these "ambassadors" to spread the word.
- It empowers store managers to run marketing initiatives suited to the local market. For example, the Santa Monica store in California sponsors yoga sessions on the beach.
- Its staff are encouraged to take up to two yoga classes a week at approved studios. This keeps staff happy and healthy, while profiling the lululemon brand in public.
- While the brand has gone global, the focus is not on volume but on the brand, store experience, and community involvement.

The hard work in building a strong brand has paid off. Its products are priced at a premium over competitors. But its customers do not care; they are price-insensitive. They willingly pay over $100 for a pair of workout pants or an athletic shirt.

Lululemon's yoga-inspired clothing is famous the world over.

Achieving the full profit potential
of each customer relationship should be the fundamental
goal of every business.

ALAN GRANT AND LEONARD SCHLESINGER

Why Price Is Important: Reason #2

Price and Your Overall Marketing Strategy Are Inextricably Related   Although lululemon's story is inspiring, it is the exception—lululemon is capable of charging price premiums because its management understands that without a strong brand strategy, they cannot be successful in the price arena. Most managers, however, fail to grasp that there is a strong correlation between **marketing strategy** and price.

From 2003 to 2005, global **private label brand** market share grew by 13%. For many brands, price premiums have eroded. Consumers are 50% more price-sensitive than they were 25 years ago. Seven out of ten consumer goods managers cite pricing pressure and shoppers' declining loyalty as their primary concerns.[2] Three examples will illustrate why you should think carefully about your marketing strategy and its relationship to price.

For 50 years, Vlasic was a beloved brand of pickles. In the late 1990s, it started offering its product in 3.79 L (1 gal.) jars. Wal-Mart began selling the product for an unbelievably low price of $2.99. Soon, Wal-Mart made up 30% of Vlasic's business. The super-cheap, large-sized jar cannibalized Vlasic's other channels (for example, grocery stores) and shrank its margins by 25%. Like many other brands, Vlasic was stuck. It needed to increase its price, but it needed Wal-Mart for its volumes. It could not have both (very few companies dealing with Wal-Mart have been able to secure a higher price). It filed for bankruptcy in 2001.

In contrast to the Vlasic example, consider the case of Nike. When Foot Locker (a major sports retailer) cut Nike orders by about $200 million to protest the terms Nike had placed on prices and selection, Nike cut its allocation of shoes to Foot Locker by $400 million. How did this scenario play out? Who do you think surrendered? Foot Locker, of course. Consumers, frustrated because they could not find shoes they wanted, stopped shopping at Foot Locker. Sales at a competitor increased. Foot Locker got the message.[3]

Finally, a brilliant strategy can fail if the price does not correspond. One company offered a new data-management system that could save companies hundreds of millions of dollars a year. It released the core software with an enterprise licensing fee of less than $100 000. Potential customers would not take the company's claims seriously. After all, if the product worked the way they claimed, the software should have been priced in the same range as other alternatives, which cost $1 million or more.[4]

So the message from the preceding examples should be crystal clear—there is a strong relationship between price and your marketing strategy. A company like Rolex knows this very well. That is why its watches are priced at a premium to match a premium brand position it wants to occupy in the marketplace. We will have more to say about this later in the chapter.

Rolex matches its brand and pricing strategy.

Why Price Is Important: Reason #3

Price Has the Most Impact on Your Profits

As shown in Figure 6.1, there are many levers you can pull in your company to influence profits. These are price, costs (both variable costs and fixed costs), and volume. A **variable cost** (such as raw material or labour) varies with production volume, while a **fixed cost** (such as monthly rent on office space) has to be incurred regardless of volume.

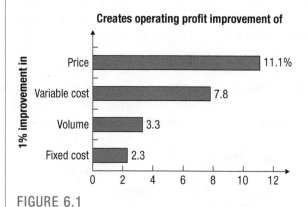

FIGURE 6.1

A comparison of profit levers

Source: McKinsey, based on average economics of 2463 companies, as reproduced in Michael V. Marn, Eric V. Roegner, and Craig C. Zawada, *The Price Advantage* (Hoboken, NJ: John Wiley & Sons, 2004), p. 5.

But research reveals that price has the most impact on your profits. In fact, a 1% improvement in price results in an 11% improvement in operating profits. Conversely, a price that is 1% less than optimal results in 8% less operating profit![5]

As we will see later in this chapter, there is a right way and a wrong way to approach the pricing decision. Many firms use the wrong way—they start by looking at their costs to arrive at a price. This approach is wrong because the end price can be too low or too high. The right way is to start with customer needs (as with every smart business move), and match them with the value created by the organization's products.

Why is it so vital to get pricing right? Because pricing right is the fastest and most effective way for companies to grow profits.

MARN, ROEGNER, AND ZAWADA

CHAPTER CHALLENGE 6.1

ARE YOU ON THE RIGHT TRACK?

If pricing decisions are so important, why is price an underutilized marketing mix variable? Why do firms "leave money on the table"?

(*Were you on the right track? Check your answers in Appendix 2.*)

Where We've Been

■ We have seen that decisions on price are critical for any company because they are the reward for building strong brands. Pricing decisions and marketing strategy are strongly related, and price has the most impact on profits.

Where We're Going

■ We will learn why the majority of firms, in spite of knowing how critical the price decision is, set their prices too low for new products.

CHECKPOINT

Why Do Most Firms Set Their Prices Too Low?

The previous section can be summarized by a key observation: even if you think your pricing is 90% effective, it is worth striving for 91%.

The research reveals that most firms set their prices too low, resulting in untold loss of profits. To understand why this is the case, take Chapter Challenge 6.2 before reading further.

OBJECTIVE 2

KEYPOINT

The implications are clear: even if you think your pricing is 90% effective, it is worth striving for 91%!

CHAPTER CHALLENGE 6.2

ARE YOU ON THE RIGHT TRACK?

You sell T-shirts for $10 in a crowded tourist area, where there are many other stalls also selling the same item. Your cost per T-shirt is $7, giving you a profit of $3 per item. If you do nothing, you will sell 1000 T-shirts. If you cut your price to $9.50 (your profit is now $2.50 per item), you will sell 1200 T-shirts. Which option would you choose? Remember, your profits are $3000 in each case ($3 × 1000 in the first case and $2.50 × 1200 in the second case).

(*Were you on the right track? Check your answers in Appendix 2.*)

> *We are very poor at setting prices. We say 'let us increase our prices by 5% . . . throw it on the wall and see what happens.'*
>
> MANAGER IN THE PHARMACEUTICAL INDUSTRY (WHO WISHES TO REMAIN ANONYMOUS)

Why Do Firms Set Prices Too Low? Reason #1

They Use a "Seat-of-the-Pants" Approach to Pricing In many firms, prices are set by looking at last year's price list and adding a certain percentage increase. Or managers guess and tinker with prices. This seat-of-the-pants approach to pricing works like this: managers set an initial price within a middle range (neither too high, nor too low) and then make incremental adjustments depending on whether market demand is lower or higher than expected. Such an approach to pricing sacrifices long-term profits by as much as 20%.[6]

Managers are not very good at tinkering with prices either. Research has shown that when demand is lower than expected, managers respond with an excessively large price drop. And when demand is higher than expected, prices do not move up correspondingly. In general, managers are slow to change prices in response to market information.[7]

Why Do Firms Set Prices Too Low? Reason #2

They Blindly Chase after Market Share   If you chose the second option (dropping the price by 50¢ to sell an additional 200 T-shirts) in Chapter Challenge 6.2, you chose the wrong option. But do not worry—you are in good company; most managers would also have chosen the second option. This is how the thinking goes: "It is only a price cut of 50¢. And, look at the benefit I am accruing—the chance to sell more items and steal market share away from my competitors. Besides, I can *always* raise prices at a later date if I want to."

This thinking is flawed for these reasons:

- What is the most likely reaction of your competitors when you drop your price? You guessed it—they will retaliate by dropping their price also. So the lower price advantage you sought will be lost. Worse, you will have initiated a **price war** in the industry. If this cycle continues (competitors dropping prices to gain market share), the entire industry is in jeopardy. Witness the sad state of affairs confronting North American car manufacturers. In their quest to lure customers, they have periodically dropped prices (in the form of ever-increasing discounts), giving their Japanese competitors a chance to gain a stronger foothold in their own backyard.

- There is a strong possibility that your **brand image** could be hurt if you drop your price. A weak brand image, in turn, will make it harder for you to attract customers, thus defeating your objective of gaining market share.

KEYPOINT

Dropping your price in the hopes of securing more volume is short-lived because your competitors will likely match your price.

⬛ The major reason why most firms lower their price is to secure a higher market share. But this rarely happens. Using data from 1200 companies from around the world, Michael Marn and his colleagues have demonstrated that a 5% price decrease would require a 17.5% volume increase to simply maintain your profit level.[8] Such an increase is highly unlikely. For a 5% decrease to generate a 17.5% volume increase, every percentage point drop in price would have to drive up unit volume by 3.5% (this is referred to as **price elasticity**). In the researchers' experience, a 1% price decrease usually results in a volume increase of only 1.7% or 1.8%!

Finally, the reason why most firms chase after market share is because, from a strategic perspective, they simply do not know what else to do.[9] Therefore, building market share becomes their *de facto* "strategy." While building market share is important (to develop a loyal customer base, set industry standards, and secure channels of distribution), a blind devotion to chasing market share, to the detriment of price and profit, does not make sense.

Why Do Firms Set Prices Too Low? Reason #3

They Rely Too Much on Costs to Make Pricing Decisions   Seventy percent of the world's firms rely on an inferior pricing method called **cost-plus pricing**. In cost-plus pricing, the firm takes its cost and attaches a certain margin to arrive at the final price. Therefore, if the cost of the T-shirt is $7, and the firm wants a profit margin of 43% ($3), it charges a price of $10 for the item. While the biggest advantages of cost-plus pricing are its simplicity and ability to cover costs, its many disadvantages make it a very poor way to arrive at a price.

The biggest drawback of cost-plus pricing is that it does not take into account customer needs or brand strategy. Prices should be based on what customers are willing to pay. This, in turn, is based on how differentiated your offering is (how successfully you have built a brand). Cost-plus pricing does not consider any of these factors; it only takes into account your cost. As a result, your prices may be too high or too low. Either way, cost-plus pricing results in a less-than-optimal pricing strategy.

CHAPTER CHALLENGE 6.3

ARE YOU ON THE RIGHT TRACK?

If cost-plus pricing is an inferior way to make pricing decisions, why do the majority of the world's firms continue to use it? (Hint: you should be able to answer this question based on your knowledge of marketing research and branding strategies.)

(*Were you on the right track? Check your answers in Appendix 2.*)

CHECKPOINT

Where We've Been

■ We have learned that setting a price is a critical marketing decision you will have to make because it impacts your profitability.

■ Yet most firms are very poor at making the right pricing decision for three main reasons: they use a "seat-of-the-pants" approach to pricing, they blindly chase market share, and they rely overly on costs to make pricing decisions.

Where We're Going

■ We will see the right and wrong way to approach pricing decisions.

OBJECTIVE 3

Two Approaches You Can Take to Making Pricing Decisions

There are two main approaches to pricing decisions: an internal focus and an external focus. These are depicted in Figure 6.2.

The internally focused approach puts costs *before* customers. The customer-focused approach rightly puts the focus on customers *first* and costs *last*. As we have seen throughout this book, firms that do not put their customers first underperform compared to their competitors, or they go out of business. Pricing strategies are no exception. Firms that put their customers last by following a narrow **product focus (orientation)** do not capture the full benefit of optimal prices.

Organizations that use an internally focused approach to pricing start with their product (a good or a service). They look at what it costs them to provide the good or service to arrive at a price for their offering (this is called cost-plus pricing). They then try to attract customers willing to pay the asking price by communicating the value to them. But as we have seen, this approach can lead to setting a price that is out of touch with customer needs. Let us take an example.

KEYPOINT

Contrary to popular belief, it is possible to simultaneously cut costs and maintain (or increase) customer value.

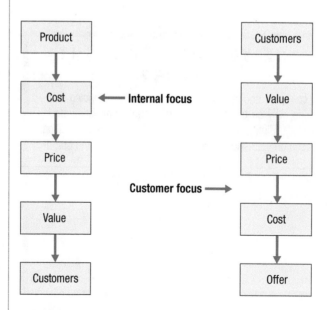

FIGURE 6.2

The wrong and right way to approach pricing decisions

In 1987, the wife of a senior Motorola technology leader was upset because she could not call home from a boat in the Bahamas. Eleven years and more than $2 billion later, Motorola introduced Iridium, a satellite phone that allowed users to call anywhere from anywhere on the planet. However, there was a catch: the phones were bulky, they were costly ($3000), and they were too expensive to use ($7 for one minute). As a result, the market segment that would value such an offering was very small. The project failed and Motorola sold the network for $25 million, about a penny on the dollar of the original investment.[10]

Businesses that use a customer-focused approach to pricing start by researching customers and their perceptions of value for any given product category. They then assign a price to the value they are going to offer the target segment. Finally, they examine their costs to ascertain whether they can make a certain profit margin. If they can make their profit margin, they take their offer to the marketplace. If they find that they are not able to make their required margin, they choose one of the following options: they examine ways to cut costs without sacrificing customer value (this is called **target costing** and will be described later in the chapter), or they abandon their quest entirely.

KEYPOINT

Contrary to popular practice, costs should play a relatively minor role in the pricing decision.

Hear Jacqueline Sava, founder and CEO of Soakwash, talk about how she follows the customer-focused approach to set prices.

MARKETING DRIVES SUCCESS

6.2 CIRQUE DU SOLEIL

Objective: Winning Organizations Start with the Customer to Arrive at a Price

Cirque du Soleil ("Circus of the Sun") is an entertainment giant based in Montreal. It was founded in 1984 by two former street performers, Guy Laliberté and Daniel Gauthier. Each Cirque show is a synthesis of circus styles from around the world and has its own central theme and storyline that brings the audience into the performance by having no curtains, continuous live music, and performers changing the props. Throughout the 1990s and 2000s, Cirque expanded rapidly from its beginning as a single show with 73 employees in 1984. It currently has 3500 employees from over 40 countries, doing 15 shows touring every continent, and an estimated annual revenue exceeding US$600 million.[11] The multiple permanent Las Vegas shows alone play to more than 9000 people a night—5% of the city's visitors—adding to the 70+ million people who have experienced Cirque.

The secret to Cirque's success lies in its ability to understand customer needs and perceptions of value. Their main market segment is a customer who likes to go to the circus to watch acrobatic acts but does not like the animal acts.[12] With an accurate understanding of customer value, Cirque du Soleil

Cirque du Soleil provides customer value through an accurate understanding of customer needs.

has cut its costs by eliminating costly animal acts while providing the same (or enhanced) value to the customer, resulting in enhanced profitability and brand recognition.

Where We've Been

- We have learned that setting a price is a critical marketing decision you will have to make because it impacts your profitability. Yet most firms are very poor at making the right pricing decision.
- You can approach the pricing decision the right way or the wrong way.

Where We're Going

- We will examine a pricing process you can use to confidently make pricing decisions.

CHECKPOINT

OBJECTIVE 4

A Pricing Process to Help You Confidently Make Pricing Decisions

A step-by-step pricing process to help you confidently make pricing decisions is depicted in Figure 6.3.

The most striking feature of this process is that, no matter where you start, you will end up in the same place! Therefore, although the discussion of the pricing process assumes we are pricing a new product, you can use the process just as effectively to make re-pricing decisions—evaluate prices of existing goods and services and make adjustments.

Pricing with Confidence Step #1: Segment the Market by Assessing the Value Created by Your Product

We saw in Chapter 3 that if you are not segmenting your customers, you are trying to be all things to everybody. In the end, you will be nothing to no one. This sentiment is especially true when developing pricing strategies—every business needs to discipline itself, recognize that all customers are not going to equally appreciate (and pay for) the value created by its product, and segment its customers by focusing on the eight areas identified in Table 6.1.[13]

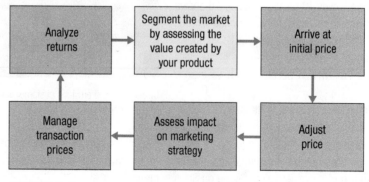

FIGURE 6.3

A pricing process to help you confidently make pricing decisions

TABLE 6.1 Assessing the Value Created by Your Product

Identify the problem customers want to solve The depth interview guide presented in Chapter 2 is very useful here. Also, some of these factors (e.g., what strategic objectives do customers want to achieve) are more applicable to business customers.	▪ What are the greatest challenges customers face? ▪ What strategic objectives do they want to achieve? ▪ What customer segments do they serve? ▪ Who do they compete against? ▪ How do they differentiate their offerings? ▪ What benefits do they seek from the product category?
Identify the current solution.	▪ What alternatives currently exist in the marketplace? ▪ How good a job do they do in helping customers achieve their objectives?
Define problems solved by your product.	▪ How does our product compare with existing alternatives? ▪ To what extent does our product improve performance against key customer objectives?
Calculate financial impact (use **Total Cost of Ownership analysis** illustrated at the end of this section).	▪ How does our product affect revenues and costs compared to current solutions?
Identify barriers to adoption.	▪ What and whom within the customer's organization would our product impact? ▪ What are the **switching costs**?[1]
Identify likely adopters.	▪ Who will benefit most from a switch to our product? ▪ Who will most likely resist the switch to our product?
Look for variations in the way customers value the product.	▪ Do customers vary in their intensity of use (heavy users versus light users)? ▪ Do customers use the product differently? ▪ Does product performance matter more to some customers, even if the use is the same? ▪ Can we customize pricing for segments that value our product differently?
Assess customers' price sensitivities (price elasticity).	▪ Is the buyer the end user? (If the buyer is not the end user, sensitivity to price increases.) ▪ In this market, does a higher price signal higher quality? ▪ Is the customer able to compare price and performance of alternatives? ▪ Are customers motivated to shop around? ▪ Is the company's reputation a consideration? ▪ Are there other intangibles affecting the customer's decision?

[1] Switching costs are costs incurred by a customer to switch options (financial or non-financial). For example, although many people dislike their current bank, they do not switch to a different bank because of the headaches involved in transferring accounts from their current bank to the new one.

Total Cost of Ownership Analysis   The key idea behind Total Cost of Ownership (TCO) analysis is that price is just one component of a customer's total cost of "owning" a product (good or service). And if we can reduce the customer's total cost of ownership, the customer will be less price-sensitive to the **acquisition cost** (the price initially paid to acquire the good or service). TCO analysis can be applied in both business-to-business and business-to-consumer settings to assess the financial impact on the customer of our product.

TABLE 6.2	**Total Cost of Ownership Analysis**		
TCO = acquisition costs + possession costs + usage costs + disposal costs			
Acquisition costs	**Possession costs**	**Usage costs**	**Disposal costs**
Price	Storage	Training	Disposal
Paperwork and processing	Interest	Labour costs	Recycling
Shopping	Quality control	Product replacement	Repurchase
Mistakes in order	Taxes and insurance Shrinkage and obsolescence Depreciation	Internal handling	Switching costs

TCO analysis attempts to break down the customer's total cost into four components identified in Table 6.2.

Here are some examples of organizations assessing the financial impact of their product by using the TCO framework:

■ Catalogue retailers like Land's End reduce customers' shopping costs by letting them shop online or over the telephone.

■ Programs called **Vendor Managed Inventory** eliminate customers' paperwork and processing costs because the supplier manages the customer's inventory and ships the product without any effort on the customers' part.

■ FedEx's "virtual warehouse" concept eliminates the need for a customer to carry inventory. FedEx's airplanes, in essence, are the customer's "warehouse."

■ Mercedes cars depreciate at a slower rate than their competitors' cars, so owners get a higher resale value.

■ SPSS, a statistical software manufacturer, offers online training programs to eliminate customer frustration with using their product.

■ Weldwood of Canada, a supplier of lumber and plywood to the construction industry, picks up packaging materials from construction sites and recycles them.

■ Marketing Research and Intelligence Association, a professional body of marketing researchers, makes it simple to renew your membership by directing you to a website. Renewal takes 30 seconds. Contrast this with past practice, where they would send a renewal notice in the mail and the member had to fill in a form and mail the envelope back with a payment.

6.3 GOOD HEALTH MULTIVITAMINS

Objective: Assessing the Value Created by Your Product Helps in Making the Right Pricing Decision

Carl, the brand manager for Good Health Multivitamins,[14] had an important decision to make. He was considering increasing the price of his brand, even though it was already priced 15% more than his competitors. He was wondering what would happen if the price premium were raised to around 20%–25% over his competitors. Table 6.3 presents an analysis leading to his decision to go ahead with the price increase.

A concern for health makes many consumers of multivitamins price-insensitive.

TABLE 6.3   Assessing the Value Created by Good Health Multivitamins

Identify the problem customers want to solve.	Consumers of multivitamins take the product as a form of "insurance" to protect themselves from ill health. Very few consumers are able to accurately tell whether their multivitamins actually work; they tend to take them on faith.
Identify the current solution.	There are many competing brands on the market, each making the same claim of providing good health. Store brands (private label brands) are cheaper than nationally branded multivitamins.
Define problems solved by your product.	Good Health has worked hard to position itself as a premium and efficacious brand of multivitamins. Consumers trust this brand.
Calculate financial impact.	The financial impact of ill health is incalculable. Consumers are willing to do what it takes to remain healthy.
Identify barriers to adoption.	Some customers may be lost if the price is increased, although the loss is likely to be minimal.
Identify likely adopters.	Current and possibly new customers.
Look for variations in the way customers value the product.	There are sophisticated customers in this product category who research multivitamins. However, our brand is a mass market brand; our customers do not tend to shop around.
Assess customers' price sensitivities.	■ The buyer is the end-user, so sensitivity to price is low. ■ A higher price signals higher quality in this product category. This is because most consumers do not know much about multivitamins (they are classified as "naive" consumers). ■ Customers find it hard to compare among competing products because they lack knowledge of ingredients and their functions.

Based on the eight areas identified in Table 6.1 (page 127), a company should segment customers. This is an important step because customer segmentation allows you to customize prices to segments. By customizing prices, a company can earn much greater profits than it could with a single segment/single product/single price policy.[15] Yet many managers fail to appreciate this idea. Instead, they attempt to target an "average" customer. *Such a customer does not exist.* A company's pricing will be much more effective if it develops a profile of customer segments and matches its offerings and prices to suit the needs of each segment. A sample segmentation profile is offered in Table 6.4.[16]

TABLE 6.4 **Segmenting Customers for Optimal Pricing Decisions[17]**		
Price customers	**Value customers**	**Relationship customers**
■ Primarily value the cheapest priced product	■ Will consider paying for added product benefits if a case can be made	■ Tend to be brand loyal because they actively compare alternatives and are satisfied with their choice; or they are brand loyal due to intangibles such as liking for a brand
■ Do not care about added benefits of our product over competitors	■ Are primarily interested in product performance features (e.g., the ability of the product to save them money)	■ Tend to be averse to risk; do not like switching suppliers
■ Want the basic product at the basic price		■ Tend to be price-insensitive

Pricing with Confidence Step #2: Arrive at Initial Price

A procedure called Economic Value Added (EVA)[18] analysis is useful in arriving at the initial price (Figure 6.4). Let us take an example to illustrate this method.[19] A manufacturer of dental instruments is developing a new product (to replace reusable dental instruments with disposable ones) and wants to know how to price it (notice in this example that the manufacturer is thinking about price even at the developmental stage, not *after* the product has been developed).

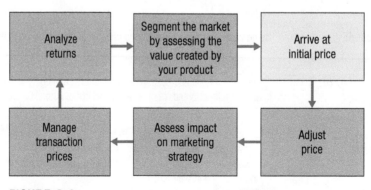

FIGURE 6.4

Pricing process step #2: Arrive at initial price.

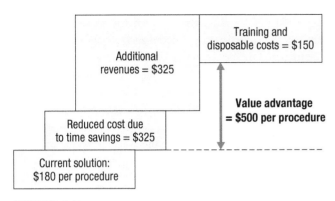

FIGURE 6.5

Use customer value data to determine your price.

Source: Mark Burton and Steve Haggett, "Rocket Plan," *Marketing Management*, September/October 2007, pp. 32–38.

Through customer interviews and operational studies, the manufacturer determines that such a device would improve procedure-room utilization by reducing cleanup time. The innovation would also enable oral surgeons to differentiate themselves by advertising that they use the safest and most advanced equipment (thus enhancing their revenues). However, the manufacturer also determines that there would be a cost to switch from the current solution (training staff, disposing of current equipment) to the new one.

Calculating the initial price involves determining the following and is illustrated in Figure 6.5:

- The cost per procedure of current solutions (called the reference value) is estimated to be $180.
- The cost savings due to greater procedure-room utilization is estimated to be $325.
- Enhanced revenue from new patients is estimated to be $325.
- Training and disposal costs are estimated to be $150.
- The added value provided by the new product is $500 ($325 + $325 − $150).
- Therefore, the price for the new product can be set anywhere between $180 and $680 ($180 reference value + $500 additional value created by new product).

Pricing with Confidence Step #3: Adjust the Price

The pricing method using Step #2 is called **value-based pricing**. The price range arrived at has to be adjusted based on many factors to arrive at the final price (Figure 6.6).

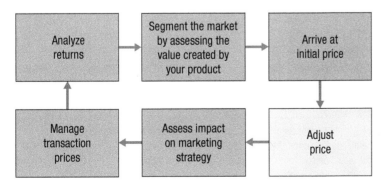

FIGURE 6.6

Pricing process step #3: Adjust the price.

Costs should never determine price, but costs do play a critical role in formulating a pricing strategy.

NAGLE AND HOLDEN

Price Feasibility   To narrow down the range, the dental equipment manufacturer considered such psychological factors as risk incurred by the customer in switching to a new technology, and pride in being on the cutting edge. The manufacturer also decided to make the price attractive to sway uncertain buyers. It settled on an initial price of $400 per instrument. Although this price is not at the higher end of the price range, the manufacturer felt that it gave them good profits and gave customers an incentive to switch. Of course, depending on market reaction once the product is actually introduced, the manufacturer might adjust the price up or down.

Costs   There are three main areas we should look at when determining the role of costs in pricing.

The first step in pricing is to understand **incremental costs**: those that actually determine the profit impact of the pricing decision.[20] Incremental costs represent the increment to cost (positive or negative) that results from the pricing decision. Let us take an example to understand the important role of incremental costs in the pricing decision.

The manager of a symphony orchestra faces the following costs per performance:

Fixed overhead costs (rent, etc.)	$1500
Rehearsal costs	$4500
Performance costs	$2000
Variable costs (e.g., printing programs)	$1 per patron

The manager has set ticket prices currently at $10. If she sells out her entire 1100-seat hall, her total revenues per performance would be $11 000 ($10 × 1100). Her total costs are $9100 per performance [$1500 + $4500 + $2000 + ($1 × 1100)], leaving her with a profit of $1900 ($11 000 − $9100) per performance.

Unfortunately, the symphony only manages to sell 900 seats per performance, leaving her with a profit of only $100 ($9000 − $8900). (Total revenue = $10 × 900 = $9000) [Total cost = $1500 + $4500 + $2000 + $900 ($1 × 900) = $8900] Her average cost per ticket is $9.89 ($8900 / 900), very close to the selling price of $10 per ticket. She believes that simply raising her prices will not solve the problem. In fact, it would worsen her situation, as a higher price would result in even fewer tickets sold, lesser revenues, and losses. Instead, she is considering three proposals to increase profits. These are depicted in Table 6.5.

Which of the proposals should the symphony adopt? The analysis is shown in Table 6.6.

Although the revenue gain is the smallest for the first proposal, its net profit contribution is the highest among all proposals, making it the most attractive option. *This is because*

TABLE 6.5 **Three Proposals to Increase Symphony Profits**		
Proposal 1 Student rush	**Proposal 2 Sunday matinee**	**Proposal 3 New series**
Priced at $4 per ticket and sold to students 30 minutes before each show. The manager expects she could sell 200 such tickets.	A Sunday matinee repeat of the Saturday night performance. Each ticket would be priced at $6. The manager believes she could sell 700 tickets, but 150 of those would be sold to people who normally would have attended the Saturday night performance. Therefore, the net patronage increase would be 550.	A brand new series of performances, with tickets priced at $10. She estimates that she could sell 800 tickets, but 100 of those would be sold to people who would stop attending the old series. Therefore, the net patronage increase would be 700.

TABLE 6.6   Analysis of the Three Proposals to Increase Profits

	Proposal 1 Student rush	Proposal 2 Sunday matinee	Proposal 3 New series
Price per ticket	$4	$6	$10
× Unit sales	200	700	800
= Revenue	$800	$4200	$8000
− Other sales foregone	(0)	($1500)	($1000)
Revenue gain	$800	$2700	$7000
Incremental rehearsal costs	0	0	$4500
Incremental performance cost	0	$2000	$2000
Variable costs	$200	$550	$700
Incremental costs	$200	$2550	$7200
Net profit contribution	$600	$150	($200)

Source: Thomas K. Nagle and Reed K. Holden, *The Strategy and Tactics of Pricing* (Upper Saddle River, NJ: Prentice Hall, 2002).

a change in pricing affects incremental costs for the three proposals in a different fashion. Although the revenue gain is the highest for the new series proposal, the impact on incremental costs is also the highest, making it the least profitable option from a net profit contribution perspective. This is why it is so important to consider incremental costs when making pricing decisions.

In reality, many managers focus on **average costs**, which are readily available from the accounting function. However, a focus on average costs would lead to the wrong conclusion: with the student rush option, average costs per ticket are $8.27 [($1500 + $4500 + $2000 + $1100) / 1100]. The student rush tickets, priced at just $4, are less than half the average cost per ticket! Most managers would be tempted to conclude that Proposal #1 is an unattractive option.

The second area in which costs become important is in calculating a **break-even point**, which is the point at which the firm "breaks even"—it neither makes a profit nor makes a loss, but it recovers its **total costs**. Let us take an example.

An entrepreneur is introducing a salad dressing made entirely of organic materials and free of preservatives. She estimates that her fixed costs (rent, salary for a manager) for the year are going to be $150 000. Her per-unit variable costs (raw material costs, labour costs per hour) are expected to be $0.97. She is thinking of setting a price of $1.50 per bottle of salad dressing. How many units should she sell before she breaks even? The calculations are shown in Table 6.7.

TABLE 6.7   Computing a Break-Even Point

Fixed cost	$150 000
Unit price per bottle	$1.50
Variable cost per unit	$0.97
Contribution margin	$0.53 ($1.50–$0.97)
Break-even point	283 018 bottles ($150 000 / $0.53)

TABLE 6.8	**Computing a New Break-Even Point**
Fixed cost	$150 000
Unit price per bottle	$3.50
Variable cost per unit	$0.97
Contribution margin	$2.53 ($3.50 − $0.97)
Break-even point	59 288 bottles ($150 000 / $2.53)

"283 018 bottles!" she thinks. "That's impossible. I cannot sell that many bottles. I wonder how many bottles I would have to sell if I raised my price per bottle by $2? I read somewhere that the trend these days is toward healthy eating and healthy living. I think consumers will be willing to pay $3.50 for a bottle of organic and preservative-free salad dressing." Her new break-even point is calculated in Table 6.8.

"I can sell close to 60 000 bottles per year," she thinks to herself. The advantage of calculating break-even points is that doing so enables a firm to play with a different range of prices to compute how many units it would have to sell simply to cover all costs.

The final method of using costs is called **target costing**,[21] which enables a company to establish an initial price, set a profit margin, and control costs to ensure that the required profit margin is met. Cirque du Soleil used this method. Let us take another example.

The packaging division of International Paper (IP) makes, among other things, cardboard boxes. In some markets (such as Houston, Texas), the humidity levels are so high that the boxes turn to mush. The traditional solution has been to put more wood fibre into the box to strengthen it. However, this adds to the cost and eats into the profit margin. It is not possible to raise prices, as customers are price-sensitive. The solution? Force product designers to look for ways to make the box stronger, while having less fibre. IP designers found the solution. They inserted a thin plastic sheet between layers of cardboard to give the box strength. They were successful in achieving two seemingly contradictory goals— make a stronger box while reducing the amount of raw material that went in it. Target costing has long been used successfully by leading Japanese electronics and vehicle manufacturers.

Short-Term Strategies and Tactics

A company can utilize two main tactics in the short term when considering what price to set: **price skimming** and **price penetration**. Firms that have invested heavily in product development (such as pharmaceutical companies and electronic goods manufacturers) use a technique called price skimming, where they set a high initial price for the product (to recoup their investment). The product is aimed at certain segments of the market (customers who view the product as a "must-have"). In time, with increasing competition, the price is reduced. With price penetration, a company chooses the exact opposite route. It sets the price of the product low to capture market share (and keep competitors out). If the product becomes popular, the price can be raised over time.

Competitor Reactions

It would be short-sighted to settle on a price without thinking about competitors and their potential reactions. A manager has to put himself in the shoes of his competitors and ask, "What would I do if I were the competitor?"

Potential New Entrants into the Marketplace

The final price has to be set based on knowledge of potential competitors that could enter the marketplace and their likely moves. Competitors enter a marketplace when they see incumbent firms enjoying profitable success. If these newcomers do not have differentiated offerings, they will compete

KEYPOINT

Your goal should be to understand the issues involved with costs; mastery will come with practice.

The founder of Dessert Lady talks about the role of costs and other factors in pricing decisions.

by lowering the price of their products and proclaiming to customers that their offering is just as good, only cheaper. However, the incumbent can rest a little easy if it knows that it has been successful in building a strong brand for itself.

Pricing with Confidence Step #4: Assess Impact on Marketing Strategy

Throughout this book we have stressed that successful organizations reach into their marketing tool box (marketing mix) and select a combination of product, price, channel, and marketing communications strategies to create maximum appeal for the target market segment. These organizations recognize that each element of the marketing mix has a unique role to play, and each element supports the other elements to create a seamless "package" for the customer. If even one of the marketing mix elements is at odds with the others, the end result is customer confusion, brand diffusion, and possible failure. Pricing strategies are no exception.

So far in this chapter, we have seen how to set a price by thinking about customer needs, the economic value added by the offering, and adjustments to price based on such factors as competitor reactions and costs. But, the business should also think about the long-term marketing strategy impact of the selected price (Figure 6.7). This is because prices impact not only how customers view the firm, but also to what extent they talk to others about it. As we will see in Chapter 8, word of mouth creates twice more value for a firm than such marketing-induced efforts as advertising.

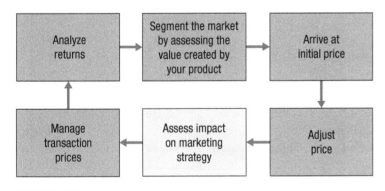

FIGURE 6.7

Pricing process step #4: Assess impact on marketing strategy.

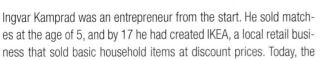

6.4 IKEA

Objective: A Business Should Think about the Long-Term Marketing Strategy Impact of Its Prices

Ingvar Kamprad was an entrepreneur from the start. He sold matches at the age of 5, and by 17 he had created IKEA, a local retail business that sold basic household items at discount prices. Today, the Swedish furniture retailer's empire stretches to 260 stores around the globe, with annual sales of €21 billion.[22]

continues…

IKEA's secret to success is a clear understanding of what marketing strategy it wants to pursue: good quality at a low price. Its prices typically are 30% to 50% below competitors'. While the prices of other companies' products tend to rise over time, IKEA's goal is to *reduce* the price of an item continually throughout its production run. IKEA's corporate mantra is "Low price with meaning." The goal is to make things less expensive without ever making customers feel cheap.[23] This is how IKEA does it:

■ Step 1: Pick a price. Based on its extensive knowledge of its customers' needs, IKEA first starts with a price for any given product. It has three price ranges: high, medium, and low.

■ Step 2: Pick a manufacturer. After settling on a target price for a product, IKEA determines what materials will be used and what manufacturer will do the assembly work, even before the new item is actually designed.

■ Step 3: Design the product. IKEA designers and engineers focus on using materials as efficiently as possible, analyzing the function of each furniture piece to determine which materials and construction techniques will work best for the least amount of money.

■ Step 4: Ship it. In 1956, an IKEA designer watched as a customer struggled to fit a table into his car. The solution was simple—remove the legs. From that moment on, IKEA has shipped flat packages that can be stored in the trunk of a car or on its roof.

■ Step 5: Sell it. To keep its prices low, IKEA stores do not have many salespeople. Customers have to pick up and assemble their own furniture. To make it appealing, IKEA stores are designed like theme parks, with child-care facilities, cafeterias, model homes, and information kiosks where customers can determine the best decor for their living space.

IKEA's strategy is clear: good quality at a low price.

Pricing with Confidence Step #5: Manage Transaction Prices

As part of the pricing process, a business needs to manage its transaction prices (Figure 6.8). So far, we have been focused on setting a price. However, the *listed* price may not be the *actual* price that the company realizes (or puts in its "pocket"). This is because the set of pricing terms and conditions the company offers its customers can be quite elaborate. They include such things as volume discounts, discounts for early payment, competitive discounts, and special terms and discounts offered by a salesperson to secure the contract. These special terms and discounts given to different customers are a form of price abuse that is prevalent throughout the industry. An example of this **price waterfall** is shown in Figure 6.9.[24]

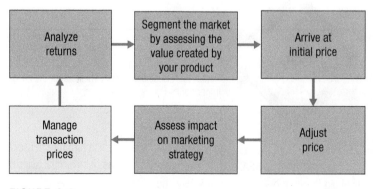

FIGURE 6.8

Pricing process step #5: Manage transaction prices.

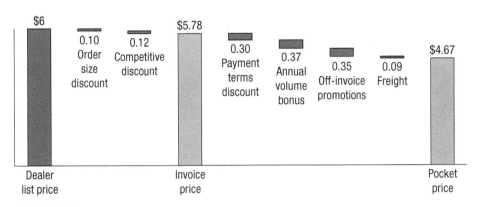

FIGURE 6.9

Price waterfalls demonstrate price leakage in a business.

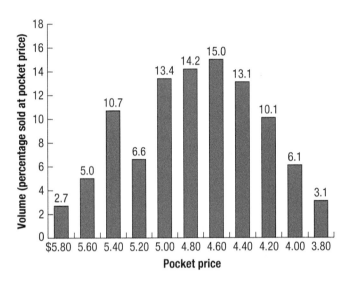

FIGURE 6.10

A pocket price band demonstrates pricing abuse in a firm.

As can be seen if Figure 6.9, although the list price is $6.00, the actual **pocket price** is only $4.67. Although there is only one list price, there can be many final prices. This is called a **pocket price band** and is depicted in Figure 6.10.

A company can realize many price advantages by simply examining its price waterfall and pocket price band to uncover price leakages. As we can see from Figure 6.10, only 2.7% of customers pay a price even close to the list price ($6.00). Yet most managers spend the majority of their time on arriving at the list price. They ignore the hole in their pocket—substantial foregone profits due to special terms and conditions offered to customers by salespeople.

Pricing with Confidence Step #6: Analyze Returns

There is one final variable every business must take into account—the cost to serve a customer (Figure 6.11). In an *ideal* world, high-cost-to-serve customers pay a higher price and low-cost-to-serve customers pay a lower price. But it does not work this way in the *real* world. What we may find instead is low-cost-to-serve customers paying higher prices, while high-cost-to-serve customers pay a lower price. It all depends on how loudly the customer complains, how much power and influence the customer wields, and how fearful the salesperson is of losing a "strategic account." An example will illustrate this point.[25]

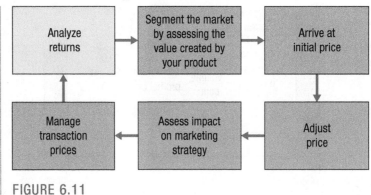

FIGURE 6.11

Pricing process step #6: Analyze returns.

> *We went to two of our customers, representing total sales of $10 million, and told them that they would have to pay a higher price based on our cost to serve them. They refused to take the price increase. We let them go. We had to shut down several of our production lines and lay off a few employees. When we compared financial numbers with the previous year's, we found that our profits had stayed the same!*
>
> FLORENCE FURLONG, SOLO CUP

MARKETING DRIVES SUCCESS

6.5 MARKETING COMMUNICATIONS INC.

Objective: Pay Attention to the Cost to Serve Your Customers

Marketing Communications Inc. (MC) was founded by three partners to help corporate clients with their ecommerce (website-enabled business transactions) needs. MC had only one golden rule when deciding on accepting a customer: a customer was a good customer if they had a *minimum* of $30 000 to spend on a project; nothing else mattered. MC was growing at a rate of 50% each year. In two years they moved locations three times, each time to newer and fancier digs. They were riding high! Although their sales curve looked liked a rocket taking off, their profit curve told a different story—it was sloping downward; they were losing money. How could a company with such spectacular growth rates be losing money? Simple. They were not taking into account cost to serve their customers.

MC had many "important" customers (called "strategic accounts") that imposed heavy demands on the firm. For example, these customers would call at the last minute and make changes to their job specifications. As a result, employees would have to work overnight to complete the job—all at no extra charge to the customer. It was a badge of honour at MC to announce to colleagues the next day, "I was up all night working on the Jones project!" MC would simply swallow the additional incurred charges, just to keep the customer happy. Had

someone bothered doing the analysis, they would have noticed that the so-called "strategic customers" were actually losing the company money—they were high-cost-to-serve customers, but they were paying the same as everyone else.

MC could no longer keep up this arrangement. On the advice of a consultant, they segmented their customers into three groups, taking into account price paid by the customer and cost to serve the customer. Group A customers were high-cost-to-serve customers, but they also paid MC a high price. These were the true "strategic accounts." MC made sure they were served with their best salespeople. Group C customers, on the other hand, were the price shoppers; some of these customers were also the most demanding. MC dropped some of these customers and decided not to allocate face-to-face salespeople to the remaining customers. Instead, Group C customers would be served electronically (through MC's website and by telephone). As MC got its costs in line with the price paid by customers, its profits began to climb.[26]

The lesson is clear: a business must match its services to customer needs. Wells Fargo understands this concept—private banking services are a highly customized product.

continues...

Wells Fargo matches cost to serve its customers with price received.

Chapter Summary

1. **Learn why price is a *key* marketing decision you will have to make.**

   Your price is a barometer—it tells you whether or not you have been successful in your branding strategies. *The* best way to improve your profitability is to get your pricing strategy right. A 1% improvement in price results in an 11% improvement in operating profit.

2. **Learn why the majority of firms, in spite of knowing how critical the pricing decision is, set their prices too low, sapping their company of untold profits.**

   Many managers take a seat-of-the-pants approach to pricing. They begin thinking about what price to charge for their good or service *after* it has been designed. They do not take a systematic and disciplined approach to pricing. Moreover, they let costs *drive* the pricing decision, instead of focusing on the value their offering is creating in the marketplace. Finally, a blind chase after market share makes them sacrifice price.

3. **Learn the right and wrong way to make pricing decisions.**

   The internal (myopic) approach to pricing ignores customer needs. Instead, the firm starts with the product and its costs, assigns a price to the offering, and then goes to the marketplace seeking ways to convince customers to buy its product. The external approach to pricing starts with customers and their needs. Based on this, the firm assigns a price to the value created by its offering. It *then* examines its cost to ensure it is receiving the right margins.

4. **Learn a pricing process to confidently make pricing decisions and avoid mistakes made by your competitors.**

   The six-step pricing process starts with segmenting customers based on their needs and the value created by the product. The next step is to assign a price to the value creation. The initial price is then adjusted based on firm costs, short-term tactics, and marketplace factors. The price impact on overall marketing strategy is assessed before launching the pricing strategy. Securing a price improvement does not always refer to a price increase. Therefore, smart firms examine transaction prices—the actual price paid by a customer. This is done to avoid typical price leakages in an organization. Finally, each customer group is analyzed to assess cost-to-serve, to ensure that the price paid by customers is commensurate with the value they are receiving.

1. A central message in this chapter is that a business succeeds when its prices match the value it creates for customers (lululemon is a good example). This is known as value-based pricing. Provide two other examples of firms, one business-to-consumer firm and one business-to-business firm, that successfully practise value-based pricing. In each case, state the customer segment the company is targeting, the value it provides, and the pricing strategy being pursued.

2. We have said that pricing concepts apply equally well to nonprofit organizations. Based on your research, profile one nonprofit organization you believe clearly embodies the strategies and tactics outlined in this chapter.

3. What is meant by pocket price? Why do different companies have differently shaped price bands?

4. Sarah Finley, owner and manager of Sweet Tooth Temptations, a small retailer of homemade chocolate truffles, would like you to answer these questions based on the information provided.

   Her annual fixed costs are $25 000. She pays a chocolate maker $30 000 in salary. Her variable costs are $0.25 to make a chocolate truffle, which retails for $0.75.

   a. Calculate her current break-even volume.

   b. If her fixed costs go down by 1%, how much profit improvement will she see (if price and sales units remain the same at the break-even point)?

   c. Increasing sales volume by 1% over break-even point, while keeping costs and prices constant, will see what improvement in profit?

   d. What is the percentage change in break-even volume required if price is increased by 10%?

RUNNING CASE

ARBOL INDUSTRIES DEVELOPS SMART PRICING STRATEGIES

As we saw in the last chapter, Arbol Industries has been successful in building a brand in a marketplace typically dominated by commodity products. In this case, we will see how, using the concepts from this chapter, they designed pricing strategies to take advantage of their bold branding strategies.

Arbol segmented their customers into these groups:

- lumber and plywood customers: home builders, industrial users, and repair and remodelling customers
- paper customers: residential customers and business customers

They developed profiles of each customer group based on their perceptions of value created by Arbol products.

There are two types of home builders: builders of tract homes (non-custom homes) and builders of custom homes. Tract home builders are price-sensitive because they cannot charge price premiums over their competitors. Custom home builders, on the other hand, are price-insensitive because their customers demand homes built to exacting specifications, and they are willing to pay for the customization. Industrial customers are the most price-sensitive group, as the end products they make (stakes to grow grape vines and wooden pallets) do not add much value to their customers. Repair and remodelling customers tend to be price-insensitive; they want the best materials for their projects.

Residential consumers of paper tend to buy the cheapest paper. On the other hand, business customers tend to be price-insensitive

depending on the final product they are going to create: they buy cheaper paper for photocopy machines, but more expensive paper for creating documents for board members.

Based on these customer profiles, Arbol developed pricing strategies to appeal to each group. This is shown in Table 6.9.

Once the initial prices were set, Arbol adjusted the prices based on its knowledge of customer perceptions, competitor reactions, cost, and other factors. Arbol managers knew they were taking a risk because competitors could undercut their prices in an effort to gain market share. But this is a risk Arbol was willing to take based on the marketing strategy they wished to pursue in the industry—they wanted to break out of the "commodity" mentality that had plagued this industry for decades.

Case Assignment

One of the key points we have made in this book is that there is no such a thing as a commodity; anything can and should be differentiated. Arbol Industries clearly exemplifies such thinking. Based on research, profile another business in a different "commodity" industry. Show how they have used the pricing process outlined in this chapter to (1) segment their customer base and (2) arrive at pricing strategies aimed at different segments.

TABLE 6.9 Arbol Matches Its Pricing Strategies with an Accurate Understanding of Customer Needs

	Tract home builder	Custom home builder	Industrial customer	Repair and remodelling customer	Residential paper customer	Business paper customer
Products offered	Basic lumber and plywood	■ Pre-assembled doors and windows based on custom specifications ■ Consulting services	Basic lumber and plywood	Lumber and plywood bundled with tools, nails, glue, etc., for projects (e.g., building a deck)	Cheapest grade paper	■ Heavier, brighter paper for sharper text and graphics ■ Sold under HP and Xerox brand names
Pricing strategy	Charge prices based on commodity index	■ Premium pricing strategy ■ Prices charged are 15% higher than commodity index prices	Charge prices based on commodity index	Bundled offering priced 25% over competitor products	Charge based on competitor prices	Priced 20–50% over competitor products

SUGGESTED READINGS
If You Want to Learn More about Confidently Setting Prices, Read These Publications

Michael V. Marn, Eric V. Roegner, and Craig C. Zawada, "The Power of Pricing," *The McKinsey Quarterly*, 2003, Issue 1, pp. 26–39.

Thomas K. Nagle and Reed K. Holden, *The Strategy and Tactics of Pricing* (Upper Saddle River, NJ: Prentice Hall, 2002).

NOTES

1. Laura Bogomolny, "Toned and Ready—Lululemon Transitions," *Canadian Business*, April 24–May 7, 2006.

2. The material in this section, along with the Vlasic and Nike examples, is from Leonard M. Lodish and Carl F. Mela, "If Brands Are Built over Years, Why Are They Managed over Quarters?" *Harvard Business Review*, July–August 2007, pp. 104–112.

3. Another example, as related to the author, concerns Coca-Cola and a famous grocery chain. Coca-Cola refused to agree to shelf space reductions and price concessions being demanded by the chain. In retaliation, the chain ordered Coke off its shelves. The standoff lasted six months. The end result was the same as with the Nike example—the retail chain, confronted with irate customers, asked Coca-Cola to come back.

4. Michael V. Marn, Eric V. Roegner, and Craig C. Zawada, "Pricing New Products," *The McKinsey Quarterly*, 2003, Issue 3, pp. 40–49.

5. Michael V. Marn, Eric V. Roegner, and Craig C. Zawada, "The Power of Pricing," *The McKinsey Quarterly*, 2003, Issue 1, pp. 26–39.

6. Robert Meyer, John Walsh, and Rajeev Tyagi, "Intuitive Dynamic Pricing under Demand Uncertainty," *Marketing Science Conference*, St. Louis, Mo., March 1993. Cited in *Harvard Business Review*, March/April 1994, Vol. 72, Issue 2, p. 11.

7. *ibid*.

8. Michael V. Marn, Eric V. Roegner, and Craig C. Zawada, *The Price Advantage* (Hoboken, NJ: John Wiley & Sons, 2004).

9. In my consulting work I encounter this situation frequently. I find firms want to become bigger by gorging on customers (gaining market share), without a clear idea of why they want to pursue such a path. I call this strategy "not knowing what you want to be when you grow up."

10. Mark Burton and Steve Haggett, "Rocket Plan," *Marketing Management*, September/October 2007, pp. 32–38.

11. cirquedusoleil.com

12. John Rockwell, "The Soleil Never Sets," *The New York Times*, May 5, 2006.

13. Adapted from Burton and Haggett, *ibid*, and Robert J. Dolan, "How Do You Know When the Price Is Right?" *Harvard Business Review*, September–October 1995, pp. 174–183.

14. Company name is disguised. I worked on this example with an ex-MBA student of mine.

15. Robert J. Dolan, *ibid*.

16. Material adapted from Ajay K. Sirsi, *Marketing Led—Sales Driven: How Successful Businesses Use the Power of Marketing Plans and Sales Execution to Win in the Marketplace* (Victoria, BC: Trafford Press, 2005).

17. The example shown here is only a sample. Please refer to Chapter 3 for more detail on segmentation efforts.

18. Thomas K. Nagle and Reed K. Holden, *The Strategy and Tactics of Pricing* (Upper Saddle River, NJ: Prentice Hall, 2002).

19. Example provided by Burton and Haggett, *ibid*.

20. This material and example is taken from Nagle and Holden, *ibid*.

21. Robin Cooper and W. Bruce Chew, "Control Tomorrow's Costs Through Today's Designs," *Harvard Business Review*, January–February 1996, pp. 88–97.

22. Ikea.com website.

23. Lisa Margonelli, "How IKEA Designs Its Sexy Price Tags," *Business 2.0*, October 2002, Vol. 3, Issue 10, p. 106.

24. Marn, Roegner and Zawada, "The Power of Pricing," *ibid*.

25. This example was provided in Chapter 3 and is based on a consulting project I did a few years ago. The name of the company has been disguised.

26. Many of my clients who have undertaken such an exercise have seen their revenues drop, but have enjoyed dramatic improvements in profits.

CHAPTER
Channel Strategies

CHAPTER INTRODUCTION

In this chapter you will

Throughout this book, we have emphasized that winning companies balance two seemingly contradictory philosophies. On the one hand, they know they have to be market oriented—they have to think about customer needs when making decisions. But on the other hand, they also know that in many cases they have to "lead" customers to make the right decision. Left on their own, customers may choose a path that increases a company's costs of doing business. But sometimes, leading customers down a certain path can have unanticipated and unintended consequences. Let us illustrate with an example.

In the 1970s, banks introduced bank machines as an alternate distribution channel to give customers more control over their money and to reduce their cost to serve the customer (the customer did not have to go to a high-cost channel—a bank teller—to withdraw money or make a deposit). Later, banks got into online banking for the same reasons—to steer customers to a lower-cost channel to reduce the cost to serve the customer. However, these developments have had the unintended effect of actually *raising* the cost to serve the customer because customers make many more transactions than they used to.[1]

This discussion succinctly illustrates the importance of this chapter: companies have to think carefully about guiding customers to the right channels to boost revenues, while keeping their cost to serve customers in check. If a business can achieve these twin goals, it can substantially improve its profitability and success.

But determining the right mix of channels is not an easy task. For example, under what circumstances does it make sense to use the internet to reach customers? (Companies mistakenly believe that the internet, given its low cost, is *always* a great channel to reach customers.) When should a company send out salespeople to meet customers face to face versus serving customers with in-house salespeople? Should a company open retail stores to serve customers? How should it treat its suppliers? These are some tough questions every business must grapple with. As we have seen, wrong decisions about channel strategy can have severe negative consequences.

1. Learn how to use channel strategies to attract and keep customers.

2. Learn how to use channel strategies to build advantage over your competitors.

3. Learn how to use channel strategies to leverage brand strategies.

4. Appreciate the negative consequences of making wrong channel decisions.

5. Learn a step-by-step process that will help you to design the right channel strategy for your good or service.

Too much of a good thing is wonderful.

MAE WEST

I disagree with Ms. West; in my world we have too much and it is not good. There is an explosion of customer segments, products, channels, and media. Just when I am under severe pressure to improve the return on marketing expenditures, I no longer know how to serve my customers in a cost-effective fashion.

PRESENT-DAY MARKETING MANAGER

The dilemma faced by the present-day marketing manager is real. The explosion in customer segments, products, channels, and media has made marketing more complex, more costly, and less effective.[2] Fortunately for the marketing strategist, help is at hand.

As we will see in this chapter, thinking about the right channel strategy is key to business success, even if your business has a weakness in other areas of marketing strategy. The astute reader will observe that channel strategies have been discussed in other parts of this book as well. For example, in Chapter 3 we saw how a business has to rethink segmentation to succeed in the emarketplace. This is because rules that apply in conventional markets do not necessarily apply on the internet. In Chapters 10 and 11, we will see how smart companies satisfy customers and build a customer-focused company by getting very close to their customers. They do this by inserting themselves into their customers' network of suppliers and customers, a concept called **supply chain**, which will be discussed later in this chapter.

Thinking about Channel Strategy Is Important

OBJECTIVE 1

KEYPOINT

You cannot think about channel strategies in this chapter alone. Channel strategies impact *every* aspect of a business.

Channels Help a Business Attract and Keep Customers

When marketing was a young discipline, marketing writers were concerned about the right channels to use to move agricultural commodities from the farm to the marketplace.[3] Essentially, they were concerned about how to move *goods* from manufacturer to consumer.[4] This emphasis on understanding the role of channels to move *goods* made perfect sense in the early days, as the *service* economy was not yet on the horizon. Unfortunately, that bias still exists in marketing today, although services are a major part of the economies of most countries.

Although moving goods from manufacturer to consumer is still an important role played by channels, we will see in this chapter that channels move services as well. And finally, we will see that the most important thing channels move is *information*. Successful businesses use information to attract and keep customers. They recognize that the movement of goods and services is tangential.

CHAPTER CHALLENGE 7.1

ARE YOU ON THE RIGHT TRACK?

What does it mean to say that "the prime purpose of a channel is to effectively deliver the customer value proposition"?
(*Were you on the right track? Check your answers in Appendix 2.*)

7.1 ZARA

Objective: Winning Organizations Use the Movement of Information in Their Channels to Attract and Keep Customers

Zara, a division of Spain's Inditex Group, is a popular fashion retailer with stores in 68 countries. In Canada, Zara has stores in Vancouver, Edmonton, Calgary, Toronto, and Montreal.

Zara has a severe disadvantage compared to other specialty retailers: it has higher production costs and lower prices, a recipe for disaster. But Zara is very successful. Its gross margins are 55% greater and it has sales of approximately 20% more units per square foot than its competitors. Also, it sells around 80% of its products at full price.[5]

How does Zara do it? It uses the flow of information in its channels to attract and keep its customers. Zara divides its clothes into three categories. "Classic" garments change infrequently, "Fashion" clothes change seasonally, and "Trend" clothes change rapidly in response to rapidly changing styles. This last category of clothes may only stay in the store for a few weeks and accounts for half of Zara's volumes. Therefore, Zara divides its clothing lines according to how fast styles and consumer tastes change.

Zara has developed its channel strategy to support its customer strategy. "Classic" garments are made by low-cost suppliers in Sri Lanka or Malaysia. These suppliers are given designs, specifications, and ample lead times. "Fashion" clothes are made by Zara's own factories or vendors in Europe. Because "fashion" clothes change each season, it makes sense to have suppliers close by. "Trend" clothes are made in Zara's high-speed factories or by vendor partners.

For the "fashion" and "trend" lines, Zara has kept its production cycle very short and *very* responsive to market information flowing through its channels. Its retail stores gather information on which products customers try on, what they ask for, problems they have with clothes (for example, zippers that do not work properly), and what products customers ultimately buy.

Information from the retail stores is sent to designers, its own manufacturing facilities, and a small set of closely managed suppliers. Because it strategically uses up-to-date customer information and shares this information with its supply network (this is called a supply chain, a concept we will examine in more detail later in the chapter), Zara is able to overcome higher production and distribution costs by charging full price for its products and avoiding markdowns.

Zara uses channel information to attract and keep customers.

OBJECTIVE 2

The prime purpose of a channel is to effectively deliver the customer value proposition.

Channels Can Be Used to Build Advantage over Your Competitors

By properly understanding customer needs and channel dynamics, a business can build a significant competitive advantage. While still in college, Michael Dell started a computer company built on a simple idea—he would bypass the dealer network and sell computers directly to customers. In 2007, Dell Inc. had sales of $57 billion and a net income of $2.7 billion.[6] Michael Dell, who dropped out of college to run his company full time, has a personal net worth of around $17 billion.

Even Michael Dell could not have envisioned the revolution in channels he unleashed in 1984. Here is how Dell has positioned itself to be the most successful computer manufacturer in the world:

■ Traditionally, Dell has sold all its products to consumers or corporate customers using a direct-sales model via the telephone or the internet.

■ Dell only builds the product after it receives an order from the customer. This enables it to customize each order, keep records on customer needs, and stay ahead of its competitors by knowing customer trends in advance.

■ The direct channel model enables Dell to maintain a negative cash conversion cycle. This means that Dell receives payment for products before it has to pay its suppliers for materials.

■ The direct channel model allows Dell to practice just-in-time (JIT) inventory management. While competitors have to keep computer parts in inventory (thereby sinking part of their costs in keeping inventory), Dell only orders parts as needed, thus keeping its inventory costs at a minimum.

■ JIT inventory management provides an added benefit—as customer needs change, Dell can introduce new models faster than its competitors, who have to first deplete their inventory (or sell it at a reduced price).

■ Dell has taken an old (and outdated) channel concept called **vertical integration** and turned it on its head. Michael Dell calls this **virtual integration**.[7] Virtual integration works by providing accurate, up-to-the-minute *information* to channel partners so they all work in a synchronized way to serve the customer. Because Dell has direct access to its customers, it has information on their needs and trends. This enables it to forecast with some degree of accuracy what products it is going to make. It shares this information with suppliers (for example, manufacturers of chips or panels) and logistics partners (for example, UPS).

Virtual integration means you basically stitch together a business with partners that are treated as if they are inside the company.

MICHAEL DELL

■ Dell's competitors have tried to imitate Dell, but without success. This is because their current channel members will not allow a model that bypasses them to serve the customer directly. This is called **channel conflict** and will be explored in more detail later in this chapter.[8]

Channels Can Be Used to Compensate for Weaknesses in the Marketing Mix

How do you compete when your rivals are bigger than you are and have larger resources (such as advertising budgets) than you do? Answer: you look to your channels. Papa John's International, a pizza chain, trails its bigger rivals Pizza Hut and Domino's. As a result, it has had to be very creative in its approach. Papa John's relies on channels of distribution to overcome weaknesses in its marketing mix.

In 2001, Papa John's was the first of the three to introduce online ordering. Its competitors did not offer this service until five years later. Recently, Papa John's has trumped its rivals by introducing another innovation in its channels—text messaging to order pizzas.[9] This is how it works. Consumers first create an account online where they can save as many as four different "favourite" orders that include any combination of pizza, sides, and drinks; delivery address or takeout information; and payment type.

When hunger pangs strike, a customer can simply tap in FAV1, FAV2, FAV3, or FAV4. The consumer only pays standard text messaging fees. Papa John's has not only given its customers greater choice in ordering, but it has also opened up a new channel to present customers with promotional offers such as coupons or updates on new menu items.

> *We are smaller. We have to be more nimble.*
>
> JIM ENSIGN, VP OF MARKETING COMMUNICATIONS, PAPA JOHN'S

Papa John's may be smaller than its rivals, but it uses channels to be a clever competitor.

Channel Strategies Help Leverage Branding Strategies

OBJECTIVE 3

Channels Can Be Used to Differentiate a Brand

How do you compete against a rival who has the strongest brand in your product category? Smart use of channels may provide the answer. Let us take an example to illustrate. Nokia, based in Espoo, Finland, is taking on Apple's iPhone, not by making changes to its **core**

Nokia is relying on channel strategies to differentiate its brand.

Pascal Guyot/AFP/Getty Images

Devices alone are not enough anymore, consumers want a complete experience.

OLLI-PEKKA KALLASVUO,
CEO, NOKIA

product, but by focusing on the **potential product** (these concepts were discussed in Chapter 5). It is differentiating its brand by using channels of distribution in creative ways.

Nokia wants to capitalize on a marketplace trend—the lines between companies making phones, computers, music players, digital cameras, and other gadgets are blurring.

However, other companies that have tried to capitalize on this trend have failed. For example, Britain's Vodafone Group, the world's largest global service provider, spent $38 billion on third-generation mobile licences, hoping that consumers would use mobile networks to download music. But only 15% of its 206 million subscribers has used its Vodafone Live! content portal.[10] Most Europeans "sideload" music to phones from their computers, instead of "downloading" music directly from the airways.

Nokia believes it can succeed where others have failed. It has bought Loudeye, a rival to Apple iTunes, and it has acquired navigation software maker gate5 and media-sharing site Twango. With these purchases, it hopes to help users of the 200 million music-capable Nokia mobile phones already on the market to download music and swap photos and videos. It has a big advantage over the Apple iPhone—users can download music to their phones anywhere, whereas iPhone users need a Wi-Fi hotspot to perform the same task. This should make mobile phone network operators like Vodafone, Orange, and smaller operators very happy.

KEYPOINT

Nokia's strategy is clever because it makes mobile phone network operators its channel partners.

CHAPTER CHALLENGE 7.2

ARE YOU ON THE RIGHT TRACK?

What do well-designed channels move? (Hint: you should be able to answer this question in one word.)

(*Were you on the right track? Check your answers in Appendix 2.*)

Channels Can Be Used to Build Brand Loyalty

The alert reader will have recognized that well-designed channels primarily move, not goods or services, but *information*. Earlier we saw how the flow of information plays a crucial role in Zara's strategic success. Zara, through its stores, collects information on customer needs, trends, likes, and dislikes. This information is shared with its supplier partners (manufacturers of clothes and suppliers to those manufacturers). Zara's supplier partners make clothes that customers will like and, through Zara's retail stores, the clothes reach the customer. This flow of information from customer to suppliers (and back again to customers) is called a **supply chain**. Let us examine this topic in more detail.

KEYPOINT

Well-designed channels primarily move, not goods or services, but information.

7.2 SATURN

Objective: Supply Chain Strategy Can Be Used to Build Customer Loyalty

In the mid-1980s, GM was building a different kind of car company, named Saturn, to compete against Japanese car manufacturers. The Saturn brand was created based on the concept of a better car, not as defined by an engineer, but as defined by the customer. Instead of competing against the Japanese on a car's quality, Saturn not only offers customers a quality car, but also provides a different experience at the retailer (this is the name Saturn gives its car dealers). It is widely known how customers are treated during the car buying process. Unlike at other dealers, their experience at a Saturn dealer is a pleasant one. Customers do not haggle over the price, there are no high-pressure sales tactics, and the salesperson is there to help customers make a choice and to facilitate the transaction.

However, what is not widely known is what happens *after* the car is bought. At most dealers, when a customer brings a car in for repair (either following an accident, for maintenance, or for breakdowns), the customer has to leave the car for a few days. The length of delay depends on the availability of parts. Typically, the dealer has to order the part from the manufacturer. Saturn, on the other hand, scores the highest marks among car brands for fixing a car quickly and correctly the first time.[11] Saturn knows that customers do not like waiting more than a day to get their cars back. Wisely, it has secured tremendous brand loyalty based on the customer's experience at the retail level.

Saturn succeeds because it has given careful thought to its supply chain strategy. Its secret lies in developing a service supply chain strategy based on its customers' needs. And it uses its channel partners to execute the strategy.

Here is Saturn's recipe for supply chain design:

1. Start with an accurate understanding of customer needs. Saturn knows that vehicle owners do not want to wait more than a day to get their cars repaired. Saturn aims for same-day car repairs, except for major repairs and bodywork jobs.

2. Make channel members your partners in success.

   a. Each Saturn dealer is given a region. There are no other dealers in that region, so retailers can focus on the brand instead of competing with other dealers through discounting the brand.

   b. Saturn knows that retailers (dealers) want vehicle owners to come to the dealership to get their cars repaired. But vehicle owners often do not go back to the dealership once the car has been purchased. Because Saturn's supply chain strategy ensures that dealers have the necessary parts, car owners know their cars will be fixed in less time. As a result, Saturn leads the industry in number of repairs performed at the dealership.[12]

   c. Saturn's supply chain strategy is depicted in Figure 7.1. It is designed to enable retailers to win. Saturn ensures this by helping retailers fix cars as quickly as possible. This, in turn, creates brand loyalty, which drives sales of new cars. Further, retailers can modify or reject Saturn's recommendations on what parts to carry. If a part does not get sold in nine months, Saturn takes the part back and compensates the retailer.

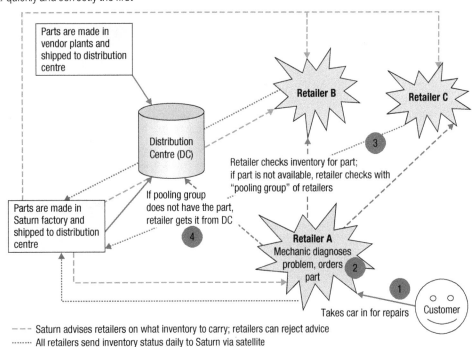

FIGURE 7.1

Saturn's supply chain strategy builds customer loyalty.

The author discusses the brilliance of Saturn's supply chain strategy in more detail.

CHAPTER CHALLENGE 7.3

ARE YOU ON THE RIGHT TRACK?

Define the potential product being sold by Saturn.
(*Were you on the right track? Check your answers in Appendix 2.*)

Where We've Been

- We have seen why thinking carefully about channel strategy is so important to business success.
- Well-designed channels attract, satisfy, and keep customers by effectively delivering the customer value proposition.

Where We're Going

- We will see the negative consequences that accrue to a business if it fails to think carefully about its channel strategy.

CHECKPOINT

OBJECTIVE 4

What Happens If a Business Fails to Think Carefully about Channel Strategy?

Poor Channel Decisions Will Cost Dearly

The cost of going to market (the combined cost of sales and marketing expenses across all channels) is often a company's single largest expense. This is shown in Table 7.1. This cost is usually larger than a company's research and development budget, and is sometimes

TABLE 7.1	**Channel Costs Are a Major Expense for Any Business**	
Sales	$1 000 000	
[minus] Cost of goods sold	300 000	Raw material costs to actually produce goods
[equals] Gross profit	700 000	
Operating Expenses		
Selling, General and Administrative (SG&A)	300 000	These are *channel* costs associated with sales, marketing and administrative overhead.
Research and development (R&D)	70 000	
Other expenses	50 000	
Total Operating Expenses	420 000	SG&A + R&D + Other expenses
Operating profit	280 000	Operating profit = gross profit − total operating expenses
Taxes	60 000	
Net profit	220 000	Net profit = operating profit − taxes

larger than the total cost of making all products combined. It can consume over 40% of total revenues, and rarely consumes less than 15% to 20%.[13]

As can be seen in Table 7.1, channel costs are 30% of sales ($300 000 ÷ $1 000 000). A mistake made in selecting the proper channel strategy can cost a company a lot of money.

Poor Channel Decisions Will Result in Lost Market Share and Profits

If you do not understand your customer's needs, you will suffer the consequences. As can be seen in Figure 7.2, there is a mismatch between a priority customer's channel preferences and Company X's channel strategy. As a result, the company has lost market share to competitors, who have more closely aligned their channel mix with the customer's needs. Competitor C, especially, has gained market share in comparison to the others.

A similar situation has occurred in another industry.[14] The corporate housing industry was established to satisfy a customer need. Corporate employees who were assigned to a project in a city different from their own had no choice but to stay in a hotel for the duration of the project—anywhere from a few weeks to a few months. Employees do not like staying in a hotel for this length of time: they want to live in a space they can customize and where they can cook their own meals. The corporate housing industry satisfies this need by providing temporary accommodations that range from simple apartments to fully furnished living spaces, complete with maid services.

The corporate housing industry had a great channel strategy—they sold directly to corporate customers. However, they did not treat their customers well; they overcharged for a bad offering. The end result? A new channel member, the broker, has inserted itself between the corporate housing provider and the corporate customer. Many major real estate firms, for example, have a brokerage service. What is the broker's promise to the corporate customer? "We are unbiased. We look after *your* best interests by searching for the

Pay attention to customer preferences

Disguised example of industrial company

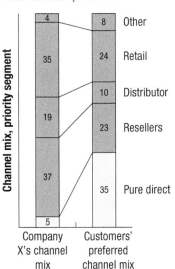
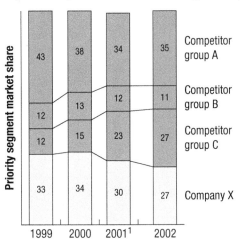

FIGURE 7.2

Mismatch between customer needs and channel strategy results in lost market share.

Source: Exhibit 1 from Joseph B. Myers, Andrew D. Pickersgill and Evan S. Van Metre, "Steering Customers to the Right Channels," *The McKinsey Quarterly*, 2004, No. 4, pp. 37–47.

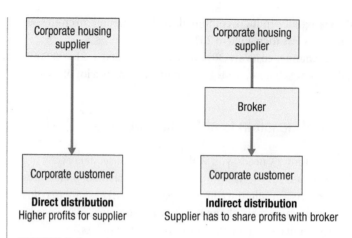

FIGURE 7.3

Failure to treat customers properly results in lost profits.

best deal possible among competing corporate housing suppliers." This new arrangement is shown in Figure 7.3.

Poor Channel Decisions Will Result in Wasted Effort

KEYPOINT

Low-cost channels may appear attractive, but they may not be the right choice for a business.

Tom, a business consultant, could not believe his good luck! He had just received a letter from a database company that offered to sell him, for only $149, a CD containing the names and email addresses of thousands of CEOs across the country. Tom was struggling to break into the consulting business, and this was just the opportunity he was looking for! He could send an email to thousands of prospective customers, sit back, and wait for business to come in.

Of course, the astute reader will have recognized the fatal flaw in Tom's reasoning. Corporate customers who need consulting services do not respond to email solicitations. Instead, they rely on such channels as word of mouth. Tom should save the $149; he is going to need it!

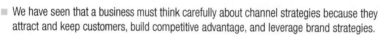

Where We've Been

■ We have seen that a business must think carefully about channel strategies because they attract and keep customers, build competitive advantage, and leverage brand strategies.

■ Poorly conceived channel decisions result in wasted effort and loss of market share and profits.

CHECKPOINT

Where We're Going

■ We will examine a step-by-step process to make smart channel decisions.

OBJECTIVE 5

How to Pick the Right Channels for Your Business

Before we examine a step-by-step process to help you pick the right channels for your business, let us address an issue that is perhaps brewing in your mind. If channel decisions are so important, why not simply add more channels to serve the customer? After all, research has shown that customers with access to multiple channels spend, on average, 20% to 30% more than customers with access to a single channel.[15] Therefore, it would appear that to make money, a company should add more channels to serve the customer.

In reality, this is not the case. Multi-channel marketing is much harder than it appears. Also, adding more channels may actually decrease a company's profits by increasing the cost to serve the customer. We saw at the beginning of this chapter that in some industries (for example, retail banking), adding more channels has increased the cost to serve the customer, as customers make more transactions.

Once a company adds channels, it becomes very hard to reduce the number of channels because customers become used to the new channels. Removing channels will lead to dissatisfied customers. *An organization is much better off not offering the additional channels in the first place.* It is for this reason that a business should use a methodical process to arrive at channel decisions. Let us take an example before examining the process to design channels.

ING is a Dutch financial services company that pioneered online banking. It has succeeded because of its focus on one channel and the fact that it was the first organization to offer such a channel option to customers. ING also owns an insurance company called Belair. It tried to duplicate its success in online banking by launching a similar product called belairdirect—an online insurance provider.

Interestingly, it has found that while customers will bank online, they prefer to buy insurance through a traditional channel—the insurance broker. Accordingly, it provides two channel options for insurance customers, online and brokers.[16] ING is smart—it bases channel decisions on customer needs, a topic we turn to next.

KEYPOINT

By adding more channels, a business sets up customer expectations. Reducing the number of channels leads to customer dissatisfaction.

KEYPOINT

Having more channels *does not* mean more sales.

A Step-by-Step Process to Determine the Right Channels for Your Business

A step-by-step process to make effective channel decisions is shown in Figure 7.4.

Effective Channel Decisions Step #1: Define Realistic Channel Range   Very few businesses take a strategic approach to channel design. Rather, managers spend the majority of their time focusing on low-cost channels. As we have seen in this chapter, low-cost channels may not always be the most appropriate given customer needs and product category.

The first step in channel design is to realistically define a set of channels. To do this, use the grid shown in Table 7.2, where a set of channels for a financial planning firm is developed. After doing the analysis, four channels are identified as realistically possible: internet, direct mail, brokers, and retail stores. Although telesales (telephone sales) is a good fit

When choosing distribution channels, companies need to rely on design principles that are aligned with their overall competitive strategy and performance objectives.

ANDERSON, DAY, AND RANGAN

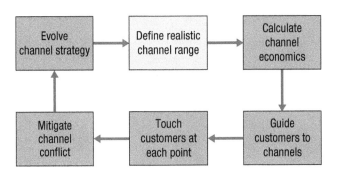

FIGURE 7.4

A step-by-step process to design channel strategy.

Keshia Khan, Marketing Manager of G&K Services, talks about the challenges involved in considering a new direct-to-customer channel.

TABLE 7.2   Defining a Realistic Channel Set: Financial Planning Firm

All possible channels	Will customers use the channel?	Is channel a good fit with our product?	Will channel impact our brand positively?	Is channel a good fit with our overall strategy?
Internet	Yes. Traditionally, customers have not used the internet to buy financial planning services. But this is changing as more firms develop an internet presence and consumers become more familiar with this channel.	Yes	Yes	Yes. Our strategy is to give customers financial advice "packages" while keeping our cost to serve low.
Direct mail	Yes	Yes	Yes	Yes
Telesales	Yes	Yes	No. There is a negative association with telesales in the minds of customers.	No. We want to maintain the image of a prestige brand. Telesales will not fit our strategy.
Field sales	No. Field sales are not appropriate for this product category.	No. Field sales are more appropriate for products with high revenue per transaction.	Yes	No. This is a very high-cost channel.
Brokers	Yes	Yes	Yes	Yes
Distributors	No	No. This is not an appropriate channel for this product category.	No	No
Retail stores	Yes	Yes	Yes	Yes

with the product and certain customer segments may use it, this channel is rejected because it will impact the brand negatively and it is not a good fit with the firm's overall strategy.

Effective Channel Decisions Step #2: Calculate Channel Economics   Once a realistic set of channels is identified based on customer needs, product characteristics, and firm strategy, the next step is to calculate **channel economics** (Figure 7.5), which consists of examining channel profitability and the channel's capacity for generating sales.[18] The computations necessary for determining channel economics are shown in Table 7.3 for a hypothetical firm operating in a business-to-business environment.

If we only looked at cost per transaction, field sales would be the least attractive option (at $1000 per transaction), while the internet would be the most attractive channel (at only $10 per transaction). But looking at only the *cost* side of channel economics would be misleading; we have to consider *revenues* generated by the channel as well. To do this,

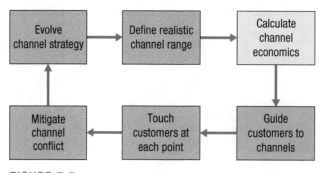

FIGURE 7.5

Channel Decisions Step #2: Calculate channel economics.

TABLE 7.3   Calculating Channel Economics

	Field sales	Telesales	Retail store	Internet
Yearly channel expenses (a)	$1 000 000 (salaries and commissions)	$500 000 (salaries and commissions)	$150 000 (salaries, retail operating costs)	$50 000 (ecommerce start-up, operating costs)
Number of transactions performed per year by channel (b)	1000	5000	1000	5000
Cost per transaction (a ÷ b)	$1000	$100	$150	$10
Total sales generated by channel	$7 000 000	$2 000 000	$750 000	$100 000
Channel profitability = expense/revenue (E/R)	14%	25%	20%	50%
Channel sales capacity	$14 000 000	$3 750 000	$950 000	$150 000
Expense/capacity (E/C)	7%	13%	16%	33%

E/R = yearly channel expenses ÷ total sales generated by channel
E/C = yearly channel expenses ÷ channel sales capacity

we calculate channel profitability, which is measured by the E/R ratio (expense divided by revenue). As can be seen from Table 7.3, field sales is the most profitable channel, with an E/R ratio of only 14%. The internet, on the other hand, is not a very profitable channel, with an E/R ratio of 50%.

Although channel profitability is a compelling statistic, it does not paint the complete picture. Another figure we have to examine is the channel's capacity for generating sales. In Table 7.3 we see that although the sales force (field sales) is currently generating $7 000 000 in sales, it is actually capable of generating $14 000 000 in sales a year.

The sales force is not operating at its full capacity, perhaps because sales professionals need more training, better demonstration kits, and so forth. If we compute another ratio (E/C), total channel expenses divided by channel capacity, field sales is at 7% (for every $1 in revenue generated, this channel option costs $0.07). While the internet continues to be the least profitable channel (E/C ratio of 33%), telesales looks more attractive than retail, with an E/C ratio of 13%.

Once you have identified a group of acceptable channels and completed the channel profitability calculations, there are two broad approaches that can be taken to make the final selection of channels. The first approach is to choose the channel with the highest profitability (field sales in the example in Table 7.3). The second approach is to choose a group of channels. This latter approach has two advantages. First, it gives the customer a choice. Second, it allows a company to evolve its channel strategies over time (discussed further in Step #6). Such flexibility may be important in taking advantage of changing customer preferences and market conditions.

KEYPOINT

To calculate channel economics, examine channel profitability and the channel's capacity for generating sales.

Effective Channel Decisions Step #3: Guide Customer to Channels   Once a company opens up a suite of channels to customers, it must *proactively* steer the right customer to the right channel (Figure 7.6). This is because customers have different preferences for different channels as they move through the purchase process. A failure to understand customer preferences may result in mismatching channels with customer needs. Inevitably, such mismatching means that the company is either under-serving or over-serving customers. The end result? Wasted resources and lost profits. To steer the right customers to the right channels, a company should match the purchase process with customer needs and channel fit. This is shown in Figure 7.7.

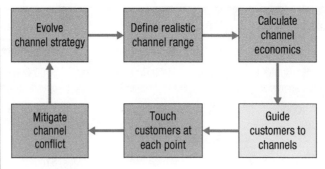

FIGURE 7.6

Channel Decisions Step #3: Guide customers to channels.

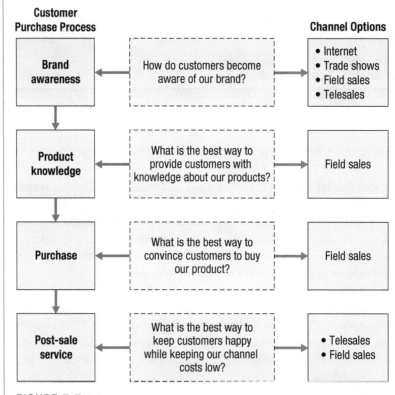

FIGURE 7.7

Match the purchase process with customer needs and channel fit.

A typical customer goes through four steps in the purchase process: brand awareness, product knowledge, purchase, and post-sale service (we will have more to say about this in the next chapter on marketing communications, as well as in Chapter 9 on translating marketing strategy into sales action). Although the company can use a high-cost channel such as field sales to build brand awareness, this may be a waste of resources. So the decision is made to build brand awareness using lower-cost channels such as the internet and tradeshows. However, the company may feel that customers need a lot of hand holding and reassurance during the product knowledge and purchase stages of the buying process. Therefore, the decision to use field sales is made.

Finally, even though the customer can be serviced after the sale by field sales and telesales channels, the decision is made to serve the customer using telesales. This is because the company feels that customers will be quite comfortable with the telesales channel. Besides, the telesales channel is more than up to the task of not only serving customers, but also cross-selling other products offered by the company.

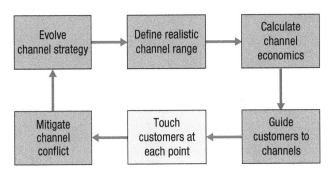

FIGURE 7.8

Channel Decisions Step #4: Touch customers at each point.

Effective Channel Decisions Step #4: Touch Customers at Each Point There is one major problem associated with offering customers a choice of channels—left to their own devices, customers will often choose a higher-cost channel, mainly due to habit. For example, customers will choose to do transactions with a bank teller, rather than visit the internet. Or customers will choose to check in at the airline counter, rather than choose the self-serve option. There are many things a company can do to simultaneously provide high-quality service while migrating customers to the right channel (Figure 7.8).

Migrating Customers to the Right Channel Option 1: Provide Customer Incentives and Disincentives This option is the proverbial "carrot-and-stick" approach. Customers are given discounts if they use preferred channels such as the internet. For example, ING, the Dutch online bank, offers customers a higher savings rate and does not charge fees for services (such as withdrawals) traditionally imposed by other banks. Their famous slogan is "Save your money."

Or customers are "punished" for using higher-cost channels. You can certainly conduct a bank transaction face to face with a bank teller. But you will have to wait in a long line. This is because the bank has only two tellers serving customers. Of course, you can always go to the internet (or the bank machine) and conduct the same transaction in a fraction of the time.

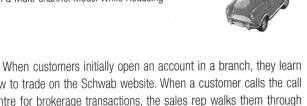

7.3 CHARLES SCHWAB

Objective: How to Maintain a Multi-channel Model While Reducing the Cost of Providing It

Schwab's investors open around 70% of all new accounts in Charles Schwab branches.[19] Schwab wants affluent investors to continue to use these branches, as these customers want advice and are more amenable to cross-selling efforts. So Schwab makes it easy for these customers to schedule appointments at branches. But customers who want to manage their own investments are of low value to Schwab *if* they are served in branches. So the company makes it easy for these customers to do business via the internet or a Schwab call centre.

When customers initially open an account in a branch, they learn how to trade on the Schwab website. When a customer calls the call centre for brokerage transactions, the sales rep walks them through the transaction over the internet. Schwab continues to use its branches to *acquire* customers, but uses other channels to *keep* them. For example, investor education seminars are often held at third-party locations.

 continues...

Schwab touches its customers at every point.

Migrating Customers to the Right Channel Option 2: Make It Easy for Customers During channel migration, customers initially require a lot of hand holding. Companies that make it easy for customers to switch channels reap the dual benefits of channel migration and customer satisfaction. Many airlines have introduced self-serve check-in counters, where customers can not only obtain a boarding pass, but tag their bags as well. At most major airports airline personnel are at hand, ready to guide customers step by step through the check-in process.[20]

Customers using a lower-cost channel

Migrating Customers to the Right Channel Option 3: Provide a Safety Net When an organization begins to move customers from one channel to another, confusion, uncertainty, and doubt are not just customer reactions. The organization's sales force and its channel partners face the same fears as well. These need to be managed. W.W. Grainger (Marketing Drives Success 7.4) illustrates this brilliantly.

Effective Channel Decisions Step #5: Mitigate Channel Conflict   Formulating channel strategy often results in conflict among channel members. Specialized toy retailers such as Toys "R" Us were dismayed and angry to learn that toy companies like Mattel were supplying the same toys to Wal-Mart, which was selling the items at a cheaper price. To compete more effectively, Toys "R" Us closed some stores and launched related product lines. It now owns Toys "R" Us Toy Box (toy stores operating within supermarkets in the United States, Hong Kong, and Singapore), Babies "R" Us (clothing, toys, furniture, and accessories for babies), Kids "R" Us (children's clothing), Bikes "R" Us (bike stores located within Toys "R" Us, operating only in the United Kingdom), and Imaginarium (retail stores focused on learning toys).

MARKETING DRIVES SUCCESS

7.4 W. W. GRAINGER

Objective: Channel Partners and the Sales Force Need Hand Holding During Changes in Channel Strategy

W. W. Grainger, Inc. is a leading supplier of facilities maintenance products in North America. It supplies over 800 000 products in such categories as tools, test instruments, fasteners, materials handling, and safety products to other business customers. Grainger serves 1.8 million customers through a network of 425 branches, 18 distribution centres, and multiple websites. The company is best known for its huge 3700-page catalogue of products for sale, also available on CD and on the web.

When Grainger wanted to shift its customers from its face-to-face sales force to a web-based ordering system, it knew it would have to proceed carefully.[21] Its sales force visited customers to show them how to order parts over the internet, thus ensuring a high degree of customer satisfaction while reducing its channel costs. Grainger knew there could be a backlash from its sales force, as commissions were being taken away because of the channel migration. So it revamped its sales compensation structure to ensure that sales professionals would get commissions for all sales in their territory, regardless of channel.

Now the sales force spends its time on higher-value activities such as prospecting for customers, keeping customers satisfied, and building customer loyalty. The new compensation structure ensures that sales professionals associated with the web-based channel pass on information and leads to the face-to-face sales channel. Without an equitable compensation structure, there is a tendency for one part of an organization to hoard information, resulting in internal competition for control over the customer.

Grainger differentiates itself from competitors who are burdened with high-cost sales forces and underused websites.

> *The supply chain is a company's circulation system, you have to fix it to keep the blood flowing.*
>
> JORGEN VIG KNUDSTORP,
> CEO, LEGO GROUP

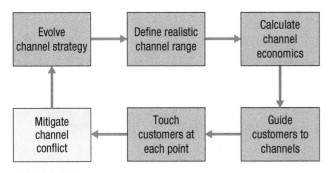

FIGURE 7.9

Channel Decisions Step #5: Mitigate channel conflict.

Mitigating channel conflict should form an important part of any channel strategy (Figure 7.9). Fortunately, with careful thought, channel conflict can be not only mitigated but also eliminated. Here are some examples.

Sony sells the same item (say a DVD player) through multiple channels such as club stores (for example, Costco), department stores, specialty electronics retailers, Sony stores, and the internet. How does it ensure that there is no channel conflict? Or how does it ensure that consumers do not browse for items in a high-cost channel (such as the Sony store) and then buy the same items for less on the internet? Simple. Sony makes it hard for the consumer to comparison shop by tweaking features on each item, depending on which channel it is sold in. So one channel will have one feature, while another channel will have a different feature. In this way, the different channels are not really competing for the "same" product, thus reducing channel conflict.[22]

Draeger Canada is owned by Drägerwerk AG of Germany, a supplier of medical and safety equipment. Its core channel is a dealer network. While dealers have several advantages, a crucial disadvantage with dealers is that they represent many manufacturers. Thus, Draeger's products could potentially get lost among competitor products. To bypass this problem, Draeger has its own sales force that calls on customers. But here is the brilliant part of its channel strategy—while the sales force builds **brand awareness**, provides product knowledge, and develops customer relationships, customers still have to buy the product from a dealer, thus avoiding channel conflict. Draeger has designed a win-win situation. It gets the advantages of a dealer network (wide distribution coverage) while avoiding the disadvantages.

Effective Channel Decisions Step #6: Evolve Channel Strategy   As we have stressed throughout this book, a firm's marketing strategy, or go-to-market approach, has to be dynamic. It has to change with changing customer needs and market conditions. Channel strategies are no exception (Figure 7.10). Let us take an example.

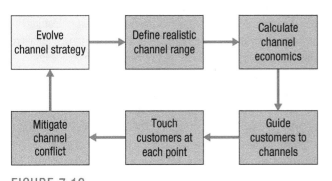

FIGURE 7.10

Channel Decisions Step #6: Evolve channel strategy.

CHAPTER CHALLENGE 7.4

ARE YOU ON THE RIGHT TRACK?

In your own words, provide a definition of supply chain. (*Were you on the right track? Check your answers in Appendix 2.*)

7.5 LEGO

Objective: An Organization Has to Make Changes to Its Channel Strategy over Time or Risk Failure

Although on the surface the Lego Group of Denmark did not appear to be in trouble, in reality it was. Lego sales are over €1 billion a year. The world's children spend 5 billion hours a year playing with Lego bricks.[23] Older children play with Mindstorms, a line of do-it-yourself robot kits.

In spite of this outward success, Lego's financial picture told the real story. The company had lost money four out of seven years from 1998 to 2004. Sales dropped 30% in 2003 and 10% in 2004, when its profit margin stood at −30%. Lego Group executives estimated that the company was destroying €250 000 in value *every day.*[24]

Lego executives realized that while they had been busy trying to halt the red ink by focusing on the brand, innovation, and product quality—traditional Lego strengths—the world of channels had changed. But Lego's channel strategy had not kept pace with the changing environment. Lego's supply chain was at least 10 years old, and it was not geared for a world in which big companies like Wal-Mart and Carrefour dominated the retail scene. The focus on brand, innovation, and product quality did nothing to stop the losses, so they decided to revamp their channel strategy. They believed that a focus on channel strategy would energize the entire company and bring it to profitability.

The CEO and his team approached the supply chain problem holistically. They analyzed their product development, sourcing, manufacturing, and distribution process. They found that not only had their products become more complex, but they were also delivering less and less profit. Essentially, Lego's famous product designers were designing new products without regard to cost of production. For example, a designer might need a specially coloured resin for a new product. But the resin was only sold in three-tonne lots. The designer would buy the entire amount, use only few kilograms of it, and the company would be stuck with €10 000 worth of material it would never use.

The team found that the Lego Group was dealing with over 11 000 suppliers—nearly twice as many as Boeing uses to build its airplanes! This "supplier creep" had happened over a period of years as each product designer, lacking centralized procurement procedures, built up a network of ad hoc relationships with vendors. Finally, the team found that the company paid as much attention to the thousands of stores that together generated only one-third of its revenue as it did to the 200 larger stores that accounted for the other two-thirds. Sixty-seven percent of all orders from smaller retailers were for less than one carton—an incredibly labour-intensive and expensive proposition to fulfill.

One of the first channel challenges the Lego Group tackled was the resin issue. By halving the number of colours used on toy figures, they

The Lego brand is famous all over the world.

cut their resin costs in half and managed to shrink their supplier base by 80%. A process was put in place to help designers regarding creation of new colours, shapes, and requirements for ordering raw materials. Designers were taught that having more raw material is not necessarily the best way to produce innovative products. Rather, limited raw material forced designers to be more creative in using existing material.

The final step was to treat big retailers differently from the smaller ones. Lego began working closely with bigger retailers to conduct joint forecasting, inventory management, and product customization. This enabled the production group to coordinate production schedules on a cycle; previously, without proper forecasts, production was an ad hoc (and expensive) affair. Lego decided to continue dealing with smaller retailers, but only on regular and standardized terms. It reduced its costs to serve these customers by providing discounts for early orders and halting the practice of shipping less than full cartons.

Lego's channel strategy has paid off handsomely. It has saved €50 million since 2004. In 2005 it recorded its first profit—€61 million—since 2002. Profits in 2006 (latest figures available from Lego's website) were 2.4 times the profit in the previous year! Most importantly, the supply chain transformation is a tonic to the corporation, enabling it to become a more innovative and creative competitor.

A quote from CEO Knudstorp aptly summarizes Lego's effort: "I think one of the big mistakes companies often make in this kind of initiative is approaching the supply chain as one topic, innovation as another, product quality as a third. The better way to think about it is that all these issues are connected. Innovation is also a supply chain issue, and sometimes the supply chain can provide ideas for consumer- or customer-driven innovation."

Chapter Summary

1. Learn how to use channel strategies to attract and keep customers.

Smart businesses like Zara recognize that channels are not just used to move goods and services from producer to consumer. First and foremost, a well-designed channel moves and shares information about customer needs and trends. This information can be strategically used to satisfy customer needs. This, in turn, helps to attract and keep customers.

2. Learn how to use channel strategies to build advantage over your competitors.

A business secures advantage over its competitors when it does not merely imitate them, but does something different in the marketplace. A frequently overlooked aspect of business is channel strategy. Companies like Dell and Schwab succeed because they use unique channels to satisfy their customers. Over time, channel uniqueness has given them additional advantages over their competitors such as better information about their customers, the ability to let customers customize the interaction with the company, the ability to predict trends in the marketplace, and lower-cost channels to serve customers.

3. Learn how to use channel strategies to leverage brand strategies.

Channel strategies can help a business focus on the potential product. In this way, the business can differentiate its brand. Nokia is aiming to do this with its channel strategy of providing music, video, and other content to its customers. Saturn is also focusing on the potential product by using channel strategies to build customer loyalty.

4. Appreciate the negative consequences of making wrong channel decisions.

Among all the expenses incurred by a business, channel costs can comprise up to 40% of sales. Therefore, wrong channel decisions will cost you dearly. Making the right channel decisions not only helps a business save money, but also enhances customer satisfaction. A channel strategy that is out of alignment with customer needs will result in lost profits, market share, and wasted effort.

5. Learn a step-by-step process that will help you to design the right channel strategy for your good or service.

The six-step process starts with identifying a possible set of channels based on fit with customer needs, brand, product category, and firm strategy. The next step is to calculate channel profitability for each potential channel. A business can choose to select the lowest-cost channels or, preferably, a group of profitable channels that can serve customers. The next step is to steer customers to the right channels by thinking about the customer purchase process.

Because customers tend to choose high-cost channels if they are left on their own, a business should provide the right incentives and disincentives to migrate customers to the right channels and provide them with support during the migration. Channel conflict can be mitigated or eliminated by being sensitive to the needs of channel partners. The final step is to revisit the channel strategy to ensure its currency in an ever-changing marketplace.

CRITICAL THINKING QUESTIONS

1. In what way has the "explosion" in customer segments, products, channels, and media made marketing more complex and more costly for today's marketing strategist? Provide a concrete example to illustrate your point.

2. We said that you cannot think of channel strategies in the chapter on channels alone. Rather, channel strategy impacts every aspect of a business. Explain this by providing a concrete example.

3. Provide an example of a business that is using channel strategies to attract and keep customers. Provide another example of a business that is using channel strategies to differentiate its brand. In each case, explain how the business is using channel strategies to accomplish its objective.

4. Many high-end brands (such as Armani) have evolved their channel strategies and are now selling their goods on the web. Do you think this is a good idea? Explain why or why not.

5. Define a realistic set of channels for (a) a company selling expensive watches, (b) a business consulting firm, and (c) a company selling janitorial products to other businesses. Use the example in Table 7.2 on page 156 as a guide.

RUNNING CASE

ARBOL INDUSTRIES EVOLVES ITS SUPPLY CHAIN

Just like the Lego Group, Arbol Industries reexamined its supply chain with a view to finding some cost savings. What it found instead was a way to re-energize a sleepy company. Arbol's supply chain for one of its products, plywood, is shown in Figure 7.11.

Arbol Industries leases millions of acres of forest land, typically from the government. A contractor is awarded the job of sourcing and cutting trees, and delivering them to Arbol plywood manufacturing plants. At these plants, the trees are sorted according to their quality of fibre, the trees are stripped of bark and other materials (a process called dressing), and they are cut into required lengths. The cut pieces are transported to another part of the plant where the plywood is manufactured.

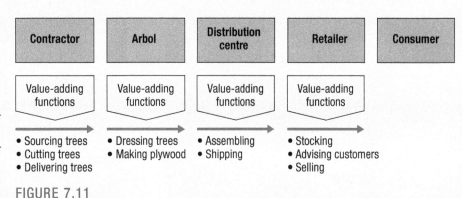

FIGURE 7.11

Arbol Industries' value chain

The finished plywood, along with other products, is shipped to the Distribution Centre, from where trucks carry products to such retailers as Home Depot. The retailer displays the product, advises customers, and sells the product.

This sequence, from raw material to sale, is known to you as a *supply chain*. However, when we examine the value added to the product at each stage (for example, the contractor adds value by sourcing and delivering the proper trees; Arbol adds value by making plywood; the retailer adds value by displaying the product), the supply chain concept is known by the term **value chain**. Thus, a value chain *is* a supply chain, but its emphasis is on examining how value is created (or destroyed) by a channel member.

Many manufacturers mistakenly see themselves as solo, static businesses, islands unto themselves. They do not realize that a business is really a network of interconnected, value-adding functions, whose primary purpose is to serve the needs of the end customer. Looking at value chains enables a business to get out of this silo mentality and build relationships with its channel partners to enhance the value-adding functions. This is exactly what happened at Arbol.

Initially, management undertook an evaluation of its supply chain to examine product flows. A routine investigation at a large retailer revealed the following: consumers of plywood are ignorant about different grades of plywood; they mistakenly believe plywood is a commodity. Therefore, when they buy plywood they tend to purchase the cheapest possible offering. While this discovery was disconcerting enough, Arbol discovered another startling fact—the retailer's sales personnel were also ignorant about different grades of

plywood. This ignorance naturally prevented them from giving consumers the best advice, thus hurting the retailer's brand and its sales.

To solve this problem, Arbol undertook a national program at the retailer to educate its sales personnel on plywood, how to tell different grades of plywood from one another, and proper applications of plywood, all with the intention of creating further value to the end consumer as well as the retailer. The program was a hit! The retailer reported higher sales and happier customers. This initial success led to other programs. Arbol Industries and the retailer started working even closer together, jointly forecasting sales, inventory management, and new product innovations.

But the supply chain evolution did not stop there. Arbol decided to look in the other direction of the supply chain as well. It noticed that once the contractor supplied raw trees to a manufacturing plant, the trees had to be sorted by fibre grade and then scheduled for production. This process consumed a lot of time and money. Just as Arbol worked closely with the retailer, it began working closely with its supplier as well. It did this by making its supplier a partner in its production process. Contractors now presource trees by grade at the forest level. Trees arrive at the manufacturing facility presorted, ready for production.

Just like the Lego Group, Arbol Industries achieved a strategy transformation by examining and evolving its channel of distribution.

Case Assignment

Draw a supply chain for a greeting card company (for example, Hallmark, American Greetings, or Carlton Cards). Next, using the concept of a value chain, specify the value created by each player in the network. Will another channel (ecards) affect this supply chain positively or negatively? Be specific in your answer.

SUGGESTED READINGS

For Brilliant Insight into Channel Strategy, Customer Focus, Market Segmentation, and Business Innovation, Do Not Miss These Publications

Joan Magretta, "The Power of Virtual Integration," *Harvard Business Review*, March–April 1998, pp. 73–84.

Keith Oliver, Edouard Samakh, and Peter Heckmann, "Rebuilding Lego, Brick by Brick," *Strategy + Business*, Autumn 2007, pp. 58–67.

NOTES

1. Joseph B. Myers, Andrew D. Pickersgill and Evan S. Van Metre, "Steering Customers to the Right Channels," *The McKinsey Quarterly*, 2004, No. 4, pp. 37–47.

2. David C. Court, "A New Model for Marketing," *The McKinsey Quarterly*, 2004, No. 4, pp. 4–5.

3. See for example, Louis Dwight and Harvell Weld, *The Marketing of Farm Products* (New York: Macmillan, 1926), pp. 1–23.

4. See for example, Arch Shaw, "Some Problems in Market Distribution," *Quarterly Journal of Economics*, Vol. 26, August 1912, pp. 706–765.

5. Rich Kauffeld, Johan Sauer, and Sara Bergson, "Partners at the Point of Sale," *Strategy + Business*, Autumn 2007, pp. 46–57.

6. Form 10-k, Dell Inc., U.S. Securities and Exchange Commission.

7. Joan Magretta, "The Power of Virtual Integration," *Harvard Business Review*, March–April 1998, pp. 73–84.

8. Current channel members such as dealers could sue manufacturers if they tried to bypass them and go directly to the customer. A similar fate has befallen North American auto manufacturers, who cannot delete bloated product lines for fear of retaliation from channel members (car dealers).

9. Emily Steel and Suzanne Vranica, "Tapping in Your Papa John's Pizza Order," *The Wall Street Journal*, November 13, 2007, p. B4.

10. Jennifer L. Schenker, "Nokia Aims Way beyond Handsets," *BusinessWeek*, September 10, 2007, p. 38.

11. Morris A. Cohen, Carl Cull, Hau L. Lee, and Don Willen, "Saturn's Supply Chain Innovation: High Value in After-Sales Service," *MIT Sloan Management Review*, Summer 2000, pp. 93–101.

12. Morris Cohen, *ibid.*

13. Lawrence G. Friedman and Timothy R. Furey, "The Bottom Line: The Economics of Channel Selection," *Direct Marketing*, Vol. 62, No. 7, November 1999, pp. 54–61.

14. This example was given to me by a client in the corporate housing industry.

15. Myers, et al., *ibid.*

16. This fact was provided to me by an ex-student who works for belairdirect.

17. Attributable to Friedman and Furey, *ibid.*

18. This section is adapted from material in Friedman and Furey, *ibid.*

19. This example is based on material in Myers et al., *ibid.*

20. I remember when airlines introduced kiosks to obtain boarding passes. I never used them because of habit. One day, as I was waiting in line to check in, an airline staff member took me out of the line and walked me through the self-serve process. It was simple! It saved me time! Since then, I have always used the kiosks to obtain my boarding pass.

21. Myers et al., *ibid.*

22. This example was given to me by the General Manager of Sony Canada.

23. Lego website, www.lego.com

24. This example is based on Keith Oliver, Edouard Samakh, and Peter Heckmann, "Rebuilding Lego, Brick by Brick," *Strategy + Business*, Autumn 2007, pp. 58–67.

CHAPTER 8

Marketing Communications Strategies

CHECKPOINT

Where We've Been

- We have seen that winning companies deeply understand customer needs and choose which customer segments they want to serve (they know they cannot possibly satisfy all needs).

- They differentiate their offering from their competitors by thinking carefully about branding strategies.

- They realize the full profit potential of each customer by employing the right pricing strategies.

- They spend a lot of time crafting and evolving their channel strategies.

Where We're Going

- This chapter will focus on marketing communications strategies.

Sasahara/Associated Press

CHAPTER INTRODUCTION

In this chapter you will

Life was simple for a marketer until about 1985. At that time, by placing one ad on the major television networks, you could reach 80% of your customer base. Today, you would have to develop 20 messaging and media programs to get the same reach.[1] Also, the ad would have to run on 100 TV channels to achieve the same effect! Sending the right message to the right person in the right way and at the right time is getting to be a very difficult, but crucially important, task for marketers.

What has caused this situation? For one thing, markets have atomized into countless market segments driven by demographic factors and product preferences. At the same time, consumption of TV and newspapers—darling media of mass marketers—has been steadily declining since the 1970s. Replacing them is the proliferation of digital and wireless communication channels across millions of websites, cellphones, personal digital assistants, video game consoles, and computer terminals. Add to this mix the thousands of specialty magazines and cable TV and radio channels, and the conditions are ripe for targeted, not mass, communication.

> *Monolithic blocks of eyeballs are gone. In their place is a perpetually shifting mosaic of audience microsegments that forces marketers to play an endless game of audience hide-and-seek.*
>
> ERIC SCHMITT,
> FORRESTER RESEARCH INC.

It may appear to you that the days of mass marketing were better than the current reality of micromarketing because a marketer's job was a lot easier. This may be true, but the good news is that the new reality creates many more opportunities. Companies who master the secrets of the new marketing communications landscape will be much more successful than their competitors who do not adjust to the new paradigm.

1. Be primed for success by learning about the realities of the new marketing communications paradigm.

2. Learn valuable lessons on how to successfully get your message across to *any* target customer.

3. Learn a step-by-step process to develop winning marketing communications strategies.

4. Learn metrics to measure your marketing communications efforts to help you get the most out of your budget.

5. Learn how to take advantage of social media to reach your target customers successfully and with minimal cost.

OBJECTIVE 1

To Be Successful, a Business Must Learn the Realities of the New Marketing Communications Paradigm

Companies who have mastered the complexities of the new marketing communications paradigm have been very successful. Let us take an example.

MARKETING DRIVES SUCCESS

8.1 PROCTER & GAMBLE (P&G)

Objective: Success Derives from a Mass- to Micromarketing Shift

No brand represents mass marketing as much as P&G's Tide. It is the quintessential one-size-fits-all product. Right? Wrong. P&G, the company that put the "mass" in mass marketing, is shifting emphasis from selling to the mass market to selling to millions of particular consumers. Tide, its best-selling laundry detergent, has been extended into a family of 14 finely differentiated products, each appealing to a different market segment.

Even though P&G has cut its spending on TV commercials for Tide by nearly 16%, Tide advertising has become even more targeted—for example, with more allocation for Chinese, Italian, and Punjabi customers in Canada and Latino customers in the United States. The advertisement shown, for example, is targeted at those customers concerned about saving energy and the environment. P&G spends about 10% of its sales on advertising, about the same as in 1998, but its unit sales growth is three times as much.[2] This shows that P&G is more successful today in leveraging its marketing communications. It has achieved this by learning, adapting, and using the new marketing communications landscape to its advantage.

Every one of our brands is targeted.

JAMES R. STENGEL, P&G

P&G has taken the "mass" out of mass marketing by targeting its brands.

TABLE 8.1   The Changing Landscape of Marketing Communications

	Old	New
Target	Customers were the main target	Multiple audiences are the target now: customers, employees, suppliers, competitors, society, government, media
Customer needs	Passive; accepted what they were given	Active; customers control and shape content and dissemination of the message using such means as the internet
Needs	To fit in	To stand out from the crowd; they want customized messages
Media choice	Major networks, magazines	Virtually unlimited media choice due to the internet, specialty channels, and print media
Ads	Designed to appeal to a broad audience	Targeted to narrow market segments
Brands	Big, mass-marketed brands such as Coca-Cola and Tide	Niche brands, mass customization
Communication	Fragmented	Integrated marketing communications
Objectives	Short-term promotions	Long-term brand health
Metrics	None or traditional metrics such as reach and frequency	Sophisticated metrics such as brand equity

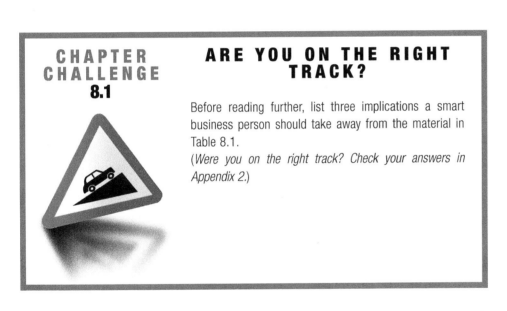

CHAPTER CHALLENGE 8.1

ARE YOU ON THE RIGHT TRACK?

Before reading further, list three implications a smart business person should take away from the material in Table 8.1.

(*Were you on the right track? Check your answers in Appendix 2.*)

The Old and the New of Marketing Communications

If you want to succeed in the new world of marketing communications, you have to first learn what makes it tick. The old and new paradigms are contrasted in Table 8.1.[3]

To succeed in the new world of marketing communications, you need to heed these important points:

1. Customers can no longer be the only target. Rather, the aim of marketing communications should be to build relationships with customers, employees, suppliers, society, government, and the media.

2. Customers want messages that are targeted at them. They will not respond to messages that are geared to a mass audience. The percentage of mass-marketed ads actively ignored on television ranges from 4.8% for beer to 45% for fast food.[4]

3. Customers have the power to create and distribute content, thanks to software packages that let users manipulate images, the internet, and social networking outlets such as MySpace and Facebook. The implications for a brand are serious—take charge of your brand's identity or someone else will. (The chances are, someone already has.)

4. There are many tools available to the marketing communications strategist. Each tool has its strengths and weaknesses. The best way to select the right combination of tools is to use a method called **integrated marketing communications** (IMC), a technique that will be described later in this chapter.

5. Marketing communications strategies should be designed to build long-term brand health, not short-term gains.

6. Measure the **return on investment** (ROI) of marketing communications expenditures by using the right metrics.

Where We've Been

■ We have learned about the new realities of the marketing communications landscape.

CHECKPOINT

Where We're Going

■ We will learn the secrets of how to create a "sticky" message.

OBJECTIVE 2

How to Communicate Anything to Anyone, Anytime

The model in Figure 8.1 shows you how to communicate any idea to anyone at any time. Let us examine the lessons it offers.

Start with the Message You Intend to Communicate

Often, a company will want to communicate an idea to a target audience (customers or employees). "Maximize shareholder value," "We provide superior customer service," and

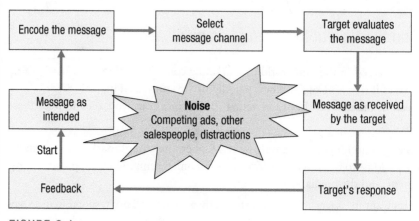

FIGURE 8.1

How to communicate anything to anyone, anytime

8.2 FEDEX

MARKETING DRIVES SUCCESS

Objective: Stories Are a Great Way to Get a Message Across

Researcher Chip Heath provides an example of an employee at FedEx, who could not open one of his pickup boxes on his route because he had forgotten the key back at the office.[5] His deadline was tight and he knew if he went back to the office for the key, the packages in the box would miss the plane. He used a wrench to unbolt the box from its foundation and took it back to the office, where he knew he could open it. This is the kind of behaviour a company that bases its competitive advantage on absolute reliability wants from its employees.

Telling this story to other employees and customers is a far better way to package the message than telling them to "Maximize shareholder value" or "Provide superior customer service." In fact, research has shown that our brains are hard-wired to better understand a message through stories, rather than reams of data.

Telling stories is a far better way to package a message.

"We listen to customer needs" are examples of messages that a company may want to communicate. The problem is, communication is successful *only* when the target believes you; that is, the message as received by the target equals the message as intended. Therefore, statements like "Maximize shareholder value" are quite meaningless to customers or employees, as they are vague and do not resonate with them.

Encode the Message

Once the intended message has been developed, conduct research on the target audience to understand their needs and the frames of reference they will use to evaluate your message. Without an accurate understanding of what your message will be up against, you are setting yourself up for failure. Let us take an example.

The marketing vice-president of ABC Telephone Company wants to communicate to his customers that they are customer focused. So he inserts full-page advertisements in newspapers and magazines showing pictures of happy, smiling customers. Unfortunately, customers do not believe this message because, in *their* minds, ABC is a 150-year-old company that until recently was a monopoly, and it is complacent and does not care much for its customers' welfare.

For this reason, the intended message has to be properly "packaged" (psychologists use the term **encoding**, which basically means packaging) based on an understanding of the target audience's needs.

Encoding the message also refers to the *physical* package of the message as well. Smart Uniforms,[6] a supplier of uniforms and janitorial supplies to business customers, equipped their sales force with a suitcase containing miniatures of their entire product range (including uniforms, mops, and buckets). The intention was correct: to better communicate with customers by actually showing them products instead of merely describing them. The idea backfired because they used the wrong encoding mechanism. First, the suitcases were too heavy to carry. Second, sales professionals would not carry the suitcase, as they felt embarrassed to open it in front of their peers and customers.

> *When you inspire the accountants you know you're onto something.*
>
> CHIP HEATH ON CRAFTING A "STICKY" MESSAGE

Olsen sells high-end, European-designed clothing.

Deliver the Message Using the Right Channel

If the channel used to communicate the message is wrong, communication will fail. Let us take an example.[7] Olsen is a brand of high-end, European-designed clothing. The clothes are sold in high-end department stores and Olsen retail stores. One day, a store manager called her store clerks in for a meeting. "We need to advertise," she announced. "So we are going to advertise in buses and subway cars." A junior employee gingerly raised her hand. "But," she said, "our customers are well-to-do women—they probably do not ride buses or subways." To which the manager replied, "I know, but that is all we can afford."

Get Feedback

Once the message has been delivered, the target evaluates the message by filtering it through pre-existing filters in the brain. What remains is the message as received in the form of feelings, beliefs, and attitudes. Based on the message as received, the target responds accordingly. Therefore, the target may say, "I know you are a customer-focused company because you have been working hard on training your employees. So I believe in you and I want to continue being a customer of your company." Or, the target may say, "I do not believe you are a customer-focused company. You have been a monopoly for 150 years. You cannot teach an old dog new tricks, you know. I think I will switch phone companies."

Either way, you should get feedback on the effectiveness of your communication based on such sources as market research (we will discuss this later in the chapter), sales reports, employee feedback, and media reports. This feedback is critical because it should be used to make changes to your messaging strategy.

CHAPTER CHALLENGE 8.2

ARE YOU ON THE RIGHT TRACK?

Of course, the Olsen manager has chosen the wrong channel to communicate her message. But she has done something even worse. Do you know what that is?
(*Were you on the right track? Check your answers in Appendix 2.*)

CHAPTER CHALLENGE 8.3

ARE YOU ON THE RIGHT TRACK?

The target evaluates the message by subjecting it to pre-existing filters in the brain. Where do these filters come from?

(*Were you on the right track? Check your answers in Appendix 2.*)

If you want to create a "sticky" message, learn the key lessons from this section, which are summarized in Table 8.2.

TABLE 8.2   How to Communicate Anything to Anyone, Anytime: Key Lessons

■ To be truly effective, communication should be a continuous activity. Communicate, get feedback on the effectiveness of your communication, learn from your mistakes, and make changes to your communications. Unfortunately, most organizations miss this crucial point. They communicate sporadically with their target audiences.

■ Find the right encoding mechanism to suit the needs of your target.

■ Find the right message channel to suit the needs of your target market.

■ Measure your target's pre-existing filters (brand perceptions and associations) before you start communicating. You have to know your target's pre-existing biases. Without this, you are flying blind.

■ Measure the effectiveness of your communication efforts. Learn from your mistakes.

■ Remember, you are not alone in trying to win the attention of your target (e.g., customers). The target is distracted by competing messages. So keep your message, simple, to the point, and differentiated.

CHECKPOINT

Where We've Been

■ We have learned about the new realities of the marketing communications landscape.

■ To effectively communicate you have to heed the lessons offered by the communications model.

Where We're Going

■ We will learn a step-by-step process to create winning marketing communications strategies.

OBJECTIVE 3

A Step-by-Step Process for Designing Winning Marketing Communications Strategies

Figure 8.2 depicts a step-by-step process to use in designing winning marketing communications.

Designing Winning Marketing Communications Strategies Step #1: Conduct Market Research

As we saw in the model of effective communications (Figure 8.1), without an accurate understanding of the needs and beliefs of the target audience, marketing communications efforts will fail. Therefore, the very first step is to conduct research on the target audience, brand, and competitors. Some research questions to be posed at this stage are as follows:

- What does the target audience already know about my brand and competing brands? Earlier, we called this a pre-existing filter (perceptions developed based on past usage, word-of-mouth communications, and associations) used by a customer in evaluating your message.

- What encoding mechanism will work best with the target audience?

- What channel will work the best in reaching this target?

- What "noise" is already out there that may distract the target from my message? Before reading further, complete Chapter Challenge 8.4.

Designing Winning Marketing Communications Strategies Step #2: Make Strategic Decisions

The output from Step #1 is used to make some strategic decisions regarding the marketing communications: What objectives do we want to achieve? What is the overall messaging strategy? What resources (budgets) do we have? How will we measure success?

If you do not carefully think about these issues, you will end up wasting precious resources. Here is an example.[8] ABC Telephone Company is celebrating its 150th year. The marketing function has proposed the following marketing communications to senior

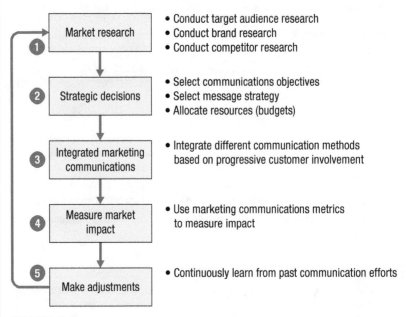

FIGURE 8.2

A disciplined process for developing winning marketing communications

CHAPTER CHALLENGE 8.4

ARE YOU ON THE RIGHT TRACK?

What does Campbell's know about its target customer, and how has it used this knowledge in its advertisement?

(*Were you on the right track? Check your answers in Appendix2.*)

Campbell's accurately understands the needs of its target customer.

management, shown in Table 8.3. Respond to Chapter Challenge 8.5 on page 180 before reading further.

Developing a Marketing Communications Budget: The Good, the Bad, the Ugly   In many organizations, a certain percentage of sales (say 5%) is devoted to marketing communications. This approach does not make any sense because marketing communications budgets should be based on what marketing communications strategy the business is trying to achieve (Step #2). Once a firm knows who the target audience is, what objectives it is trying to achieve,

---

TABLE 8.3   Memo

From: Kristine Lang, Marketing Manager
To: Senior Management, ABC Telephone Company
Subject: 150th anniversary celebrations

To celebrate ABC's 150th anniversary, we are pleased to announce the following year-long marketing communications:

January
Peach Perkins will be launching a three-day concert. Banners announcing our 150th anniversary will be on display during the entire three days. Our staff will attend the first night, along with their families. We will provide them with a drink ticket each.

March
Each week we will run full-page newspaper ads announcing our 150th anniversary and celebrations.

May
A light shaped in the number 150 will stay lit all year atop the stock exchange building.

July
At the Chamber of Commerce meetings, we will take turns making 20-minute presentations on our company and our achievements.

September
We will take a staff photo in front of the state legislature building. We can use this in our newspaper ads.

October
We will participate in TECH TOUCH WEEK, where we will have a booth, sponsor technology workshops, and have a career fair.

November
We will announce an education scholarship. We may have a luncheon where we will invite recipients of past awards of our corporate sponsorship efforts.

December
We will organize a scavenger hunt, co-sponsored with the Chamber of Commerce.

Total cost of marketing communications campaign: $250 000

CHAPTER CHALLENGE 8.5

ARE YOU ON THE RIGHT TRACK?

If you were the manager evaluating the marketing communications proposal in Table 8.3, what would you tell the employee who developed the proposal?

(*Were you on the right track? Check your answers in Appendix 2.*)

and what the messaging strategy is, it can develop a budget (see also Step #4 on page 184).

In reality, most managers cannot provide a good rationale for their marketing communications budgets. This frustrates the finance function (we will have more to say about return on investment on marketing expenditures in Chapter 12), which slashes the budget, provides marketing with a new budget, and asks them to meet sales targets nevertheless. This, in turn, frustrates the marketing function, which believes that finance has no right to interfere with marketing's "magic."

Designing Winning Marketing Communications Strategies Step #3: Use Integrated Marketing Communications

Rob Schmeichel of Farm Credit Canada discusses the marketing communications budget-setting process.

Once you have done the research and made some strategic decisions on communications, the next step is to use integrated marketing communications (IMC) to select a set of communication tools that will deliver the right message to your target market. There are five guiding principles behind IMC, and they are listed in Table 8.4.

Table 8.5 shows the different tools in the marketing communications tool box and their pros, cons, and uses.

Given that the marketing communications tool box contains so many different tools, how do you decide when to use what tool? The answer lies in the fact that as customers become progressively more involved with your brand, they need to be communicated to with different tools. We will first discuss the process of customer progression. This is shown in Figure 8.3 on page 182.

Every business would like to have satisfied and loyal customers. But before customers can become loyal, they go through a process of increasing involvement with the brand. All customers, at one point or another, are unaware of your brand. Once they become aware of the brand, customers must gain knowledge about it (features and benefits). Brand knowledge is a necessary, but not sufficient, step. This is because objective knowledge alone does not make customers want to try the brand; they must develop a liking and preference for it over the other brands they are considering. In other words, customers must develop an emotional connection with the brand.

Brand liking and preference leads to conviction that the brand is the best choice. This state of customer readiness, of course, leads to customers actually choosing your

TABLE 8.4	**Guiding Principles of Integrated Marketing Communications**
Guiding principle 1	There are many tools in the marketing communications tool box.
Guiding principle 2	Each tool has its uses, advantages, and disadvantages. An indiscriminate use of tools will result in waste of money.
Guiding principle 3	Customers move through a process to become progressively involved with your brand.
Guiding principle 4	Different communication tools should be used at each step of customer involvement.
Guiding principle 5	The end result should be a set of communication tools that support and enhance the overall brand message.

TABLE 8.5   Marketing Communications Tool Box

Tool	Pros	Cons	Uses
Advertising	■ Very useful for building brand awareness	■ Expensive ■ Hard to measure results (although new techniques are emerging; see next section)	■ Build brand awareness
Public relations	■ Credible ■ Cheap	■ Hard to measure results	■ Build brand awareness ■ Build positive brand associations
Promotions	■ Induces customers to try a product (example: coupons or offers)	■ Can devalue brand if used indiscriminately ■ Not suitable for all product categories	■ Build trial usage
Marketing collateral material	■ Helps build brand relevance and differentiate a brand (example: brochures)	■ Can get expensive	■ Support brand efforts ■ Support sales force efforts
Sales force	■ Is both a channel of distribution *and* a marketing communications tool ■ Builds direct relationships between customer and brand ■ Helps overcome customer resistance by building brand relevance and brand differentiation	■ Expensive	■ Overcome customer resistance ■ Build customer relationships ■ Generate revenue
Interactive tools	■ Helps build brand relevance and differentiate a brand (example: website)	■ Needs constant updating to avoid looking dated	■ Support overall brand strategies ■ Build brand relevance ■ Help differentiate a brand
Direct marketing	■ Builds brand awareness, relevance, and brand differentiation (example: direct customer solicitation through mail)	■ Expensive	■ Build customer relationships ■ Build brand relevance ■ Build brand differentiation
Event marketing and sponsorship	■ Builds brand awareness and relevance	■ Expensive ■ Hard to measure return on investment	■ Support overall corporate brand-building efforts ■ Support corporate sustainability efforts (community involvement, good corporate citizenship)
Trade shows	■ Builds brand awareness and relevance	■ Expensive	■ Build brand awareness ■ Generate new customer leads ■ Build brand relevance
Social media	■ Builds brand awareness and relevance (example: word of mouth, consumer networks like Facebook)	■ Hard to measure return on investment ■ Need to update constantly to avoid being outdated	■ Build positive brand image ■ Keep in touch with current market trends

brand. Customer usage of your brand leads them to evaluate it. At this stage, they are either satisfied with the brand and they continue toward becoming loyal customers, or they are dissatisfied with their brand experience and they switch brands. Loyal customers do not need to be made aware of your brand; they inherently have high levels of brand awareness.

Integrated Marketing Communications is Based on Customer Brand Involvement
How do we use the customer's progressive brand involvement to choose from an array of marketing communications tools? This is shown in Figure 8.4 on page 183. To fully appreciate the material in Figure 8.4, you must not forget that different marketing communications tools have different advantages, disadvantages, and uses (Table 8.5).

Customer brand involvement

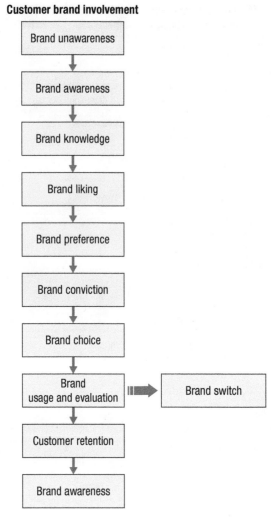

FIGURE 8.3

Customers become progressively more involved with a brand.

As we can see in Figure 8.4, tools such as advertising, public relations, direct marketing, and trade shows are excellent to build brand awareness. But as we have also seen, brand awareness is not enough; the customer has to progress to brand knowledge. This is where many companies make a mistake—they spend a lot of money building brand awareness by using expensive tools such as advertising, but they don't move the customer to the next stage of brand involvement. This is a mistake because, over time, as the effectiveness of advertising wears out, brand awareness falls. What do these companies do? You guessed it—they spend more money on advertising. This makes them addicted to expensive forms of marketing communications tools.

Instead, organizations must keep in mind their end goal—to develop a pool of loyal customers. Therefore, they should use such tools as their sales force, interactive tools (websites), marketing collateral materials (brochures), direct marketing methods (catalogues), and event marketing and sponsorships to build brand knowledge, liking, preference, and conviction. Promotional techniques (coupons and offers) are good ways to induce customers to try a brand. A company's sales force is also an excellent communication tool to break down customer resistance and get customers to try the brand.

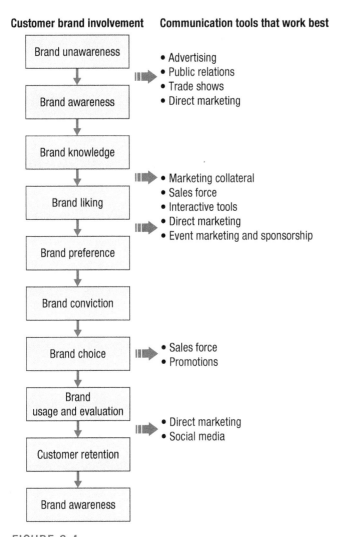

Customer brand involvement

- Brand unawareness
- Brand awareness
- Brand knowledge
- Brand liking
- Brand preference
- Brand conviction
- Brand choice
- Brand usage and evaluation
- Customer retention
- Brand awareness

Communication tools that work best

- Advertising
- Public relations
- Trade shows
- Direct marketing

- Marketing collateral
- Sales force
- Interactive tools
- Direct marketing
- Event marketing and sponsorship

- Sales force
- Promotions

- Direct marketing
- Social media

FIGURE 8.4

Different marketing communications tools are relevant at different stages of customer brand involvement.

At this stage, organizations tend to make another mistake—they ignore their customers once the sale is made. However, as we have seen, this is a crucial stage for customers, as they are evaluating their brand choice. Using such marketing communications as direct marketing and social media, a business can positively shape the customer's evaluation of the brand.

KEYPOINT

Customer defection is not an axiom. A business forces its customers to defect when it ignores them after the sale is made.

The author discusses how Goodyear successfully uses integrated marketing communications to position its brands.

Where We've Been

- We have learned that designing winning marketing communications strategies is a five-step process.
- We have examined the first three steps: conduct research, make strategic decisions, and use integrated marketing communications.

Where We're Going

- Step #4 will describe how to measure the impact of marketing communications.

CHECKPOINT

OBJECTIVE 4

KEYPOINT

Marketing strategists who do not bother measuring the return on marketing communications investment are simply being arrogant and are setting themselves, and the marketing function, up for failure.

Designing Winning Marketing Communications Strategies Step #4: Measure the Impact of Marketing Communications

As we saw in Figure 8.2, it is not enough to merely spend money on marketing communications. To be truly effective, a business must measure the impact of marketing communications, learn from successes and failures, and make adjustments to begin the next cycle of communications.

However, a survey of top executives in 2006 shows that only 57% of companies measure the impact of their marketing communications efforts. But as shown in Figure 8.5, the rewards for measuring the impact of marketing communications are substantial.

In the previous chapter on channels, we discussed how to measure the return on one marketing communications tool, the sales force. Metrics to measure the return on advertising are shown in Table 8.6.

Marketing communications metrics are important!

- In firms where there are metrics for marketing communications, there is a 13% dissatisfaction rate with marketing.
- In firms where there are no metrics, the dissatisfaction rate is 37%.
- 57% of companies measure the results of their marketing efforts.
- Companies that measured their marketing results increased their annual marketing budgets an average of 11.2% in 2004.
- Companies that did not measure marketing results decreased their budgets by 6%.

FIGURE 8.5

The rewards for measuring the impact of marketing communications are substantial.

Source: Compiled from information released by Blackfriars Communications Inc.

TABLE 8.6	**Advertising Metrics**
Content evaluation	■ Does the advertisement communicate the strategic objectives? ■ Does the advertisement reflect the positioning strategy of the brand (company)? ■ Will the advertisement resonate with the target market?
Advertising awareness	■ Can the target market recall the advertisement unaided?[1] ■ Can the target market recall the advertisement aided?[2]
Recall tests	Respondents are asked if they can recall specific points made in the advertisement: ■ What did the ad actually communicate? ■ What was the primary message in the ad? ■ What did the respondent like about the ad? ■ What did the respondent dislike about the ad? ■ What is the level of purchase intention (intention of becoming a customer of the brand)?
Business results	■ Sales increase ■ New customers attracted ■ Increased sales from current customers[3]

[1] In **unaided recall** of an advertisement, the respondent is asked if he or she recalls seeing an ad for a brand (company) by simply providing the respondent with the product category. For example, "Do you recall seeing an ad for an insurance company?"

[2] **Aided recall** of an advertisement is used when the respondent cannot recall using the unaided method. For example, "Do you recall seeing an ad for State Farm Insurance?" Of course, unaided recall is a more powerful indicator of advertisement effectiveness.

[3] Of course, it is hard to attribute increase in sales or new customers attracted purely to the advertising effort. However, if an organization sees positive business results each time it advertises, it can make the argument that the sales increase is due to the advertising efforts.

8.3 PROJECT APOLLO[9]

Objective: New Metrics for Old Media

When marketers buy ads on the web, they can track everything from the number of clicks an ad receives from a certain geographic area to how long a person watches a video clip on a website. This data helps decision makers objectively evaluate the impact of online advertising on sales. But evaluating the impact of TV advertising has always been a matter of guesswork or the establishment of **correlational** evidence, as discussed in Table 8.6. However, many ad research firms are hoping to change this with a new breed of metrics to measure the impact of advertising.

Arbitron, a radio-ratings firm, has been putting together a database it calls Project Apollo. A cellphone-sized Portable People Meter pings whenever a person carrying it is exposed to properly encoded radio or TV advertising, whether they are at home, in a bar, or at a friend's place. Combined with data provided by ACNielsen's Homescan program, in which participating households use a different device to scan their product purchases into a database, Project Apollo aims to link exposure to advertising with product purchases.

Project Apollo has shown that applying its data to ad campaigns can make them 40% cheaper. And analysis of one unidentified household product's TV ads showed that those seen by its lightest users proved so wasteful that, once product sales and manufacturing costs were factored in, the campaign lost $24 million on those ads.[10]

IAG Research, which uses online methods to measure how well TV viewers remember commercials, is adding questions about internet ads to its surveys. Toyota, for example, is trying to understand answers to such questions as "What is the optimal mix between TV and the internet?" and "Where are the synergies?"

IAG conducts online surveys with over two million consumers, who visit a website called RewardTV to answer questions about TV shows they watch. In the midst of the questions, IAG sprinkles in questions about the ads that appeared during the TV program. Participants earn points that they can redeem toward prizes, as well as the chance to win bigger prizes such as $10 000 or free gasoline for three years.

Event marketing includes both small and large events such as sponsorship of industry events, trade shows, and VIP events. The case of Arbol Industries at the end of this chapter offers valuable lessons on how to measure the impact of this important marketing communications tool.

Finally, it is very hard to directly measure the impact of community involvement activities such as sponsorships of community events (for example, CIBC sponsors Run for the Cure to fund breast cancer research). Such marketing communications tools are best considered as a corporate expense. Therefore, the proper thing to measure in these cases is corporate brand equity. A tool to measure brand equity was discussed in Chapter 5 on product and brand strategies.

Livia Grujich, co-founder of OnQ Communications, discusses the rise of public relations (PR) as a marketing communications tool and how to measure the impact of PR.

CHECKPOINT

Where We've Been

■ We have learned that designing winning marketing communications strategies is a five-step process

■ We have examined the first four steps: conduct research, make strategic decisions, use integrated marketing communications, and measure the impact of marketing communications.

Where We're Going

■ Step #5 will describe how to learn from past communication efforts and make adjustments.

Designing Winning Marketing Communications Strategies Step #5: Make Adjustments

KEYPOINT

The world's best brands communicate constantly and consistently.

We saw in Figure 8.1 that communication works best when it is continuous. Unfortunately, as we have also discussed, many organizations communicate in a discontinuous fashion. That is, they communicate, and then they stop. After a gap, they communicate again. This is a waste of resources, as they do not reap the full benefits of communication efforts. The best approach is to learn from past communication efforts, make changes, and communicate again. Marketing Drives Success 8.4 provides an example.

MARKETING DRIVES SUCCESS

8.4 AFLAC

Objective: The Best Brands Learn from Their Marketing Communications and Make Changes

Aflac provides supplemental insurance to employees. Since 2000 it has used the Aflac duck to communicate its services to prospective customers. The company used the duck because a duck's quack sounds like "Aflac." This was a ploy used by the company to make an obscure insurance company very recognizable. And it has worked. Brand awareness shot up from less than 13% to over 90% in two years after the duck was introduced. In the same time period, sales went from $555 million to $919 million.[11]

In North America, the duck has a little attitude. Typically, the scenario goes like this: humans are discussing their insurance, but cannot remember the name of the company. The duck tries to jog their memories by quacking the Aflac name and gets aggravated when they cannot remember.

However, the company found that in Japan the duck needed to have a different temperament. There, the duck smiles and sings along to songs while stamping its feet to music. The company has learned that what works domestically may not work elsewhere. The Japanese want the duck to be much more of a reassuring character.

Aflac has learned from its marketing communications efforts.

Where We've Been

- We have learned the realities of the new marketing communications paradigm.
- We have learned valuable lessons on how to successfully get your message across to *any* target customer.
- We have examined a step-by-step process to develop winning marketing communications strategies.
- We have examined metrics to measure your marketing communications efforts to help you get the most out of your budget.

CHECKPOINT

Where We're Going

- The final section of this chapter will teach you how to take advantage of **social media** to reach your target customers successfully and with minimal cost.

OBJECTIVE 5

Taking Advantage of Social Media

In 2006, *Ad Age* magazine named the consumer as the "Agency of the Year"—not surprising given the power customers have these days over how they consume communications. We began this chapter by saying that until 1985, life was good for a marketer. Consumers were happy with top-down marketing communications generated by the marketer, mostly in the form of TV, radio, and print advertising.

These days, however, customers not only consume marketing communications information, but they also *create* it through powerful new means called social media such as blogs and websites like Twitter, YouTube, Facebook, and MySpace. Any business that hopes to control information is in for a rude awakening. And it is not just customers who are creators of information. Every email or memo can be blogged, making any employee, regardless of rank, a voice for the company. Fearful as all of this sounds, companies that embrace this new breed of media will benefit greatly.[12]

> *The new order favours those who network, create buzz, and promote their brand.*
>
> STEPHEN BAKER AND
> HEATHER GREEN

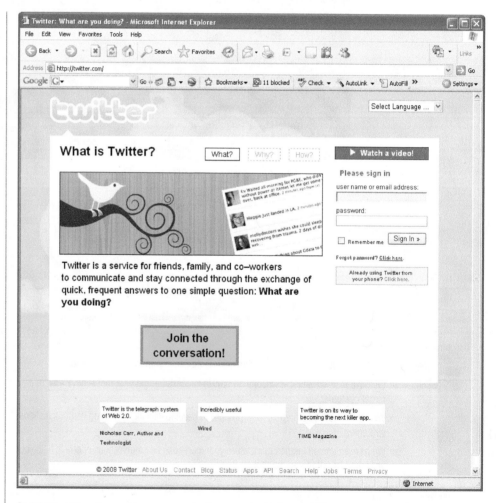

Social networking sites enable consumers to share communications quickly.

8.5 DOVE[14]

Objective: Drive Brand Loyalty by Creating a Brand Community

In 2004, Dove made headlines when it created an advertising and public relations effort called "Campaign for Real Beauty." Dove took a stand against conventional advertising that portrays an unnatural concept of womanly beauty by showcasing freakishly slim and beautiful models (often helped by generous touch-ups from Photoshop software!). Dove's intention was to instill self-esteem in young girls. The marketing communications strategy has been a brilliant success, adding over $1 billion to the brand's value.

Now, Dove is spending millions of dollars on a new website, www.dove.msn.com, that offers women entertainment, advice, advertising, blogs, and a chance for consumers to connect with each other. The question, of course, is whether consumers will turn to Dove for advice, knowing that it is trying to sell them its products.

What made "Campaign for Real Beauty" a success was that it was not specifically linked to any Dove prod-

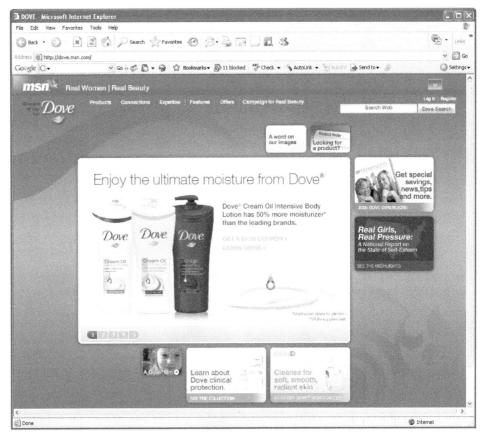

Dove builds brand loyalty by building a community of users.

ucts. The campaign received much publicity on popular shows such as *The View, Entertainment Tonight, Ellen,* and *The Today Show.* Tens of millions of people watched Dove's "Evolution" video, which showed an average-looking woman completely transformed by makeup and airbrushing, on online video-sharing sites such as YouTube.

Dove is not alone in using non-traditional media to communicate its brand. Its main rival, P&G, has more than one online community aimed at women. One of its sites, Capessa, which appears on Yahoo, is a forum for women to discuss subjects such as parenting, pregnancy, and weight loss. Another success story has been a social marketing site from Sprint and Unilever's Suave, In the MotherHood, where mothers submit short scripts about their lives and see them acted out by Hollywood stars. So far, the web series has had 15 million views.

> *Dell's service on Twitter has brought in half a million dollars of new orders in the past year.*
>
> AS TOLD BY A DELL EMPLOYEE
> (AND TWITTER USER)
> TO *BUSINESSWEEK*

KEYPOINT

You will learn more about the power of social media to attract, satisfy, and keep customers in Chapter 11.

Livia Grujich, an expert on social media, talks about how your business can take advantage of low-cost and effective alternate media.

In 2006, two marketing managers at Best Buy worked weekends to create an in-house social network, Blue Shirt Nation. It now has more than 20 000 participants. Eighty-five percent of them are sales associates working the floor. In a company with an annual turnover rate of 60% among employees, this group's turnover is only 8.5%. A promotional drive on the site persuaded 40 000 employees to sign up for a retirement account! Such a bottom-up process is far more effective than a top-down corporate communication process.[13]

To be successful in the world of social media, a company has to give customers something interesting to talk about (such as Dell's new fire-engine-red laptop), encourage communication, listen to customer feedback, and engage in a transparent conversation with customers.

Although P&G has many sites devoted to taking advantage of social media, there are some angry customers at Tide.com, the website devoted to P&G's detergent. The site allows customers to share their views on all aspects of Tide. Customers are not happy with the packaging, as is evident from the quote. If P&G does not respond to customers' concerns, the many advantages of social media will work against it.

> *The spout is useless. The detergent doesn't come out of the spout; it runs out the sides around the spout. It drips down the front of the bottle.*
>
> CUSTOMER ON TIDE.COM[15]

Chapter Summary

1. Be primed for success by learning about the realities of the new marketing communications paradigm.

A marketer who is not up to date on the new realities of marketing communications is going to fail. The old paradigm of top-down, one-way marketing communications is dead. The new paradigm is bottom-up (customer created), two-way communications. It is not just the customer who is the sole target of marketing communications. Rather, other stakeholders such as employees, society, media, and regulators have become important communication targets. Besides traditional sources of advertising such as TV, radio, and print, there is an explosion of media outlets today, thanks to the internet. Finally, the objective of marketing communications these days is the long-term health of the brand.

2. Learn valuable lessons on how to successfully get your message across to *any* target customer.

There are six lessons you have to learn to successfully communicate any message to anyone at any time. First, communication has to be a continuous activity. Second, the message has to be properly encoded. Third, the message has to be sent using the right channel. Fourth, you have to measure your target's pre-existing filters. Fifth, you have to get feedback from your communications efforts to help you make changes. And finally, to cut through the clutter, your message has to be simple, to the point, and differentiated.

3. Learn a step-by-step process to develop winning marketing communications strategies.

The five-step process starts, naturally, with research on customers, brand, and competitor messages. Based on the findings, strategic decisions regarding the target market, communication objectives, and resources are made. Integrated marketing communications (IMC) is a framework that enables a business to tactically implement communication strategies. IMC is based on the principles that different tools have different uses, and a tool should be used depending on the level of customer involvement with a brand.

4. Learn metrics to measure your marketing communications efforts to help you get the most out of your budget.

Regardless of budget or ambition of marketing communications objectives, you should always measure the impact of marketing communications. While metrics for social media are harder to define as yet, those for more traditional media like advertising have made great strides. Common metrics for advertising are content evaluation, brand awareness, recall, and sales. Metrics for events are number of customer interactions, sales leads, brand awareness and perceptions, and customer response. Metrics for public relations include counting the number of brand mentions in the media, number of impressions (based on media circulation), and brand awareness.

5. Learn how to take advantage of social media to reach your target customers successfully and with minimal cost.

Social media enable customers to share any kind of communication by virtue of networking capabilities. Social media include word of mouth communications, YouTube, Facebook, MySpace, Wikipedia, blogs, and Twitter. There are some key strategies to keep in mind in order to take advantage of social media. A company has to give customers something interesting to talk about (such as Dell's new fire-engine-red laptop), encourage communication, listen to customer feedback, and engage in a transparent conversation with customers.

CRITICAL THINKING QUESTIONS

1. A non-profit organization that provides translation services to police departments wants to communicate the range of services it offers to police officers. Police officers often need translation services while on the job (for example, a police officer may be called to a site of a domestic dispute, where the couple does not speak English). In this case, the officer would call the company and a live person would offer translation services in any of 50 different languages. Accordingly, the organization develops a glossy brochure that is distributed to all officers. Do you agree with brochures as an encoding mechanism? Why or why not?

2. Dove has built tremendous brand loyalty by aligning itself with a shared attitude among consumers—beauty as portrayed by the fashion and cosmetics industry is not "real." In the process, it has added over $1 billion to its brand value. What advantages and disadvantages do you see with this approach? (You can learn more about Dove's marketing communications by visiting www.dove.msn.com or www.campaignforrealbeauty.com and watch videos such as "Onslaught" and "Evolution".)

3. You are giving advice to an entrepreneur who wishes to use low-cost but effective marketing communications. What tools would you suggest he use? What cautions would you advise him to take when using the suggested tools?

4. Do you think social media such as Twitter, Facebook, MySpace, and blogs are the new frontiers of marketing communications? Or is this new breed of media a phenomenon that will never be as effective as traditional media (advertising)? Pick a position and present your arguments.

5. Find an example of a marketing communications effort that failed. Make a list of lessons learned from the failure.

RUNNING CASE

ARBOL INDUSTRIES MEASURES THE IMPACT OF EVENT MARKETING

As Arbol Industries became more "marketing led," management's interest naturally gravitated toward measuring the impact of spending on marketing communications. Although Arbol did not spend much money on traditional advertising, it did spend a lot of money on trade shows. Its employees normally attended three or four major industry trade shows a year.

A little digging into the preparation and follow-up for trade shows revealed a most interesting phenomenon—there was virtually no disciplined preparation, nor was there any follow-up. It goes without saying that there were no metrics in place to measure the impact of trade shows.

Typically, someone in either sales or marketing would alert everyone about an upcoming trade show by asking, "Who wants to go to the National Home Builders' Trade Expo next month?" The interested individuals would get the travel agency to make the necessary travel arrangements. They would contact the event organizers, get a booth, pick up marketing collateral (brochures, samples, and gifts), and attend the trade show.

The trade show attendance was viewed as an opportunity to get out of the office, meet old acquaintances, keep up on industry trends, and gather competitive intelligence by visiting competitors' booths. Arbol managers would take turns manning the booth, handing out marketing collateral material to interested individuals, and answering any questions. They would ask for an individual's business card. These would be collected at the end of the trade show. The intention was that someone would follow up with interested individuals. This happened, but it was hit or miss. Sometimes, no one would follow up, and the leads generated at the trade show would be lost.

As management investigated further, things looked even worse. The Arbol Industries trade show booth was not designed with the customer in mind. It was a classic case of an internally focused company designing a product (a trade show booth) without any customer input.

As a result, Arbol completely rethought its approach to event marketing. The recommendations for this important marketing communications tool are given in Figure 8.6.

No longer would it think of events as situations where mere attendance would suffice. Instead, Arbol began to view events as a crucial way to build relationships with current and prospective customers, and as a medium to increase sales.

Case Assignment

Besides trade shows, event marketing includes corporate sponsorships of events. You are the marketing manager of a company that sponsors an annual jazz festival in the summertime. Top management is asking what the return on this marketing communication vehicle is. How would you respond?

Recommendations for events

- Measure effects of all kinds of events, not just trade shows.
- View events as **sales tools**.
  - Make event relevant to your customers.
  - Make a compelling offer.
    - Instead of handing out pens with the corporate logo, hand out case studies and white papers offering solutions to customer problems.
  - Nurture and follow up until the deal is closed. Once the event is over, the relationship with the prospect is just beginning.
    - Use tools to follow up with the customer (webcasts, articles, etc.).
    - Use number of new deals closed as a crucial metric to evaluate events.
- Measure every element of the event for its possible contribution to, or detraction from, your marketing objectives.
  - Staff
    - Was the staff knowledgeable?
    - Did we have the right mix of staff at the event?
  - The exhibit
    - Are we giving customers the information *they* are looking for? Or are we being internally focused? Arbol Industries found that while event attendees wanted solutions to current problems they were facing, Arbol was focused on providing them with information on future technologies.

FIGURE 8.6

Arbol's new approach to event marketing

SUGGESTED READINGS

If You Want to Learn How to Make the Most Use of Marketing Communications, Read These Publications

Stephen Baker and Heather Green, "Beyond Blogs," *BusinessWeek*, June 2, 2008, pp. 44–50.

Charlene Li and Josh Bernoff, *Groundswell: Winning in a World Transformed by Social Technologies* (Boston: Harvard Business School Press, 2008).

Lenny T. Mendonca and Matt Mille, "Crafting a Message That Sticks: An Interview with Chip Heath," *The McKinsey Quarterly*, 2007, November, pp. 1–8.

NOTES

1. David C. Court, "A New Model for Marketing," *The McKinsey Quarterly*, 2004, No. 4, pp. 4–5.
2. Anthony Bianco, "The Vanishing Mass Market," *BusinessWeek*, July 12, 2004, pp. 61–68.
3. This material is based on Anthony Bianco, *ibid*, and Noel Capon and James M. Hulbert, *Marketing Management in the 21st Century* (Upper Saddle River, NJ: Prentice Hall, 2001).
4. Survey conducted in 2003 by CNW Marketing Research Inc. and reported in Anthony Bianco, *ibid*.
5. Lenny T. Mendonca and Matt Mille, "Crafting a Message That Sticks: An Interview with Chip Heath," *The McKinsey Quarterly*, 2007, November, pp. 1–8.
6. I have disguised the name of the company, but the example is real.
7. This example was given to me by an undergraduate student who worked at an Olsen retail store.
8. This example is from one of my consulting projects, but with disguised information.
9. This section is based on Jon Fine, "A Better Measure of Old Media?" *BusinessWeek*, July 9 & 16, 2007, p. 20, and
10. Emily Steel, "Web vs. TV: Research Aims to Gauge Ads," *The Wall Street Journal*, March 19, 2008, p. B3.
11. At the time of writing, Project Apollo has been scrapped because of lack of sponsorship. The initial cost for a company to participate was $1 million, later dropped to $350 000.
12. James R. Gregory, *The Best of Branding: Best Practices in Corporate Branding* (New York: McGraw-Hill Professional, 2003), page 131.
13. This section is based on Stephen Baker and Heather Green, "Beyond Blogs," *BusinessWeek*, June 2, 2008, pp. 44–50 and material provided by Livia Grujich of On Q Communications Inc. Thank you, Livia!
14. Baker and Green, *ibid*, cite this example from *Groundswell*, a new book about social media.
15. Suzanne Vranica, "Dove Rolls Out Web Channel for Women," *The Wall Street Journal*, April 10, 2008, p. B6.
16. As reported in Jonathan Birchall, "Dangerous e-liaisons With the Customer," *Financial Times*, June 5, 2008, p. 12.

Delivering Customer Value

describes how to implement marketing strategies by engaging the entire organization.

CHAPTER 9 Provides a framework to successfully translate marketing strategy into sales action.

CHAPTER 10 Describes how to build a business where all functions are focused on the customer.

Understanding Customers ← PART 1, P. 1

Creating Customer Value ← PART 2, P. 67

Delivering Customer Value ↑ PART 3, P. 195

Managing Customer Value ↓ PART 4, P. 231

SUCCESS

CHAPTER 9

Marketing Planning to Sales Execution

Where We've Been

- We have seen how successful businesses understand customer needs, segment their customers, and select attractive target customers.

- For each target customer segment, successful businesses craft a winning marketing strategy based on the marketing mix elements of product, price, channel, and marketing communications strategies.

Where We're Going

- This chapter will focus on successful sales implementation.

- Winning businesses know that crafting superior marketing strategies will not guarantee marketplace success—these strategies have to be implemented by other functions.

- The next chapter in this part discusses how to build a business where all functions are focused on the customer.

We're a Warren Buffett company.
We have ideas. We bring solutions.

Wherever you're heading,
we'll be there.

A Berkshire Hathaway Company

A LOT OF COMPANIES CAN DELIVER YOUR OFFICE FURNITURE. BUT ONLY ONE CAN DELIVER YOU IDEAS ABOUT HOW TO MANAGE IT.

What's your office furniture situation? Call us.
We'll send someone who can help.

CORTline 1.888.360.CORT or CORT.com

CHAPTER INTRODUCTION

In this chapter you will

The customer was reluctant to buy. "Your competitor can offer me the same product, but at a cheaper price," he told the salesperson. The salesperson was desperate. It was the month end and he had to make his sales quota to get his annual bonus. "Okay," he said, "This is what I can do. I will give you a further 3% discount on the price and throw in six months of free customer service." They signed the deal.

Back at head office, the marketing manager was fuming. "This is typical," she told her colleagues, "We in marketing work hard to build and protect a strong brand, while *they* in sales destroy it by offering price discounts!"

This scenario takes place every day across thousands of business organizations. The cause? Not thinking enough about how to make the transition from marketing strategy to sales execution. Without a process to align the sales and marketing functions, the organization will not be able to achieve its strategic goals.

1. Appreciate the dangers of not aligning the marketing and sales functions.

2. See why there is a misalignment between marketing and sales in many organizations.

3. Learn how to align the sales and marketing functions to achieve competitive success.

OBJECTIVE 1

Dangers of Not Aligning the Marketing and Sales Functions

In many companies, sales forces and marketers feud like Capulets and Montagues—with disastrous results.

KOTLER, RACKHAM, AND
KRISHNASWAMY

The scenario outlined in this chapter's introduction is all too common, has severe negative consequences for the business, and is entirely avoidable. Therefore, it is not surprising that this topic has garnered attention recently. The American Marketing Association has identified this as a crucial arena for determining organizational success and many articles have been written on it.[1] The fault lies neither with sales nor with marketing—the organization does not have a process to translate marketing strategy into sales action. Let us examine in more detail the dangers of not aligning the marketing and sales functions.

Marketing Is from Mars, Sales Is from Pluto

When the marketing and sales functions are not aligned, they operate independently of each other, with disastrous consequences for the organization. When sales are down, marketing blames the sales function for failing to implement a brilliant **marketing plan**. The sales function, in turn, blames the marketing function for being out of touch with marketplace realities and setting prices too high.[2] As we saw in Chapter 6 on pricing, lacking clear direction from the marketing function, the sales function may take matters into its own hands and engage in pricing practices that result in lower **pocket (realized) prices**. Either way, the loser is the organization. Let us take an example.[3]

The marketing function in a company spends $250 000 on a new segmentation model based on psychological factors such as customer attitudes. The sales force refuses to use it because they are quite happy with the current segmentation model—one based on customer buying habits. The end result? Both sides are at a stalemate, each thinking it is right. The new segmentation model sits unused.

Table 9.1 summarizes the negative consequences that accrue when the marketing and sales functions are not aligned.

TABLE 9.1	**What Happens When Marketing and Sales Are Not Aligned?**
Blame game	When sales are down, marketing blames the sales function for failing to implement a brilliant marketing plan. The sales function, in turn, blames the marketing function for being out of touch with marketplace realities and setting prices too high, resulting in sales lost to the competition.
Who owns the customer?	Marketing feels it owns the customer relationship, while sales feels *it* does. So the marketing function guards the marketing plan without revealing its content to the sales function, while sales blocks marketing from having direct contact with the customer.
Pricing abuses	The **price waterfall** chart in Chapter 6 highlights the problem when marketing does not provide clear direction to the sales function—the sales professional may offer price discounts and other incentives to the customer to secure the business. This reduces the price earned by the business.
Longer sales cycles	In businesses where alignment is lacking, longer sales cycles are common. In businesses where there is alignment between marketing and sales, one prime task of marketing is to build the brand and make the customer price-insensitive. This, in turn, enables the sales professional to close the sale faster, shortening the **sales cycle**.
Higher sales and market entry costs	Related to the above point, when sales does not have marketing support, sales and market entry costs go up.

9.1 IBM

Objective: When Sales and Marketing are Aligned, the Corporation Sees Improved Performance

At IBM, before the sales and marketing functions were aligned, they operated independently of one another. The sales force was only concerned about fulfilling product demand (selling), not creating it. The marketing function, on the other hand, was not actively linking marketing efforts to sales generated. Therefore, the sales group could not see the contribution of the marketing function. Marketing would introduce new products and train the salespeople, but there would be no uptake in the marketplace. This is because the new products were being introduced at a time when the sales force was not prepared to capitalize on them.

Recognizing the danger of this situation, IBM integrated its sales and marketing groups by creating a new function called channel enablement. This new function's role is to create value for the customer by focusing everyone's attention on the customer, regardless of functional affiliation. At the CRN Channel Champion awards program in 2008, IBM won the Channel Champion award in six categories. The award, based on a survey of customers, is given to a supplier that is most successful in creating solutions for them.

The end result has been a substantial improvement in performance metrics at IBM: sales cycles are shorter, market entry costs are lower, and the cost of sales is lower.[4]

STOP COUNTING CLICKS. START MAKING MONEY.

IBM helped Staples create a better, more efficient online experience, which increased their online conversion rate by 60%. Start turning browsers into buyers at ibm.com/do/retail STOP TALKING START DOING

IBM, like many businesses, has taken steps to align its sales and marketing functions.

CHAPTER CHALLENGE 9.1

ARE YOU ON THE RIGHT TRACK?

It is common knowledge that the sales and marketing functions must work together. If this is the case, why don't they?

(*Were you on the right track? Check your answers in Appendix 2.*)

Victoria Jurincic of Amgen discusses why misalignment between marketing and sales is bad for the business.

Where We've Been

■ We have learned that when the marketing and sales functions are not aligned, the business faces negative consequences.

Where We're Going

■ Let us examine why the misalignment between marketing and sales exists in the first place.

CHECKPOINT

OBJECTIVE 2

Why Does the Misalignment between Marketing and Sales Exist?

There are three main reasons why there is a misalignment between marketing and sales in many organizations.[5]

CHAPTER CHALLENGE 9.2

ARE YOU ON THE RIGHT TRACK?

After reading Marketing Drives Success 9.2 on Robeez, opposite, answer this question: Why is it a concern that the retailer is selling a pair of shoes for $29.95?

(*Were you on the right track? Check your answers in Appendix 2.*)

Misalignment Reason #1: Different Thought Worlds

Marketing and sales have different viewpoints on an organization's strategy. These viewpoints are distinct yet complementary, and every business needs both.

Misalignment Reason #2: Marketing and Sales Roles Not Defined

In many organizations there is no formal definition of what role should be played by marketing and sales. In fact, as we saw in Chapter 1, in many businesses the role

9.2 ROBEEZ

Objective: Marketing and Sales Thought Worlds Are Different

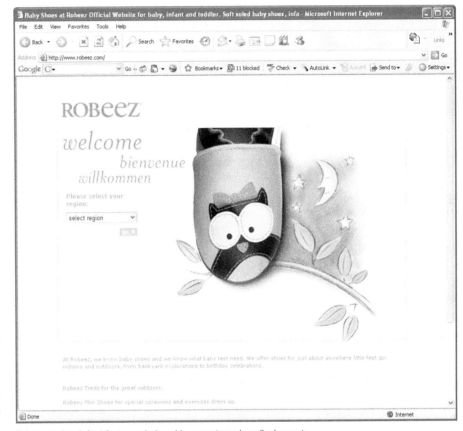

Robeez makes infant footwear beloved by parents and medical experts.

One day Sandra Wilson from Burnaby, B.C., cut up an old leather handbag and sewed a pair of booties (shoes) for her 18-month-old son. She took her handiwork to a gift show. By the end of the day, she had secured a few orders for her creative designs. She was in business! This was how her business, Robeez, was born.[6] Robeez makes creative footwear for infants, among other products. Pediatricians say that wearing booties helps infants' feet develop better.

For the first few years of Robeez's existence, Sandra focused exclusively on securing sales. Her sales team focused on signing up customers (retailers) willing to carry Robeez's products. Robeez was a classic sales-driven company; neither Sandra nor her team gave a thought to marketing until one day when an employee said, "We want our shoes to sell for $35 a pair, but the retailer down the street is selling them for $29.95."

This is when the team began thinking about such issues as building and protecting a brand, and other marketing concerns such as maintaining price integrity. The Robeez example is emblematic of most businesses—they start off by being sales, not marketing, driven.

Perhaps you are beginning to see why, in many organizations, there is no alignment between marketing and sales. The Robeez example demonstrates that marketing and sales have different thought worlds.

Sales is more focused on the here and now—revenue generation (making sales)—while marketing is more focused on the longer-term strategy of brand building, brand extensions, and protecting price integrity.

of marketing is improperly defined to only include sales generation (also called lead generation). Lacking clear role definitions, the two functions compete for resources and ownership of the customer. This was shown in Table 9.1.

Misalignment Reason #3: No Process to Align Marketing and Sales

Human beings are creatures of habit; they like their comfort zones. Managers in corporations are no different; they like to operate in their functional boxes. As we have seen in this book (and as we will see in Chapter 10), this is problematic because if employees operate in functional silos without co-operating with each other, the customer does not get served.

Aligning the sales and marketing functions is a very challenging but crucial task, given that the thought worlds of sales and marketing are inherently different, and the roles of these functions are unclear in many organizations. Therefore, it is necessary to design a process to link them. Without a process, the marketing and sales personnel will rarely start working together on their own.

MARKETING DRIVES SUCCESS

9.3 GRAND & TOY

Objective: Marketing and Sales Are Two Sides of the Same Coin

How do you transform a 125-year-old company from a purveyor of commodities (pens, paper, and furniture) to a provider of customer value? By harnessing the power of marketing and sales, of course. Grand & Toy was founded in Toronto in 1882 and today is Canada's largest office solutions company. Eighty percent of its sales come from business-to-business marketing.[7]

Grand & Toy realized that its customers were looking for long-term benefits, not saving a few pennies on a pen. In a brilliant move to create more value for its customers, Grand & Toy restructured the organization into five business units—technology, interiors, office supplies, digital imaging, and services—each staffed by experts in the field who can provide the customer specialized knowledge to solve a particular problem. For example, customers buying office furniture can get advice on interior design for free, thus saving customers additional expense and giving them an additional reason to do business with Grand & Toy.

Each account at Grand & Toy is serviced by a dedicated account manager. This sales professional takes care of understanding his or her customers' business goals and objectives in order to identify specific business needs and be a true customer advocate, thus bringing solutions to customers, not merely selling a product. At Grand & Toy, an account manager is called a Business Solution Advisor to better reflect this strategic role. This job is to be a customer advocate.

Grand & Toy wants customers to know that it is *the* place to go to build their business. To make this possible, Grand & Toy has brilliantly understood customer needs. For example, small business owners want to be free to focus on growing their business. But essential activities such as HR take up a lot of their time. They cannot afford to outsource these services because they can be expensive. By going through their Business Solution Advisors, these businesses can afford services such as HR solutions, insurance, and web hosting and design. Of course, backing up the Business Solution Advisor is a pool of experts within each of the business units, thus harnessing the unique power of sales and marketing to serve the customer.

Grand & Toy reorganized itself to create more value for the customer.

Where We've Been

■ We have seen that when there is misalignment between marketing and sales, the business faces severe negative consequences.

■ There are three main reasons why the misalignment between these functions exists in the first place.

Where We're Going

■ Let us examine how to align the marketing and sales functions, thus translating marketing planning into sales execution.

How to Align the Marketing and Sales Functions

OBJECTIVE 3

Although there are three main reasons for misalignment between the marketing and sales functions, the first one—the different thought worlds of marketing and sales—is not necessarily a bad thing. A successful organization needs the distinct yet complementary skill sets of marketing (longer-term focus on brand building) *and* sales (shorter-term focus on revenue generation). Research has shown that the distinct orientations of marketing and sales lead to better market performance.[8] The organization suffers when only *one* skill set is emphasized and it does not harness the power of marketing and sales in its go-to-market strategy.

Let us see how to align the marketing and sales functions by examining the other two reasons for misalignment: lack of clear role definitions and lack of a process.

Define the Role of Marketing and Sales in the Organization

All customers go through a predictable sales cycle called a **buying (or purchasing) funnel**, which posits that customers initially become aware of a need, they are initially unaware of a brand's existence, they give consideration to a few brands, they make a purchase, they evaluate their purchase, and they become loyal to the brand (or not, depending on their experience with it). This funnel, shown in Figure 9.1 (you encountered this concept in Chapter 8 and you will see it again in Chapter 12), is a good visual to understand the unique roles marketing and sales should play.[9]

We can see from the buying funnel that marketing is responsible for "creating" a need (go back to this material in Chapter 2, if you have to refresh your memory), building **brand awareness**, imbuing the brand with properties (**brand associations**) that will resonate with the market segment, and positioning the brand in such a way that it becomes the preferred alternative.

This is shown very clearly in the advertisement for Kennametal, a supplier of engineering solutions to a range of industries from aerospace and defence to specialty applications.

The role of marketing is to educate the customer on the importance of taking a holistic view of the business: instead of buying from a cheaper alternative, it is wiser to align with a supplier who can reduce the customer's total cost of manufacturing (this concept, called **Total Cost of Ownership**, was discussed in Chapter 6). The role of marketing is to position the Kennametal brand uniquely in the marketplace by giving it certain associations. The end result? The customer has brand awareness and brand knowledge even before the salesperson calls, making the sales process a lot easier, thus reducing sales costs. In this way, marketing is providing the sales force with a competitive edge in the marketplace.

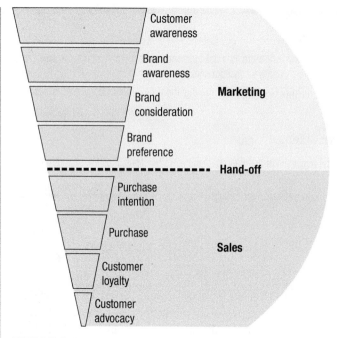

FIGURE 9.1

Every business has to define the unique roles played by marketing and sales.

Source: Philip Kotler, Neil Rackham, and Suj Krishnaswamy, "Ending the War between Sales and Marketing," *Harvard Business Review*, July–August 2006, p. 77.

At the point of hand-off in Figure 9.1, the sales function takes over and steers purchase intention to the brand (by answering questions and easing customer concerns), handles purchase details (payment, credit terms), and follows up with the customer to ensure satisfaction with the purchase, which leads to loyalty and, hopefully, to converting the customer to a strong advocate of the brand (you will find more on this topic in Chapter 11).

The schematic in Figure 9.1 is a good starting point, but it suggests that there is a distinct hand-off point between marketing and sales. In reality, both marketing and sales should have a role to play all through the sales cycle. Let us examine how.

As we saw in Chapter 1, all winning businesses understand-create-deliver-manage customer value. If this is the process they follow, surely we should be able to use it to

KEYPOINT

A critical role of marketing is to provide the sales force with a competitive edge in the marketplace.

CHAPTER CHALLENGE 9.3

ARE YOU ON THE RIGHT TRACK?

Name at least three brand associations marketing is trying to create in the Kennametal advertisement opposite.
(*Were you on the right track? Check your answers in Appendix 2.*)

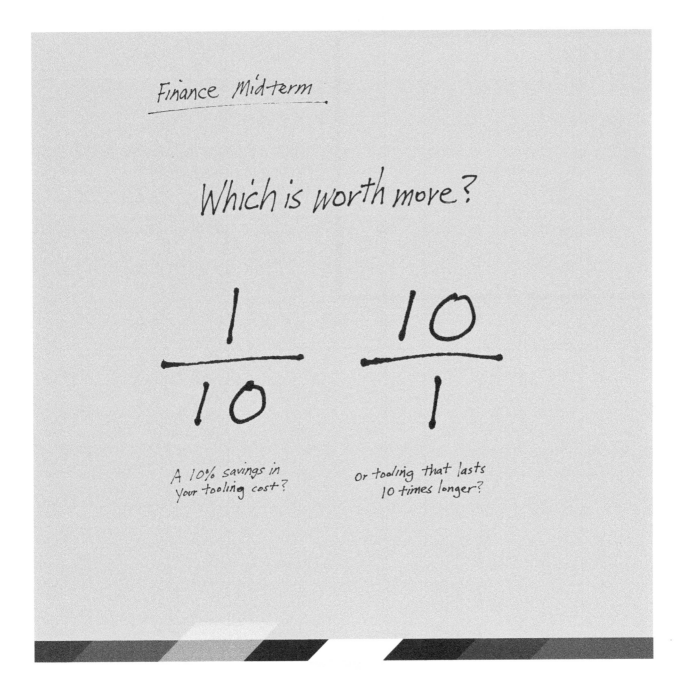

Kennametal has clearly defined marketing and sales roles.

define what roles should be played by marketing and sales at each step. This is shown in Table 9.2.

As can be seen from Table 9.2, the interaction between marketing and sales is ongoing and seamless. Each function has a role to play in the understand-create-deliver-manage

CHAPTER CHALLENGE 9.4

ARE YOU ON THE RIGHT TRACK?

According to Figure 9.1, the marketing function has no role to play during the stages of customer loyalty and advocacy. Do you agree? Why or why not?

(*Were you on the right track? Check your answers in Appendix 2.*)

customer value process. In other words, the purpose of a sales force is not just to communicate the value created by marketing, but also to play an active role in *creating* value.

Design a Process to Translate Marketing Planning to Sales Execution

Aligning the marketing and sales functions (translating marketing planning to sales execution) requires careful thought regarding the roles of these two functions. However, simply defining roles is not sufficient. A *process* to align marketing and sales has to be put in place. Without a process, no amount of wishing will

TABLE 9.2	**The Role of Marketing and Sales in Successful Businesses**			
	Understand customer needs	**Create customer value**	**Deliver customer value**	**Manage customer value**
Role of marketing	Conduct formal marketing research	Develop marketing plan	Accompany the sales function on periodic sales calls	Measure customer satisfaction
	Visit customers	Develop customer value propositions (see next section for details)	Implement the marketing plan	Share customer satisfaction results with key decision makers
	Perform market segmentation			Develop action plan based on customer satisfaction research
	Perform competitive analysis			Conduct review of segments, customers, product mix
	Measure segment, customer, product attractiveness			Manage the brand
				Conduct **sales review** jointly with the sales function (see next section for details)
				Champion the customer and influence all functions to be customer focused
Role of sales	Make sales calls to customers	Develop sales plans (see next section for details)	Implement the sales plan	Participate in customer satisfaction measurement
	Develop specialized knowledge of customer's industry and business		Deliver customer **value propositions**	Provide feedback on market and customers to key decision makers
				Conduct sales review jointly with marketing (see next section for details)
				Manage customer relationships for long-term profitability

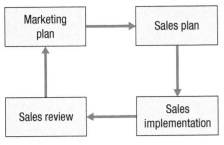

FIGURE 9.2

A process to translate marketing planning into sales action

accomplish the task.[10] We have already hinted at this process (in Chapters 1 and 4, for example), but let us examine it in more detail in Figure 9.2.

Figure 9.2 shows that the marketing plan should be translated into a sales plan (a template to develop a sales plan appears in Table 9.3). Essentially, the language of marketing has to be translated into the language of sales, enabling the sales function to implement sales strategies. Finally, the organization has to engage in a sales review to (1) compare actual sales figures to targets, (2) evaluate how well the sales plan is being implemented, and (3) provide feedback to other functions on what the sales function is observing in the marketplace regarding competitors, customers, and market trends.

The sales review is accomplished in two ways. First, the sales function reviews sales efforts during internal sales meetings and makes adjustments as necessary.[11] Second, the sales function meets formally with marketing (and other functions) once every quarter to provide feedback on sales figures, sales implementation, and market feedback. In this way, the entire organization learns from its implementation efforts, enabling the marketing planning process to start all over again. This is yet another way that the marketing plan becomes a living, breathing document (we discussed this in Chapter 4). Finally, it is in this way that the sales function not only communicates value to the customer, but also is responsible for creating it.[12]

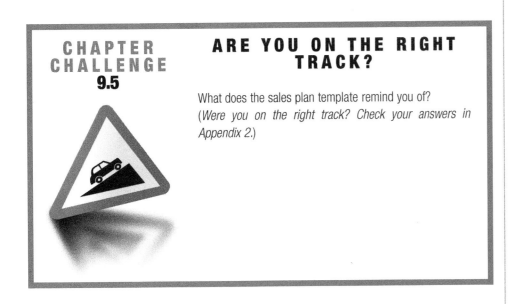

CHAPTER CHALLENGE 9.5

ARE YOU ON THE RIGHT TRACK?

What does the sales plan template remind you of?
(*Were you on the right track? Check your answers in Appendix 2.*)

Make Segmentation the Glue   In Chapter Challenge 9.5, if you said that the sales plan template reminds you of the marketing plan template, you would be absolutely correct. In fact, many sections of the sales plan are directly lifted from the marketing plan. It makes

TABLE 9.3   Sales Plan Template

1. **Executive Summary**
   - Key sales issues facing the business
   - Key sales opportunities
   - Key sales objectives and outcomes
   - Key sales strategies
   - Key resources required

2. **Table of Contents**

3. **Opportunity Analysis**
   - Our historical performance in segment or geography[1]
   - Market, customer, product, and competitor analysis
   - Top issues and opportunities in this segment or geography
   - Target customers by priority
   - Target prospects[2] by priority

4. **Performance Targets**
   - Volume targets by market segment/geography
   - Revenue targets by market segment/geography
   - Market share targets by segment/geography
   - Profitability targets by market segment/geography
   - Other

5. **Sales Strategies**
   - Value propositions[3] by market segment
   - Value propositions by customer
   - Products offered
   - Pricing
   - Marketing communications
   - Supply chain
   - New business development
   - Sales force deployment
   - Sales organization effectiveness
   - Other

6. **Sales Plan Implementation and Control**
   - Detailed tactical plans for each sales strategy
   - Detailed control plans to monitor sales execution

7. **Sales Budgets and Key Resources**
   - Budgets
   - Resource requirements

[1] Some sales functions are organized by segment, some are organized by geography, while others may be organized using a hybrid model.
[2] Potential customers
[3] A value proposition is an offering (goods and services) targeted at a particular market segment or customer. Examples are provided in Table 9.5 on page 210.

perfect sense that the sales plan is similar to the marketing plan. This is because, as we have discussed previously, many aspects of the marketing plan are implemented by the sales function, and there should be seamless interaction between the two functions in the understand-create-deliver-manage customer value process (Table 9.2). So the sales plan *is* the marketing plan, albeit written in the language of sales (sales opportunities, sales objectives, and sales strategies).

How, exactly, do we translate marketing planning into sales action? The key lies in **market segmentation**. As we discussed in Chapter 3, a prime reason we segment markets

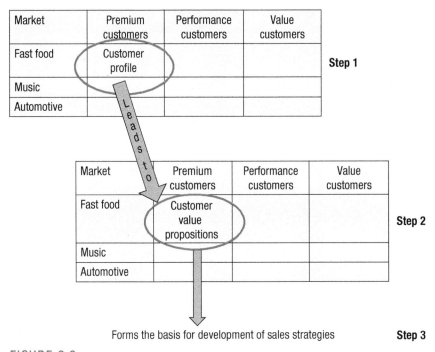

FIGURE 9.3

Market segmentation is the key to translating marketing planning to sales execution.

(besides the other reasons we discussed) is to provide the sales function with direction. Without such direction, the sales force may engage in actions (such as discounting the price) that are detrimental to the brand and the organization (this aspect was discussed in Chapter 6).

By giving the sales force direction, we avoid any tension the salesperson may feel between serving the customer (who has needs and imposes demands on the salesperson) and serving the company (which has explicit sales and pricing goals it wants to achieve).[13]

To see how market segmentation provides direction to the sales force, look at the logic in Figure 9.3, which reproduces the segmentation matrix from Chapter 3.

Step 1, of course, is to profile the customer in terms of needs and price sensitivity (reread the material in Chapter 3, especially around Tables 3.1 and 3.2, if necessary). When we profile a customer based on needs and willingness to pay, development of value propositions (goods and services we are prepared to offer the customer) becomes straightforward (Step 2). A clear understanding of what can and cannot be offered to the customer (value propositions) provides unequivocal direction to the sales force, captured in the form of sales strategies (Step 3).

Although the example in Figure 9.3 is from a business-to-business setting, the logic applies equally well to consumer markets. When you are in the market to buy a car, the salesperson will sell you a model based on your needs and wallet considerations. You cannot have a car, complete with all the trimmings, unless you are willing to pay. While Figure 9.3 provides the overall logic for how marketing planning is translated into sales action, Tables 9.4 and 9.5 provide details.

Profiling customers (Table 9.4) enables development of customer value propositions (Table 9.5).

Development of clear value propositions by customer type enables the development of sales strategies, thus providing the sales professional with clear direction on how to serve a customer. Therefore, if a customer in the Automotive-Value cell wants services that he is not willing to pay for, the salesperson knows she cannot offer this value proposition without jeopardizing the organization's strategic marketing objectives.

KEYPOINT

The sales plan is the marketing plan, but written in sales language.

Michael Jurincic of Bayer discusses how to engage a sales force.

TABLE 9.4   Market x Customer Segmentation: Customer Profile

Market	Premium customers	Performance customers	Value customers
Fast food industry	■ Customer wants custom solutions ■ Customer wants security of supply ■ Customer is willing to pay price premiums	■ Customer wants cost containment solutions ■ Customer wants security of supply ■ Customer will consider price premiums if case is made	■ Customer wants a basic product ■ Customer is very price-sensitive ■ Customer will not consider paying price premiums
Music industry	■ Customer wants highest-grade product ■ Customer values supplier relationships ■ Customer is price-insensitive	■ Customer wants product grade to produce high impact on retail shelf ■ Customer wants supply chain solutions ■ Customer will consider price premiums if case is made	■ Customer wants basic product ■ Customer wants standardized ordering ■ Customer will not consider paying price premiums
Automotive industry	■ Customer wants innovative product solutions ■ Customer wants proactive technical support ■ Customer will pay price premiums	■ Customer wants user-friendly products ■ Customer wants quick turnaround on orders ■ Customer will consider price premiums if case is made	■ Customer values product consistency above all else ■ Customer wants sales materials ■ Customer is price-sensitive

TABLE 9.5   Customer Value Propositions

Market	Premium customers	Performance customers	Value customers
Fast food industry	We will provide the customer with ■ Grade A product ■ custom solutions team at no extra charge ■ dedicated sales team	We will provide the customer with ■ cost containment solutions ■ security of supply ■ value creation for end consumer ■ other services, not free of charge, but priced on a case-by-case basis	We will provide the customer with ■ Grade C product line ■ no face-to-face selling, ordering done via call centre ■ extra services, offered at a price to be determined on a case-by-case basis
Music industry	We will provide the customer with ■ Grade AA product line ■ dedicated sales team, led by key account manager ■ quarterly review of revenue and cost goals ■ 24-hour turnaround on all customer requests	We will provide the customer with ■ Grade AB product line ■ guarantees on retail shelf impact ■ supply chain solutions	We will provide the customer with ■ Grade C product line ■ standardized ordering via our website ■ no free services ■ no discounts or terms
Automotive industry	We will provide the customer with ■ Grade A+ product line ■ market research support ■ free and unlimited access to our product innovation team	We will provide the customer with ■ Grade BB product line ■ quick turnaround guarantees ■ ability to do short production runs	We will provide the customer with ■ product consistency guarantees ■ sales materials via brochures and technical material ■ no free services ■ no discounts or terms

MARKETING DRIVES SUCCESS

9.4 GE

Objective: Market Segmentation Is the Glue Binding Marketing and Sales

GE is well known for its leadership in adopting industry best practices. However, even until recently it would give a salesperson little more guidance than a territory, a set of sales targets, and wishes for good luck.[14] But today, by using a more scientific approach to increasing sales force effectiveness, some GE divisions (for example, U.S. Equipment Financing) have added $300 million in new business in one year alone.

The GE division began by revising the way customers were segmented. Using data contained in past company transactions, the division not only segmented customers by industrial classification codes and type of equipment leased, but also by prospective-customer characteristics that would highlight the likelihood of a customer wanting to do business with GE. The group then ranked customers from high to low on their likelihood of doing business with GE.

They found something very interesting. The top 30% of prospective customers were three times more likely to do business with GE than the bottom 70%. Essentially, the top group was made up of very attractive customers to pursue. Yet before this segmentation exercise, only about half of these customers had previously been classified as high priority by sales managers! By using the new approach, the company had identified 10 000 new high-priority prospects that it would have otherwise overlooked. Sophisticated market segmentation enabled GE to harness the power of marketing (segmentation) with sales action (ability to pursue attractive prospects, armed with a knowledge of their needs and attitudes toward GE).

GE uses market segmentation to align its sales and marketing functions.

Chapter Summary

1.　Appreciate the dangers of not aligning the marketing and sales functions.

When sales and marketing are not aligned, several scenarios raise their ugly heads. When sales are down, marketing blames the sales function for failing to implement a brilliant marketing plan. The sales function, in turn, blames the marketing function for being out of touch with marketplace realities and setting prices too high, resulting in lost sales.

Marketing feels it owns the customer relationship, while the sales function feels *it* does. So the marketing function guards the marketing plan without revealing its content to the sales function, while sales blocks marketing from having direct contact with the customer.

A sales professional may offer price discounts and other incentives to the customer to secure the business. This reduces the price earned by the business. Marketing fumes that its brand-building efforts are being undermined by the sales function.

2.　See why there is a misalignment between marketing and sales in many organizations.

There are three main reasons why there may be misalignment between marketing and sales. Inherently, marketing and sales have different thought worlds: marketing is more concerned with the long-term health of the brand, while sales is more concerned about shorter-term issues such as revenue generation (sales).

While having different thought worlds is not necessarily a bad thing, it can have negative consequences if the power of marketing planning is not harnessed with the impact of sales action via a process. Finally, the reason why many organizations have not aligned their marketing and sales efforts is because there is no clear role definition for these two functions. Without a role definition, the contribution of each function is hard to measure.

3.　Learn how to align the sales and marketing functions to achieve competitive success.

Naturally, the first thing to do to align the sales and marketing functions is to define their respective roles. While it may be tempting to view marketing as being responsible for all activities from customer and brand awareness to building brand preference, and sales as being responsible for all activities leading to the actual purchase and beyond, such a distinct "hand-off" model is too limiting.

It is better to use the understand-create-deliver-manage customer value framework used by all winning businesses to define what activities must be performed by *each* function at *each* stage. Such an approach enables a business to realize that marketing and sales are two sides of the same coin—a business needs both orientations to be successful.

Clear role definition is a necessary first step in aligning these two functions. The other step is to design a process to translate marketing planning into sales action. The key in achieving this translation lies in making market segmentation the glue that binds marketing and sales.

Step 1 is to profile customers based on their needs and price sensitivities (willingness to pay). Step 2 is to develop customer value propositions that clearly provide the sales force with direction on what can and cannot be offered. In Step 3, customer value propositions form the basis for the development of sales strategies (captured in the sales plan).

CRITICAL THINKING QUESTIONS

1. Provide an example of a business where the sales and marketing functions are not aligned. Outline the negative consequences befalling the organization as a result of this misalignment.

2. Conversely, provide an example of a business where the sales and marketing functions are aligned. Outline the positive consequences accruing to this business as a result of the alignment.

3. We have seen in this chapter that marketing and sales can have different thought worlds. Identify two other functions that might have thought worlds that are different from marketing's. Outline the differences between the thought worlds of

marketing and these two functions. What are some consequences of these differences?

4. Using the understand-create-deliver-manage customer value framework, outline the role of marketing and the two functions you have identified in the question above.

5. Pick any two product categories (for example, cars and business suits). For each, develop a profile of common customer segments. Identify what value propositions are targeted at each customer segment. Finally, outline how the value propositions help a sales professional to do his or her job.

RUNNING CASE

ARBOL INDUSTRIES ALIGNS ITS SALES AND MARKETING FUNCTIONS

Arbol Industries was well on its way to realizing the CEO's vision of making a transformation from a cost-focused company to a customer-focused company. It was conducting regular research into customer needs, sending cross-functional teams to analyze a customer's business to uncover opportunities for value creation. It was developing marketing plans, which were the foundation for the development of functional plans.

Yet the marketing manager had begun noticing something at meetings. The sales team, during reviews of sales orders gained and lost, would often make comments like, "The only reason we lost that order is because we are more expensive than our competitors." The marketing manager was worried because Arbol was well on its way to translating marketing plans into sales and other functional plans. The sales team should know that if a customer complained about Arbol's higher prices and was willing to sign up with a cheaper competitor, it was a sign that (a) it was perhaps not a customer Arbol wanted to secure or (b) the sales professional was doing an inadequate job of communicating Arbol's value propositions.

The marketing manager realized that it was not realistic to expect the sales function to develop sales strategies based on a reading of the marketing plan alone. A process would need to be devised to engage the sales force more directly.

With input from senior management and the sales team, a new process was put in place to better align marketing and sales. First,

Arbol's CEO formally announced the distinct but complementary roles of marketing and sales based on the understand-create-deliver-manage customer value framework. Next, marketing developed a customer segmentation matrix and, with the help of the sales team, populated it with four items: current customers, their needs, customer value propositions to be delivered (similar to Tables 9.4 and 9.5 on page 210), and a list of attractive prospective customers. Finally, marketing and sales, along with other functions, developed a plan to meet at least once a quarter to review sales efforts. This gave the sales team ongoing opportunities to provide marketplace feedback to the rest of the organization.

The alignment effort was a big success! In fact, during the first year alone, Arbol recorded a 10% organic growth in its business, an increased sales pipeline of prospective customers, and a 20% increase in sales conversions (closing sales). While their competitors were struggling with low-margin customers, Arbol's marketing–sales alignment efforts were being rewarded with attractive customers.

Case Assignment

Besides the techniques mentioned in this case on how to better align the sales and marketing functions, identify at least one other way in which a business can accomplish the same objective.

SUGGESTED READINGS

If You Want to Know More about How to Translate Marketing Planning to Sales Execution, Read These Publications

Philip Kotler, Neil Rackham, and Suj Krishnaswamy, "Ending the War between Sales and Marketing," *Harvard Business Review,* July–August 2006, pp. 68–78.

Ajay Sirsi, *Marketing Led—Sales Driven: How Successful Businesses Use the Power of Marketing Plans and Sales Execution to Win in the Marketplace* (Victoria, BC: Trafford Publishing, 2005).

N O T E S

1. See for example, Joel Claret, Pierre Mauger, and Eric V. Roegner, "Managing a Marketing and Sales Transformation," *The McKinsey Quarterly*, August 2006, pp. 111–121; Belinda Dewsnap and David Jobber, "The Sales–Marketing Interface in Consumer Packaged-Goods Companies: A Conceptual Framework," *Journal of Personal Selling & Sales Management*, Volume 20, No. 2, 2000, pp. 109–119; Belinda Dewsnap and David Jobber, "A Social Psychological Model of Relations between Marketing and Sales," *European Journal of Marketing*, Volume 36, No. 7–8, 2002, pp. 874–894; Christian Homburg and Ove Jensen, "The Thought Worlds of Marketing and Sales: Which Differences Make a Difference?" *Journal of Marketing*, Volume 71, July 2007, pp. 124–142; Philip Kotler, Neil Rackham, and Suj Krishnaswamy, "Ending the War between Sales and Marketing," *Harvard Business Review*, July–August 2006, pp. 68–78; Ajay Sirsi, *Marketing Led—Sales Driven: How Successful Businesses Use the Power of Marketing Plans and Sales Execution to Win in the Marketplace* (Victoria, BC: Trafford Publishing, 2005).

2. Kotler et al., *ibid.*

3. This example was given to me by a client of mine.

4. Kotler et al., *ibid.*

5. Ajay Sirsi, *ibid.*

6. Sandra Wilson related this to me.

7. Natasha Renaud of Grand & Toy; Annette Bourdeau, "The Shake-Up," *Strategy*, September 2007, pp. 11–17. The author would like to thank Natasha Renaud for her invaluable insights on this topic.

8. Homburg and Jensen, *ibid.*

9. Kotler et al., *ibid.*

10. I know of cases where the organization has brought in motivational speakers, who urge functions (especially marketing and sales) to work together. While nobody within the business would argue against working together, people go back into their functional silos as soon as the motivational speaker leaves.

11. The frequency of this review depends on how frequently the sales organization meets. Many sales functions meet on a weekly basis, while others meet less frequently.

12. John R. DeVincentis and Neil Rackham, "Breadth of a Salesman," *The McKinsey Quarterly*, Number 4, 1998, pp. 32–43.

13. For a good perspective on this, see Erin Anderson and Vincent Onyemah, "How Right Should the Customer Be?" *Harvard Business Review*, July–August 2006, pp. 59–67.

14. This example is taken from Dianne Ledingham, Mark Kovac, and Heidi Locke Simon, "The New Science of Sales Force Productivity," *Harvard Business Review*, September 2006, pp. 124–133.

CHAPTER  10

Building a Customer-Focused Business

CHECKPOINT

Where We've Been

- We have seen that winning businesses know that crafting superior marketing strategies will not guarantee marketplace success—these strategies have to be implemented by other functions.

- In the previous chapter, we saw that marketing strategies have to be translated into sales action.

Where We're Going

- In this chapter, we will discuss why all functions within a business have to be focused on the customer.

CHAPTER INTRODUCTION

In this chapter you will

Tammy was excited. A confirmed health nut, she had bought a new brand of good-for-you soup at her local health food store, and she could not wait to get home to make it for supper. But she could not understand the directions on the can—did it indicate to add water or not? She was uncertain. Fortunately, the can also recommended calling a toll-free number in case the consumer had any questions. Tammy dialed. The following conversation took place.[1]

TAMMY:	"Can you please tell me if the Healthy and Tasty brand needs the addition of water? I am unclear upon reading the label."
PERSON AT THE OTHER END OF THE LINE:	"What product? We don't have any brand by that name."
TAMMY:	"Is this not The Healthy Tasty Company?"
PERSON AT THE OTHER END OF THE LINE:	"Yes, it is. But, I'm telling you we don't have such a brand. Now, is there anything else I can help you with?"
TAMMY:	"No, thank you. You have done enough already."

1. See that without customer focus, marketing strategies fail.

2. Learn to avoid mistakes made by your product-centric competitors by truly understanding what customer focus is.

3. Learn how to build a customer-focused business.

4. Learn to avoid common traps when implementing customer focus.

Every person reading this book has gone through a frustrating experience similar to Tammy's. It is a sure bet that Tammy will never buy from this company again. And she will relate her experiences to all her friends. The Healthy Tasty Company has lost a customer for life and, due to Tammy's word-of-mouth communications, possibly many more potential customers as well. The company could have prevented this by ensuring that *all* employees in the corporation were focused on the customer.

OBJECTIVE 1

KEYPOINT

Without a total, organization-wide focus on the customer, the best marketing strategies will fail.

Bill, a consumer, talks about his contrasting customer service experiences at Home Depot and Lowe's.

Without Customer Focus, Marketing Strategies Fail

What happened at The Healthy Tasty Company can be explained rather easily. The marketing function ran a series of **focus groups** with consumers to understand their health habits and uncover new product concepts. Thrilled with the results, they introduced a new product—a healthy but tasty soup—into the marketplace. Glossy ads in magazines enticed customers to the store. The marketing function thought it had done its job. But it had not. It had failed to anticipate customer needs. It had failed to train its call centre personnel thoroughly on the new product. It had failed to train other parts of the company to focus on the customer.

As a result, while one part of the company was creating value, another part was destroying it. The lesson is clear—without a total, organization-wide focus on the customer, the best marketing strategies will fail.

> *Marketers that devote at least 50% of their time to advanced, customer-centric marketing processes and capabilities will achieve marketing ROI [return on investment] that is at least 30% greater than that of their peers, who lack such emphasis.*
>
> GARTNER GROUP REPORT

MARKETING DRIVES SUCCESS

10.1 GE HEALTHCARE[2]

Objective: Without Customer Focus, Marketing Strategies Fail

GE Medical Systems (now GE Healthcare) created a consulting unit, Performance Solutions, as a way to bolster revenues in its medical diagnostic machines division. The consulting arm would help health care institutions such as hospitals to increase efficiency and productivity.

Other suppliers (for example, Siemens—you encountered this example in Chapter 1) were doing the same thing as a way to differentiate themselves in a product category that was becoming a commodity. Although the consulting unit was successful initially, four years later its revenues were in decline.

This is because GE had two distinct sales functions: the sales professionals who sold the actual machines and those who offered consulting services. The two functions focused on what each did best—machine sales or consulting advice. What was lacking was a shared viewpoint of the customer. As a result, the equipment salespeople had a hard time explaining the value of the consulting service business. Therefore, they could not contribute to the growth of consulting services.

Further, they were reluctant to allow the Performance Solutions salespeople (the consulting unit) to contact their customers (a common

continues...

problem in many organizations where different functions compete to "own" the customer; we saw this in Chapter 9 as well). Finally, because GE offered consulting services in conjunction with its own products, only certain customers benefited from the consulting value proposition. For non-GE customers, the value added by the consulting group was tenuous.

In the end, GE redesigned the consulting unit to better meet the needs of its customers. For one thing, it no longer limited consulting services to GE products only. It also better aligned the two sales organizations to focus on the customer. The focus on the customer

paid off. In just one year after reorganization, the consulting business generated $500 million in revenue!

What turned out to be an ultimate success story did not start out that way, because GE fell into a classic trap—it designed the value proposition through the lens of its own products, rather than a focus on the customer. It was right in thinking that customers would value the consulting services. Its mistake was in the execution. It failed to recognize that when different parts of the company do not focus on the customer, they do not have the same goals. As a result, in spite of best intentions, the whole is *not* greater than the sum of its parts.

All GE businesses have a customer focus.

CHAPTER CHALLENGE 10.1

ARE YOU ON THE RIGHT TRACK?

GE Healthcare tried to differentiate a commodity product by offering consulting services. What do we call such an effort? (Hint: we discussed this concept in Chapter 5.)

(*Were you on the right track? Check your answers in Appendix 2.*)

Where We've Been

■ We have seen that if every function is not focused on the customer, marketing strategies will fail.

■ A focus on the customer pays off.

Where We're Going

■ In the next section, we will see what exactly customer focus is.

CHECKPOINT

OBJECTIVE 2

What Is Customer Focus?

> *It is the customer who determines what a business is, what it produces, and whether it will prosper.*
>
> PETER DRUCKER

One reason why many companies are not customer focused is that the concept of **customer focus** is hard to understand. Many people mistakenly think, "What is the big fuss? Customer focus is a simple concept to grasp. It just means that a business should concentrate on its customers." This thinking is flawed. True, customer focus means to concentrate on the customer. But exactly how and by whom is it accomplished? In other words, the concept of customer focus is intuitively appealing and understandable, but hard to concretely grasp and implement.

To understand what customer focus is, we need to understand its opposite. Table 10.1 provides a contrasting view of product-centric versus customer-centric (customer-focused) approaches.[3]

TABLE 10.1   Product-centric vs. Customer-centric Approaches

	Product-centric approach	Customer-centric approach
Basic philosophy	Sell products; we will sell to whoever will buy	Serve customers; all decisions start with the customer
Business orientation	Transaction oriented; there will always be another customer	Relationship oriented; building long-lasting customer relationships is the key
Product positioning	Highlight product features and benefits	Highlight what the product can do to meet customer needs
Organizational structure	Product profit centres, product managers, product sales team	Customer segment centres, customer relationship managers, customer segment sales team
Organizational focus	Internally focused, new product development, new account development, market share growth	Externally focused, customer relationship development, profitability through customer loyalty
Responsibility for customer relations	Marketing department has sole responsibility	All employees are customer relationship builders; every customer brand touch point is important
Performance metrics	Number of new products, profitability per product, market share by product/sub-brands	Share of wallet[1] of customers, customer satisfaction, customer lifetime value[2]
Management criteria	Portfolio of products	Portfolio of customers
Selling approach	How many customers can we sell this product to?	How many products can we sell to this customer?
Customer knowledge	Captures and distributes what a company knows about a customer	Captures and distributes what a customer thinks about a company

[1] Refers to what percentage of the customer's expenditure in a product category is held by the business. For example, if a customer spends $100 on office paper and buys from three companies, what percentage of $100 does Brand A command versus its competitors?

[2] Refers to the present value of all future purchases made by a loyal customer. For example, if a customer only ordered pizza from Pizza Hut for the rest of her life, how much would she be worth to the company today?

Source: Adapted from Denish Shah, Roland T. Rust, A. Parasuraman, Richard Staelin, and George S. Day, "The Path to Customer Centricity," *Journal of Service Research*, Volume 9, No. 2, November 2006, p. 115.

MARKETING DRIVES SUCCESS

10.2 McDONALD'S

Objective: Customer Focus is a Multi-dimensional Issue[4]

McDonald's brilliantly demonstrates what customer focus is. At *any* McDonald's, regardless of the location, the service a customer gets is the same—fast, friendly, accurate, clean, and reliable. What most customers do not know is that, behind the scenes, McDonald's obsesses about the customer.

At its Hamburger University outside Chicago, managers and store owners (franchisees) are taught minute details on how to serve the customer so that the end result is a consistent customer experience.

For example, they are taught the correct arm motion to use when salting fries, the right amount of ketchup to put on a bun, and when to replace a worn-out tile on the floor.

Everything McDonald's does is focused on making the customer's experience with it a lot better. It is for this reason that McDonald's was the first organization in its industry to offer breakfast. As the advertisement shows, it wants to capture an increasing portion of the customer's wallet by offering the customer a range of meal options.

continues...

It is also for this reason that McDonald's got into selling upscale coffee (it sells a higher grade of coffee in its stores and has opened cafés called McCafé to compete with Starbucks). In the United Kingdom and in New York, it owns a chain of upscale sandwich stores called Pret A Manger. It constantly tries new ventures and is not afraid to take risks based on customer trends. For example, McDonald's also owned a Mexican restaurant called Chipotle Grill and a restaurant chain called Boston Market, but sold them.

Finally, McDonald's also demonstrates customer focus by ensuring that everyone within its organization understands what it is trying to achieve. For example, although McDonald's considers its popular Dollar Menu a key part of its strategy, it is proving to be unpopular with some franchisees, who fear they will lose money because of rising food ingredient costs. Accordingly, McDonald's is working hard to find an alternative that will satisfy the needs of both customers and franchisees.

CINNAMON MELTS

the new fragrance for your mouth

BREAKFAST   BRUNCH   LUNCH   SNACK   DINNER

i'm lovin' it.

©2008 McDonald's

McDonald's is a customer-focused business.

CHAPTER CHALLENGE 10.2

ARE YOU ON THE RIGHT TRACK?

Before reading further, describe three to five traits of a business that is customer focused.
(*Were you on the right track? Check your answers in Appendix 2.*)

Along with the material discussed in Figure 1.7 from Chapter 1 (page 19), a picture of what customer focus is begins to appear. Customer focus is

- a management philosophy—in customer-focused businesses, senior management is deeply committed to making all decisions based around the customer

- a clear and shared understanding of the customer throughout the organization

- the commitment by each and every employee to make every customer interaction with the brand an opportunity to reinforce brand values

- not merely collecting and disseminating data on the customer using customer relationship management (CRM) tools

- redefining how success is measured in an organization

CHECKPOINT

Where We've Been

- We have learned that customer focus is a management philosophy about the customer that is shared by every employee within the business.

Where We're Going

- In the next section, we will see how to design a customer-focused business.

How to Build a Customer-Focused Business

OBJECTIVE 3

Building a customer-focused business takes courage, senior management commitment, and a different way of organizing and running the business. The case of Arbol Industries at the end of this chapter illustrates this point perfectly. The overall process to make a move from a product-centric business to a customer-centric (customer-focused) business is shown in Figure 10.1.[5] As can be seen, building a customer-focused business requires four key building blocks: senior management commitment, organizational realignment, support systems and processes, and revised financial metrics.

The Greystone Property Management example will provide details on each of the four building blocks of customer focus.

Every company wants to get close to its customers, but wishing doesn't make it so.

Gulati and Oldroyd

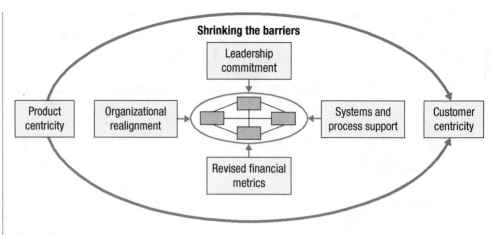

FIGURE 10.1

How to become a customer-focused business

Source: Denish Shah, Roland T. Rust, A. Parasuraman, Richard Staelin, and George S. Day, "The Path to Customer Centricity," *Journal of Service Research*, Volume 9, No. 2, November 2006, p. 119.

> *Customer-oriented values and beliefs are uniquely the responsibility of top management.*
>
> FREDERICK WEBSTER

10.3 GREYSTONE PROPERTY MANAGEMENT

Objective: Building a Customer-focused Business Requires Four Key Building Blocks

Greystone Property Management (you met Greystone in Chapter 4) manages high-rise residential properties for landlords (wealthy individuals and corporate clients such as pension funds).[6] Property management suppliers do regular maintenance on the buildings (for example, ensuring that the boilers and air conditioning units are in proper working order), rent out apartment units, collect rent, disburse monies for maintenance and repair, keep building turnover low, and refurbish apartment units to maintain and grow asset values. Greystone's CEO wanted to move his company from a product-focused entity to a customer-focused business.

Building a customer-focused business starts with *senior management commitment* (customer focus building block #1). A commitment to developing a deep understanding of customers is one action senior managers can take to demonstrate to the rest of the organization that customer focus is a key priority.[7] Talking about the importance of customer focus is one thing—actually allocating resources to understanding customers and making it a priority to listen to customers is another.

Greystone's CEO required all senior managers to visit their properties once a month to talk to customers (tenants and landlords) and

employees. Visionary CEOs have this one trait in common. For example, Bill George, the ex-CEO of Medtronic (a maker of medical devices), insisted that all engineers and designers attend at least one surgical procedure a year to watch how their customers (surgeons) used their products and to obtain live feedback from them.[8]

Without leadership commitment, the other three requirements for customer focus become irrelevant because it is the senior leadership that has to keep the spirit of customer focus alive in the business.

Previously, a customer (landlord) would have to deal individually with each Greystone business function. For example, if a customer wanted to know what the total expenditures on a building were for a given month, she would have to call the accounts payable department. Similarly, if she wanted to know what maintenance operations were being planned, she would have to call the maintenance function.

Worse, if a person went on vacation or quit the company, the customer lost a valuable contact within Greystone, and she would have to rebuild relations with the new individual. This caused tremendous frustration to customers. This lack of functional alignment around the customer is shown in Figure 10.2.

FIGURE 10.2

Greystone was not a customer-focused business.

The CEO and the senior leadership team realigned the organization around the customer. This is shown in Figure 10.3.

The *organizational realignment* (customer focus building block #2) was a success. Now, the customer was served by a team, not by several individual departments. Further, the customer had a single point of contact, the account manager, to whom she could direct all inquiries. If an employee went on vacation or quit the company, the team would seamlessly pick up the slack.

The CEO did not stop there. He astutely realized that without a glue to bind the organizational realignment, it would fall apart. So

Greystone developed *systems and process support* (customer focus building block #3) to further align the customer service teams. Specifically, Greystone took two steps. It cross-trained each team member to do other team members' jobs. Previously, each function focused on its own role, ignoring the needs of the customer. Now, each team member had a holistic picture of the customer, her needs, and what needed to be done to protect and grow her property. Additionally, the senior management team invested in a software program to enable each team member to view any detail regarding a particular property—number of tenants, cash flow, building operations, and so forth. This enabled each employee to better handle customer inquiries.

The final step Greystone executives took was to institute a set of *revised financial metrics* (customer focus building block #4) to ensure that the customer focus model was working smoothly and equitably. Previously, employees had absolutely no incentive to help each other and act as a team because they were measured and compensated based on individual department metrics. For example, the operations team was rewarded on keeping costs low, and the finance team was rewarded on lowering accounts receivable cycles.

Greystone put in place a set of revised financial metrics based on the performance of each team. The metrics included customer satisfaction, tenant satisfaction, and property profitability. Each team was given a percentage of profits generated from each property, and the team decided how best to allocate the profits based on team member performance. In essence, Greystone succeeded in making each team a self-motivating entity. This lowered costs of managerial supervision and raised employee morale because team members felt as if they were running a small business.

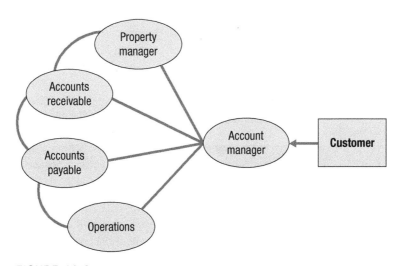

FIGURE 10.3

Greystone realigned its functions to focus on the customer.

Gloria Mogavero, senior executive at a global real estate services firm, talks about how to build a customer-focused business.

> *Getting closer to customers is not just a matter of installing a better CRM [customer relationship management] system or finding a more effective way to measure and increase customer satisfaction levels.*
>
> GULATI AND OLDROYD

CHECKPOINT

Where We've Been

■ We have seen what customer focus is, why it is important, and how to build a customer-focused business.

Where We're Going

■ In the next section, we will see that there are some common traps businesses should avoid when building a customer-focused business.

OBJECTIVE 4

Common Traps to Avoid in Building a Customer-Focused Business

In the previous section, we saw that there are four building blocks to a customer-focused business: senior management commitment, organizational realignment, support systems and processes, and revised financial metrics. Even if one of these building blocks is missing, customer focus efforts fail. There are many traps a business must avoid in its journey to become customer focused. These are shown in Table 10.2.

A common trap senior managers fall into is to wish for customer focus without providing the proper soil for it to take root and grow. We have seen that customer focus is a philosophy, a strategic priority. Unfortunately, many senior managers do not understand this. Instead, they take a tactical approach to customer focus. Let us take two examples.[9]

One route senior managers take is to hire motivational speakers to talk to employees about the importance of customer focus. Nothing is wrong with this approach, as long as it is viewed as an event that kicks off the customer focus journey. Unfortunately, many firms stop there, falsely thinking that employees will change their ways and miraculously

TABLE 10.2　**Traps to Avoid in the Customer Focus Journey**	
Trap	**Danger**
Wavering senior management support	■ Senior managers are hot and cold about customer focus. ■ Senior managers say one thing, but do something else. ■ Senior managers do not devote resources to customer focus. ■ Senior leadership changes; new guard changes direction
Lack of support systems and processes	■ No data on customer needs ■ Data on customer needs not shared across functions
Wishing for functional alignment	■ Not putting in place a process to ensure that every function is focused on the customer
Unrevised metrics	■ Old metrics that do not support focus on customer
Not willing to stay the course	■ Giving up after initial setbacks

start working together. This will never happen. This is because, while employees may believe in the message of customer focus and the need to work together, they don't know how to begin. They are lacking a process and a set of tools we have described in the previous section.

At a meeting of heads of different functions within a business, the senior executive stood in front of the group and laid a few empty cans of Coca Cola in a line on the table. He then proceeded to bash the cans in with a bat. "What did I just do?" he asked. Nobody said a word; they were looking fearfully at him. "I just got rid of our business silos," he said. "Tell the rest of the organization that, from this day forward, we will work together as one and focus on the customer."

Do you need me to tell you that this organization never achieved its goal of customer focus?

> *Customer and stakeholder relationships are the only source of truly sustainable competitive advantage. Yet most companies do not have a process to manage and grow this asset.*
>
> ANDERS GRONSTEDT

MARKETING DRIVES SUCCESS

10.4 BRITISH AIRWAYS

Objective: Senior Management Has a Crucial Role to Play in Fostering Customer Focus[10]

British Airways was privatized in 1987 in a bid to transform a loss-ridden, state-owned airline into a competitive, customer-focused business. Coming from outside the airline industry, CEO Sir Colin Marshall took a very unorthodox approach to achieving the transformation. He realized that other competitors were viewing air travel as a commodity business, thinking of an airline as a "bus of the skies," and focusing on cost-cutting to achieve profitability. Marshall bet that customers would be willing to pay a slight premium to be treated with respect and get services that would make travel more pleasant.

Under his leadership, British Airways began focusing on the customer's total experience to make changes to how it operated its business. It worked with the British government to install fast-track immigration channels at major airports like Heathrow and Gatwick. It opened new lounges where customers arriving on long overnight flights could get a full meal, take a shower, get their clothes pressed, and conduct business—all before public transport and offices were open. Even passengers flying in economy class were not forgotten— seating and meal options were greatly enhanced.

The focus on the customer has paid off. Except for one year, British Airways has made profits for the past decade. And yet, it has found that customer focus is a moving target. Although it won the award for best airline of the year in 2006 and 2007, it has also been voted by the Airport Transport Users Council as the worst European airline for baggage handling. This only shows that no business can take customer focus for granted—past successes do not guarantee future successes. New CEO Willie Walsh has his job cut out for him!

Senior management commitment enabled British Airways to become a customer-focused business.

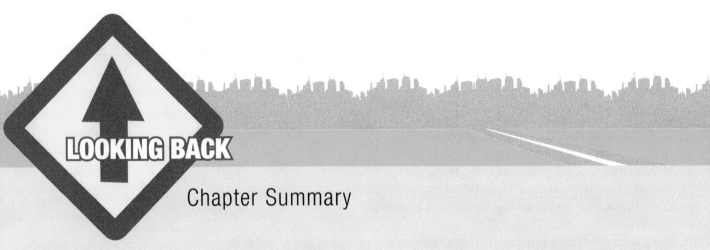

Chapter Summary

1. See that without customer focus, marketing strategies fail.

As we have seen in this book, although the marketing function may develop marketing strategies (which customers to target, what value propositions to offer), it is not the marketing function that implements many of these strategies. The vignette at the beginning of this chapter showed that the function handling customer inquiries failed to help the customer; it failed to implement the marketing strategy of satisfying the customer. It is for this reason that all functions within a business have to focus on the customer.

2. Learn to avoid mistakes made by your product-centric competitors by truly understanding what customer focus is.

Customer focus is diametrically opposite to product focus. Customer focus is

- a management philosophy—in customer-focused businesses, senior management is deeply committed to making all decisions based around the customer

- a clear and shared understanding of the customer throughout the organization

- the commitment by each and every employee to make every customer interaction with the brand an opportunity to reinforce brand values

- not merely collecting and disseminating data on the customer using CRM tools

- redefining how success is measured in an organization

3. Learn how to build a customer-focused business.

One reason why firms do not achieve customer focus is that everyone thinks the concept is intuitive and is common sense. Everyone in a business has to focus on the customer—what is so complicated about this obvious truth? The problem is, building customer focus takes courage, time, and culture change. There are four fundamental bricks that have to be put in place to build a customer-focused business: senior management commitment, organizational realignment, support systems and processes, and a revised set of financial metrics.

4. Learn to avoid common traps when implementing customer focus.

There are five main traps a business should avoid in implementing customer focus: wavering senior management support, lack of support systems and processes, wishing for customer focus, unrevised metrics, and unwillingness to stay the course in the face of setbacks.

1. If every function is not focused on the customer, marketing strategies fail. What suggestions do you have to ensure alignment between different functions in an organization? (Hint: this was discussed in Chapter 9.)

2. Provide an example of a business that you believe is customer focused. Be sure to justify your choice by providing details on what this organization does to deserve your nomination.

3. Provide an example of a business that you believe is not customer focused. Again, be sure to justify your choice.

4. What advice would you give a business that is convinced it needs to become customer focused but does not know where to start?

RUNNING CASE

ARBOL INDUSTRIES BUILDS A CUSTOMER-FOCUSED BUSINESS

Arbol Industries' marketing manager was worried. He had just received the results of the company's first ever customer satisfaction survey (see the next chapter on how to measure customer satisfaction). The results were not encouraging. The data showed that Arbol was not focused on the customer. Rather, some decisions were being made based on internal, not customer, considerations.

Here was one typical comment made by several customers who were buying dimensional lumber: "You ship me a product that is 4.27 m (14 ft.) in length. This is an odd size because most applications require a product that is 3.66 m (12 ft.) in length. I have to saw off 61 cm (2 ft.) just to use your product. This causes a lot of waste in material and resources."

The marketing manager talked informally to a few salespeople to gain further insight into this problem. The matter was even worse than the survey comments. One salesperson told him, "We are not just being arrogant about ignoring customer needs, we are being plain dumb. If we were smart, we would listen to what our customers are telling us. They are telling us that they will pay us for a product that is 4.27 m in length if we ship them a 3.66 m product! Does this make any sense to you?"

It didn't make any sense to the marketing manager either. So he went to the head of production and broached the issue with him. "Why do we ship the customer the wrong product?" he asked. "Well," came the reply, "it may be the wrong product to *you*, but it is the right product for *me*." The production manager went on to explain. "I understand what our customers are saying, I really do. But, I don't care what their needs are. This is because I am measured and compensated based on how efficiently our factories run, not on customer satisfaction. And I get greater efficiencies when I run 4.27 m products through the system, not 3.66 m logs."

It became abundantly clear to the marketing manager what the problem was—Arbol Industries, for all the progress it had made during the past months, was not customer focused. It was internally focused. So the marketing manager brought the issue with up the CEO during one of their meetings. Together, they thought about how to make Arbol a customer-focused company.

The first step they took was to form a committee comprising the heads of all functions—marketing, sales, supply chain, production, finance, and human resources. They called this the Operating Committee (OC). The president of Arbol, who was also their chief operating officer (COO), was put in charge of the OC.

Previously, when the functional heads met, they would act as if they had nothing in common. They would report on what their function was doing to meet *functional* objectives. With the realignment, the OC behaved differently. Now, each functional head reported on what the function was doing to meet *organizational* objectives. In essence organizational, not functional, objectives became the glue binding them together.

Next, they redesigned metrics used to measure and reward functions. Previously, each function looked after its own interests and made decisions that would optimize its goals. As was made clear in the 4.27 m log example, sometimes these goals were in conflict with the needs of the customer and the rest of the organization. The team instituted enterprise-wide metrics.

These new metrics placed the needs of the customer first and measured such items as customer satisfaction, loyalty, and share of wallet (refer to Table 10.1 on page 221). The new metrics recognized that it might be important to sub-optimize one function in order to meet a customer goal. So the production manager felt happy because he was being measured on metrics that emphasized factors other than factory efficiency. The marketing manager was happy because he was being measured on achieving customer satisfaction. This was true for all functions.

Finally, Arbol's senior management actively communicated the new arrangement throughout the organization. But they did not stop there. To demonstrate their commitment to focus on the customer, a new position was formed—the factory marketing coordinator. At each of Arbol's 15 manufacturing plants, a factory marketing coordinator ensured that marketing strategies were being understood and implemented by all functions. This critical position liaised between the marketing function at head office and the factory. As one senior manager put it, "People working on the factory floor have to know what our marketing strategy is and the crucial role they play in implementing it."

The changes worked! Arbol saw a steep increase in customer satisfaction, and this made a tremendous positive impact on its financial position.

Case Assignment

Research another business that moved from an internal focus to become a customer-focused business. Write a short report on the steps this company took to become customer focused.

SUGGESTED READINGS
If You Want to Achieve Customer Focus in Your Business, Do Not Miss These Publications

Robert Ricci, "Move from Product to Customer Centric," *Quality Progress*, November 2003, pp. 22–29.

Denish Shah, Roland T. Rust, A. Parasuraman, Richard Staelin, and George S. Day, "The Path to Customer Centricity," *Journal of Service Research*, Volume 9, No. 2, November 2006, pp. 113–124.

NOTES

1. As recounted by Tammy to the author. The name of the company has been disguised.

2. Ranjay Gulati, "Silo Busting: How to Execute on the Promise of Customer Focus," *Harvard Business Review*, May 2007, pp. 98–108.

3. I am treating *customer centric* and *customer focused* as interchangeable terms. Some authors use one term versus the other.

4. Based on conversations with ex-students and Richard Gibson, "Franchisees Balk at Dollar Menu," *The Wall Street Journal*, November 14, 2007, page B3A.

5. This section is based on Denish Shah et al., "The Path to Customer Centricity," *Journal of Service Research*, Volume 9, No. 2, November 2006, pp. 113–124 and Robert Ricci, "Move From Product to Customer Centric," *Quality Progress*, November 2003, pp. 22–29. For additional insight, refer to Ajay Sirsi, *Marketing Led—Sales Driven: How Successful Businesses Use the Power of Marketing Plans and Sales Execution to Win in the Marketplace* (Victoria, BC: Trafford Publishing,

2005). Chapter 7 in that book presents an annual planning calendar to align all functions to focus on the customer.

6. This example is based on a consulting project, but I have disguised the name of the client.

7. George S. Day, *The Market-Driven Organization* (New York: Free Press, 1999).

8. Paul Kaihla, "Best Kept Secrets of the World's Best Companies," *Business 2.0*, 2006, Volume 7, No. 3, p. 94.

9. I have witnessed both examples as part of ongoing consulting engagements.

10. Based on Steven Prokesch, "Competing on Customer Service: An Interview with British Airways' Sir Colin Marshall," *Harvard Business Review*, November–December 1995, pp. 100–112; Rebecca Smithers, "British Airways—Fly the Flag, Lose Your Bag," *The Guardian*, June 23, 2007; Charles R. Weiser, "Championing the Customer," *Harvard Business Review*, November–December 1995, pp. 113–116; Skytrax Research website; PR Newswire website.

Managing Customer Value

describes how to reap the benefits of successful marketing strategies.

CHAPTER 11 Provides strategies on how to attract and satisfy customers to build customer loyalty.

CHAPTER 12 Describes how marketing can be the engine of business transformation.

Understanding Customers ← PART 1, P. 1

Creating Customer Value ← PART 2, P. 67

Delivering Customer Value ← PART 3, P. 195

Managing Customer Value ↑ PART 4, P. 231

SUCCESS

CHAPTER 11

Customer Attraction, Satisfaction, and Retention Strategies

CHECKPOINT

Where We've Been

- We have seen how successful businesses understand customer needs, segment their customers, and select attractive target customers.

- For each target customer segment, successful businesses craft a winning marketing strategy based on the marketing mix elements of product, price, channel, and marketing communications strategies.

- Winning businesses know that crafting superior marketing strategies will not guarantee marketplace success—these strategies have to be implemented by other functions.

- Winning businesses translate marketing strategies into sales and other functional strategies.

- In this way, winning businesses build a customer-focused business.

Where We're Going

- In this chapter, you will learn how to attract, satisfy, and retain your customers.

- The next chapter will discuss how to build a marketing organization that is an engine for corporate transformation.

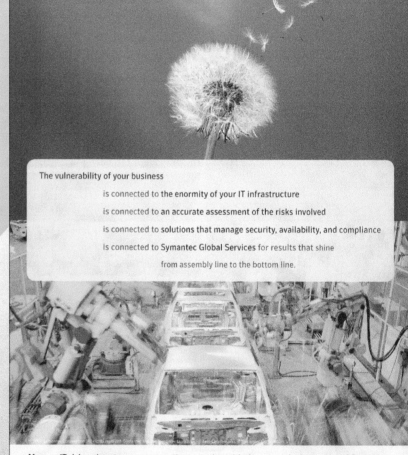

CHAPTER INTRODUCTION

In this chapter you will

$34 508.69. That is how much Tammy, our loyal Starbucks customer from Chapter 5, is worth (in today's dollars) to Starbucks during her lifetime. In other words, $34 508.69 is the present value of all future expenditures she will make at Starbucks consuming lattes and snacks. Tammy's financial planner has often told her, "If you only saved the money you spend on Starbucks, you could have $88 984.56 in your bank in 20 years!" But Tammy does not care. She likes Starbucks and she will not change her habits.

If Starbucks was a smart company (and it is), it would stop looking at Tammy as a one-time transaction. Rather, it would make sure she was a completely satisfied customer, knowing full well that customer satisfaction leads to customer loyalty (retention). And loyal customers are *very* profitable to any company.

1. Learn an important secret all winning businesses have.

2. Learn how to attract customers to your business without spending a lot of money.

3. Learn how to measure and use customer satisfaction data to get ahead of your competitors.

4. Learn how to keep your customers forever (the ones you want to keep, that is).

5. Learn how to attract, satisfy, and keep customers on the internet.

CHAPTER CHALLENGE 11.1

ARE YOU ON THE RIGHT TRACK?

List five things Starbucks must be doing right to enjoy Tammy's loyalty.

(*Were you on the right track? Check your answers in Appendix 2.*)

Starbucks finds creative ways to keep Tammy's loyalty.

Winning Businesses Know That Satisfying Customers Is the Secret to Success

There is a growing body of research conclusively showing that satisfied customers spend more, and this positively impacts overall business performance and creates **shareholder value**.[1] In other words, winning businesses know that satisfying customers is the secret to business success.

In a groundbreaking study, researchers showed the relationship between customer satisfaction and financial success by creating a portfolio of stocks bought and sold in response to the American Customer Satisfaction Index (ACSI)—an indicator of customer satisfaction with 200 companies in more than 40 industries. The research showed that companies with higher customer satisfaction scores have produced higher stock returns, and that their stock values and cash flows have been less volatile.[2] These results are shown in Figure 11.1.

As we will see later in the chapter, satisfying customers is also the best way to attract and keep them.

A study of 200 companies shows a clear correlation between higher levels of customer satisfaction and higher stock prices.

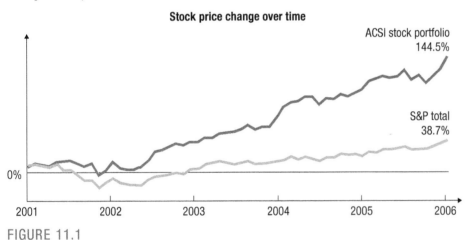

Stock price change over time

ACSI stock portfolio
144.5%

S&P total
38.7%

0%

2001   2002   2003   2004   2005   2006

FIGURE 11.1

Satisfying customers pays off.

Source: Christopher W. Hart, "Beating the Marketing with Customer Satisfaction," *Harvard Business Review*, March 2007, pp. 30, 32.

11.1 ACE HARDWARE

Objective: Smart Companies Satisfy Customers without Adding Costs

Ace Hardware has found a way to increase customer satisfaction without adding extra costs. When a store gets busy, a "customer quarterback" takes on the role of customer coordinator with only one goal: to help customers. The customer quarterback greets incoming shoppers, talks to them, and assesses their body language to decide whether they are just browsers, mission shoppers (customers with a specific mission and no time), or customers wanting to work on a home renovation project.

Using an earpiece, the customer quarterback radios ahead so the right expert is waiting in the right aisle for the customer. When there is an influx of customers, the customer quarterback instructs all employees to drop everything and focus on helping customers. This scheme was developed by 12 Ace employees who spent one year analyzing how to increase the time employees spent with customers without adding extra employees.[3]

Smart companies know that the secret to success is customer satisfaction.

> *As long as repeat business is important, and as long as customers have a chance to go somewhere else, employees must deliver high levels of customer satisfaction for a company to be successful.*
>
> CLAES FORNELL

CHAPTER CHALLENGE 11.2

ARE YOU ON THE RIGHT TRACK?

Ace Hardware demonstrates how a business can increase value to customers without increasing costs. The trick is to understand customer needs. Name one other business profiled in this book that is successful using the same strategy of increasing value while not increasing costs.

(*Were you on the right track? Check your answers in Appendix 2.*)

Where We've Been

■ We have learned that winning businesses have a secret: they know that satisfying customers is the smart thing to do.

CHECKPOINT

Where We're Going

■ In the next section, we will see how to attract customers without spending a lot of money.

Attract Customers to Your Business without Spending a Lot of Money

OBJECTIVE 2

As we discussed in Chapter 8, attracting customers (building brand awareness) can be a very expensive proposition if approached incorrectly. Many companies spend a lot of money on advertising to build brand awareness and attract customers. But as we saw in Chapter 8, over time the impact of advertising diminishes, leading companies to spend more on advertising to attract customers. This is not a smart way to run a business.

Let us discuss a smart alternative. In the previous section, we saw that satisfying customers is profitable. The truth is, a business has no other choice in a society that is socially networked. Using **social media** (refer to Chapter 8 if you need to refresh your memory), customers can instantly communicate with the world about problems with a brand. Let us take an example.[4]

Michael Whitford uploaded a video to a social networking site in which he considers a golf club, an axe, and a sword before deciding on a sledgehammer to bash his non-functioning Apple MacBook to small pieces. In the video he says that Apple declined to repair the computer, still under warranty. More than 340 000 people viewed the video. Two months later, Apple replaced his laptop.

> *Here's some free advice: Go to Google, enter any of your company's brands followed by the word "sucks," and you will see the true consumers' reports. Brace yourself, for it won't be pretty. Googling Wal-Mart turns up 165 000 results; Disney, 530 000; Google, 767 000. What's your number?*
>
> JEFF JARVIS

If social media are so powerful in getting companies to do the right thing, can companies take advantage of them to *attract* and *keep* customers? Absolutely. Research shows that word of mouth creates twice as much long-term value for the firm, while marketing-induced efforts such as advertising only create a short-term gain.[5] Let us take an example.

11.2 DELL

Objective: Smart Companies Take Advantage of Social Media to Attract, Satisfy, and Keep Customers

In 2007, Jeff Jarvis wrote about his negative experiences with a Dell computer on his blog BuzzMachine, under the headline "Dell sucks." Dell not only resolved Jeff's problems, but also harnessed the power of social media to its advantage. Here are some ways in which Dell uses social media to attract, satisfy, and keep customers:

- It enables customers to rate its products on its own website.

- It reaches out to bloggers to fix their problems.

- It organizes customers' advice so customers can learn from each other.

- It has started IdeaStorm, where customers have offered 8600 suggestions in a year, voted on them 600 000 times, and left 64 000 comments.[6] Dell has implemented some of the ideas.

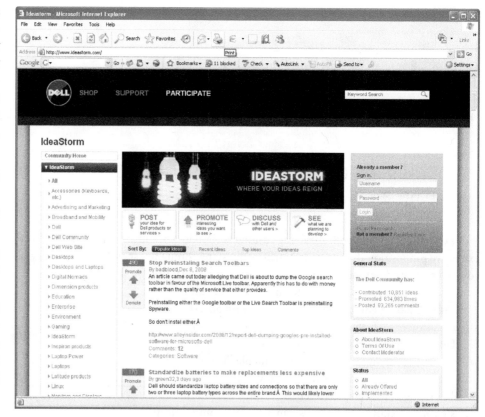

Dell uses the power of social media to attract, satisfy, and keep customers.

CHECKPOINT

Where We've Been

- We have seen that satisfying customers is one of the smartest things a company can do because customer satisfaction is the best way to attract and keep customers.
- Customer satisfaction has tremendous impact on business cash flow, profitability, and shareholder value.
- Using social media, a business can attract, satisfy, and keep customers without adding excess costs.

Where We're Going

- In the next section, we will see how to measure and use customer satisfaction data.

How to Measure and Use Customer Satisfaction Data

OBJECTIVE 3

Measuring Customer Satisfaction

 Financial planner Ennio Longo discusses how he attracts and retains customers.

A typical way to measure customer satisfaction is to survey customers. There are usually five sections in a satisfaction survey:

1. an overall customer satisfaction score
2. satisfaction with goods and services offered by the firm
3. intention to repurchase from the firm
4. willingness to recommend the firm to others
5. customer demographic information

Table 11.1 presents an *abbreviated* customer satisfaction survey.

TABLE 11.1 A Typical Customer Satisfaction Survey

Overall customer experience
Please rate your overall satisfaction with ABC Inc.:

Very satisfied	Satisfied	Neither satisfied nor dissatisfied	Dissatisfied	Very dissatisfied
5	4	3	2	1

Performance ratings
Please rate your satisfaction with the following:

Very satisfied	Satisfied	Neither satisfied nor dissatisfied	Dissatisfied	Very dissatisfied
5	4	3	2	1

Product performance	5	4	3	2	1
Product variety	5	4	3	2	1
Sales force product knowledge	5	4	3	2	1
Sales force responsiveness	5	4	3	2	1
Price-value ratio	5	4	3	2	1

Intention to repurchase and recommend
Please indicate your level of agreement or disagreement with the following statements:

Strongly agree	Agree	Neither agree nor disagree	Disagree	Strongly disagree
5	4	3	2	1

I plan to continue buying from ABC Inc.	5	4	3	2	1
I will recommend ABC to another person who is in the market for the same product.	5	4	3	2	1

Using Customer Satisfaction to Get Ahead of Your Competitors

There are certain hidden gems in customer satisfaction research that not too many people know about. Heed this advice and get ahead of your competitors.

As can be seen from Table 11.1, overall satisfaction is measured on a 5-point scale.[7] In most businesses if, say, 80% of customers gave the business a score of 4 (satisfied), champagne bottles would be uncorked. The reasoning would be that 80% of customers are satisfied. Only 20% of customers are less than satisfied. That is a good thing, correct? Wrong.

The research shows that customers who give you a score of 5 (very satisfied) are six times more likely to repurchase from you compared to customers who give you a score of 4 (satisfied).[8] So it is not enough to satisfy customers; a business should focus on completely satisfying them. This is not all. The different levels of satisfaction have tremendous impact on customer loyalty.[9] This is shown in Table 11.2. We will have more to say about this topic in the section on how to build customer loyalty.

KEYPOINT

Stop wasting your time trying to convert customers who give you a score of 1–3 to a 4. Focus instead on converting the 4s to a 5.

TABLE 11.2	**Customer Satisfaction Impacts Customer Loyalty**	
Satisfaction score	**What it means**	**Impact on customer loyalty**
5	Very satisfied customer	Very loyal customer
4	Satisfied customer	Customer will easily switch to competitor
1–3	Dissatisfied customer	Very disloyal customer

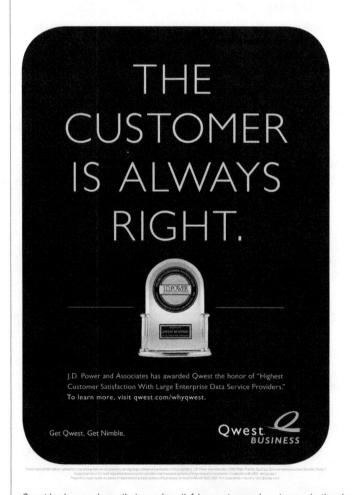

Smart businesses know that merely satisfying customers is not enough; they have to be completely satisfied.

As we have seen, in a typical customer satisfaction survey, we measure intention to repurchase and willingness to recommend. However, recent research has shown that the average satisfaction score is the best indicator of business performance, followed by the top two box scores (percentage of customers who scored a 4 or 5). Intention to repurchase has some impact on predicting future business performance, but intention to recommend has no impact.[10]

Finally, some businesses measure both customer satisfaction and customer complaints. But they tend to treat these as separate items. Recent research shows that this could be a mistake. Researchers studied the impact of customer satisfaction and customer complaints on a firm's stock value gap (the gap between the firm's market value and its optimal value based on benchmarking against best-of-class competitors). They found that customer complaints have a greater impact on the stock value gap compared to customer satisfaction. Further, customer complaints raise the stock value gap more than customer satisfaction.

CHAPTER CHALLENGE 11.3

ARE YOU ON THE RIGHT TRACK?

Why do we say in Table 11.2 that satisfied customers will easily switch to a competitor? (*Were you on the right track? Check your answers in Appendix 2.*)

MARKETING DRIVES SUCCESS

11.3 FOOT LOCKER

Objective: Learn from Customer Complaints

Do you remember the example in Chapter 6 on the standoff between Nike and Foot Locker? When Foot Locker (a major sports retailer) cut Nike orders by about $200 million to protest the terms Nike had placed on prices and selection, Nike cut its allocation of shoes to Foot Locker by $400 million. As we saw, Foot Locker customers complained about the lack of variety. Foot Locker listened to them. Now the relationship between the two firms is stronger than ever.

Foot Locker listened to customer complaints and renewed its relationship with Nike.

Where We've Been

■ We have seen that customer satisfaction is responsible for attracting and keeping customers, and for generating greater and less volatile cash flows, greater business profitability, and greater shareholder value.

■ Although measuring customer satisfaction is a standard practice, there are hidden gems in how to use satisfaction data.

CHECKPOINT

Where We're Going

■ In the next section, we will see how to build customer loyalty.

OBJECTIVE 4

KEYPOINT

Do not treat customer satisfaction and customer complaint in isolation; view them as a duet.

How to Keep Customers Forever

When we say "how to keep customers forever," we of course mean the customers you actually *want* to keep (this point was discussed in detail in Chapters 3 and 6). Why is building customer retention (loyalty) so important to a business? The answer is easy. Loyal customers

■ are more profitable

■ cost less to serve as they are already familiar with the brand and like it

■ are generally more price-insensitive

■ engage in greater positive word-of-mouth communications, thus helping a business attract more customers

■ are more willing to forgive a business for negative experiences

■ are less willing to listen to inducements from competitors

■ are more willing to try new offerings by the business

MARKETING DRIVES SUCCESS

11.4 AIR PRODUCTS AND CHEMICALS INC.[11]

Objective: Building Customer Loyalty Is a Journey

With sales of over $10 billion annually, Air Products is a global organization that supplies industrial gases, chemicals, and services to a wide range of markets, from semiconductor production to businesses that serve the home healthcare market by providing oxygen therapy to patients in their homes. Air Products also provides the liquid hydrogen and liquid oxygen that provide fuel for the Space Shuttle External Tank.

Under the leadership of chairman John P. Jones, the company embarked on a remarkable journey to build customer loyalty. Its customer loyalty process, which can be used by any business, is shown in Figure 11.2.

FIGURE 11.2

Air Product's customer loyalty process

Source: Robert Ricci, "Move From Product to Customer Centric," *Quality Progress*, November 2003, p. 24.

Developing Customer Loyalty Step #1: Listen to Customers

The first step to building customer loyalty is to truly listen to customers. We have already discussed one important way to listen to customers—the customer satisfaction survey in Table 11.1. Other ways to listen to customers are through sales reports and customer complaint data.

If listening to customers is simply a matter of customer satisfaction surveys, customer complaint data, and sales reports, why do many businesses do a poor job of it? This is because in order to listen to customers, you have to think like a customer. Unfortunately, this is where many businesses fall short—they are internally focused. This is shown in Figure 11.3.[12] Once a business starts to *think* like a customer, it is ready to *listen* to the customer, not before.

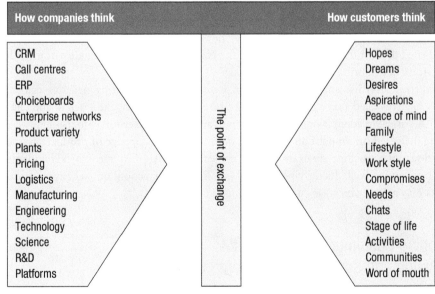

FIGURE 11.3

To listen to your customers, think like a customer.

Source: C.K. Prahalad and Venkatram Ramaswamy, "The Co-creation Connection," *Strategy + Business*, Issue 27, Second Quarter 2002, p. 53.

TABLE 11.3	**Step 2: Classify Customers on a Loyalty Index**		
Customer loyalty classification	Score given by customer on overall satisfaction	Score given by customer on repurchase intention	Score given by customer on willingness to recommend
Secure	5	5	5
Favourable	4	4	4
Indifferent	3	3	3
At risk	1–2	1–2	1–2

Developing Customer Loyalty Step #2: Understand and Communicate

Based on the customer satisfaction data collected, customers should be classified into loyalty categories. One such classification is shown in Table 11.3. Customers are labelled as "secure" if they indicate they are very satisfied (score 5 on overall satisfaction), will definitely continue buying from the same company (score 5 on this dimension), and will definitely recommend the product to others (score 5 on this dimension). Lower ratings result in other customer classifications, as shown in Table 11.3.[13]

The customer classification should be communicated to all employees within the organization. Although there is a potential for misinterpretation of information, the payoffs outweigh the downsides. Besides, through proper training, information misinterpretation can be mitigated. Throughout this book we have seen that in winning organizations, all employees, not just those in sales or marketing, have a clear picture of the customer.

Developing Customer Loyalty Step #3: Focus on Opportunities

Once customers are classified according to their loyalty index, it is time to take action. Each customer category will require a different set of actions (listen to the author as he provides details on this topic). One important issue to keep in mind is that the "at risk" customers should not be thought of as delivering low margins and, therefore, of little value. In reality, these customers can be very attractive to keep. They are at risk because something negative has happened to dent their relationship with the company. Taking immediate action with these customers will bring immediate payback.

Recent research has supported this idea. Researchers investigating negative critical incidents have revealed that a critical incident causes a customer to take stock of the relationship. A critical incident is one that is so important, the customer remembers it. Flowers not being delivered on time for an important occasion or the stoppage of production due to breakdown of a machine are examples of a critical incident. Of course, critical incidents can be positive as well. Identifying and taking immediate action on negative critical incidents may actually increase customer satisfaction and loyalty.[14]

KEYPOINT

Negative critical incidents, if handled properly, can enhance customer satisfaction and loyalty.

Developing Customer Loyalty Step #4: Take Action and Sustain Improvement

Air Products knows that the final step of sustaining improvement is the most important step. Although Air Products has kept the basic approach the same, it has modified its customer data collection instruments, made changes to elements that were not adding value to the process, driven more customer-segment-based information and actions, and integrated customer loyalty data with other linkages such as employees and operational effectiveness. Arbol Industries has done the same thing; you can read about its efforts in the case at the end of this chapter.

Air Product's experience with customer loyalty has paid off. Customers rated as "secure" or "favourable" have generated significantly higher returns than customers who are "indifferent." Its stock price has seen steady improvement since it embarked on the process to build customer loyalty. Such successes spur more commitment to the customer loyalty process. This is an important point to never forget—building customer loyalty should not be thought of as a one-time project. Rather, it is an ongoing journey.

> *The customer loyalty process is about more than just conducting a survey. It is an ongoing process that requires the organization to take time to understand what the customer is truly saying.*
>
> ROBERT RICCI

 Hear the author discuss how smart businesses are building customer loyalty by using satisfaction data wisely.

CHECKPOINT

Where We've Been

⬛ We have seen that building customer loyalty is a process.

Where We're Going

⬛ In the final section of this chapter, we will see how to attract, satisfy, and keep customers on the internet.

Attracting, Satisfying, and Keeping Customers on the Internet

△ OBJECTIVE 5

In Chapter 3, we saw that traditional segmentation methods do not work on the internet. Instead, a new form of segmentation called occasionalization is very useful to segment and build loyalty with customers on the web. The occasionalization segmentation is shown in Table 11.4.

TABLE 11.4 The Web Requires a Different Segmentation Approach

Segment	Session length	Number of sites	Example
Quickies	1 min.	1.8	Quick, daily check of the weather forecast
Just the facts	9 min.	10.5	Visiting online stores to buy hard-to-find foreign movies
Single mission	10 min.	2.0	Longer visits to research a single topic, for example, recommended restaurants in a city
Do it again	14 min.	2.1	Lingering visits to a few familiar sites, for example, paying bills online
Loitering	33 min.	8.5	Leisurely visits to a few "sticky" or time-consuming sites, for example, reading the daily news
Information please	37 min.	19.7	In-depth information gathering on a particular topic by visiting many related sites, for example, researching what car to buy and financing options
Surfing	70 min.	44.6	Aimless wandering around the web

Source: Horacio D. Rozanski, Gerry Bollman, and Martin Lipman, "Seize the Occasion! The Seven-segment System for Online Marketing," *Strategy + Business,* Issue 24, Third Quarter, 2001, pp. 42–51.

Traditional segmentation methods do not work on the internet because traditional methods make use of customer characteristics. As we saw in Chapter 3, customer characteristics are poor predictors of customer behaviour. Even mass customization (the ability to customize offerings to each and every customer) fails if based on user characteristics. Let us take an example.[15]

An advertiser can very easily send different banner ads to a 24-year-old graduate student and a 54-year-old CEO visiting the same business news site. But if the content and placement of those ads aren't appropriate to the type of *usage session* the student or the CEO is in, the ads will fail to deliver on their objectives of attracting and keeping the customer. So even though the student likes country music, if he is in a "quickies" session (see Table 11.4 for descriptions of usage segments), he is not going to be interested in any offers on new music CDs, however attractive they may be.

So just how can a business use the occasionalization segmentation approach to attract, satisfy, and keep customers? This is shown in Table 11.5.

TABLE 11.5	**Occasion-Based Marketing Strategy to Attract and Keep Customers on the Web**			
1. Consumer group	**2. Marketing goals**	**3. Usage occasion**	**4. Internet site**	**5. Marketing tactics**
Select the target customer group.	Select a marketing goal.	Decide which type of occasion works best for the selected marketing goal.	Select the sites the target customer is most likely to visit.	Design and use occasion-specific tactics.
■ 14–17 ■ **18–24** ■ 25–32	■ Extend brand awareness ■ Interact with customers ■ **Establish brand position**	■ Quickies ■ Just the facts ■ Single mission ■ Do it again ■ **Loitering** ■ Information please ■ Surfing	■ amazon.com ■ espn.com ■ yahoo.com ■ **mtv.com**	■ **Create pop-ups that link to co-branded content** ■ Set up a chat room to spread "buzz" about the product

Source: Adapted from Horacio D. Rozanski, Gerry Bollman, and Martin Lipman, "Seize the Occasion! The Seven-segment System for Online Marketing," *Strategy + Business,* Issue 24, Third Quarter, 2001, pp. 42–51.

Chapter Summary

1. Learn an important secret all winning businesses have.

All winning businesses know that the secret to customer attraction and customer retention (loyalty) is customer satisfaction. A growing body of research attests to this fact. Customer satisfaction is responsible for higher and less-volatile cash flows, higher rates of customer loyalty, greater word of mouth leading to attraction of new customers, greater business profitability, and increased shareholder value.

2. Learn how to attract customers to your business without spending a lot of money.

The not-so-smart way to attract customers is to constantly spend money on advertising. The smarter way is to satisfy customers. By using social media (such as Facebook and blogs) to its advantage, any business can harness the power of social networks to attract new customers. But to do this, a business has to be serious about listening to customers and responding to their concerns. Actually, a business has no other choice in a socially networked world. This is because negative experiences with a company can be shared by anyone with anyone across the globe. All it takes is a post on the internet.

3. Learn how to measure and use customer satisfaction data to get ahead of your competitors.

A typical customer satisfaction survey consists of (1) overall satisfaction with the company, (2) satisfaction with goods and services provided by the company, (3) intention to repurchase, (4) willingness to recommend the company to others, and (5) customer demographic information.

There are certain key points to keep in mind in order to use customer satisfaction data wisely. Merely satisfying customers is not enough; a business has to make its customers very satisfied. This is because only very satisfied customers are loyal. The lesson to be learned here is that you need to spend time thinking about how to convert satisfied customers to very satisfied customers, instead of converting dissatisfied and indifferent customers to satisfied status.

4. Learn how to keep your customers forever (the ones you *want* to keep, that is).

To keep your customers forever, you first need to think like a customer. Many companies think in terms of enterprise networks or technology, but their customers think in terms of needs and expectations. Such an internal view of the world does not enable a firm to listen to its customers, which is the first step in the process of building customer loyalty.

The second step is to understand and communicate customer profiles. This is typically done by categorizing customers as "secure," "favourable," "indifferent," or "at risk." The third step is to treat each of these customers differently. For example, strategies to keep loyal customers should be different from strategies for the "at risk" customers. The final step in building customer loyalty is to take action and sustain improvements.

5. Learn how to attract, satisfy, and keep customers on the internet.

Attraction, satisfaction, and retention strategies on the internet require a thorough understanding of how to segment customers, as traditional segmentation methods do not work on the internet. A usage-based method called occasionalization is useful in this regard. Using this segmentation approach, any business can attract and keep customers on the internet by (1) selecting the target customer group, (2) selecting a marketing goal, (3) deciding which type of occasion works best to achieve the marketing goal, (4) selecting the sites the target customer is most likely to visit, and (5) designing and using occasion-specific marketing tactics.

CRITICAL THINKING QUESTIONS

1. Why is satisfying customers also the best way to attract and keep them? Provide an example of a company that succeeds in attracting and keeping its customers by satisfying them.

2. According to the American Customer Satisfaction Index (ACSI), if satisfaction declines, customers are not likely to buy unless there is a price cut. Why do you think this might be the case? Can you provide an example to demonstrate this point?

3. Design a customer satisfaction survey and compare the results for two businesses in the same industry. Administer the survey to at least 10 customers from each business.

4. You have been hired as a consultant by a business that wishes to build customer loyalty. Write a short proposal outlining what steps you will take in helping this business build a base of loyal customers.

5. Mercedes Benz would like to attract a younger target market, consumers aged 25–30. Outline an internet strategy for this purpose using the occasionalization segmentation method.

RUNNING CASE

ARBOL INDUSTRIES TAKES STEPS TO SATISFY AND KEEP CUSTOMERS

As we saw in the last chapter, Arbol received a rude awakening upon seeing the results of its customer satisfaction work. Although it had made tremendous progress in becoming a marketing-led company, it was not customer focused. In the previous chapter, we saw the steps Arbol management put in place to make it customer focused. They did not stop there. "Being customer focused is just the first step," mused Arbol's marketing manager. "We will really begin to see the payoff when we build a base of loyal customers." Let us see in this chapter, and in the next chapter, what Arbol did.

Initially, the marketing manager did not know where to start. Although he thought hard about the problem, he was getting nowhere. "Oh well," he thought, "I'll tackle the problem when I get back from vacation." He was very excited about going on his vacation. He and his wife had saved for an entire year to spend a week at the Four Seasons resort along Maui's Wailea Beach. The entire package would cost several thousand dollars, but this was a special occasion—their 25th wedding anniversary.

He spent the first couple of days doing nothing but eating nice food and watching the Pacific Ocean. But then he began noticing something. All the employees at the resort looked like they were actually happy serving guests. It was not an act they were putting on. The service was helpful without being subservient, and instinctive rather than programmed.[16] "How can someone be happy serving other people?" he wondered.

Being a curious kind of person, he began chatting informally with the staff and management. He learned that the staff were happy because Four Seasons invests in their employees by giving them training, free meals, free nights at any property depending on tenure, and profit-sharing. When he returned to his office, he began researching how companies build a loyal and profitable customer base.

The marketing manager started by adopting a framework called the Service Profit Chain (Figure 11.4).[17]

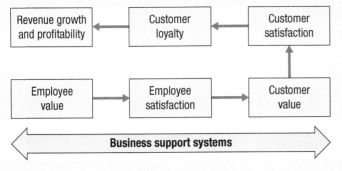

FIGURE 11.4

Arbol Industries' recipe for building loyal customers

This is the logic Arbol followed:

- A business is more successful (measured by revenue growth and profitability) when it has loyal customers. This is because loyal customers buy more, are generally price-insensitive, and have lower costs to serve.
- Customer satisfaction drives customer loyalty.
- Customers are satisfied when they perceive that their needs are being met through the value propositions being delivered by the company.
- It is the employees in a company who design and deliver customer value propositions.
- Satisfied employees deliver superior customer value.
- Employees are satisfied when the organization is successful in creating value for them.

Arbol started by conducting satisfaction surveys with their customers as well as their employees to understand what these important stakeholders thought of the company. As we saw in Chapter 10, Arbol realized it was not focused on the customer; it was a product-centric company. We also saw the steps it took in building a customer focus orientation. The employee satisfaction results were even more revealing. While employees were not unhappy, there was a lot that could be done to create value for them. For instance, employees wanted more business training, better coordination between different functions, greater say in the running of the company, and more access to senior management.

The marketing manager immediately got together with the human resources manager, and together they mapped out what kind of training to provide employees. They resolved to create Arbol University, a training facility to teach employees marketing strategy, customer service, leadership, and financial skills. All courses would be taught by Arbol senior managers, thus making them more visible to employees.

To resolve the other two employee issues, the marketing manager, along with other functional heads, developed an annual planning calendar to translate the marketing plan into functional plans (customer service, finance, human resources, and operations).[18] As we saw in Chapter 9, Arbol had already started the process of translating marketing plans into sales plans.

To give employees a greater say in running the company, senior management resolved that all key employees should have a holistic picture of each key customer. So just as Greystone did (refer to Chapter 10), Arbol invested in business support systems in the form of software to enable each employee to see the profile of each key customer and to view customer needs information and the value propositions in place with each customer. This enabled employees to make suggestions to improve customer satisfaction.

The end result? Every employee knew what the key elements of the marketing strategy were—what customers Arbol was serving, potential customers being targeted, customer value propositions offered to customers, how Arbol planned to differentiate itself from competitors, and how it was going to be successful.[19] This enabled them to serve their customers better, which improved customer satisfaction. In turn, enhanced customer satisfaction drove customer loyalty. When Arbol conducted the same survey the following year, the efforts were visible—both employee and customer satisfaction levels had gone up! In the next chapter you will see that Arbol went a step further to measure and build customer loyalty.

The marketing manager knew they were on the right path. But he also knew that improving customer satisfaction and loyalty was *not* a project, but a journey. He had learned the lesson well during his vacation. He wondered if he could get Arbol to pay for another trip to the Four Seasons resort for "research purposes."

Case Assignment

Research the Four Seasons hotels and resorts on the internet. Write a short report on how they build customer satisfaction and loyalty by investing in satisfying employees.

SUGGESTED READINGS

If You Want to Build Loyal Customers, Grow Revenues, and Improve Profitability, Do Not Miss These Publications

James L. Heskett, Thomas O. Jones, Gary W. Loveman, W. Earl Sasser, Jr., and Leonard A. Schlesinger, "Putting the Service-Profit Chain to Work," *Harvard Business Review*, July–August 2008, pp. 118–129.

Robert Ricci, "Move from Product to Customer Centric," *Quality Progress*, November 2003, pp. 22–29.

NOTES

1. Thomas S. Gruca and Lopo L. Rego, "Customer Satisfaction, Cash Flow, and Shareholder Value," *Journal of Marketing*, Volume 69, July, pp. 115–130.

2. Christopher W. Hart, "Beating the Marketing with Customer Satisfaction," *Harvard Business Review*, March 2007, pp. 30, 32; and Claes Fornell, Sunil Mithas, Forrest V. Morgeson III, and Mayuram S. Krishnan, "Customer Satisfaction and Stock Prices: High Returns, Low Risk," *Journal of Marketing*, January 2006, pp. 3–14.

3. Jena McGregor, "Customer Service Champs," *Business Week*, March 3, 2008, pp. 37–58.

4. Jena McGregor, *ibid.*

5. Julian Villanueva, Shijin Yoo, and Dominique M. Hanssens, "The Impact of Marketing-Induced versus Word-of-Mouth Customer Acquisition on Customer Equity Growth," *Journal of Marketing Research*, Volume XLV, February 2008, pp. 48–59.

6. Jena McGregor, *ibid.*

7. There is no hard and fast rule to this. I have used 7-point scales as well in measuring customer satisfaction.

8. Thomas O. Jones and W. Earl Sasser Jr., "Why Satisfied Customers Defect," *Harvard Business Review*, November–December 1995, pp. 88–99.

9. Jones and Sasser, *ibid.*

10. Neil A. Morgan and Lopo L. Rego, "The Value of Different Customer Satisfaction and Loyalty Metrics in Predicting Business Performance," *Marketing Science*, Volume 25, No. 5, September–October 2006, pp. 426–439.

11. Robert Ricci, "Move from Product to Customer Centric," *Quality Progress*, November 2003, pp. 22–29.

12. Taken from C.K. Prahalad and Venkatram Ramaswamy, "The Co-creation Connection," *Strategy + Business*, Issue 27, Second Quarter 2002, pp. 50–61.

13. This is not the exact classification method used by Air Products. It is based on the satisfaction survey in Table 11.1.

14. Jenny van Doorn and Peter C. Verhoef, "Critical Incidents and the Impact of Satisfaction on Customer Share," *Journal of Marketing*, Volume 72, July 2008, pp. 123–142.

15. From Horacio D. Rozanski, Gerry Bollman, and Martin Lipman, "Seize the Occasion! The Seven-segment System for Online Marketing," *Strategy + Business*, Issue 24, Third Quarter, 2001, pp. 42–51.

16. The marketing manager was not imagining what he saw at the Four Seasons resort; their attention to guests is legendary. Many articles have been written about them, including "The 100 Best Companies to Work For 2008," *Fortune*, February 4, 2008, pp. 64–66.

17. James L. Heskett, Thomas O. Jones, Gary W. Loveman, W. Earl Sasser, Jr., and Leonard A. Schlesinger, "Putting the Service-Profit Chain to Work," *Harvard Business Review*, July–August, 2008, pp. 118–129.

18. Refer to Ajay Sirsi, *Marketing Led—Sales Driven: How Successful Businesses Use the Power of Marketing Plans and Sales Execution to Win in the Marketplace* (Victoria, BC: Trafford Publishing, 2005). Chapter 7 in that book presents an annual planning calendar to translate marketing plans into functional plans.

19. Many businesses are afraid to share their strategy with their employees for fear that it may be leaked to competitors. This is a mistake for two main reasons. First, without a knowledge of what the organization's strategy is, employees cannot create value for customers. Second, as we have seen throughout this book, it is very hard for competitors to merely imitate your strategy and be successful (think about Southwest Airlines discussed in Chapter 2).

CHAPTER 12

Building the Marketing Organization of the Future

CHAPTER INTRODUCTION

In this chapter you will

The marketing function was worried. The present CEO was due to retire in October and, according to the rumour mill, the incoming CEO, who had an engineering background, did not "get" marketing. The present CEO, who had a marketing background, had enthusiastically built up the marketing function during his tenure. For years, the marketing function had spent money without ever documenting its contribution to the organization's success. The successes were there, but the marketing function had not bothered to put in place a set of metrics to measure the marketing return on investment (ROI).

The new CEO began asking questions. "What, exactly, is the value you [the marketing function] add to this corporation?" When I look at what you people do, all I see are items on the expense side." Predictably, this story did not end well. The CEO eliminated the *entire* corporate marketing function.

What could have been a triumph for the marketing function ended instead in tragedy.[1]

1. See why marketing is critical to business success.

2. Learn that marketing has to demonstrate its productivity and return on investment.

3. Learn how to demonstrate marketing productivity.

4. Learn what marketing metrics need to be put in place to measure marketing ROI.

5. Learn how to evaluate your own marketing function to set it up for success.

6. Learn what you need to do to ensure your personal success in the new world of marketing.

Marketing Is Critical to Business Success

OBJECTIVE 1

The marketing function that got "fired" could not only have avoided its fate, but it could have also gone on to play a crucial role in being the engine of corporate transformation.[2] For a start, it could have instituted simple metrics to track the return on its expenditures, as shown in Table 12.1.

Are you starting to get the picture? Let us take two examples to show how marketing *can* be the engine for corporate transformation.

TABLE 12.1   "You Are Fired"

What the marketing function spent money on	What it could have demonstrated	What the CEO saw instead
All promising managers (around 300 of them from across the globe) were sent to a prestigious business school for a week-long executive training course. Total cost: $6 million	■ Did marketing planning efforts improve? ■ Did the quality of marketing plans improve? ■ Did managers become better leaders?	Expense
A world-famous authority on new product development gave a two-day course. Speaker's fee: $40 000.	■ How many new products were launched post-course? ■ How many of them were true innovations? ■ How much revenue was generated as a result?	Expense
A pricing consultant was hired to teach managers how to make better pricing decisions. Consulting fees: $250 000	■ What percentage of products were successful in garnering price premiums above industry benchmarks? ■ Were we successful in halting abusive pricing practices? (See Chapter 6 on transaction prices.)	Expense

MARKETING DRIVES SUCCESS

12.1 PUROLATOR COURIER LTD.

Objective: Marketing *Can* Be the Engine of Corporate Transformation[3]

Mike O'Leary sells guitar accessories from his base in Victoria, Canada, to music stores across Canada. For years, his products took a circuitous route to end up in music stores: from the Chinese factory to a warehouse in Chicago to Victoria (located on Vancouver Island) to music stores. Such a lengthy channel of distribution sent his shipping costs through the roof, increasing the price of his products. When the Canadian dollar rose against the U.S. dollar, O'Leary discovered that his customers could buy more cheaply by buying directly from U.S. suppliers on the internet. What was he to do?

Enter Purolator Courier Ltd., a company that wants to be more than just a shipper of packages. As we saw in Chapter 5, focusing on the **core product** (shipping packages) alone is a sure recipe for disaster. Purolator's Global Supply Chain Services arm is in the business of helping businesses like O'Leary's to reduce their costs by solving their **supply chain** puzzles.

Unlike large corporations such as Home Depot, small and medium-sized businesses lack sophisticated distribution systems to take advantage of globalization. They have no choice but to face higher distribution costs. Purolator wants to change all that by taking over their supply chain entirely, enabling them to focus on running their business.

Purolator's solution was music to O'Leary's ears: direct-to-store distribution. Instead of receiving products from overseas in Victoria and then shipping them across Canada, Purolator would take over his entire distribution by receiving the products in a container in Vancouver, unpacking them in a state-of-the-art facility in Richmond (near Vancouver), and then shipping them directly to his customers. As a result of Purolator's innovation, O'Leary has been able to drop his prices by 30%, making him competitive with the internet-based suppliers. Not only that, but Purolator has freed him from distribution headaches, allowing him to focus on building sales.

continues

Purolator wants to be more than just a shipper of packages.

Purolator's Global Supply Chain Services business shows what marketing thinking can do to transform an entire business, in this case from moving boxes (a low value-add business) to providing innovative solutions to customers (a high value-add business). No wonder the research supports this.

Research by consulting firm Booz & Company shows that marketing is increasingly more important to corporate success. Yet across the nine industries studied by the firm, a high percentage of respondents believe marketing's most important contribution lies in areas not typically associated with marketing such as driving innovation and cross-functional collaboration.[4] Other research shows that marketing is more important than research and development (R&D) or operations in determining firm performance.[5]

In recognition of marketing's increasingly important role in corporate performance, a new position has been introduced in business organizations in recent years: the chief marketing officer (CMO). The CMO is on equal footing with other top executives in the firm such as the chief financial officer (CFO) and the chief operating officer (COO). These senior executives report to the CEO of the company.

 Shakeel Bharmal, former general manager (GM) of Purolator's Global Supply Chain Services business, talks about how marketing has the power to be the engine of corporate transformation.

CHAPTER CHALLENGE 12.1

ARE YOU ON THE RIGHT TRACK?

If Purolator was a smart company (and it is), what is the next step in its evolution to help a business like O'Leary's?

(*Were you on the right track? Check your answers in Appendix 2.*)

MARKETING DRIVES SUCCESS

12.2 BATA

Objective: Marketing Can Be the Engine of Corporate Transformation by Focusing on Corporate Sustainability

Many people believe that **corporate sustainability** refers to an organization's efforts to protect the environment. In reality, it is much more than that. Corporate sustainability is a set of actions any organization can take to demonstrate its commitment to comporting itself in an ethical manner and treating its employees, customers, society, and the environment with respect.

Thomas John Bata[6] was guided by his late father's moral testament: that the Bata Shoe Company was to be treated not as a source of private wealth, but as a public trust, a means of improving living standards within the community and providing customers with good value for their money. The company successfully expanded into new markets in Asia, the Middle East, Africa, and Latin America not only by contributing to the economies of the new markets it entered, but also by making a positive difference in the lives of employees and their communities by providing medical, educational, and social facilities for Bata employees.

Thomas John Bata was a visionary and a pioneer in thinking about corporate sustainability, but he has good company today. Many organizations are committed to using marketing as a means of corporate and societal transformation.

Thomas Bata was a pioneer of corporate sustainability.

Nature's Path and Mountain Equipment Co-op minimize their environmental impact.

Where We've Been

■ We have seen that marketing has the power to be the engine of transformation within a business.

Where We're Going

■ We will see that marketing has to demonstrate its productivity and return on investment to be accepted as the engine.

CHECKPOINT

Marketing Has to Demonstrate Its Productivity and Return on Investment

OBJECTIVE 2

As we discussed in Chapter 1, a business becomes more productive when it reviews four things every year:

- customer satisfaction
- segments
- customers
- product mix

A yearly review of these four items is like taking a car for regular maintenance check-ups. The four items are like indicators that determine how productive any business will be (remember Tim from Chapter 1?). Customer satisfaction review was discussed in Chapter 11. We will discuss the other three items in the next section.

What is meant by marketing return on investment (ROI)? As we have seen throughout this book, a marketing organization makes investments in marketing research (Chapters 2 and 3); product and brand innovation (Chapter 5); distribution innovation (Chapter 7); marketing communications (Chapter 8); and customer attraction, satisfaction, and retention strategies (Chapter 11). Any shrewd business person will ask, "What is the return from all this investment?" As we saw at the beginning of this chapter, without demonstrating marketing ROI, a marketing function can get into serious trouble. It is necessary to put in place marketing metrics to demonstrate ROI. This will be discussed later in this chapter.

Where We've Been

■ We have seen that although marketing can and should be the engine for corporate transformation, it will not achieve this status unless it demonstrates its productivity and ROI.

Where We're Going

■ In the next section, we will see how marketing can demonstrate its productivity.

CHECKPOINT

OBJECTIVE 3

Marketing Productivity

As discussed, a prime marketing role is to drive productivity in four areas: customer satisfaction review (discussed in Chapter 11), segment review, customer review, and product mix review.

Segment Review

As Tim demonstrated in Chapter 1, he is constantly on the lookout for new segments (markets) to serve. We also saw this attitude being demonstrated by Arbol Industries in Chapter 3—it is constantly evolving its segmentation to focus on newer markets: home builders, industrial customers, and repair and remodelling customers. Without such a focus, a business becomes stale because it serves the same markets over and over again. Worse, as the needs of the market shift over time, the business is caught unawares. We saw what happened to the buggy whip manufacturer and Harry, the manufacturer of transformers, in Chapter 5.

MARKETING DRIVES SUCCESS

12.3 JOHN DEERE

Objective: Conducting a Segment Review is a Prime Marketing Responsibility

John Deere noticed that cast iron plows did not help farmers to work the sticky soil found in the prairies, so in 1837 he successfully introduced the first commercially successful steel plow. From the beginning, Deere's aim was to make farmers more productive; his prime motivator was not a singular focus on profits. From these humble beginnings, Deere & Company has grown into a successful global supplier of farm equipment, lawn and garden equipment, construction and forestry equipment, engines and components, and financial services, with over 57 000 employees and over $24 billion in sales (FY2007—24.1 billion net sales and revenues).[7]

How Deere got there is a story built around segment reviews. Deere started by making farm equipment. But farmers needed money to buy its products, so Deere got into providing them with credit (financial services). Downturns in the agricultural sector forced it to look beyond its core. Deere realized that urban "farmers" (home owners) also needed "farm" equipment to maintain their gardens and yards. So it took the technology developed for conventional farm equipment like tractors and created products for the residential market. When golf

began acquiring a lot of popularity, Deere saw another segment opportunity. It started making equipment to maintain golf courses.

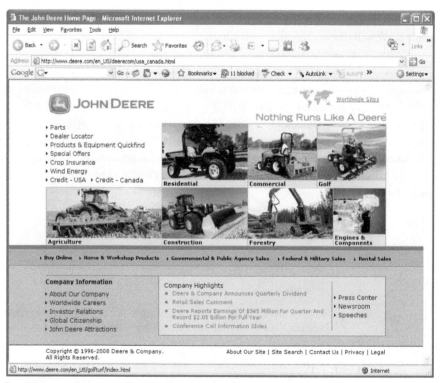

Deere is successful because it constantly reviews its segments.

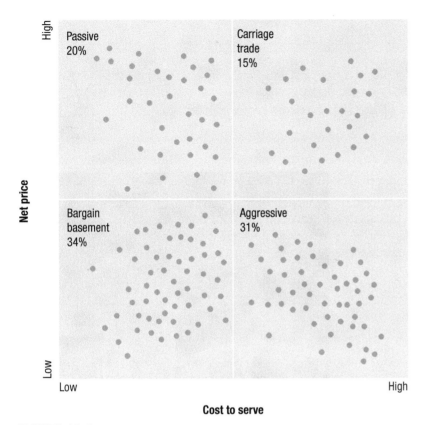

FIGURE 12.1

Customer reviews reveal interesting and ugly facts.

Source: Benson P. Shapiro, V. Kasturi Rangan, Rowland T. Moriarty Jr., and Elliot B. Ross, "Manage Customers for Profits, Not Just Sales," *Harvard Business Review*, September–October 1987, p. 105.

Customer Review

In Chapter 6 on pricing, we saw that all customers are not created equal. In fact, if a business closely examines its customers along two dimensions—cost to serve them and price paid by them—many interesting and ugly facts become apparent. This is shown in Figure 12.1.

As can be seen in the figure, when we plot the cost to serve versus net price paid by the customer (this is data for an industrial packaging materials supplier[8]), 31% of customers can be classified as "aggressive." These customers have a high cost to serve, but do not want to pay very much. As we saw in Chapter 6, the cost to serve certain customers is high because they are demanding, and the business provides them with extra services (for example, custom orders or rush jobs) at no extra charge. It is very important to examine these relationships to bring cost to serve in line with compensation received. The case of Arbol Industries at the end of this chapter demonstrates how Arbol tackled this problem.

> *Some customers are needy, but greedy. I fire them and hope they go to my competitors.*
>
> TIM FROM CHAPTER 1

Product Mix Review

A review of segments and customers should naturally lead a business to examine its basket of goods and services, with the goal of ensuring that the basket is current and resonates with its customers.

MARKETING DRIVES SUCCESS

12.4 HP

Objective: A Business Should Continually Examine Its Product Mix

All manufacturers of information technology (IT) equipment (such as computers, servers, and printers) would like to serve a highly attractive customer segment—small businesses (those with less than 100 employees), but they struggle with how to do this. Small businesses, unlike large-enterprise customers, do not spend millions a year on IT equipment, but collectively their spending adds up. In a supplier's focus to serve large customers, smaller businesses often get lost in the shuffle.

Most manufacturers like HP, IBM, and Cisco serve small customers through a channel called "value-added resellers," who buy equipment from suppliers and work with small businesses to set up IT systems. While HP wants to continue working with this channel, it also wants to serve the needs of small businesses by offering them a more personal touch. To accomplish this objective, it has retooled its sales strategies and product mix. For example, it has extended its Total Care customer website to small customers, which provides them with diagnostic tools to "self-help" their technology portfolio.[9] It has also developed new products aimed at providing higher value to these customers while keeping their costs in check.

HP re-examines its product mix to serve small businesses.

CHAPTER CHALLENGE 12.2

ARE YOU ON THE RIGHT TRACK?

Why does a regular review of segments, customers, product mix, and customer satisfaction make a business more productive?

(*Were you on the right track? Check your answers in Appendix 2.*)

Where We've Been

■ We have seen that although marketing can and should be the engine for corporate transformation, it will not achieve this status unless it demonstrates its productivity and ROI.

■ To demonstrate marketing productivity, every business should conduct a yearly review of four items: customer satisfaction, segments, customers, and product mix.

Where We're Going

■ In the next section, we will see what metrics need to be put in place for marketing to demonstrate its ROI.

CHECKPOINT

Metrics to Measure Marketing Return on Investment (ROI)

OBJECTIVE 4

The quote by Webster and his colleagues says it all: although marketing skill sets (competencies)—such as understanding customer needs, creating innovative goods and services, and charging for them—will never go away, the critical question is *who* in the corporation will be in charge of these necessary competencies. Therefore, it is imperative that any forward-thinking marketing organization pay a lot of attention to instituting metrics to demonstrate marketing ROI.[10]

Before metrics can be put in place to measure marketing ROI, the business has to make some fundamental decisions.[11] These are shown in Table 12.2. As can be seen from the table, if there is lack of agreement on items such as marketing's role or time frame, the efforts to institute marketing metrics will fail.

It helps to think of instituting marketing metrics in terms of a framework such as the purchasing funnel shown in Figure 12.2 (this is a concept you encountered in Chapters 8 and 9).

> *Financial pressures, a shift in channel power, and marketing's inability to document its contribution to business results have combined to force reductions in marketing spending and influence, and to accelerate a transfer of funds and responsibilities to the field sales organization.*
>
> WEBSTER JR., MALTER, AND GANESAN

TABLE 12.2	**Marketing Metrics Decisions**
Marketing's role	Is there agreement on what the role of marketing is within the business? For example, is there agreement that marketing is long-term and strategic, while sales is short-term and tactical?
Objectives	Do the CEO and chief marketing officer (CMO) have the same objectives for marketing ROI? For example, if the CEO if focused on revenue growth, while the CMO is focused on brand health, their objectives do not match.
Time frame	Is the business interested in measuring the short-term impact on sales or a longer-term impact on brand equity, customer satisfaction, and customer loyalty?
Authority	Does marketing have the capacity to control or influence decisions on things it will be measured on (for example, pricing decisions)?

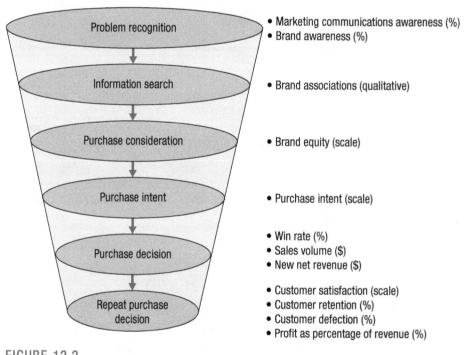

FIGURE 12.2

Key marketing metrics to demonstrate ROI

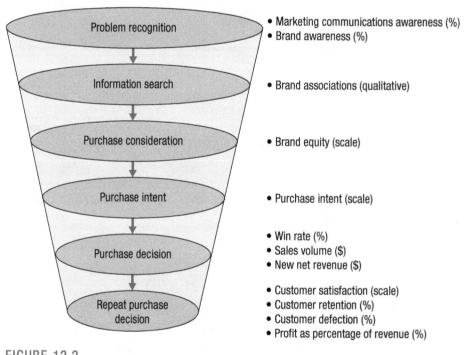 Gloria Mogavero talks about the importance of marketing metrics to firm performance.

The author discusses different types of metrics that can be put in place to measure marketing's effectiveness.

The purchasing funnel acknowledges that while customers have a problem to solve (a couple is looking for a car seat for their child, or a business wants data management software), they are initially unaware of your offering. Customers progress through the purchasing funnel by searching for information, considering different offerings (brands), forming an intention to purchase, actually making the purchase, and, finally, making the decision to repurchase (or not) based on their experience with the brand.

At each stage of the purchasing funnel, different marketing metrics should be put in place to measure marketing ROI. Not surprisingly, at the early stages of the purchasing funnel, metrics such as awareness of marketing communications (advertising) and brand are important. Toward the middle, measures of **brand equity** play a role in determining purchase, as they involve a customer's **brand perceptions**, which influence which brand will be selected. In the long term, metrics such as customer satisfaction, customer retention, and profitability determine the success of marketing efforts.

CHAPTER CHALLENGE 12.3

ARE YOU ON THE RIGHT TRACK?

Why does the quote at the start of this section reveal that when marketing cannot demonstrate its contribution to business performance, marketing funds are diverted to the sales force?

(*Were you on the right track? Check your answers in Appendix 2.*)

CHECKPOINT

Where We've Been

■ We have learned that every marketing organization should put metrics in place to demonstrate its productivity and ROI.

Where We're Going

■ In the next section, we will see how to evaluate a marketing function's influence within the organization.

How to Evaluate the Marketing Function's Influence in an Organization

OBJECTIVE 5

As we have seen, marketing has the power to lead an organization provided certain conditions (such as metrics to demonstrate marketing ROI) are in place. Table 12.3 provides a survey that can be used to evaluate the extent to which an organization is "marketing led."[12]

Experience demonstrates that in organizations where the marketing function scores below 60, there are some fundamental reasons why marketing does not have a higher status. For example, senior management may not really understand what marketing is all about. As we discussed in Chapter 1, there are many misconceptions about marketing: marketing is about advertising; marketing is only about activities that generate immediate sales. In such instances, a marketing function should undertake to educate the rest of the organization on what the true potential of marketing can be.[13]

KEYPOINT

If you want your business to be marketing led, make sure you have the right people on the team. Marketing showmanship without strategic marketing talent is all too common.

TABLE 12.3 Evaluating the Marketing Function's Influence

Give marketing a score from 1 to 10 on each of the 10 dimensions below. Follow instructions at the end of the survey to rate your marketing function.
1 = Rarely
10 = Always

Marketing works hand in hand with the CEO to establish the company's strategy.	1 2 3 4 5 6 7 8 9 10
Marketing leads the effort to conduct market research on customers, competitors, and the industry.	1 2 3 4 5 6 7 8 9 10
Marketing develops a marketing plan, which is translated into sales and functional plans.	1 2 3 4 5 6 7 8 9 10
Marketing leads efforts on product innovation and new business development.	1 2 3 4 5 6 7 8 9 10
Marketing makes major strategic decisions in areas such as brand positioning, channel strategy, pricing, and communications.	1 2 3 4 5 6 7 8 9 10
Marketing leads major advertising, promotions, public relations, and social network campaigns.	1 2 3 4 5 6 7 8 9 10
Marketing approves large growth-oriented investment decisions such as entering new markets and launching new products.	1 2 3 4 5 6 7 8 9 10
Marketing provides a range of support services (market research, communications strategy, customer service) to business units.	1 2 3 4 5 6 7 8 9 10
Marketing is the customer's champion within the organization.	1 2 3 4 5 6 7 8 9 10
Marketing leads the efforts to disseminate and implement standardized marketing best practices across all business units.	1 2 3 4 5 6 7 8 9 10

Score

90 or above means the organization is marketing led.

60–90 means there is some recognition that marketing plays a vital role in corporate transformation. Focus on dimensions with low scores and take corrective actions.

Below 60 means that the organization is not marketing led, and there is low recognition of marketing's value within the organization. Identify root causes (e.g., too little expertise in the marketing function, lack of understanding of the role of marketing) and take corrective action.

CHAPTER CHALLENGE 12.4

ARE YOU ON THE RIGHT TRACK?

Make a list of five reasons why marketing may have limited visibility in an organization.

(*Were you on the right track? Check your answers in Appendix 2.*)

Where We've Been

■ We have seen how to evaluate a marketing function's influence within an organization.

Where We're Going

■ We will see what you need personally to succeed in the marketing organization of the future.

CHECKPOINT

What You Need to Succeed in the Marketing Organization of the Future

We have seen in this book that the discipline of marketing has been bombarded with some major external changes in recent years. Some of these changes are

- explosion of media outlets
- proliferation and fragmentation of markets
- the internet
- complex supply chains
- sophisticated customers
- commoditization of goods and services
- a focus on corporate sustainability

As a result of these changes, the skills required to be a successful marketer have changed as well.

In the Past, the Ideal Marketing Candidate Would Have

- had a broad understanding of marketing
- understood customers' needs and translated that into brand strategies
- been gregarious and outspoken (this stereotype persists even today—students mistakenly believe that to be successful in marketing, a person has to fit this profile)
- fit the cliché of "work hard, play hard"
- been motivated by responsibility, assurances of climbing the corporate ladder, and a fear of failure

However, the Ideal Marketing Candidate of the *Future* Will

- need to understand not only customer needs, but also how value systems (network of suppliers and customers) work
- move from project to project, as a member of a cross-functional team
- perhaps report to someone who is not trained in marketing
- spend periods of time in non-marketing roles (finance, supply chain, production, etc.), thus developing a broad appreciation of the business
- be required to have a strong knowledge of supply chains, customer engagement, and contracting skills
- have to be genuinely excited about, and practise, corporate social responsibility
- have to be comfortable dealing with unstructured environments and making decisions with limited data
- have to be creative and flexible, with a long-term perspective
- be called on to use both right- and left-brain skills.[14]

Chapter Summary

1. See why marketing is critical to business success.

Because it is the only function within a business that has an external (customer) orientation, marketing has the power to transform an entire corporation, forcing it to stop being internally focused and to think about customers, employees, and society. The Purolator example amply demonstrates this. The Global Supply Chain Services arm is helping transform Purolator from a mover of boxes (a low value-add business) to a provider of supply chain solutions (a high value-add business). The Bata example demonstrates the power marketing has in being a force for corporate sustainability efforts.

2. Learn that marketing has to demonstrate its productivity and return on investment.

A business becomes more *productive* when it reviews four things every year:

- customer satisfaction (levels and causes of customer satisfaction and dissatisfaction)
- segments (markets served by the business)
- customers (customers served)
- product mix (goods and services the business serves customers with)

Marketing return on investment is the demonstration of all the benefits that accrue to the business because of its investments in such activities as marketing research, product development, marketing communications, and training and development.

3. Learn how to demonstrate marketing productivity.

Marketing demonstrates its productivity by regularly reviewing, as part of its annual marketing planning efforts, four items: customer satisfaction, segments (markets) served, customers served within those markets, and goods and services customers

are served with. When marketing demonstrates its productivity, it naturally follows that the business becomes more successful.

4. Learn what marketing metrics need to be put in place to measure marketing ROI.

To understand marketing metrics, it is useful to think in terms of frameworks. A useful framework is the customer purchasing funnel, which reveals that customers are initially unaware of your brand. From that point on, they progress through a funnel that leads them to evaluate different offerings (brands), consider and purchase a brand, use it, and then make decisions on repurchase.

At each stage of the purchasing funnel, different marketing metrics can be instituted. At the top of the funnel, we put in place metrics to measure awareness of marketing communications (such as advertising) and brand awareness. Toward the middle, when the customer is considering different alternatives, we put in place metrics to measure how the brand is perceived. Finally, at the end of the funnel, we measure customer satisfaction, retention, defection (churn), and customer profitability.

5. Learn how to evaluate your own marketing function to set it up for success.

Table 12.3 provides a 10-item survey to measure marketing's influence within a business. These 10 items fall into the following categories: driving organization strategy and resource deployment; directing efforts related to market research, product development, pricing, and communications; influencing operations (what other functions do); offering marketing support services to business units; championing the customer; and disseminating marketing best practices throughout the organization.

6. Learn what you need to do to ensure your personal success in the new world of marketing.

In the new world of marketing, the old rules of personal success will not apply. Instead, you should focus on

- acquiring skills in statistics, analytics, and new media
- developing both creative as well as technical marketing expertise
- acquiring experience in non-marketing roles such as finance, sales, supply chain, and human resources

- developing decision-making skills in uncertain environments
- learning to work with other functions as part of a team
- acquiring interpersonal skills to lead others
- developing a deep appreciation for corporate sustainability efforts

CRITICAL THINKING QUESTIONS

1. As we saw in this chapter, research has shown that marketing is more important than research and development (R&D) or operations in determining firm performance. Why do you think this is the case?

2. Provide three examples of businesses where the marketing function has indeed been the engine of corporate transformation. Be sure to justify your choices. [Hint: you may pick examples from this book!]

3. If it is evident that a good marketing function should put in place metrics to demonstrate its value to the business, why do marketing functions have a hard time implementing this?

4. Use the survey in Table 12.3 to evaluate the marketing function of a business. Use the results to advise the marketing function on what changes it needs to make to enhance its status within the business.

5. A friend says to you, "If you want to succeed in marketing, you need to be creative." Knowing what you know about marketing, how would you respond?

6. Table 12.4 provides details on what skills you need to succeed in marketing. Use the table to assess gaps in your skills. Write a short report on what you personally need to do to succeed in the new world of marketing.

RUNNING CASE

ARBOL INDUSTRIES MANAGES CUSTOMERS FOR PROFITS, NOT JUST SALES

Arbol Industries' success described in Chapter 1 was not accidental; they earned it by working hard and making the right choices. Let us summarize in Table 12.5 how they continued to make money in an industry that was losing money and how their overall return on investment continued to surpass that of their competitors.

The final step Arbol took was to change the way they looked at customers. As we saw in Figure 12.1, a great deal can be revealed once a business plots its customers on cost to serve and net price paid. Ideally, all customers should plot along a diagonal—strong, positive correlation between cost to serve and net price paid. But as we have seen, this does not happen in practice due to pricing abuses (refer to Chapter 6).

In order to manage their customers by their profits and not just sales, Arbol developed a customer scorecard shown in Table 12.6.

The customer scorecard enabled Arbol to developed detailed profiles of their customers. These profiles enabled Arbol to manage their customers for their profitability, and not just for the sales revenues they were generating. This approach made a huge impact when it came time to renegotiate customer contracts. Let us take an example.

A manufacturer of mobile homes was not happy because Arbol was asking for a price increase during the contract renewal process. The customer refused to take the price increase. Arbol, in turn, refused to serve the customer any longer. The two parted ways. The standoff lasted three months. Who do you think surrendered? The customer, of course. The customer came back to Arbol and accepted the new contract terms.

Why did this situation play out the way it did? Simple. Arbol had done its homework. Its accurate profiling of the customer using its scorecard method revealed the true profitability of the customer. Arbol knew it did not want to keep the customer; it was willing to let the customer go. Within the three-month period, the customer went shopping and compared Arbol's value propositions and price levels to other suppliers. The customer found that no other supplier could match Arbol on the price-value ratio.

As the marketing manager put it, "Increased profits are gained by attracting and retaining customers who are loyal, profitable, and find our products and services more valuable than those of our competitors."

TABLE 12.5 Arbol Industries Earned Its Success

Actions Arbol took	Chapter	Impact
They made the commitment to become a marketing-led business.	1	They made the shift from being an internally focused business to an externally focused business.
They began by understanding customer needs.	2	They realized that there were many opportunities for them to create customer value and charge for it.
They did not accept current industry segmentation.	3	A different segmentation approach enabled Arbol to find hidden opportunities to serve customers in a superior fashion.
They developed a marketing plan for the business and brand plans for individual products.	4	The marketing plan became their "playbook," enabling them to be a disciplined business.
They introduced product innovations by focusing not on the core product, but on the potential product.	5	They decommoditized a commodity product (lumber, plywood).
They changed their pricing strategies to fit customer segment needs.	6	They were able to match price received for value created.
They introduced innovations in their supply chain strategy.	7	They cut costs while simultaneously serving the customer better.
They looked for return on investment on their marketing communications.	8	They eliminated waste while serving customers' needs better.
They translated marketing plans into sales and functional plans.	9	They ensured that everyone was on the same page regarding strategy and implementation.
They broke down functional silos.	10	They became a customer-focused business.
They created value for their employees.	11	Employees, in turn, could better satisfy customers and build customer loyalty.
They managed customers for profits, not just sales.	12	They became more profitable.

TABLE 12.6   Arbol Industries' Customer Scorecard

Scorecard item	Description
Revenue	Annual sales to customer
Cost to serve	Total cost to serve customer (sales costs, extra costs like custom orders)
Pocket price	Also called the realized price (see Chapter 6); this is the actual price paid by the customer after taking into account customer discounts and other deductions
Current profitability	Pocket price minus cost to serve
Customer potential	Incremental customer revenues and profits that could be generated in the future
Account dominance	Also called share of wallet; this refers to how much business a customer gives one supplier versus another
Customer satisfaction	Satisfaction measured on a scale
Customer retention	A measure of customer loyalty; this refers to how long the customer has been with Arbol

Case Assignment

Arbol Industries' marketing function was clearly the engine that drove the tremendous success experienced by this company. You have been hired by a marketing function that wants to be the "engine of corporate transformation" within its own organization. Write a short report on what steps this marketing function needs to take to accomplish its objective.

SUGGESTED READINGS

If You Want to Build a Marketing Organization That Is an Engine of Corporate Transformation, Do Not Miss These Publications

Ian Davis, "What is the Business of Business?" *The McKinsey Quarterly*, 2005, Number 3, pp. 105–113.

Nirmalya Kumar, *Marketing as Strategy: Understanding the CEO's Agenda for Driving Growth and Innovation* (Boston: Harvard Business School Press, 2004).

Edward Landry, Andrew Tipping, and Jay Kumar, "Growth Champions," *Strategy + Business*, Issue 43, Summer 2006, pp. 60–69.

Benson P. Shapiro, V. Kasturi Rangan, Rowland T. Moriarty Jr., and Elliot B. Ross, "Manage Customers for Profits, Not Just Sales," *Harvard Business Review*, September–October 1987, pp. 101–108.

NOTES

1. I was witness to this example in one of my consulting engagements.

2. Nirmalya Kumar, *Marketing as Strategy: Understanding the CEO's Agenda for Driving Growth and Innovation* (Boston: Harvard Business School Press, 2004).

3. Based on Marcus Gee, "How One Musician Ships Goods from Asia for a Song," *The Globe & Mail, Report on Business*, July 23, 2008, p. B9.

4. Paul Hyde, Edward Landry, and Andrew Tipping, "Making the Perfect Marketer," *Strategy + Business*, Issue 37, Winter 2004, pp. 37–43.

5. Hyde, Landry, and Tipping, *ibid*, and Alexander Krasnikov and Satish Jayachandran, "The Relative Impact of Marketing, Research-and-Development, and Operations Capabilities on Firm Performance," *Journal of Marketing*, Volume 72, July 2008, pp. 1–11.

6. Based on Thomas John Bata's obituary in the *Globe and Mail*, September 2, 2008.

7. Information from www.deere.com website.

8. Benson P. Shapiro, V. Kasturi Rangan, Rowland T. Moriarty Jr., and Elliot B. Ross, "Manage Customers for Profits, Not Just Sales," *Harvard Business Review*, September–October 1987, pp. 101–108.

9. Kevin Allison, "TerraCycle Offers HP Example of Small Success," *Financial Times*, Asia Edition, May 15, 2007, p. 20.

10. Frederick Webster Jr., Alan J. Malter, and Shankar Ganesan, "The Decline and Dispersion of Marketing Competence," *MIT Sloan Management Review*, Summer 2005, pp. 35–43.

11. From Scott Wilkerson, "Time for Teamwork," *Marketing Management*, May/June 2008, pp. 41–45 and Frederick Webster Jr., *ibid*.

12. Some ideas in the table are taken from Edward Landry, Andrew Tipping, and Jay Kumar, "Growth Champions," *Strategy + Business*, Issue 43, Summer 2006, pp. 60–69.

13. I have personally witnessed situations where, once senior executives were educated on the strategic nature of marketing, they became interested in developing similar marketing competencies within their own business.

14. Partially based on Richard Rawlinson, "Beyond Brand Management," *Strategy + Business*, Issue 43, Summer 2006, pp. 52–59.

MARKETING PLAN EXAMPLE: ARBOL INDUSTRIES

Introduction

As was outlined in the case at the end of Chapter 1, Arbol Industries' main products include pulp, paper, dimensional lumber, and plywood. What follows is a marketing plan for one of their divisions—paper packaging.[1] This division supplies packaging material to customers in such industries as pharmaceuticals, fast food, and entertainment.

Executive Summary

Internal and external analysis of our markets identified several key business issues we must address next year:[2]

- Address the threat of substitutes (plastics) taking market share away from us.

- Leverage product innovation to address customer needs such as flexible manufacturing and high-impact packaging.

- Develop strategies with a select group of customers to build our contract business.

- Continue to leverage premium pricing strategy by lowering customer total cost in use and helping our customers penetrate new markets.

Based on these key issues, we have a plan to achieve $1.34 billion in sales and $295 million EBIT (earnings before interest and taxes) through sales of 32 million units, and increase market share by 4.1% next year by introducing new products, reducing costs, and flawlessly executing sales plans based on marketing strategies.

To achieve our objectives, we must focus on four key marketing strategies:

Product strategy—Create value-added products for pharmaceutical, food, and multimedia markets, and leverage total cost in use including machine utilization flexibility for food and general consumer markets.

Pricing strategy—Continue to support premium pricing strategy by delivering superior value in goods and services (web applications and sample program) to target customers.

Channel strategy—Continue building relationships with key accounts while beginning to develop relationships with target companies in target segments including manufacturing, pharmaceuticals, food, multimedia, and general consumer segments.

Marketing communications strategy—Strengthen our brand position with customers and improve our brand perception with target customers.

These are the key outcomes we expect for our business next year:

- Achieve $1.34 billion in sales and $295 million EBIT through sales of 32 million units, and increase market share by 4.1% next year.

- Introduce seven new products, contributing $155 million in sales and $30 million EBIT.

- Strengthen our position with customers and improve our perception with target customers by improving our customer satisfaction scores by 15%.

- Grow international business to receive 5% share and 1.25 million units, resulting in sales of $140 million and generating $28 million EBIT.

- Provide support to sales force in translating marketing strategies into actionable sales plans by developing more compelling value propositions to our customers, resulting in an increase of premium customers by 30%.

Table of Contents

Business Overview

The following table provides a current business overview for our product lines.

Business Overview					
Product line	Current year sales ($ million)	Market share	5-year average ROI	5-year average EBIT ($ million)	Current year capital employed ($ million)
ABC	$350	15%	22%	$85	$100
KLM	$110	32%	15%	$37	$50
XYZ	$185	10%	7%	$26	$55
DEF	$55	5%	4%	$7	$72
GHI	$250	40%	17%	$45	$173
Total	$950	30%	15.2%	$200	$450

Note: Our DEF product line continues to underperform, based on minimum return on investment (ROI) expectations of 7%.

Key Initiatives from Last Year and Lessons Learned

The following table describes the key initiatives we undertook last year and the lessons learned.

Key Initiatives from Last Year and Lessons Learned			
Initiative	Goal	Status	Lessons learned
Segmented customers by need and profitability	Q2	Completed	This is the key to our success as we face increasing numbers of low-priced competitors. Currently, we have categorized our customers into premium, performance, and value customers. Opportunities exist to refine our segmentation scheme as we move forward.
Resized machine at Bloomfield plant	Q4	Completed, but we encountered problems with product quality	Customer communication is key. We must develop contingency plans as we resize machines in our other operations.
Conducted a formal customer satisfaction survey	Q3	Completed	Although we scored well, we must continually create value for our customers.
Implemented premium pricing model across targeted segments	Q2	Completed	We lost business to lower-priced competitors. However, our strategic plan is very clear about our direction—we do not want to serve customers who are price-sensitive but demand high levels of resources from us.
Implemented sales tracking tools	Q3	Completed	Superior sales tracking by salesperson, plant, segment, customer, and product enabled us to add $15 million EBIT last year. We need to roll out this tool to all market segments in which we operate.

Market Analysis

Summary of key facts:

- The global paper packaging market is 150 billion units, with a projected 4% annual growth rate.
- There is increased pressure from alternate packaging materials such as plastics.
- Internationally, there are different product requirements.
- Asian manufacturers are building capacity, and they will penetrate North American and European markets.
- Consumers are demanding visually appealing packages; therefore, our customers (packaging manufacturers) are demanding packaging material that can absorb high-impact graphics.

- Due to mergers among packaging manufacturers, our customers are fewer but bigger.
- Our customers continue to consolidate suppliers—the trend is for them to buy from fewer suppliers.
- Powerful retailers exert control over our customers.

Competitor Analysis: Business Implications

Competitors' consolidation and increased levels of integration continue to bring challenges to our industry. Lower-priced competitors will continue to make inroads. (Please see the appendix for detailed profiles on individual competitors.)

- We need better competitive intelligence.
- We need to focus on selected retail segments and relationships with target companies in those segments.
- We need to implement the Total Solutions concept (our ability to solve any customer need using a cross-functional team).

- Discovering and capturing met and unmet customer needs should be a top priority for us.
- We need to improve our speed to market for new products.
- We need to address product quality issues against competitors capable of offering M3X technology.
- We must address the need for different product offerings for international markets.
- We need to focus our selling strategy on value-added features of our products to compete with lower-priced competitors. Our value-added features are:
  - superior machine performance
  - trouble-free raw material utilization
  - improved technical and service offerings

Customer Analysis

We operate primarily in three market segments: pharmaceutical, manufacturing, and food. Multimedia and global are new markets for us. The analysis below identifies trends and needs in each of these segments.

Market Segment Review

	Pharmaceutical	Manufacturing	Food	Multimedia	Global
Growth rate	7%	4%	10%	15%	22%
Pricing outlook (5 year)	$150/unit	$120	$320	$175	$205
Our share	25%	43%	20%	0	5%
Profitability	Average	Average	Above average	Well above average	Well above average
Segment attractiveness	Average	Medium	High	High	High
Strategic fit	High	Medium	High	High	High
Segment decision	Maintain	Maintain	Grow	Grow	Grow

Note: Multimedia and global are new segments for us. As indicated above, our analysis reveals that they are very attractive segments and we must pursue them aggressively. Currently, we have not segmented the global market along the lines of our domestic market. This is a step that will be pursued in the future.

Product Line Sales to Segments

Product line	Pharmaceutical		Manufacturing (million units and $ million annual)		Food		Total	
ABC	1.6	$150	2.5	$200	—	—	4.1	$350
KLM	3.2	$40	0.6	$40	1.7	$30	5.5	$110
XYZ	—	—	1.3	$140	2.2	$45	3.5	$185
DEF	0.25	$12	0.95	$43	—	—	1.2	$55
GHI	1.46	$125	2.0	$83	5.1	$42	8.56	$250

Note: We currently do not offer our ABC line in the food segment. Our analysis has revealed the food segment to be growing at 10% annually. Therefore, we should think about how we can secure channels of distribution for the ABC line in this segment.

The XYZ line is not offered currently in the pharmaceutical market segment. However, our analysis indicates that we should not pursue this opportunity at the present time. Instead, resources should be devoted to penetrating the multimedia segment, a growth opportunity for us.

The DEF product line is best represented in the manufacturing segment. Our decision with this segment is to maintain our presence. Currently, we serve the manufacturing segment with all of our product lines. Our analysis reveals that we should phase out the DEF line within the next five years.

Pharmaceutical Segment Trends

- The aging baby boomer population and increased longevity is impacting the strong growth (7%) in this segment.[3]

- Consumers are increasingly health conscious and are taking charge of their personal health choices.

- Last year, this market generated $350 billion in global sales, with North America accounting for 48% and Europe accounting for 24%.

- Industry consolidation is expected to continue.

- The packaging market for pharmaceuticals is estimated at 25 million units.

- This market segment accounted for 15% of EBIT last year.

- Next year, we estimate this market segment to be even more attractive with 19% EBIT.

Pharmaceutical Segment Implications

- We need to build stronger relationships with our customers to penetrate this market.

- New product development will be key to success in this marketplace. Specifically, we see a need to develop products to capture the direct-to-consumer (DTC) marketing communications programs that major pharmaceutical companies have launched.

Based on customer *needs* and *attractiveness* to us, we have categorized our customers into three segments: premium, performance, and value.[4]

Premium Customer Segment Description and Needs

- These customers require proactive sales solutions and are willing to pay us a price premium.

- They require 24/7 technical support.

- These customers want a customer service desk.

- They want us to share with them research on market trends and end-user trends and needs.

- They need new, innovative products to compete in the marketplace.

- They will not tolerate "stock outs."[5]

- They will have special requests from warehousing to packaging.

Premium Customer Segment Implications

- We should actively develop this customer segment, as it is the most attractive in terms of contracts, price premiums, and our capabilities.

- Premium customers represent 20% of our sales revenues and 35% of our profits.

- Developing this customer segment will require us to invest in research and development, customer service, and sales effectiveness.

Value Segment Trends and Needs

- These customers require basic product quality and product bundling options.

- They are not willing to consider price premiums.

- They tend to be price-sensitive and tend to switch suppliers.

Value Segment Implications

- We should continue to serve this customer segment, as they enable us to utilize our excess capacity.

- Also, this customer segment is lucrative because they buy the basic product from us. Without this segment, we would have to consider selling the basic product at a deep discount.

- However, these customers should be increasingly served electronically so we reduce our cost to serve them.

- We should conduct a customer review every year and eliminate the least profitable 3% of our value customers.

The chart below identifies a market segment by customer segment matrix. Each cell in the matrix identifies a set of needs.

	Premium	Performance	Value
Pharmaceutical	Highest-grade quality Proactive technical support Willing to pay price premiums	Consistent product quality System efficiencies May consider price premiums if case is made	Basic quality Product bundling Will not consider price premiums
Manufacturing	Custom solutions Proactive technical support Willing to pay price premiums	Cost containment Quick turnaround May consider price premiums if case is made	Consistency in product Sales materials Will not consider price premiums
Food	High-impact product Security of supply Willing to pay price premiums	User-friendly packages Security of supply Will consider price premiums if case is made	Diversified product line Competitive price

The chart below provides more details on premium, performance, and value customers.

Customer Review[6]

Customer segment	Customer	Sales ($ million)	Cost to serve ($/unit)	Customer profitability ($/unit)	Decision
Premium	Belvedere Co.	$23	$12	$25	Grow
	Briar Co.	$42	$20	$15	Grow
	Cameron Co.	$100	$44	$4	Reduce cost to serve
	Deal Inc.	$15	$35	$17	Grow
	Real Co.	$5	$45	($20)	Negotiate contract for better terms or drop
Performance	ABC Co.	$25	$25	$7	Shows signs of value customer; need further data to validate
	Bonyton Inc.	$11	$35	$12	Grow
	Bossier Ind.	$56	$26	$45	Potential to become premium customer
	Catmatsu Co.	$78	$34	$23	Grow
Value	Aim Co.	$34	$26	$17	Maintain
	Bruno Mfc.	$85	$11	$18	Maintain
	Caruthers Co.	$67	$15	$25	Potential to become performance customer
	Eigen Mfc.	$12	$46	($15)	Reduce cost to serve or drop

Customer Satisfaction Survey: Key Findings

A customer satisfaction survey conducted last year identified the following:

- Our overall satisfaction score is 4.4 (out of 5). This compares very well with the competition.

- However, our loyalty rates are below our competitors' rates.

- On-time delivery continues to be a problem for us compared to the competition. We have managed an 87% on-time delivery rate versus 92% for the competition.

- Customer technical service agents need to improve product knowledge and problem diagnosis skills.

- Customers complain that our sales force needs to be more accessible and willing to listen to customer needs.

Key Issues Analysis

Key Opportunities

- Significant opportunities exist to develop and implement strong value propositions in selected target segments.
- Opportunities exist to exploit the Total Solutions team concept with new customers.
- Opportunities exist to leverage overseas facilities and develop stronger product offerings to better compete in international markets.
- Opportunities exist to improve supply chain efficiencies.

Key Threats

- Plastics are taking share away from our material.
- Lower-priced competitors are targeting our traditional markets.
- Our larger competitors are investing more heavily in new product innovations.

Key Strengths

- We have manufacturing flexibility.
- We are very cost competitive.
- We have a broad product line offering.
- We have cross-functional expertise to create value for our customers.

Key Weaknesses

- We have domestic production only.
- We have issues with delivering products on time to customers.
- We lack complete information on our competitors.

Key Issues to Be Addressed by the Marketing Plan: Next Year

- Address the threat of plastic taking share from our material.
- Continue product innovation directed at high-end markets to create barriers for competition.
- Address cost-reduction efforts for existing products.
- Address product and service issues regarding specific needs of international markets including stiffness, shade, brightness, and yield.
- Identify target customers and prospects for each segment and develop value propositions.
- Continue to leverage premium pricing strategy.
- Increase competitive intelligence and leverage lower customer total cost in use of our products.
- Develop a marketing communications plan to strengthen our position with customers and improve our perception with prospects, addressing the gaps from the customer satisfaction survey.
- Work with sales to translate marketing strategies into actionable sales plans.

Key Issues to Be Addressed by the Marketing Plan: Future Years

- Develop strategies for new business through a select group of customers in target markets.
- Develop web tools to support efficient supply chain processes such as order status, order entry, invoice status, and tally sheets.
- Work with sales to gain more customer intimacy.

Objectives to Be Achieved

The following tables outline objectives to be achieved by segment for marketing, sales, and financial, as well as objectives for our key marketing mix elements.

Objectives to Be Achieved by Segment: Marketing, Sales, Financial

	Pharmaceutical	Manufacturing	Food	Multimedia	Global
Current sales (units)	6.51	7.35	9.0	—	2.0
Current sales ($ million)	$327	$506	$117	—	$87
Next year target (units)	7.0	7.0	11.0	3.0	5.0
Next year target ($ million)	$330	$506	$130	$150	$225
Current market share	25%	43%	10%	—	5%
Target market share	25%	43%	15%	6%	11%
Current customer mix (%)	Premium: 25 Performance: 33 Value: 42	Premium: 10 Performance: 45 Value: 45	Premium: 5 Performance: 50 Value: 45	—	Global market segmentation not yet done
Target customer mix (%)	Premium: 30 Performance: 40 Value: 30	Premium: 15 Performance: 45 Value: 40	Premium: 15 Performance: 50 Value: 35	Premium: 45 Performance: 25 Value: 30	Global market segmentation not yet done
Current EBIT ($ million)	$70	$60	$85	—	$15
Target EBIT ($ million)	$80	$65	$100	$20	$30
Current product mix (million units)	ABC: 1.6 KLM: 3.2 XYZ: — DEF: 0.25 GHI: 1.46	ABC: 2.5 KLM: 0.6 XYZ: 1.3 DEF: 0.95 GHI: 2.0	ABC: — KLM: 1.7 XYZ: 2.2 DEF: — GHI: 5.1	—	We only sell the ABC line in global markets
Target product mix (million units)	ABC: 2.0 KLM: 3.0 XYZ: — DEF: 0.1 GHI: 1.9	ABC: 3.0 KLM: 1.0 XYZ: 1.0 DEF: 0.7 GHI: 1.3	ABC: 1.2 KLM: 2.0 XYZ: 3.0 DEF: — GHI: 4.8	ABC: 1.0 KLM: 0.1 XYZ: 0.5 DEF: — GHI: 1.4	Continue selling ABC line

Objectives to Be Achieved by Segment: Marketing Mix

	Pharmaceutical	Manufacturing	Food	Multimedia	Global
Product objectives	Continue supporting this segment with current products. Introduce two new products to capture direct-to-consumer markets.	Continue supporting this segment with current products	Introduce ABC line in this market segment. Develop three new products to capture emerging fast-casual market.	Introduce all our product lines (except DEF) to this segment. Develop two new products to capture crossover media markets.	Stay the course with this segment
Pricing objectives	Maintain price premiums	Protect price premiums	Increase price margins by value-added pricing and reducing cost to serve	Serve high-end customer segment; maintain price premiums	Continue targeting high end of market
Channel objectives	Continue with current channel objectives of dealing with large customers	Develop relationships with end customers	Develop channels to sell ABC line in this segment	Develop relationships with major channel members	Develop relationships with agents
Marketing communications objectives	Maintain current communication strategy of premium-priced, high value-added supplier	Mitigate brand image problems due to machine resizing issues	Strengthen perception with current customers and grow brand awareness with prospects	Communicate our Total Solutions concept	Grow identity with regional markets
Marketing research objectives	Send follow-up customer satisfaction survey to assess if customers have noticed changes in service	Develop in-depth understanding of customer needs by cross-functional team approach	Understand customer decision making to reduce cost to serve	Develop customer panel to leverage relationships and obtain customer needs understanding	Conduct research to segment customers in this market

Marketing Strategies, Tactics, and Budgets

The following analysis outlines tactics and budgets for our product, pricing, channel, and marketing communications strategies.

Marketing Strategies and Tactics

Product Strategy
- Create value-added products for pharmaceutical, food, and multimedia segments.
- Improve product quality.

Tactics	Timing	Person/responsibility	Cost/resources required	Metric to track	Impact of strategy
Introduce two new pharmaceutical products	Q2	A. Anders	$55 000	Units and EBIT	$35 million in EBIT in three years
Introduce ABC line into food market segment	Q3	P. Drake	■ $100 000 ■ Work with supply chain to align distribution channels ■ Coordinate with sales counterpart to develop marketing and sales materials for customers	■ Units ■ Market share ■ EBIT	■ $100 million in sales in three years ■ $20 million EBIT/yr in three years
Introduce two new multimedia products	Q3	A. Anders	$75 000	Units and EBIT	$50 million in EBIT in five years
Improve product quality at Pinemountain facility	Q1	J. Ray	■ $25 000 ■ Work with production	■ Litmus test score of 7.5 ■ Customer complaints	■ Reduce customer turnover by 20% in one year ■ 10 new customers in two years

Pricing Strategy
Continue to support premium pricing strategy by delivering superior value in goods and services to target markets and customers.

Tactics	Timing	Person/responsibility	Cost/resources required	Metric to track	Impact of strategy
Gain insight into customer needs and value drivers	Q1	J. Welk	■ $40 000 ■ Deploy four cross-functional teams	Meeting segment objectives	Market share increase by 4.1%
Increase price margins in food segment	Q4	R. Draper	■ Work with IT to develop online service mechanisms ■ Total cost: $250 000	10% improvements in margins across the board next year	■ Cost savings of $2 million over three years ■ $15 million EBIT increase next year
Roll out sales tracking tools to all segments	Q3	J. Welk	■ $150 000 ■ Work with sales	% of product sold over industry average price	$7 EBIT improvement within three years

Channel Strategy
- Continue to build relationships with key end-user customers.
- Develop additional channels.

Tactics	Timing	Person/responsibility	Cost/resources required	Metric to track	Impact of strategy
Develop relationships with key end-user customers in manufacturing segment	Q2	C. Franks	■ $30 000 ■ Coordinate with cross-functional members	■ Number of direct relationships ■ EBIT	EBIT improvement by $5 million next year
Penetrate executive suite in multimedia segment[7]	Q2	C. Franks	$10 000	Five new contracts secured next year	Sales impact: $30 million
Develop electronic channel for pharmaceutical segment	Phase 1 by Q3	W. Burns	$250 000	1.2 million units next year	Sales impact: $13 million

Marketing Strategies and Tactics (continued)

Marketing Communications Strategy

Define corporate brand identity and communicate to target segments and customers.

Tactics	Timing	Person/ responsibility	Cost/resources required	Metric to track	Impact of strategy
Print campaign to current customers to reinforce message about product quality and service levels	Q2	R. Brown	$85 000	Brand equity score increase to 8.9 (from current 7.5)	Reduce customer turnover by 10% over two years
Develop sales materials to communicate Total Solutions concept	Q2	R. Brown	■ $5 000 ■ Work with sales to finalize material	Number of new customers	■ Increase premium customer mix to 30% next year

Other Tactics

Follow up customer satisfaction survey	Q4	A. Circe	$5 000	Reduction in customer complaints by 25%	■ Better customer relations ■ Process improvements in customer service

Positioning Relative to Our Competitors

Our marketing plan will enable us to build a competitive advantage in the areas of penetrating premium customers, premium price positioning, and strong product innovation, as shown in the following table. [8]

	Product Strategy	Pricing Strategy	Channel Strategy	Marketing Communications Strategy
Us	■ Marketing plan enables us to demonstrate strong product innovation ■ Enables us to penetrate new markets	■ Positions us squarely as a premium-priced, value-added player ■ Increases our premium customer mix to 30%	We have taken leadership role in the industry with electronic channels	■ This has traditionally been our weakest link ■ Marketing plan strategies and tactics should see improvement in our brand image
Competitor A	Moves us beyond this competitor in product superiority	This competitor will emulate our strategy next year	Our strategy will provide us with a competitive edge against this competitor for two years	■ Our strongest competitor ■ We will still lag behind this competitor in terms of brand image, but the gap is narrowing
Competitor B	We have always been superior to this competitor; gap should increase	This competitor will most likely try to occupy a mid-market position	This competitor will develop electronic channel capabilities, but without features in our offering	Our brand image is clearly superior to this competitor
Competitor C	This competitor has never been known for product innovation	This competitor will compete further on low prices	This competitor will eventually be forced by customers to develop electronic channels	■ Our brand image is far superior to this competitor ■ We foresee this competitor exiting some markets we operate in

Marketing–Sales Linkage

Our business has excellent alignment from the strategic plan through the marketing plan to the sales plan as identified below.

Strategic Plan	Marketing Plan	Sales Plan
Develop new products and markets	■ Introduce two new multimedia products ■ Introduce two new pharmaceutical products ■ Introduce ABC line into the food market segment	■ Target accounts: MediaGiant Inc., SMX Music, ABC Communications, Pioneer Symbols Inc. ■ Develop better customer relationships for product development initiatives ■ Establish customer value programs with food market customers
Develop key strategic alliances	■ Continue to build relationships with key end-user segments ■ Develop additional channels	■ Develop end-user strategies with key customers (Acme, Belvedere, Tamaron, and Branson)
Reduce cost across the system	■ Improve product quality at Pinemountain facility	■ Initiate esales with key customers
Define and communicate corporate identity	■ Print campaign to current customers to reinforce product quality message	■ Develop sales material to communicate Total Solutions concept

Successful implementation of our marketing plan has implications for all functions:

■ *Marketing*: Need to identify new product and market opportunities based on end-consumer needs, as well as develop the Total Solutions concept, which will add value for our customers.

■ *Sales*: Need to communicate our Total Solutions concept to our customers and incorporate our products and solutions into customer plans.

■ *Product development*: Need to continue to identify innovative products based on understanding of end-consumer needs and trends to address the threat of plastic and other emerging materials.

■ *Supply chain*: Identify cost reduction opportunities from our suppliers to our customers by making the entire process function in a more streamlined fashion. This not only adds value for our customers, but also strengthens our competitive position as well.

■ *IT*: Continue to support sales in delivering additional value to our customers in a cost-effective fashion (for example, esales). At the same time, find ways to integrate and use marketplace information available across functional groups.

Besides segment objectives outlined earlier, these are the value propositions we will offer our customers. The matrix below, in conjunction with the Target Customer List (next page), will be used by the sales function to develop sales and customer plans.

	Premium	Performance	Value
Pharmaceutical	■ Grade A product ■ Superior performance ■ Continuous availability ■ Dedicated technical service team ■ No charge for special requests	■ Product quality guarantees ■ High quality-control standards ■ Aesthetic packaging ■ Dedicated technical service team	■ Grade B product ■ Technical team available as requested ■ Customer service available as add-on
Manufacturing	■ Grade AA product ■ Cost containment guarantees ■ Inventory management ■ Dedicated technical service team ■ No charge for special requests	■ Custom Solutions Team ■ Quick turnaround ■ Lower total cost in use guarantees	■ Consistency in product ■ Sales materials ■ Guaranteed machine uptime
Food	■ Grade A product ■ User-friendly material ■ Dedicated sales team ■ No charge for special requests	■ Superior performance ■ Security of supply ■ Product quality guarantees	■ Diversified product line ■ Competitive price ■ Grade B product

Target Customer List[9]

Customer segment	Target customer	Target sales ($ million)	Pharmaceutical	Manufacturing	Food
Premium	Acme Co.	$10.4	✓		
	KLM Co.	$7.7		✓	
	Tamaron Ind.	$5.5	✓		✓
	DEF Co.	$4.5		✓	
	RST Co.	$3.9	✓	✓	
Performance	ABC Co.	$7.3	✓		✓
	Springhill Ltd.	$5.7	✓		
	AKS Inc.	$2.75		✓	
	CLT Co.	$1.34			✓
	Branson Ind.	$0.68		✓	
	Abby Intl.	$0.52	✓		
	Mack Bolts	$0.08	✓		
Value	PON Inc.	$2.2		✓	
	Reed Ind.	$1.4	✓		✓
	Flower Co.	$0.56			✓
	TSR Co.	$0.45	✓		
	Anson Ltd.	$4.1		✓	

Key Outcomes for the Business

If we execute our marketing and sales plans flawlessly, key expected outcomes next year are as follows.

	This Year	Next Year
Marketing plan budget ($ million)	$0.9	$1.08
Sales (million units)	22.86	32
Sales ($ million)	$950	$1340
EBIT ($ million)	$200	$295
Market share	30%	34.1%
ROI	15%	17%

Marketing Plan Budget

The following table outlines the budget for marketing plan implementation.

Tactic	Cost
Introduce two new pharmaceutical products	$55 000
Introduce ABC line into the food market segment	$100 000
Introduce two new multimedia products	$75 000
Improve product quality at Pinemountain facility	$25 000
Gain insight into customer needs and value drivers	$40 000
Increase price margins in food segment	$250 000
Roll out sales tracking tools to all segments	$150 000
Develop relationships with key end-user customers in manufacturing segment	$30 000
Penetrate executive suite in multimedia segment	$10 000
Develop electronic channel for pharmaceutical segment	$250 000
Print campaign to current customers to reinforce message about product quality and service levels	$85 000
Develop sales materials to communicate Total Solutions concept	$5000
Follow-up customer satisfaction survey	$5000
Total	$1 080 000

Marketing Plan Control

- Each strategy has a set of tactics associated with it.
- Each tactic (action item) has a person responsible for completion, timelines, costs, and resources required.
- For each tactic, goals are established by period (example shown in the table below) to act as milestones.

- Each month, the marketing director will receive a progress report on tactics from each individual.
- Marketing and sales, during their quarterly meetings (or more often, as necessary) will discuss marketing and sales program execution and make changes as necessary.

Product strategy: New market penetration
Tactic: Introduce ABC line into food segment
Person responsible: P. Drake

	Year 1 goal	Year 2 goal	Year 3 goal	Comments
Sales (million units)	1.2	2.3	3.1	—
Sales ($ million)	$20	$30	$50	—
EBIT ($ million)	($0.25)	$5	$25	—
Market share	1%	1.9%	3%	—
Resources required	■ Work with supply chain ■ Coordinate with sales	—	—	■ Well on track to achieve launch date of Q3 ■ Exploring factory direct route with supply chain ■ Will work with sales in Q1 to develop customer materials

Marketing Plan Appendix

Competitor A Profile

The following table outlines Competitor A's market position in each key segment.[10]

Competitor A Market Position

Segment	Tonnes	Sales	Share
Pharmaceutical	575	$403	24%
Food	300	$240	30%
Manufacturing	10	$12	15%
Multimedia	1000	$800	35%

Key Opportunities for Competitor

- This competitor can merge with Premium Packaging Co. overseas to increase presence internationally and acquire TMX multi-task manufacturing technology.
- This competitor can define a better distribution strategy.

Key Threats for Competitor

- Plastics are a threat for this competitor, just like for us.
- There is a customer trend toward material reduction.
- They have exchange rate disadvantages.
- They face growing material costs.

Key Competitor Strengths

- They are a global supplier with a strong international presence.
- They have focus and commitment to high-end markets.
- They have strong relationships with key customers.

Key Competitor Weaknesses

- They have a manufacturing disadvantage internationally, as their production is mainly in North America.
- They are distracted by integration efforts; product quality has suffered.

Leverage Points for Competitor A versus Us

- They have innovative new products in the pharmaceutical category.
- They are more advanced in customer-facing systems.
- They have less constraint in manufacturing stiffer packaging material.

Leverage Points for Us versus Competitor A

- We can focus on our superior HDC technology.
- We have offshore manufacturing experience, especially in Asia.
- We have cross-functional customer value creation capabilities, which we must exploit.

What Actions Should We Take against This Competitor?

- We should leverage our offshore manufacturing experience to gain entry into Europe.
- We should leverage our cross-functional expertise to create value for customers and cement customer relationships.

Notes

1. I have disguised the data in the marketing plan.
2. Please note that all numbers are for illustrative purposes only.
3. Only one market segment description is being provided here.
4. Only two customer segment descriptions (premium and value) are being provided here.
5. A "stock out" is a situation where an item is not available on a retail shelf. This situation causes consumer dissatisfaction and is therefore disliked by manufacturers.
6. As you can see in this section, this business has taken a hard look at its customer base (only partially displayed here) to make decisions about who to grow with, which customers to maintain, and which customers to drop. In my experience, smart businesses continually evaluate their customer base, dropping the least attractive customers on an annual basis.
7. "Penetrate executive suite" refers to a practice of building relationships with senior executives in the customer's business. This is done to strengthen customer loyalty by building relationships at multiple levels within a customer's business.
8. A marketing plan should demonstrate why it is superior and why the business will succeed in the marketplace.
9. A Target Customer List typically contains a list of attractive customers (current and potential) that the sales force will concentrate its efforts on. It is the responsibility of the marketing function to develop this list.
10. Only one competitor profile has been provided for illustrative purposes.

WERE YOU ON THE RIGHT TRACK?

ANSWERS TO CHAPTER CHALLENGES

Chapter 1: What Do Winning Organizations Do Well?

CHAPTER CHALLENGE 1.1

Strategy is an organization's ability to create superior value for its customers and, in the process, give it a competitive edge over its rivals.

CHAPTER CHALLENGE 1.2

Marketing is a disciplined process used by an organization to solve business problems.

CHAPTER CHALLENGE 1.3

The four-step marketing process is as follows: understand customer needs, create value for customers, deliver the value, and examine marketing efforts (manage customer value).

CHAPTER CHALLENGE 1.4

The first thing we notice about customers and their needs is that different customers have different needs.

CHAPTER CHALLENGE 1.5

Snap-on ensures that its tools do not break. It makes the mechanic more productive by developing diagnostic tools. It offers the mechanic flexible financing terms. The store goes to the mechanic. And finally, Snap-on relies on personal relationships to build trust with the customer.

Chapter 2: Understanding Customer Needs

CHAPTER CHALLENGE 2.1

Smart companies know that, sometimes, customers either do not know what their needs are or they have a hard time putting their needs into words. So these companies are very good at taking a latent (hidden) customer need and giving it shape.

CHAPTER CHALLENGE 2.2

1. The research may be outdated.
2. The research may be biased. Therefore, it is necessary to check the source of the research and the methodology employed.
3. The research was conducted with a particular set of objectives, which may not be the objectives for your research. Therefore, it may not be relevant to your problem.

CHAPTER CHALLENGE 2.3

Being an exploratory technique, focus groups would not be appropriate when the researcher wants to count and provide a summary of a target group. For example, let us say a restaurant wanted to develop a profile of their typical customer in terms of gender, age, income and profession, and satisfaction with food and service. Focus groups would not be appropriate in this situation.

Chapter 3: Choosing Which Customers to Serve

CHAPTER CHALLENGE 3.1

The only way to compete against a mass marketer is to segment the customer base. That is what GM did by offering five car brands aimed at five distinct customer needs (based on the customer's life stage)—Chevrolet, Pontiac, Oldsmobile (later discontinued), Buick, and Cadillac.

CHAPTER CHALLENGE 3.2

Friedman is not saying that a business must focus on profits above all else. What he means is that if a business is not in the business of understanding customer needs and creating customer value, it is wasting society's precious resources. Even non-profit organizations have to make a "profit" (excess of revenues over costs), unless they want to depend on the government for handouts forever.

CHAPTER CHALLENGE 3.3

The segmentation matrix in Table 3.2 provides direction to the sales force. Each cell in the matrix contains four items any sales professional will find invaluable: current customers in the cell, their needs, value propositions to offer them, and a list of prospective customers. It is the duty of every marketing function to provide the sales force with this direction.

CHAPTER CHALLENGE 3.4

Customers were constantly making the following comments: "You do sales conferences? I thought you were an ecommerce shop." Essentially, segmenting by product does not allow the business to take a holistic view of customers and their needs.

Chapter 4: Developing a Strong Marketing Plan

CHAPTER CHALLENGE 4.1

While the marketing plan specifies a business's go-to-market approach (segments targeted, how value is created for customers, and so forth), many facets of it are actually implemented by other functions (for example, customer service). For this reason, it is crucial to develop functional plans based on the marketing plan. In this way, all functions can focus on the customer, enabling the organization to become customer focused.

CHAPTER CHALLENGE 4.2

The four areas in Figure 4.2 are the understand-create-deliver-manage customer value process we examined in Chapter 1 to learn what marketing is.

CHAPTER CHALLENGE 4.3

In a theme park or on a cruise ship, Disney can meticulously control every aspect of the guests' experience. For example, in a Disney theme park, costumed characters are never allowed to break out of character unless they are in an area reserved only for employees. However, participatory vacations are different in that Disney has to partner with other suppliers to provide certain aspects of the experience. For example, they have to hire gondolas in Venice to ferry their guests. Can Disney control each and every aspect of the experience when it is not being provided by a Disney employee? The key challenges will be setting expectations of external suppliers and training to uphold Disney standards.

CHAPTER CHALLENGE 4.4

Either option—stay the course or accept the opportunity—would be correct. Greystone chose to accept the opportunity because it would enable the company to make a move into a business that was more lucrative than property management.

Chapter 5: Product and Brand Strategies

CHAPTER CHALLENGE 5.1

A product is the totality of the customer's experiences.

CHAPTER CHALLENGE 5.2

There are three main reasons why businesses find themselves in a predicament similar to Harry's:

1. The very factors that accounted for their earlier success (focus on making the best product) become responsible for their failure. When firms become successful, they tend to repeat actions that garnered them the success in the first place. In other words, they get stuck doing the same thing over and over again. However, the marketplace is not a static entity; it is constantly changing—customer needs shift over time, new competitors enter the market, and technological advances are made. But these "successful" firms are not able to adapt to the changing environment, as they are intent on repeating actions from their past.

   This is human nature. Very few people make changes when they are at the top. Individuals like Tiger Woods (the famous golf player) are rare. At the top of his profession, he changed his golf swing to become even better. Immediately after he changed his swing, he lost a few tournaments. It took him a while to jump to the next level on his learning curve.

2. Firms like Harry's cannot adapt to changing environments because they focus on the core product without thinking about the customer's needs. As we have seen in Chapter 5, a focus on the core product puts blinders on a business, making it oblivious to shifting marketplace dynamics.

3. Managers like Harry seldom prepare marketing plans (Chapter 4). They are content to run their business from one day to the next. If they are successful *today*, they are happy. They tend not to think about the future, expecting that the environment of today will extend indefinitely into the future as well. As a result, they don't see threats until it is too late.

CHAPTER CHALLENGE 5.3

- The potential product for industrial gloves is safety—teaching the workforce to engage in safe practices.

- Starbucks, for example, defines its potential product as "café culture." So what they are really selling is a place to relax, meet friends, read, and, incidentally, drink good coffee.

- Although the core product is athletic shoes, the potential product should be defined in terms the customer can relate to. Nike defines it in terms of enabling customers to be in control and be their best, regardless of their level of athletic prowess.

- In any given price range, all hotel rooms are essentially offering the same product—a comfortable bed, a safe room, and a warm shower. This is not enough to differentiate one brand from another. So brands like Ritz-Carlton define their potential product as helping business travellers achieve their goal of having a successful business trip. Toward this end, Ritz-Carlton keeps a log of guests' preferences and staff are authorized to go out of their way to assist business people in any way they can so the travellers can concentrate on their work. At the lower end of the price range, hotels have not really carved out niches for themselves based on the potential product. This could help explain why there are so many brands that are indistinguishable from one another.

CHAPTER CHALLENGE 5.4

Words such as "commodity" or "generic" can serve as opposites of the word "brand."

CHAPTER CHALLENGE 5.5

Our buggy whip manufacturer is making automobile parts such as starter mechanisms. He is also getting into the assembly of cars. Many business organizations got their start in this way. Peugeot, the French carmaker, started by making pepper mills (grinders). You can buy a Peugeot pepper mill at high-end kitchen stores. Matsushita, the Japanese electronics giant, started by making bicycle lamps.

CHAPTER CHALLENGE 5.6

For a brand's image to equal its identity, the brand identity implementation has to be flawless. This is not realistic at all. Here is an example that, although a little extreme, everyone can relate to. You are in your car and have stopped at a stoplight. You glance around and notice, on the lamppost on the sidewalk, a sign that reads, "For advice on wealth management strategies call ABC Co. at 800-555-5555."

Think about the brand's method of communication for a minute and you will understand why identity will never equal image. The managers at ABC Co. want to build a certain brand identity in the marketplace—they want to convey to you that they are serious, professional wealth strategists. But the method they chose to convey this message is ludicrous. Customers who want professional advice on money matters are not very likely to give ABC Co. a call because the brand image as received is that of a firm that is not very professional in its approach.

All brands face the above problem. Their marketing mix implementation is never going to be flawless. Hence, there will always be a gap between brand identify (the brand concept as intended) and brand image (the brand concept as received). So a brand strategist's perennial challenge is to ensure that the brand's identity comes close to the brand's image. This is done by measuring the brand's image, making changes to the brand's identity, and repeating the process all over again.

CHAPTER CHALLENGE 5.7

If not handled properly, the danger for Mouton Cadet is that they will fail to entice the new breed of customer while alienating the loyal customer base that wants a "fussy" French brand.

Chapter 6: Pricing Strategies

CHAPTER CHALLENGE 6.1

Very few business organizations take a systematic and disciplined approach to pricing. Decisions on price are made *after* the product (good or service) is designed and is ready for introduction. At this stage, it is too late to think about customers, their needs, and their price sensitivities.

CHAPTER CHALLENGE 6.2

You have to be honest with yourself and make a choice. Continue reading to find out if you made the right choice.

CHAPTER CHALLENGE 6.3

There is a good reason why firms rely so heavily on costs to make pricing decisions. The only time a business is going to pursue bold pricing strategies is when it is successful in building a brand (differentiating itself from its competitors). As we saw in Chapter 5, building a brand requires a deep understanding of customer needs. And as we saw in Chapter 2, understanding customer needs is difficult; we have to be very clever in the kinds of questions we ask our customers. Now you see why firms rely so heavily on an "easy" variable such as cost—understanding customer needs and building a brand is hard work; firms take the lazy way and rely on costs to make pricing decisions.

Chapter 7: Channel Strategies

CHAPTER CHALLENGE 7.1

Every successful business differentiates itself from its competitors by asking a simple question: "Why should customers want to buy from us? What *unique* value do we create for customers?" The value proposition can be luxury (expensive watches), convenience (big box retailers), anonymity (internet purchases), or something else. Regardless, the channel used by the business has to match the unique value it wishes to create for the customer.

CHAPTER CHALLENGE 7.2

Well-designed channels move information.

CHAPTER CHALLENGE 7.3

Saturn's potential product is the "car buying and ownership experience." Thus, Saturn differentiates itself not by building a better car, but by providing a better car buying (for example, no high-pressure sales) and ownership (for example, cars can usually be fixed in one day) experience. Brilliant!

CHAPTER CHALLENGE 7.4

A supply chain is a network of suppliers in a channel of distribution serving the end customer. An example of a supply chain is raw material supplier (flour), bread manufacturer, wholesaler, retailer, and consumer.

Chapter 8: Marketing Communications Strategies

CHAPTER CHALLENGE 8.1

1. It is not enough to communicate with customers alone; a company should build long-term relationships with various stakeholders such as employees, suppliers, society, government, and media.
2. Communications should be viewed as means to build long-term brand health, not merely short-term promotions.
3. Customers are not going to passively sit back and accept whatever a company communicates. A company should make customers co-creators and disseminators of marketing communications messages.

CHAPTER CHALLENGE 8.2

By choosing the wrong channel for her message, the Olsen manager has devalued her brand. Loyal Olsen customers do not want to see the brand name plastered on the side of a bus.

CHAPTER CHALLENGE 8.3

These pre-existing filters are essentially brand perceptions and associations. They are formed based on past experience with the brand, reading about the brand in the media, or word-of-mouth communications through such means as the internet and social networks.

CHAPTER CHALLENGE 8.4

Campbell's knows that the time period between lunch and dinner is dangerous for anyone who wants to control their weight. This is because it is during this time that people tend to indulge in high-caloric snacks such as chips (featured in the ad). So Campbell's is relying on this research fact to position its soup as a meal (not a snack) that will get the consumer to dinner without any diet mishaps.

CHAPTER CHALLENGE 8.5

The proposal in Table 8.3 is incomplete. It lacks specific objectives. Who is the target audience(s)? What do we wish to communicate to them? How will we know we have succeeded? Without answers to these questions, we will be wasting our money.

Chapter 9: Marketing Planning to Sales Execution

CHAPTER CHALLENGE 9.1

Sales and marketing are distinct functions in a business. Typically, there is little incentive for disparate groups to work together unless they are bound by a set of commonalities (such as common goals, common objectives, and common metrics).

CHAPTER CHALLENGE 9.2

Selling the pair of shoes for just $29.95 is a huge concern because the retailer is devaluing the Robeez brand, which wants to maintain brand associations of quality, prestige, and creativity.

CHAPTER CHALLENGE 9.3

First, the Kennametal ad is designed to convey strength through the use of yellow and black. Second, the business is trying to set itself apart from its competitors by showcasing its expertise in not just saving the customer money, but also enhancing productivity. And third, Kennametal wants the customer to realize the breadth of its expertise by showcasing the different industries it operates in.

CHAPTER CHALLENGE 9.4

The marketing function can play a crucial role during the stages of building customer loyalty and advocacy by smartly utilizing marketing communications strategies. For example, car companies build loyalty and advocacy by sending frequent communiqués to customers informing them about new technologies, new models, or new offers. Some companies remind their customers how special they are by sending them birthday cards. All these tactics are designed to create happy and loyal customers.

CHAPTER CHALLENGE 9.5

The sales plan template should remind you of the marketing plan template.

Chapter 10: Building a Customer-Focused Business

CHAPTER CHALLENGE 10.1

GE Healthcare is rightly focusing not on the core product (medical diagnostic machine), but on the potential product (hospital efficiency and patient satisfaction).

CHAPTER CHALLENGE 10.2

1. Senior management is deeply committed to making all decisions based around the customer.
2. There is a clear and shared understanding of the customer throughout the organization.
3. There is commitment by each and every employee to make every customer interaction with the brand an opportunity to reinforce brand values.
4. The emphasis is not on collecting data on what the business knows about the customer, but on who the customer is, what the customer does, and what the customer thinks.
5. The definition of success is built around the customer, not around products.

Chapter 11: Customer Attraction, Satisfaction, and Retention Strategies

CHAPTER CHALLENGE 11.1

1. Starbucks is a marketing-led company, so it focuses on its customers.
2. It deeply understands the needs of its customers. For example, it knows that chic, young urbanites like Tammy would like to bring their dogs along with them, so it thoughtfully provides a hitching post and a bowl of water.
3. It knows who its target customer is. Importantly, it also knows who its target customer is not.

4. It creates a distinctive set of value propositions for the customer with coffee drinks, music, café culture, and social responsibility.
5. It is a customer-focused company. Tammy will get the same service at any Starbucks location around the globe.

CHAPTER CHALLENGE 11.2

Cirque du Soleil, profiled in Chapter 6, pursues the strategy of increasing customer value without an accompanying increase in costs.

CHAPTER CHALLENGE 11.3

Unless the customer is truly unhappy, the most probable response on a 5-point satisfaction scale is going to be a 4. Think about this for a moment. Think about your own experiences. A score of 4 basically means that the customer has no real attachment to the brand. This makes the customer vulnerable to competitive offers.

Chapter 12: Building the Marketing Organization of the Future

CHAPTER CHALLENGE 12.1

Currently, Purolator receives the products at a port, unpacks them, and ships them to O'Leary's customers, freeing him from distribution headaches. The next step for Purolator would be to advise O'Leary on how his customers' needs are changing; what products he should be ordering, in what quantity, and in what style; and where the best market opportunities are.

CHAPTER CHALLENGE 12.2

The business serves the right customers in the most attractive markets with goods and services that customers appreciate and are willing to pay for. This makes customers happy (satisfied), which leads to their loyalty. As we have discussed in Chapter 11, loyal customers are more profitable. This is why a business becomes more productive when it reviews these four items.

CHAPTER CHALLENGE 12.3

Diverting funds to the sales force is a logical move by a business frustrated by marketing's inability to demonstrate its contribution to business performance. This is because metrics to measure the contribution by sales are relatively straightforward: how much money did the sales force bring in (revenue generated)?

CHAPTER CHALLENGE 12.4

1. The role and potential of marketing is not clearly understood.

2. The organization is led by engineers or accountants. Such organizations may focus on technology and cost cutting, not on the customer.

3. The organization is sales driven. Such organizations typically focus on "making the sale" without paying attention to customer needs.

4. The marketing function is weak and lacks strategic talent.

5. Marketing has not put in place metrics to demonstrate return on marketing investment.

Glossary

acquisition cost The price paid by a customer to acquire a good or service.

aided recall Aided recall of an advertisement is used when a respondent cannot recall the advertisement using the unaided method. For example, "Do you recall seeing an ad for State Farm Insurance?"

augmented product The additions or "augmentations" that are made to the core product. Typically, these include such things as brand name, logo, colour schemes, corporate website, warranties, guarantees, toll-free numbers that customers can call to receive additional product information, call centres, and so forth.

average cost A cost figure arrived at by taking an average (mean) of all costs. The problem with average cost data is that averages hide the true picture.

basic care variables Variables that are "table stakes" or the bare minimum to enter any industry. Product quality, on-time delivery, and customer service are examples of basic care variables. Focusing on these variables alone does not offer the firm an advantage over its competitors.

brand A brand is a differentiated offering in the marketplace. Although frequently associated with "branded" goods and services, such as Mercedes Benz cars or Disney theme parks, anything can be branded if it is differentiated (in the eyes of the customer) from competitors. A one-word opposite of brand is **commodity.**

brand associations A set of perceptions a customer may have about a brand. Brand associations are represented in a customer's memory as a set of images, feelings, beliefs, and attitudes. In marketing, we attempt to measure and understand brand associations because they drive customer behaviour toward a brand.

brand awareness A measure of how aware a customer is of the existence of a brand.

brand equity The value a brand adds to a product. Picture a can of peas without a brand label. How much would you pay

for this product? Now, picture the same product, but with a Green Giant (a well-known brand) label. How much would you pay for this product? The difference between these two price levels (most consumers would pay more for the Green Giant product) is the equity of the brand (Green Giant, in this case).

brand identity A set of brand associations the strategist wants to create or maintain. The strategist has control over what identity is projected in the marketplace.

brand image The brand identity as received in the marketplace. The strategist has no control over brand image. It can only be measured. Even if the strategist relinquishes control of the brand, a certain image of the brand will develop in the marketplace. This is because customers, competitors, suppliers, media, and the government will shape the brand's image.

brand loyalty A measure of how loyal a customer is to a brand. We measure brand loyalty by asking customers (1) if they would buy the brand the next time they were in the market for the product and (2) if they would recommend the brand to someone else.

brand perceptions A set of associations about a brand held by someone. Also see **brand associations.**

break-even point Number of units that must be sold to produce a profit of zero (but a point at which all costs are recovered). [Break even = fixed cost/(unit price – variable unit cost)]

buying centre A group of people responsible for making a purchase decision in an organization. For example, the buying centre in a hospital for medical diagnostic machines may consist of a physician, nurse, administrator, and social worker.

buying funnel A framework that shows how customers go through the purchase process (also called a purchasing funnel). Customers initially become aware of a need, they are initially unaware of a

brand's existence, they give consideration to a few brands, they make a purchase, they evaluate their purchase, and they become loyal to the brand (or not, depending on their experience with it).

channel conflict A conflict that arises when one channel member behaves in a way that hurts another channel member. For example, when Mattel, the toy company, sells toys to Wal-Mart it hurts toy retailers such as Toys "R" Us. This is because Wal-Mart can sell the toys more cheaply than Toys "R" Us because it buys toys in bulk from Mattel.

channel economics A process of examining a channel's profitability (channel expenses divided by channel sales) and a channel's capacity for generating sales.

commodity Although we typically tend to associate commodities with such things as wheat, steel, or frozen orange juice concentrate, in marketing a commodity refers to something that is not differentiated in the mind of the customer. Contrast with **brand.**

competitive differentiation An act of differentiating yourself from your competitors, usually by building a brand.

core product Product features or attributes— whether the container of ketchup is made of plastic or glass, the number of seats in a restaurant, and so forth.

corporate sustainability A philosophy that a business can prosper by thinking about the welfare of its customers, employees, society, and the environment. Sustainability is the result of acting in an ethical and caring manner, without making profits the *sole* motive of a business' existence.

correlation A statistical technique of establishing if two items are related to one another. For example, are advertising and sales related? Correlation merely states that there is a relationship; it does not specify if there is a causal relationship. That is, it does not state whether advertising *causes* sales.

cost-plus pricing A pricing method whereby a profit margin is added to the cost of an item to arrive at the final price. If a T-shirt costs $7 to make and the firm wants a profit margin (markup) of 43%, the final price of the T-shirt is $10 [($7 + (.43 × $7)]. Contrast with **value-based pricing**.

cross-functional alignment A process of aligning all functions in a business (such as marketing, sales, finance, human resources, and the supply chain) to focus on the customer. This is necessary to achieve customer focus or customer centricity.

customer equity A firm's customer equity is the total of the discounted lifetime values of all its customers. Also see **customer lifetime value**.

customer focus An organizational philosophy that guides decision making. An organization that is customer focused makes decisions from the outside in. That is, the organization first considers customer needs and *then* attempts to satisfy those needs. All decisions are made keeping the customer in mind. (Contrast this philosophy with **product focus**.)

customer lifetime value The present value of all future purchases made by a loyal customer. For example, if a customer only ordered pizza from Pizza Hut, how much would that customer be worth to the company? Also see **customer equity**.

customer review A periodic activity undertaken to assess attractiveness of current customers served and potential customers that can be profitably served by a business.

customer satisfaction measurement A survey-based method to measure how satisfied a firm's customers are with its goods and services.

demographic segmentation The practice of segmenting customers using demographic variables such as age, income, and gender. Demographic segmentation may be easy, but it is rarely effective.

depth interviews A qualitative (exploratory) research technique where a moderator conducts a guided conversation with one respondent. This technique is useful in understanding customer decision making and the sources of influence on decision making.

encoding Refers to "packaging" a message using such means as a brochure or advertisement, for example.

ethnography A qualitative (exploratory) technique where the researcher engages in participant observation with customers. In essence, the researcher gains deep insight by becoming the customer.

exploratory research A set of techniques such as focus groups, depth interviews, and ethnography. These techniques are designed to explore ideas. Another name for exploratory research is qualitative research.

fixed cost The cost that has to be incurred, regardless of "production" volume. A salon owner has to pay monthly rent, regardless of how many customers are served during that month. Contrast this with **variable cost**—cost that varies by "production" volume.

focus groups A qualitative (exploratory) research technique that is a guided discussion between a group of respondents, led by a moderator. This technique is useful for generating and evaluating ideas—new product concepts, marketing communication messages, and so forth.

for-profit business A business whose primary goal is to make a profit. Contrast with **non-profit organization**.

functional plan A plan developed for a function such as human resources, operations, or the supply chain. Functional plans are based on the context provided by the marketing plan.

functional product How the product functions or performs—the taste of the ketchup, friendliness of the restaurant staff, salesperson knowledge, and so forth.

incremental cost The increment to cost (positive or negative) that results from the pricing decision. If a symphony director lowers the price of a ticket, she may sell more tickets. Her variable costs (for example, printing more programs) would go up, representing an incremental cost that is a direct result of the pricing decision. On the other hand, rehearsal costs would not be affected by how many tickets were sold for a given performance. So rehearsal costs would not be considered incremental costs.

integrated marketing communications (IMC) A framework to effectively integrate different marketing communications tools to achieve strategic objectives. IMC is based on two premises: (1) customers become progressively more involved with a brand and (2) different marketing communications tools have different uses. IMC attempts to use the proper tool at the proper customer involvement stage to achieve an overall sense of cohesion.

key issues These are a set of key considerations that must be addressed by the marketing plan. An example of a key issue from Chapter 4 is "How can we make our product more relevant to preteens?" For each key issue, a marketing strategy is developed.

listing fees A fee charged by a retailer to carry a manufacturer's goods on its shelves.

macroenvironmental trends Trends facing the business externally. Common trends examined are demographic, sociocultural, economic, technological, political, and regulatory.

marketing A disciplined process used by organizations to solve business problems: understand-create-deliver-manage customer value.

marketing mix The set of tools a marketing strategist uses to create value for chosen customers (target market). We can think of the marketing mix as comprising product strategy, pricing strategy, channel of distribution strategy (also called "place"), and marketing communications strategy (also called "promotion").

marketing plan A document developed for a time frame of one year. It encapsulates the organization's marketing strategy to illustrate how the business aims to understand-create-deliver-manage customer value.

marketing strategy A firm's go-to-market approach that outlines its product, price, channel, and marketing communications strategies (the marketing mix elements).

market segmentation A fundamental pillar in marketing. Market segmentation refers to dividing customer needs into groups (or segments) in such a way that customers within a group share similar needs, and each group is distinct from other groups in terms of its needs. Market segmentation enables an organization to accrue several benefits such as the ability to serve needs better, utilize resources more effectively, and discover unmet needs. Contrast with **mass marketing**.

market share The slice of the total market you have vis-à-vis your competitors. Market share can be calculated based on number of units or dollar amount. If 100 widgets are sold in a market in a given time period, and your firm sells 15 widgets, your market share is 15%. If the total value of widgets sold in the same time period is $1000 and your firm has sales of $225, your market share (based on dollar amount) is 22.5%. So when examining market share, it is very important to see whether the unit of analysis is units or dollars.

mass marketing Presenting the same offer to all customers. Mass marketing ignores customer needs and is, therefore, untenable. Contrast with **market segmentation**.

need-based segmentation The best way to segment customers. Need-based segmentation takes into account customers' needs, not relatively static variables such as demographics or attitudes.

non-profit organization An organization whose primary goal is not to make a profit. These organizations tackle such problems as hunger, housing, heritage conservation, and a myriad of other worthy pursuits. Although their main goal is not profit, it does not mean that these organizations can make a loss and still remain in business. Contrast with **for-profit business**.

participant observation A component of ethnographic research where the researcher does not merely observe, but also participates in an activity (for example, shopping) alongside customers to get a better understanding of their needs and motives.

pocket price Also known as realized price. The actual price received by a firm for a given transaction. Pocket prices are different from list prices because the firm may give its customers special terms (for example, discounts) and conditions to secure the customer's business.

pocket price band A chart showing various pocket prices and the percentage of sales made at each pocket price point. Pocket price bands reveal the extent of pricing abuse that occurs in a firm, costing the firm untold amounts in lost profits.

potential product The "true" solution the customer wants from the product. A very powerful concept, it enables the strategist to recognize that, although two competitors may have the same core product, it is possible to differentiate (build a brand) by carefully thinking about the potential product.

price elasticity The percentage change in volume for a given percentage change in price. Michael Marn and his colleagues have found that a price decrease of 1% typically drives up demand by around 1.7% (cited in the pricing chapter). Another term for price elasticity is price sensitivity. Of course, price elasticity varies by customer segment and product category (for example, consumers may be price inelastic for food items, but price elastic for luxury goods).

price penetration A practice where the initial price of the product is set low to attract customers. Over time, prices are raised if the product proves popular.

price skimming A practice where the initial price of the product is set high. Over time, prices are reduced. For example, firms that have invested heavily in new product development and want to recoup their costs follow this practice.

price war A situation in an industry where competitors are trying to win by outdoing each other on lowering prices.

price waterfall A chart showing the list price and various discounts subtracted from the list price to arrive at the pocket price. Price waterfalls show price "leakages" that occur in a firm.

primary research Research you have to conduct yourself. Contrast with **secondary research**, which is research that someone else has conducted and can be obtained free of charge or for a fee, depending on the source.

private label brand A brand offered under the label of a retailer. For example, Staples sells its own brand of paper products. Often, the supplier to a private label could be a national brand (such as International Paper).

product In marketing, the term "product" refers to a good, a service, a place, an idea, a person, an institution, and so forth. The product is the totality of the customer's experiences.

product focus (orientation) A narrow-minded and myopic organizational philosophy that guides decision making. An organization that is product focused makes decisions from the inside out. That is, this organization does not consider customer needs when making decisions. (Contrast this philosophy with **customer focus**.)

product life cycle A concept, challenged by some authors, that states that products predictably go through four phases—introduction, growth, maturity, and decline. As we saw in Chapter 5, this is not a *fait accompli*. In other words, while there may be a life cycle for technology or product categories (we no longer use typewriters, for example), a brand can go on forever (IBM no longer makes typewriters, but it went on to make computers and laptops, and now sells computer-related services).

product mix review A periodic assessment of the basket of goods and services used by a firm to serve customers. The intention of such a review is to ensure the basket continues to create value for customers.

profit Profit = profit margin × number of units sold. If your profit margin per item is $3 and you sell 1000 units, your profit is $3000.

profit (or loss) = total revenue − total cost.

profit margin Profit margin = price of product − cost of product. If an item sells for $10 and it costs you $7 to make that item, your profit margin is $3.

psychographic segmentation The practice of segmenting customers using attitudinal and lifestyle variables such as activities, interests, and opinions.

qualitative research A set of techniques such as focus groups, depth interviews, and ethnography. These techniques are designed to explore ideas. Another name for qualitative research is exploratory research.

return on investment (ROI) A measure of the return being generated by an investment. For example, if you invest $100 in a mutual fund that generates $8 in income for the year, the ROI is 8%. ROIs are calculated for any business investment such as capital deployed, sales efforts, advertising expenditures, and so forth.

revenue Revenue = price of product × number of units sold. If an item sells for $10 and you sell 1000 items, your revenue is $10 000.

sales cycle The length of time it takes for a sales professional to close the deal with a customer, calculated from the time the initial contact is made to the time the contract is signed.

sales review A formal review to (1) compare actual sales figures to targets, (2) evaluate how well the sales plan is being implemented, and (3) provide feedback to other functions on what the sales function is observing in the marketplace regarding competitors, customers, and market trends. A sales review is accomplished in two ways. First, the sales function reviews sales data during its internal meetings. Second, the sales function conducts a sales review with marketing and other functions.

secondary research Research that someone else has conducted that can be obtained free of charge or for a fee, depending on the source. Contrast with **primary research**, which you have to conduct yourself.

segment review A periodic activity undertaken to assess attractiveness of current market segments served and potential segments that can be profitably served by a business.

shareholder value A management philosophy that regards maximization of shareholders' equity as its highest objective. This is accomplished by increasing a firm's earnings, increasing the value of the shares, or increasing the frequency or amount of dividends paid.

share of wallet The percentage of a customer's expenditure in a product category that is held by the business. For example, if a customer spends $100 on office paper and buys from three companies, what percentage of $100 does Brand A command versus its competitors?

social media Also called new media or alternate media. The term social media refers to media made possible by the internet; for example, blogs, Twitter, Facebook, MySpace, and YouTube.

strategic plan A plan developed at the CEO's level. It is a very high-level plan delineating what markets (businesses) the organization should enter or exit. There are two key differences between a strategic plan and a marketing plan: time frame and level of detail. The strategic plan is developed for a time frame of three to five years (or longer in some organizations), while the marketing plan is developed for a time frame of one year. The marketing plan contains details on marketing strategy (product, price, channel, and marketing communications), while the strategic plan does not.

supply chain A network of channel partners, from raw material to final sale. A good supply chain not only moves goods, but also moves information. The proper movement and sharing of information is crucial for any organization to achieve its strategy. Zara and Saturn are good examples of this (Chapter 7).

survey research Data collection by means of a questionnaire. Surveys are useful in validating findings by sampling a larger set of respondents than is typical in qualitative (exploratory) research.

switching costs Cost incurred by a customer to switch from one option to another. Switching costs can be financial (cost to train employees on new database system) or non-financial in nature (headaches involved in switching banks—the customer has to transfer accounts, get new cheques printed, and so forth).

target costing A method where the firm sets a price for the product, establishes a profit margin it wants to achieve, and then tries to bring costs under control to enable it to achieve the desired profit margin. Hence, if an item is going to be priced at $10 and the firm requires a profit margin of $3, its costs cannot exceed $7. The firm has to try to provide the product for $7 or give up its quest entirely.

target market Once market segmentation is complete, the firm has to decide which segment(s) it wants to serve. This is called selecting target markets. The idea behind target marketing is simple—we cannot be all things to all people.

total cost Total cost = total fixed cost + total variable cost.

Total Cost of Ownership (TCO) analysis TCO analysis attempts to break down a customer's total costs into acquisition, possession, usage, and disposal costs. The idea behind TCO analysis is that price is just one component of a customer's total cost to "own" a good or service. And if we are successful in decreasing the customer's total costs, we can make the customer insensitive to the price paid to acquire the good or service (acquisition cost).

total revenue Total revenue = expected unit sales × price per unit.

total shareholder return (TSR) TSR represents the change in capital value of a listed/quoted company over a period (typically one year or longer), plus dividends, expressed as a plus or minus percentage of the opening value.

total variable cost Total variable cost = number of units expected to be sold × variable cost per unit.

unaided recall In unaided recall of an advertisement, a respondent is asked whether he or she recalls seeing an ad for a brand (company) by simply providing the respondent with the product category. For example, "Do you recall seeing an ad for an insurance company?"

unit price The amount of money charged to the customer for each unit of a product or service.

usage segmentation A way to segment customers based on usage. For example, beer manufacturers know that they can segment their customers into low-, medium-, and high-usage customers.

value-based pricing A pricing method that takes into account customer perceptions of value, rather than the seller's cost. Contrast this method with **cost-plus pricing**.

value chain This is the same concept as a **supply chain**. The difference lies in how we use it. The value chain enables us to examine how value is created at each step of the supply chain. Such analysis enables us identify avenues for collaboration between channel partners and elimination of redundancies, all with a view to better serving the final customer. Lego and Arbol Industries (Chapter 7) provide examples on how to use the value chain concept.

value proposition An offering (goods and services) targeted at a particular market segment or customer.

variable cost This is cost that varies with volume "produced." Items like wages paid per hour and raw material are variable costs. If a hairstylist is paid $50 per hour, the owner of the salon has to pay the stylist $500 for a 10-hour shift, but only $250 for a 5-hour shift. Contrast this type of cost with **fixed cost**, which remains fixed, regardless of "production" volume.

Vendor Managed Inventory (VMI) A program that eliminates customers' paperwork and processing costs because the supplier manages the customer's inventory and ships the product without any effort on the customer's part.

vertical integration A channel practice where a business buys another business that is its supplier or its customer. For example, an orange juice manufacturer vertically integrates when it buys an orchard (this is known as backward integration). If the manufacturer buys a retail store to sell orange juice, this is known as forward integration. Vertical integration has given way to a newer concept called **virtual integration**.

virtual integration Instead of buying a channel member, as in vertical integration, virtual integration works by providing accurate, up-to-the-minute *information* to channel partners so they all work in a synchronized way to serve the customer. Dell and Zara (Chapter 7) are great examples of companies that succeed by practising virtual integration.

win rate Calculated by dividing the number of sales won (for example, contracts secured) by the number of sales pitches made to customers.

Index

Credits

(New York: Harper & Row, 1954). **p. 17** Harter, Landry, and Tipping: George Harter, Edward Landry, and Andrew Tipping, "The New Complete Marketer," *Strategy + Business*, Issue 48, Autumn 2007, pp. 78–87; Beth Comstock: *ibid.* **p. 26** Rothenberg and Liodice: Randall Rothenberg and Robert Liodice, "Foreword: Marketing Thought Leaders: Pioneers at the Growth Frontier,"*CMO Thought Leaders: The Rise of the Strategic Marketer*, strategy + business books, July 2007; Keith Pardy: George Harter and Richard Rawlinson, "Keith Pardy: The Human Approach," *CMO Thought Leaders: The Rise of the Strategic Marketer*, strategy + business books, July 2007. **p. 27** John Hayes: Geoffrey Precourt, ed., *CMO Thought Leaders: The Rise of the Strategic Marketer*, strategy + business books, July 2007. **p. 31** Henry Ford: historical. **p. 48** J.P. Getty: historical. **p. 52** Milton Friedman: Milton Friedman, "The Social Responsibility of Business Is to Increase Its Profits," *The New York Times Magazine*, September 13, 1970. **p. 53** Yankelovich and Meer: CNN.com, January 23, 2008. **p. 58** Yankelovich and Meer (both quotations), *ibid.* **p. 76** Day and Schoemaker: George S. Day, Paul J.H. Schoemaker, "Scanning the Periphery," *Harvard Business Review*, November 2005. **p. 93** Theodore Levitt: Theodore Levitt, "Marketing Success through Differentiation of Anything," *Harvard Business Review*, January–February 1980. **p. 94** Theodore Levitt: Theodore Levitt, *Ted Levitt on Marketing* (Boston, MA: Harvard Business Press, 2006). **p. 99** Joachimsthaler and Aaker: Erich Joachimsthaler and David A. Aaker, "Building Brands Without Mass Media," *Harvard Business Review*, January–February 1997, pp. 39–50. **p. 105** James P. Andrew: David Henry, "Creativity Pays, Here's How Much," *Business Week*, April 24, 2006, p. 76; Steve Ballmer: Mohanbir Sawney, Robert Wolcott, and Inigo Arroniz, "The 12 Different Ways for Companies to Innovate," *MIT Sloan Management Review*, April 1, 2006. **p. 106** Samuel J. Palmisano: Jena McGregor, "The World's Most Innovative Companies: Their creativity goes beyond products to rewiring themselves," *BusinessWeek*, April 24, 2006, p. 63. **p. 107** Michelle Gass, Starbucks: *ibid.* **p. 119** Grant and Schlesinger: Alan W. H. Grant and Leonard A. Schlesinger, "Realize your Customers' Full Profit Potential," *Harvard Business Review*, September 1, 1995. **p. 121** Marn, Roegner and Zawada: Michael V. Marn, Eric V. Roegner, and Craig C. Zawada, *The Price Advantage* (Hoboken, NJ: John Wiley & Sons, 2004). **p. 132** Nagle and Holden: Thomas K. Nagle and Reed K. Holden, *The Strategy and Tactics of Pricing* (Upper Saddle River, NJ: Prentice Hall, 2002). **p. 138** Florence Furlong: personal interview with Ajay K. Sirsi. **p. 146** Mae West: historical. **p. 148** Michael Dell: Joan Magretta, "The Power of Virtual Integration," *Harvard Business Review*, March–April 1998, pp. 73–84. **p. 149** Jim Ensign: Emily Steel and Suzanne Vranica, "Papa John's Pizza Gets Finger Friendlier—Text-Message Ordering Creates a New Channel For Marketing the Menu, *The Wall Street Journal,* Nov. 13, 2007, p. B4. **p. 150** Olli-Pekka Kallasvuo: Jennifer L. Schenker, "Nokia barges into mobile services," *BusinessWeek*, August 31, 2007. **p. 155** Anderson, Day and Rangan: Erin Anderson, George S. Day, and V. Kasturi Rangan, "Strategic Channel Design," *Sloan Management Review*, Summer 1997, pp. 59–69. **p. 163** Jorgen Vig Knudstorp: Keith Oliver, Edouard Samakh, and Peter Heckmann, "Rebuilding Lego, Brick by Brick," *Strategy + Business*, Autumn 2007, pp. 58–67. **p. 171** Eric Schmitt: Anthony Bianco, "The Vanishing Mass Market," *BusinessWeek*, July 12, 2004, pp. 61–68. **p. 172** James Stengel: *ibid.* **p. 176** Chip Heath: Lenny T. Mendonca and Matt Mille, "Crafting a Message That Sticks: An Interview with Chip Heath," *The McKinsey Quarterly*, 2007, November, pp. 1–8. **p. 188** Baker and Green: Stephen Baker and Heather Green, "Beyond Blogs," *BusinessWeek*, June 2, 2008, pp. 44–50. **p. 198** Kotler, Rackham, and Krishnaswamy: Philip Kotler, Neil Rackham, and Suj Krishnaswamy, "Ending the War between Sales and Marketing," *Harvard Business Review*, July–August 2006, pp. 68–78. **p. 218** Gartner Group: www.gartner.com. **p. 223** Galati and Oldroyd, Ranjay Gulati and James B. Oldroyd, "The Quest for Customer Focus," *Harvard Business Review,* April 2005. **p. 224** Frederick Webster: Frederick E. Webster, Jr. (1988), "Rediscovering the Marketing Concept," *Business Horizons*, 31 (May/June), page 37. **p. 226** Galati and Oldroyd: Ranjay Gulati and James B. Oldroyd, "The Quest for Customer Focus," *Harvard Business Review*, April 2005. **p. 227** Anders Gronstedt: Anders Gronstedt, *The Customer Century: Lessons from World Class Companies in Integrated Marketing and Communications* (Routledge, 2000). **p. 236** Claes Fornell: http://www.cfornell.es/, accessed February 25, 2009. **p. 237** Jeff Jarvis: Jeff Jarvis, "Love the Customers Who Hate You," *BusinessWeek*, February 21, 2008. **p. 245** Robert Ricci: Robert Ricci, "Move from Product to Customer Centric," *Quality Progress*, November 2003, pp. 22–29.

Key Takeaways

Chapter 1

The top 10 things to keep in mind if you want to succeed in business are the following:

1. The research is unequivocal on what successful businesses do—they develop and implement superior marketing strategies.

2. Marketing is not advertising, nor is it selling. The fact that it is practised that way by some does not make it right.

3. Marketing is a disciplined process to solve business problems: understand-create-deliver-manage customer value.

4. Successful businesses start with the customer, not with the product or technology. They deeply understand their customers' needs.

5. The end goal of understanding customer needs is to segment customers and choose a set of target markets to serve.

6. Customer value is created by combining elements of the marketing mix—product, price, channel, and marketing communications strategies.

7. If sales and other functions are not focused on the customer, marketing strategies will fail.

8. Smart businesses are constantly tinkering with their business models. They realize that marketing strategies have to be examined and modified every year.

9. Marketing is a force for organizational transformation. Successful marketing functions perform 10 key tasks, ranging from finding opportunities for the business to being a change agent in the organization.

10. Organizations that are not marketing led are doomed to underperform their competitors. Many of them ultimately fail.

KEYOBJECTIVE

The main goal of this chapter is to provide you with frameworks, tools, and techniques to succeed in business.

Chapter 2

The top 10 things to keep in mind when understanding customer needs are the following:

1. Companies that do not base their decisions on customer needs make some common mistakes that cost them time, money, and resources.

2. Successful companies listen to their customers every step of the way.

3. Smart companies are not happy merely understanding customer needs: they create them. These companies are very good at producing innovations out of needs even customers have a hard time articulating.

4. Always begin marketing research effort with secondary research.

5. Qualitative research techniques are excellent for generating ideas.

6. Surveys should not be used to generate ideas. Rather, they are good tools for validating ideas.

7. True insight is received by combining qualitative and quantitative methods.

8. It is possible to decrease spending on marketing research while increasing the success rate of innovations.

9. To realize this, the most advanced companies involve their customers in co-creating value—they introduce a new product and then tinker with it, they use the entire world as their marketing research firm, and they create new market spaces.

10. Ultimately, understanding customers is not a mundane activity of routinely applying marketing research techniques in the hopes of producing results. Rather, understanding customers is a highly strategic endeavour.

KEYOBJECTIVE

The main goal of this chapter is to provide you with frameworks, tools, and techniques to understand your customers' needs.

Chapter 3

The top 10 things to keep in mind when segmenting customers are the following:

1. It's a guarantee—a business that is not segmenting its customers is wasting resources and is not as profitable as it could be.

2. Without segmentation, a business tries to be all things to all people. In the end, it stands for nothing.

3. Good segmentation should enable the business to identify customers who are underserved and new customers.

4. All customers are not created equal.

5. Segmenting by demographics or psychographics has rather limited uses.

6. The best way to segment markets is to take into account customer needs and their attractiveness to you.

7. Common segmentation pitfalls are over-segmenting, targeting too many customers with one offering, relying on complex segmentation methods, forgetting that segments change over time, always targeting the largest segment, using the same segmentation approach as competitors, not investing in emerging segments, segmenting by product and not by market, and not updating the segmentation.

8. If the sales force cannot use the segmentation, the marketing function has failed.

9. Target markets should be selected on the basis of customer profitability and other factors such as growth potential and ability to serve.

10. Do not wait to start segmentation *after* you have collected data. Start with the data you have today and evolve your segmentation over time.

KEYOBJECTIVE

Market segmentation is the pillar of business success. This chapter shows you how to segment your customers while avoiding the traps many businesses fall into.

Chapter 4

The top 10 things to keep in mind if you want to develop and implement a winning marketing plan are the following:

1. A business without a marketing plan is like a ship without a rudder—directionless.

2. You are already familiar with the main sections of a marketing plan: understand (data and analysis to identify key issues), create (marketing strategies), deliver (action plans), and manage (marketing plan outcomes and control) customer value.

3. Do not put off developing a marketing plan because you are busy with day-to-day activities. Running your business based on a sound marketing plan should be top priority.

4. Do not treat the marketing plan template as a checklist. Focus on what each section is asking of you.

5. Do not focus on data; instead, focus on what the data means to your business.

6. Do not do a SWOT analysis, as it could lead to wrong conclusions. Instead, conduct an OTSW analysis.

7. Spend a lot of time on Section 6 because it identifies the right key issues that will determine business success.

8. Take on a few strategies and implement them well, before tackling other strategies.

9. To implement the marketing plan, it has to be translated into functional plans. Marketing plans that are simply handed over to other functions do not get implemented.

10. Remember, the marketing plan is a living, breathing document. Therefore, it is necessary to revisit the assumptions that went into plan development and make changes to the plan as necessary.

KEYOBJECTIVE

The main goal of this chapter is to provide you with an easy-to-use template, tips, and techniques to develop and implement a strong marketing plan.

Chapter 5

The top 10 things to keep in mind if you want to define your brand apart from your competitors are the following:

1. To build strong brands, you must first understand the strategic significance of the term "product."

2. A product is not something you make or sell; it is the totality of the customer's experiences: the core, functional, augmented, and potential product.

3. If you define your business in terms of the core product, you will lose because customers do not buy the core product, they buy the potential product.

4. Think carefully about what brand associations (brand identity) you want to create or maintain, as this is your "brand promise" to your customer.

5. Implement brand identity using all elements of the marketing mix—product, price, channel of distribution, and marketing communications.

6. Measure the equity in your brand, as this enables you to diagnose the health of your brand.

7. Use the diagnosis to refresh your brand by repositioning it or extending it (new markets, new products, or new geographies).

8. To grow your business you *have* to innovate.

9. A common mistake made by firms is to think of innovation in narrow terms such as technology or research and development, instead of the 13 dimensions of innovation that can be used to grow the business.

10. Avoid the pitfalls of "over-innovation" by constantly examining your product mix to ensure it is not bloated with weak brands.

KEYOBJECTIVE

The main point of this chapter is to help you build a strong brand to differentiate yourself from your competitors.

Chapter 6

The top 10 things to keep in mind when you make pricing decisions are the following:

1. If you want to be profitable, pay attention to your prices. A 1% improvement in price will improve your profitability by more than 11%. So even if you think you are doing a decent job of pricing, try to make improvements.

2. Improving price does not only mean *raising* prices: it also means paying attention to price leakages within your firm. This means you should look at pocket prices and examine the shape of your price bands. Someone in your organization is giving value away without charging for it—find out where the abuse is happening!

3. Decide what you want to be when you grow up. Do you want to chase volume (market share) or do you want to be profitable? You may not be able to have both. This decision is key because it impacts your pricing philosophy.

4. Costs should play a relatively minor role in the pricing decision.

5. Start with a deep understanding of your customers' needs. Segment them based on their needs, value drivers, and their price sensitivities.

6. Arrive at an initial price based on the value you are creating.

7. Adjust the price based on
   - competitor reactions
   - new entrants into the marketplace
   - your costs
   - short-term tactics

8. Examine the impact of your price on the other marketing mix variables. Is the total "package" you are creating seamless to the customer? Are there any inconsistencies between the price and your marketing strategy?

9. Look at the cost to serve your customers. Every year, make decisions on which customers to keep based on their profitability to you. Do not be afraid to "fire" customers.

10. Finally, remember that pricing is a process. You should revisit your pricing strategies every year as part of the overall marketing planning process. Just as a marketing plan is a living, breathing document, your pricing strategies should also evolve over time.

KEYOBJECTIVE

The main goal of this chapter is to provide you with tools and techniques to confidently make pricing decisions.

Chapter 7

The top 10 things to keep in mind when you make channel decisions are the following:

1. You cannot think of channel strategy in isolation from your other marketing strategies. Channel strategies impact *every* aspect of your business.

2. Wrong channel decisions can be very expensive and can result in loss of market share and profits.

3. Low-cost channels are not always the best option.

4. Channel strategy does not mean simply adding more channels. Multi-channel strategies can be expensive if not managed correctly.

5. Look at the product category, your firm's strategy, customer needs, and brand decisions to initially arrive at a set of acceptable channels.

6. For each channel in the acceptable set, calculate channel profitability and channel capacity for generating sales.

7. Choose the right channels based on the customer decision-making process.

8. Proactively guide customers to the right channels by offering incentives and disincentives. Do not let your customers "self-select" which channel to use.

9. Remember, you are not an island; your organization is part of a network of suppliers serving the end customer. So whatever actions you take, remember to mitigate channel conflict.

10. Finally, remember that developing channel strategies is a process. You should revisit your channel strategies every year as part of the overall marketing planning process. Just as a marketing plan is a living, breathing document, your channel strategies should also evolve over time.

KEYOBJECTIVE

The main goal of this chapter is to provide you with tools and techniques to confidently make channel decisions.

Chapter 8

The top 10 things to keep in mind when you make marketing communications decisions are the following:

1. Marketing communications is not just about advertising to your customers. Rather, it is using a set of tools to build lasting relationships with a group of stakeholders crucial to the health of any company—customers, suppliers, employees, society, media, and the government.

2. It is crucial to keep in mind that anything communicated by you, your employees, or anyone else, in any shape or form, has the capability to impact your brand.

3. The ultimate goal of communications should be the long-term health of the brand.

4. Unlike in the past, customers are now in control of marketing communications through social media. You can choose to ignore this fact or to take advantage of it.

5. All good communication strategies begin with research on customer needs, brand value, and competitor positioning strategies.

6. To be effective, your message should be simple, to the point, and differentiated from your competitors' message.

7. All good communication strategies end with research on the impact of marketing communications.

8. To be effective, communication has to be continuous. Communicate-learn-communicate should be any business' mantra. Fragmented communications are a waste of resources.

9. Integrated marketing communications (IMC) is a framework that enables you to decide when to use what communication tool. It is based on the twin premises that customers escalate their involvement with your brand and different tools have different purposes.

10. Social media such as blogs, YouTube, and Facebook are here to stay. They are a cost-effective way to build relationships with your target audience.

KEYOBJECTIVE

The main goal of this chapter is to provide you with tools and techniques to confidently make marketing communications decisions.

Chapter 9

The top 10 things to keep in mind if you want to successfully translate marketing strategies into sales action are the following:

1. If marketing strategies are not being translated into sales action, it means that the marketing and sales functions are not aligned.

2. Lack of alignment between marketing and sales has disastrous consequences for the business.

3. Marketing–sales misalignment stems from three reasons: inherently different thought worlds, lack of role definition, and lack of a process to align marketing and sales.

4. The fact that marketing and sales have different thought worlds is not a bad thing in itself, but these thought worlds have to be harnessed to form a powerful whole.

5. The "hand-off" model to define marketing and sales roles is too limiting.

6. Marketing and sales should play distinct yet complementary roles in understanding-creating-delivering-managing customer value.

7. The process to align marketing and sales begins with market segmentation to profile customers and develop customer value propositions.

8. A clear understanding of customer value propositions enables the development of sales strategies encapsulated in a sales plan.

9. Essentially, the sales plan *is* the marketing plan, but written in the language of sales.

10. At least once every quarter, sales has to conduct a sales review with marketing and other functions to provide a realistic picture of the marketplace.

KEYOBJECTIVE

The main goal of this chapter is to provide you with a framework to translate marketing strategies into sales action.

Chapter 10

The top 10 things to keep in mind to get everyone in your business to focus on the customer are the following:

1. Without customer focus, the best marketing strategies will fail. This is because marketing is not just the responsibility of the marketing function. Rather, every person in the business has to live and breathe the marketing philosophy.

2. A focus on the customer pays off. Research shows that firms that are focused on the customer have a 30% greater return on investment (ROI) than their peers who do not have such a focus.

3. Customer focus is an intuitive concept to understand, but it is hard to implement unless the business understands its diametrical opposite—product focus.

4. A product-focused business highlights product features (instead of customer needs), sells products to anybody who will buy (instead of serving the customer), is transaction oriented (instead of relationship oriented), and assumes that it is the sole responsibility of the marketing function to focus on customer relations (instead of realizing that a focus on the customer is everyone's responsibility).

5. You cannot wish for customer focus—you have to have a process to build it.

6. The process starts with senior management commitment to being a customer-focused business. Senior managers have to deeply believe that customer focus is right for their business.

7. The organization has to be realigned to focus on the customer. Realignment does not necessarily mean changing the organizational structure. Rather, it means changing the pattern of workflow to focus on the customer.

8. A realigned workforce needs support systems and processes to function with the customer in mind. A critical component of support is a shared understanding of customer needs.

9. Without a revised set of financial metrics, customer focus efforts will fail.

10. Customer focus is not a project; it is a journey. Do not give up at the first signs of a setback.

KEYOBJECTIVE

The main goal of this chapter is to provide you with a framework and a set of building blocks to become a customer-focused business.

Key Takeaways

Chapter 11

The top 10 things to keep in mind if you want to attract, satisfy, and keep customers are the following:

1. All winning businesses know that customer satisfaction is key to business success. This is because customer satisfaction helps to both attract and retain customers.

2. A business with higher satisfaction scores is more profitable, generates better cash flows, and builds higher shareholder value.

3. To measure customer satisfaction, focus on five key areas: overall satisfaction, satisfaction with goods and services, intention to repurchase, willingness to recommend, and customer demographic information.

4. It is not enough to merely satisfy customers; a business must ensure that its customers are very satisfied. This is because only "very satisfied" customers are loyal.

5. Do not waste time trying to convert customers who score a 1–3 to a 4 (on a 5-point satisfaction scale). Focus instead on understanding what actions need to be taken to move the 4s up to a 5.

6. Building a base of loyal customers is very important because loyal customers are price insensitive, cost less to serve, engage in positive word-of-mouth communications, are not willing to listen to competitors, are more willing to forgive a negative experience, and are more willing to try new offerings.

7. Building customer loyalty is not a one-time project; rather, it is a journey.

8. There are four steps in building customer loyalty: listen to customers, understand and share the information, focus on opportunities, and sustain improvements.

9. Building customer attraction, satisfaction, and retention strategies on the internet requires a different approach to segmentation, one based on usage occasions.

10. There are five steps to internet strategies: select the target customer group, select a marketing goal, decide which type of occasion works best for the selected marketing goal, select the internet sites the customer is most likely to visit, and design and use occasion-based marketing tactics.

KEYOBJECTIVE

The main goal of this chapter is to provide you with tools to attract, satisfy, and keep (retain) customers.

Key Takeaways

Chapter 12

The top 10 things to keep in mind if you want to build a marketing organization of the future are the following:

1. The true potential of a marketing organization is realized when it becomes the engine to transform an entire corporation.

2. Achieving this is not easy, as many marketing organizations do not demonstrate their productivity or their marketing return on investments (ROI).

3. When marketing demonstrates its productivity, it naturally follows that the entire business is more successful.

4. To demonstrate marketing productivity, a business should review four items on a regular basis: segments, customers, product mix, and customer satisfaction.

5. Before metrics can be put in place to demonstrate marketing ROI, marketing must establish marketing's role, objectives for ROI measurement, time frames, and marketing's authority in influencing areas it will be measured on.

6. To put metrics in place, it is helpful to think in terms of the customer purchasing funnel framework, which posits that customers progress through a purchasing funnel—from being unaware of a brand to purchasing it and making repurchase decisions.

7. Common metrics to measure marketing ROI are brand awareness, brand equity, purchase intent, sales, customer satisfaction, customer retention, and profit as a percentage of revenue.

8. A survey can be used to measure how influential the marketing function is in any business. There are 10 items on the survey, which fall into the following categories: driving organization strategy and resource deployment; directing efforts related to market research, product development, pricing, and communications; influencing operations (what other functions do); offering marketing support services to business units; championing the customer; and disseminating marketing best practices throughout the organization.

9. A score of 60 or below on the survey indicates that marketing's influence in the business is minimal. Common causes are lack of understanding of marketing's role and lack of marketing expertise.

10. In the new world of marketing, the old rules of personal success do not apply. Instead, you should focus on acquiring skills that will enable you to be creative, as well as developing technical skills; working with other functional members as part of a team; and acquiring interpersonal skills to lead others.

KEYOBJECTIVE

The main goal of this chapter is to provide you with frameworks, ideas, and tools to build a marketing organization that is an engine of corporate transformation.